Contours of Being and Becoming

CONTOURS OF BEING AND BECOMING

IDENTITY, MEMORY, AND CULTURAL ENCOUNTERS

edited by
Najah Mahmi, PhD
Abdelhak Jebbar, PhD

Westphalia Press
An Imprint of the Policy Studies Organization
Washington, DC

Westphalia Press
An imprint of Policy Studies Organization
1367 Connecticut Avenue NW
Washington, D.C. 20036
info@ipsonet.org

ISBN: 978-1-63391-021-8

Cover and interior design by Jeffrey Barnes
jbarnesbook.design

Daniel Gutierrez-Sandoval, Executive Director
PSO and Westphalia Press

Updated material and comments on this edition
can be found at the Westphalia Press website:
www.westphaliapress.org

To Amira and Adam

Contents

(Cont'd.)

Preface

When we consider writing on the subject of identity through the experiences of researchers from diverse academic and cultural backgrounds, we are able, albeit implicitly, to delve into different qualitative themes that redraw new dimensions of the concept and contribute to the foundation of new readings and interpretations. Since the ability to understand even a small part of these new interpretations will enable a dual and reciprocal understanding of the self and the other, we will be faced with new and complex formulations of meanings based on diversity and aimed at mutual understanding.

This book's project falls within this context, opening up to several topics related, but not limited, to the dynamics of identity and its construction, the roles of resistance and power, embodiment and performance, hybridity and pluralism, art as a mirror of the self and the other, memory and trauma, among other concerns. The aim remains to shed light on the opportunities offered through understanding the concept in its fluid and multiple layered concretisations, and on the other hand, to comprehend its various complexities embodied in its being an active site of struggle and survival.

This project stems from an urgent need to question the human condition within the actual sites of interconnections and divisions, creating *glocal* bridges and borders. It explores thus a wide range of topics related to identity and culture, and their intersections in thought and society. Since a final and definitive decision on the nature and limits of the concept remains impossible, we consider the book's discussions as a continuation of previous discursive trials and a foundation for future ones.

Editors

The Translation of Identity in (Trans)National Literatures

Theodora Valkanou, PhD.

ABSTRACT

In an increasingly globalised context, literature seems to be at a crossroads between the national and the transnational. While promoting national literatures as manifestations of a distinct cultural identity is an established practice, the recent attention on transnationalism has shifted the focus on literatures that transcend the cultural entity of the nation-state. Either way, the notion of identity remains central in literary texts. Collective identity, in particular, is of great interest, as literary texts often contain and enact the cultural manifestations of a specific community. These representations gain further meaning when literature is translated into another language. This paper seeks to explore the constituents of the notion of collective identity as it manifests in literary texts and the role of translation in its intercultural transfer. Drawing on various conceptualisations of national and cultural identity, first, it delineates the elements that may feature as identity markers in literary texts, discussing both texts that may be representative of a national canon, as well as texts whose transnational hybridity negotiates identity creating more layers of complexity. It then proceeds to consider how translation mediates identity, offering new constructions and representations for foreign audiences. Taking into consideration not only textual and paratextual aspects, but also publishing practices, this paper discusses the journey of identities as they cross boundaries through translated literature.

Keywords: Identity, Nation-State, Transnationalism, Translation, Literature

Introduction

The concept of identity seems to be a focal point in several fields of knowledge. Philosophy, psychology, cognitive science, and sociology, to name but a few, engage in a perennial debate about its specifics. Used as a technical term in algebra and logic, it also became central in Western philosophy initially through the writings of John Locke ([1689] 1813), further developed by Immanuel Kant ([1781] 1855), and later, particularly by Georg Wilhelm Friedrich Hegel ([1812] 1969). It is a key concept in psychology, with the term "identification" first used by Sigmund Freud and the term identity later popularised and diffused by Erik Erikson in the 1950s. A core concept in the social sciences, it has lately been introduced to almost every field of the humanities, on account of the interdisciplinary nature research has assumed. Cultural and literary studies follow the same trend.

While scholarship over the centuries has managed to circumscribe the notion of identity and chart its formation, its evasiveness in the realm of cultural and literary studies remains a constant concern, as evidenced by recent work, in titles such as *Exploring Identity in Literature and Life Stories: The Elusive Self* (Barstad et al. 2019). The quest for the semiotic signifiers that constitute the discursive construct of the self in literature is never-ending. And if individual identities and subjectivities are challenging to grasp, due to their dynamic and fluid character, collective identities present yet more challenges. Matters become increasingly more complex when collective identities are not restricted to a single national space, but transcend those boundaries to include multiple sites and various cultural contexts.

Cultural identity, which is often used as an umbrella term to foster a plethora of identities, is linked to memory, history, politics, and social consciousness and is thus ubiquitous. Literary texts provide the space where the intersection between culture and identity is commonly explored and illustrated. It is in literary texts that cultural spaces, practices, and perceptions are displayed and negotiated, allowing for a temporary crystallisation of cultural identity to be witnessed. Seeing that much of the literature that circulates and is being read globally is translated, the interface between identity and translation becomes of great interest.

This interface provides the focal point for this paper, which examines the elements of cultural identity in literary texts and the role of translation in its intercultural transfer. Engaging in a discussion about the national and the transnational, the paper employs different conceptualisations of cultural identity to explore its manifestations in literature, addressing a series of questions: How can cultural identity be manifested in literature? Which elements may feature as identity markers in literary texts? How do these markers differ in texts that are considered representative of a national canon and texts which are transnational and thus are characterised by a greater degree of hybridity? Finally, how can translation mediate cultural identity for foreign audiences and what is the role of the various agents involved in the process? Through an analysis of the features which make up national and transnational identity in literature and a discussion of how identity may register in translated texts, this paper seeks to explore the translatability of cultural identity.

Identity, Culture, and Nation

The study of identity has received great attention in various disciplines, with scholars basing their work on either objectivist or subjectivist epistemological assumptions (Côté 2006), discussing identity formation and broadening their scope to include agency and culture (Côté and Levine 2002), and examining both the individual and the collective, with interest gravitating towards the latter as of the end of the twentieth century (Cerulo 1997). As for the collective, much analysis has been dedicated to cultural identity, which will be the focus of this paper. The discussion will be based on the proposition that identity is constructed and enacted within discursive practices (Davies and Harré 1991; Easthope 1983, 1999; Hall 1996; Said 2003).

This discursive view sees identities as "fluid and contingent" (Woodward 2000, 4) and thus subject to change. The move towards less rigid meanings of identity, away from static, ontological, essentialist models, which are now largely considered outdated, characterises the literature of cultural studies and the social sciences in recent decades. The fact that identity is not intrinsic in either individuals or groups, but rather a social construct has been observed by various scholars.

Stuart Hall's (1991, 1996) views have brought about an important shift in the way we consider issues of identity. Rejecting any homogeneous notion of identity and defining it as a "strategic and positional one," (1996 3) he expands his theoretical position that identity is always in flux, to consider cultural identity. According to Hall (1991), " identities are never completed, never finished; ... they are always as subjectivity itself is, in process.... Identity is always in process of formation." (47) Homi Bhabha's (1990, 1994) seminal work on hybridity also challenges essentialist conceptions of identity as static and uniform. For Bhabha (1994) identities are fluid and plural, characterised by hybridity and fragmentation, especially in colonial and postcolonial contexts. The same core concepts are found in Edward Said's (1994) work, where he maintains that there is no such thing as a pure culture: "all cultures ... are heterogeneous, extraordinarily differentiated and unmonolithic." (xxix) Thus, cultural identities, too, are found to be constructed in multiplicity and heterogeneity.

While cultural identity is increasingly being treated in terms of fluidity and heterogeneity, another concept that closely relates to it claims the same space. Cultural identity is very often associated with a sense of a national culture. Indeed, there seems to be a reciprocal relation between the two concepts of culture and nation. The two notions of cultural identity and national identity often intersect or coincide, a fact which leads to the two terms being used interchangeably in many cases. In his second definition of culture as "a concept that includes a refining and elevating element," Said (1994) observes that "in time culture comes to be associated, often aggressively, with the nation or the state; this differentiates "us" from "them"[...]. Culture in this sense is a source of identity, and a rather combative one at that, as we see in recent 'returns' to culture and tradition." (xiii)

The fact that some scholars argue that nations and nation-states need to be seen not only as political but also as cultural entities (Corrigan and Sayer 1985; Gruffudd 1995) further underlines the close relationship between the two institutions. Most theorists maintain that a shared, common culture is one of the elements that make up nations and by the same token national identities. Elaine Baldwin et al. (1999) observe that "culture is crucial to the making of national identity," (167) while Ernest Gellner (1983, 53-57) also elaborates on the importance of a shared culture for the formation of nationalities.

The impact of national identities has been extensively reported in the relevant literature. Acknowledging the fact that nations are "inventions,"[1] An-

---

1   As with culture and identity, the fact that nations, in the "modernist" sense, are "inven-

4

thony D. Smith (1991, 71), underscores the role played by nationalisms in the formation of nations and national identities, considering them as "a form of culture and identity." (72) He goes on to observe that "of all the collective identities in which human beings share today, national identity is perhaps the most fundamental and inclusive [...]. Other types of collective identity—class, gender, race, religion—may overlap or combine with national identity but they rarely succeed in undermining its hold, though they may influence its direction." (143) A similar remark is found in Hutchinson and Smith's (1994) introduction to *Nationalism*: "what is often conceded is the power, even primacy of national loyalties and identities over those of even class, gender, and race." (4)

Benedict Anderson (1991) affirms the same view when he writes, "nation-ness is the most universally legitimate value in the political life of our time," (3) while Jonathan Hall (2002) observes that "in the smaller, more interconnected and cosmopolitan world in which we live, ethnic and national categorization has assumed an ever increasing importance." (5) Brian Porter-Szücs (2009) also refers to the "centrality of the concept of 'the nation' as a means of organizing identity in the modern world," (3) while Raphael Samuel (1989) notes that "whatever the uncertainties surrounding it, the idea of nationality remains deeply embedded in the political unconscious." (xxxii) Besides, it has been argued that "the imagined community of the nation-state remains a very special case, as it seems unimaginable except as superordinate to and sovereign over all other imaginable communities." (Milner and Browitt 2002, 141)

All these views underline the fact that national identity is still largely considered more influential than other collective identities, with "nation" being used to a great extent as a means of categorisation. It is in this spirit that literary texts continue to be viewed through a national lens. National literary canons, national awards and international awards granted to writers who are considered representative of their national cultures confirm this resistant tendency. The most characteristic and persistent model is the continuing systematisation of literary texts as belonging to "national literatures," which are commonly considered to embody a sense of national cultural identity.[2]

---

tions" and came into being in the late eighteenth century has been underlined by various scholars. See Anderson (1991); Gellner (1964); Kedourie (2000).

2   The issue of cultural and national identity as manifested in literature has been the object

The idea of national literatures, a relatively recent cultural construction, owes much to the German Romantics of the late eighteenth century who disseminated the notion that literatures should be attached to specific national entities and present a particular national character accordingly. The consolidation of a national literary culture has been connected to the emergence of the novel and the newspaper, as Benedict Anderson (1983) has argued in *Imagined Communities*, but other forms of writing, from poetry and drama to popular-culture literature and children's books, have also been linked to the construction of national identity.

Until today, national literatures operate as powerful ideological apparatuses which, among other purposes, serve the process of nation-building and enhance the sense of national belonging, especially through education, where works from the national canon are taught and consolidated, imposing the cultural hegemony of a shared national identity. As Sarah M. Corse (1997) marks, national literatures "are an integral part of the process by which nation-states create themselves and distinguish themselves from other nations." (7) Hence, national literatures seem to cling to particular characteristics that reinforce national identity formation and perpetuate the notion of a distinct national character. As such, they are constructed, circulated and read, both within the nation-state itself, but also cross-nationally or internationally, on the premise that they embody and enact a distinct national identity.

For this paper, what is of interest are those elements of the literary texts that may constitute identity markers. To circumscribe those features, I shall turn to certain definitions of culture and nation to attempt to isolate the relevant concepts. From the definitions that have been proposed for culture and cultural identity[3] In numerous publications that abound every year, I have distinguished two, as the most comprehensive and relevant ones. The first one by Jackson and Garner (1999) defines culture as

---

of much research. Approaches to the topic range from theorised discourses on the relationship between a nation and its narratives (Bhabha 1990; Dirlik 2002; Wertsch 2021) to more concrete studies that focus on particular national and cultural identities as expressed in literature; Englishness, for instance (Baucom 1999; Childs 1999; Dodd 1986; Easthope 1999). Of particular interest are writings whose major concern is the impact colonialism/postcolonialism and nationalism have on literary representations of cultural identity (Eagleton, Jameson, and Said 1990; Hawley 1996; Innes 1996; Reiss 1992; Szeman 2003).

3   A. L. Kroeber and Clyde Kluckhohnen ([1952] 1963) had already listed 164 definitions by 1952.

"A set of patterns, beliefs, behaviors, institutions, symbols, and practices shared and perpetuated by a consolidated group of individuals connected by an ancestral heritage and a concomitant geographical reference location." (44) The second one defines cultural identity as "A sense of belonging to a particular culture or ethnic group. It is formed in a process that results from membership in a particular culture, and it involves learning about and accepting the traditions, heritage, language, religion, ancestry, aesthetics, thinking patterns, and social structures of culture." (Lustig and Koester 1999, 138)

Accordingly, as far as nation is concerned, theorists have proposed various definitions, underscoring that it is the sense of belonging to a particular collectivity that yields national identity. The analysis here will be based on the Western model of perceiving national identity, and more specifically on European conceptions of nation, while the variety of perspectives in non-Western models is fully acknowledged. Among the numerous lists of elements that make up a nation, Anthony D. Smith (1991) and Samuel P. Huntington's (2004) definitions are noteworthy.

According to Smith (1991), "a nation can therefore be defined as a named human population sharing a historical territory, common myths and historical memories, a mass, public culture, a common economy and common legal rights and duties for all its members," (14) while Huntington (2004), in his account of national identity writes that "while national identity was at times in the West the highest form of identity, it also has been a derived identity whose intensity comes from other sources. National identity usually but not always includes a territorial element and may also include one or more ascriptive (race, ethnicity), cultural (religion, language), and political (state, ideology) elements, as well as occasionally economic (farming) or social (network) ones." (30)

It is apparent that the concepts of culture and nation, and by the same token cultural and national identity, have many elements in common. The definitions proposed cover aspects from values and symbolic practices to economic and political structures, as they are meant to cover a variety of collectivities. Elements such as place, heritage and memory, language, and beliefs seem to be the most prevalent ones; they are bound to be of great significance for any national culture. These elements are also expected to be reflected as identity markers in literature. I would, however, like

7

to adopt Jonathan Hall's view (2002, 9-14), according to which, there is not one single one-defines-all model to be used when talking about group identity and markers of differentiation, and maintain the same to be true of national and cultural identity.

Hence, for each national culture, there will be a different combination of the aforementioned elements which may be considered as the most characteristic, and varying degrees of significance will be assigned to them. These features will then be found in the narratives and the literary representations of a culture mirroring a particular character that distinguishes it from every other national culture. Thus, certain national cultures might deem religion as a significant constituent, for instance, while others might hold myths or traditional practices as important for their cultural coherence. Either way, whatever markers are salient for each national culture will largely be reflected in the national narratives and the texts which form national literatures.

Identity Beyond Nation: Cosmopolitanism and Transnationalism

But if identity can be schematically circumscribed with the help of various definitions of culture and nation, how can it be delineated for works which defy nation as an analytical category? Two frameworks, closely related to each other, have been proposed as alternatives to the national paradigm: cosmopolitanism and transnationalism. Both are connected to the increasingly globalising processes of contemporary reality, but both have been considered to "lack a universally accepted definition." (Roudometof 2005, 113) For the purposes of this paper, the focus will be on the latter, but a few words are due for the former, as well.

Laura Chrisman (2003) observes that cosmopolitics has emerged as "a response to the proliferation of ethnic-based nationalisms." (157) Indeed, cosmopolitanism has long been treated as a universalistic concept in social theory. Thus, Bruce Robbins' (1998) claim that cosmopolitanism is "understood as a fundamental devotion to the interests of humanity as a whole" (1) could serve as a very concise definition of the concept. Similarly, Robert Fine (2007) maintains that "its basic presupposition is that the human species can be understood only if it is treated as a single subject, within which all forms of difference are recognised and respected but conceptualised as internal to the substantive unity of all human beings." (x)

Hence, cosmopolitanism underscores the notion that the subjects it is supposed to pertain to coincide with the whole of humanity and prioritises their shared mental and social belonging, transcending and rising beyond any perceived differences, albeit respecting them. Taking into consideration that identity can only be constructed and maintained through difference (Butler 1993; Cohen 1994; Derrida 1978; Gilroy 1997; Grossberg 1996; Hall 1996; Laclau 1990; Woodward 2000), it is soon clear that this approach leaves little room for the discussion of distinguishing features which circumscribe identity.

Transnationalism, on the other hand, was first employed as an academic term as early as 1916, by cultural critic Randolph Bourne. Over a century later, the concept of transnationalism has proven very vibrant and far-ranging. It has been applied to describe cross-border trade and global business practices (Green 2019; Sommer 2020), to examine black diasporic identities (Gilroy 1993), but mainly to discuss a dual or multiple-country sense of belonging and other experiences of dislocation and migrancy. The postcolonial, diasporic or migrant condition is clearly at the heart of transnationalism. Within migration studies, it has developed as a concept to refer to "the process whereby people establish and maintain socio-cultural connections across geopolitical borders." (International Organization for Migration 2008, 500)

Transnationalism emphasises the receding role of nation-states and the sense of national identity that stems from them, due to the increased movement of people, goods and ideas across national borders. While related to cosmopolitanism, transnationalism is deemed more appropriate for the scope of this paper. One of the differences between cosmopolitanism and transnationalism is that the former focuses on the universal and is more often than not a choice, a conscious, deliberate ideological stance connected to flexibility that spans across borders, while the latter is more adequate to discuss the particular lived experience of individuals as members of social spaces that connect geographical and cultural origins and destinations. Transnationalism implies a spatial and cultural duality or multiplicity, and is better suited to include the underprivileged and the coerced, while cosmopolitanism has often been linked to privilege (Cronin 2006).

Hence, I would argue that the voluntariness that cosmopolitanism is associated with might make it more suitable for the discussion of individual identities, while transnationalism embraces a broader social space. This social space obviously does not coincide with the nation-state, but is rather embedded in the concept of civil society (Kaldor 1999; Peck 2020; Portes 2001) or is spread across multiple sites, as is often common with migrant subjects who negotiate their identities, culturally cross-fertilising several localities. As Glick Schiller et al. (1992) state, discussing immigrants whose social activity links their country of origin to the host country, "transmigrants develop and maintain multiple relations—familial, economic, social, organisational, religious, and political, that span borders. Transmigrants take actions, make decisions, and feel concerns, and develop identities within social networks that connect them to two or more societies simultaneously." (1–2) Following the line of thought of Vertovec (1999), Levitt and Glick Schiller (2004), and Erdal and Oeppen (2013), transnationalism is considered here to embrace not only ways of being but also ways of belonging, both of which are intrinsically related to identity.

By definition, transnationalism goes beyond the concept of a specific national identity, to embrace features that imply a duality or multiplicity of collective identities that span across spatial boundaries. This expansion from a single space to a plurality of alternatives poses new challenges for the treatment of identity. Stephen Vertovec's (2001) assertion that "transnationalism and identity are concepts that inherently call for juxtaposition" (573) underscores the perceived paradoxical relation between the two notions. Nevertheless, if there is one thing that is known about identity is that, despite it being slippery, it is also ubiquitous regardless of the forms it might take. This means that in the absence of national identity as a distinguishing feature, other forms of shared identities are bound to take its place. Being shaped by parameters that operate beyond the centralising forces of the nation-state, these identities are dynamically constructed, constantly negotiated and reasonably hybrid.

These hybrid identities, which are born from the "diverse and uneven flows and connections that underpin interdependence across borders" (Yeoh and Collins 2022, 1) also shape a more recent current in literature that embraces the coexistence and multiplicity of distant spaces, different cultures, and complementary identities. While the model of examining literature within national frames still holds, the need to account for more multifaceted approaches both in literature and in literary criticism is becoming more pressing. Acknowledging the persistence of a nationalist ideal in the conventional structures of literary study in the United States, for example, Paul Jay (2010) emphasises "how contemporary criticism became increasingly preoccupied with difference in ways that undermine the neat, superficial cultural homogeneity informing the study of national literatures" (25) and maintains that literary and cultural studies have taken a "transnational turn."

This shift is best reflected in the cross-cultural narratives of transnational literature. Themes of migration and displacement, hybridity as a result of multiple cultural influences, but also the global perspectives of a constantly changing world are all to be found in transnational writing. Contested memories, shifting power dynamics, and interconnected histories are also at the heart of transnational narratives, as a constant reminder of the ripple effects of events such as wars, migration, and colonisation. The characters that populate the transnational literary landscape tend to be multifaceted and open to ambiguity, offering nuanced portrayals of the human experience, reflecting in their complexity their diverse journeys and backgrounds.

The literary settings found in transnational texts are fluid and dynamic, portraying the movement of characters across different locations. Whether from one continent to another, from rural to urban, from the colony to the metropolis, the diversity of the landscapes helps to shape the characters' experiences. As Stephen Clingman (2009) puts it in his discussion of transnational texts, "the grammar of identity emerges from difference and distance—in space, in time, within and beyond the self. The grammar of identity is in that regard combinatory, not exclusive or substitutive, or surrounded by impermeable walls." (240-41) Not surprisingly, recent transnational literature might also refer to the impact of technology, media, and digital practices, as they might reflect the contemporary realities of people who move across borders in a digital age.

As such, transnational literatures dismantle the traditional notion of national belonging and the perceived homogeneity it implies in every possible way. As Jay (2021) points out, "a transnational perspective usually understands identity and culture in dialectical terms." (10) This means that rather than confirming points of convergence, as the national paradigm does, a transnational approach to writing would depend on elements of identity which might be diverse or even conflicting, but complementary in many ways.

Every single one of the markers which circumscribe a semiotic signifier of collective national belonging is re-experienced, re-negotiated and re-told in new hybrid narrative forms.

Place is a very telling example. The rootedness suggested by a specific locality, one of the cornerstones in the representation of national identity in literary texts, is replaced in transnational narratives by a multiplicity of locations where subjects fashion and enact their identities in unprecedented and unexpected ways: common and dissimilar trajectories cross each other to produce new meanings and ways of belonging. The fluid nature of cultural practices and identities across globalised settings, eloquently described in "Travelling Cultures" by James Clifford (1992) no longer takes place in a self-contained location, but is rather to be found in mobility, transnational exchange, and asymmetry and is accordingly reflected in transnational literary texts.

Similarly, the other identity markers which emerge as salient, based on the definitions of culture and nation discussed in the previous section, take different forms in transnational literature. One important aspect to consider, nonetheless, is that the markers found in the model of a national paradigm are not discarded; each one of them is rather multiplied and re-arranged in what might resemble a kaleidoscopic mode. Each one will no longer be perceived as indicative of a certain national character, but will rather bear traces of all the cultures the transnational subjects are part of, adding more nuanced meanings to texts and their readings. Myths are retold, religion, when found in a new context where it is not dominant, might be perceived and represented differently, and old values from the homeland will clash or merge with new ones.

Language, in particular, is arguably the most interesting and complex feature in transnational writing; the use of multiple vernaculars, pidgin formations, and codeswitching are typical. Apart from multilingualism, the act of self-translation is central and indicative of the complicated choices transnational subjects need to make when deciding which aspects of their hybrid identities they will put forth in each setting. Echoing Salman Rushdie's (1991, 17) "translated men" (sic) and Homi Bhabha's (1988) "third space," which "challenges our sense of the historical identity of culture as a homogenizing, unifying force," (21) transnational literary texts bear witness to the transmigrants' complex experience of simultaneously inhabiting various cultural spaces and the need to accommodate not only the plurality of linguistic and cultural codes, but also of identities.

At the same time, new constituents of identity come to the fore, as collective identities are bound to rise to take the place of national identity where the latter is not pertinent. These may be uncommon, unique to the writer or the text, or they may take the form of larger analytical categories. In this case, what might unite writings within the transnational frame is an intersectional set of identity markers. The trajectories of writers and texts bear no or little connection to a single national entity; rather, they might resonate across constantly evolving conceptions of race, ethnicity, class, gender and sexuality, among others. As a consequence, the texts will depict particular images, characters, relevant vocabularies and conditions that shed light on the common experiences that unite subjects who share the aforementioned identities across transnational settings. In this case, these shared identities will arguably become salient in texts, allowing for intertextual connections that transcend the national and inviting readings that will generate new meanings of being and belonging. If these texts are meant to be read in another language the representation of these salient identities will largely depend on the way they will be translated.

Identity in Translation: The National and the Transnational

As a major component of interlinguistic communication, translation, besides linguistic transcoding, always implies a complex process of cultural transfer, as well (Bassnett 2013; Bassnett and Lefevere 1998; Hermans 1985; Hönig and Kußmaul 1984; Lefevere 1992; Reiss and Vermeer 1984; Snell-Hornby 1990). Ever since the 1980s with the "cultural turn" in translation studies (Lefevere and Bassnett 1990, 1), the cultural aspects of translation have come to the fore. The shift of focus towards the interaction between translation and culture has also led to an increased interest in the relation between identity and translation (Cronin 2006; Ellis and Oakley-Brown 2001; House, Martín Ruano, and Baumgarten 2005; Sidiropoulou 2005; Wolf 2008), especially in conjunction with the notion of cultural translation.

Cultural translation entails several issues that arise when cultures come into contact: power relations between cultures and their literary systems, the representation of the foreign, the degree of translatability, and, by consequence, the extent to which cross-cultural understanding can be achieved. Within translation studies, the term "cultural translation" has been most commonly used in a rather straightforward, literal sense. Kate Sturge, for example, defines it as "those practices of literary translation that mediate cultural difference or try to convey extensive cultural background, or set out to represent another culture via translation." (67) It is often considered as a process that not only allows for the foreign to come across, but is actually one that ought to highlight cultural specificity (Berman [1985] 2021; Snell-Hornby 1995; Venuti 1995).

Literary translation practice, however, often seems to prioritise domesticating strategies to make literary texts more accessible to target-culture readers. These strategies dictate the assimilation of the foreign to the translation norms of the target culture, at the expense of the cultural distinctiveness of the source texts. Furthermore, it is often the case that the distance and low degree of familiarisation between two cultures make the translators' task of accentuating alterity even more demanding, corroborating the view that cultural identity is difficult to translate (Bhabha 1994, 5, 224; Brisset 2003, 338).

Some theorists even argue that cultural translatability is impossible. Gayatri Chakravorty Spivak (2008), for instance, underscores the necessity but impossibility of cultural translation, while similar points about literal translation had been made earlier both by Walter Benjamin ([1923] 2021) and later by Jacques Derrida (1998, 57). These views challenge the existence of stable, unchangeable meaning and, by extension, the existence of an intrinsic cultural identity that is knowable and could thus be objectively represented. Hence, the impossibility—according to these positions—to translate; or, in other words, to transfer into another language/culture the meaning/identity that is present in the original, since meaning and identity are always provisional and can never be fully grasped.

Similarly, Bhabha (1994) underscores the provisional nature of culture, language, and thus translation, drawing a parallel between Benjamin's "foreignness"—which he sees as akin to "the performativity of translation as the staging of cultural difference" (325)—and cultural translation, using it metaphorically. Although he uses the notion of cultural translation not as the transfer of texts, but of human experience, to refer to human migrancy, rather than to any of the traditional meanings of translation, he insists on the notion of provisionality attributed to culture, and by the same token to translation. As he puts it, "translation is the performative nature of cultural communication." (1994, 228) This notion of provisionality seems very adequate to elucidate the complex ways in which meaning is articulated in the construction of cultural identity and its manifestations both in national and transnational literatures. This provisionality of meaning does not necessarily render the cultural aspects of literary texts untranslatable, but rather more open to a multiplicity of potential meanings and more negotiable in terms of the representation of the cultural identity they entail. It also allows for the consideration of how the translation agents and the readers of the target culture might influence the reception and reconstruction of foreign cultural identities.

Nevertheless, as previously discussed, cultural identity is bound to be enunciated differently in texts that form part of national literature and texts which are considered transnational. For the former, the focus would be on the manner in which the specificity of a particular national character is transferred through the translation process. For the latter, the role of translation in highlighting identity is a lot more complex and might take different forms.

Within the texts which are viewed as "national literature," there are elements- in acordance with the identity markers discussed in the previous section, which are distinctive of national culture and its aesthetics. In an article entitled "National Literature and Interliterary System," Naftoli Bassel (1991) claims there are eight features which characterise any national literature:

> an organic connection to the historical destiny of its ethnic group; a national language as the basic medium of its existence; rootedness in the folklore and mythology of its ethnic group; stability and dynamism as an aesthetic system; the existence of an indigenous, self-aware artistic tradition interacting with other national art forms; social and aesthetic heterogeneity; a literary development and growth influenced by, or generically and typologically correlated with, other literatures and the world literary process; belonging to various interliterary (zonal,

> ethno-linguistic, regional) systems, whose spectrum is comparatively stable and well defined for each national literature." (773)

This approach connects the specific characteristics of national culture as manifested in literature with the broader context of other national literatures; it is through the contact with and the juxtaposition to these other systems that the features of national literature are highlighted and perceived as unique. Whether in the form of culture-specific items and references, historical, mythological or literary allusions, or even in the overall universe of aesthetics and values which are portrayed in the texts that form part of national literature, these features will represent a specific cultural identity associated with a particular national character.

Transnational literature, on the other hand, might as well present certain features which can be perceived as salient in expressing identity and, as such, they should receive the translator's attention. They could schematically be divided in the following way: a) the elements which also serve as cultural identity markers in national literatures, as mentioned previously, albeit in a multiple, polyphonic, syncretic form, and b) other markers, which may be central to identity formation and which often gain prominence when considered intersectionally. As discussed in the previous section, these may include race, ethnicity, class gender, and sexuality, but also (dis)ability, or immigration status, to name but a few. These identities may be articulated in the literary texts, through particular codes, specific use of language, images and cultural references that are associated with them.

How these features and the cultural identity they embody will be treated in translation depends not only on the translators, but on several translation agents and other influential factors. Their role as to how cultural identity will be represented is decisive; similar to André Lefevere's (1992) control factors which include both professionals within the literary system and "patronage," outside the literary system itself, referring to "the powers (persons, institutions) that can further or hinder the reading, writing, and rewriting of literature." (15) Besides translators, an array of translation agents, mainly publishers and editors, but also other individuals or institutions that are further removed from the translator's task, such as academics, reviewers and marketing specialists, may intervene in the way the foreign is to be presented to the target-culture audience. These agents, along with economic, sociopolitical, and ideological factors help shape the dominant translation norms in each target culture, which in turn influence the expectations and literary tastes of the readers.

The degree to which a work that forms part of a particular national literature will be presented as such, whether it will be exoticised, or will largely have its distinct national character concealed or even obliterated varies and once again this does not solely depend on translators. The choice of a domesticating or foreignising strategy will obviously condition the representation of cultural specificity, but so will other factors, such as the paratexts used (Genette 1997): not only peritextual material, such as the choice of title, the cover and illustrations of a book, or its stated inclusion in a specific series, that either highlights or obscures its national origins, but also epitextual elements, such as relevant reviews or promotional texts, for instance, which might or might not make the nationality of the author or the book a central matter.

The same forces are at work in the case of transnational literary works. Nevertheless, with transnational literature, we are not faced with the reflection of the discursive construction of national specificity in texts, which can be located and perceived relatively more neatly, but rather with the constant renegotiation of multiple and constantly multiplying identities: ephemeral, idiosyncratic and everchanging. Translation in this case becomes equally significant in portraying identity, as this does not operate on a single level, but it simultaneously connects and transcodes several geographical and cultural spaces that present themselves as a single source—text, language, culture—when, in fact, they are an intrinsic combination of assorted hybrid identities. Here, too, the role of agents and extra-textual factors, as well as the readers' expectations are significant.

Transnational texts will more often than not be idiosyncratic, displaying new salient identity features, which may clash with the readers' expectations or the dominant discourse in the target cultures into which they will be translated—most commonly assumed to be cultures of the global North.[4] A telling example that not incidentally comes from a context which is not only transnational, but also postcolonial concerns autobiographical narratives by Northern African women.

---

4   For a more detailed discussion on the pressure on writers from the Global South to cater to the North's tastes and expectations, see Wiegandt (2020).

Examining the reception of Algerian women's autobiographies in France, Patricia Geesey (2012) notes: "These narratives may be read on several levels as texts that seek to reformulate the debates on assimilation, integration, and cultural and identity politics within a new discursive territory." (174) This statement reaffirms that the identity to be sought in these texts is fluid and negotiable, and can assume different forms depending on their interpretation, which in turn is inseparable from the target culture's dominant discourse, as well as the readers' positionality and expectations. In this specific instance, among the features that define those writers' identity, circumscribing their subjectivity, is their right to name themselves, resisting assimilation. Nonetheless, as Geesey (2012) observes, publishing strategies seek to highlight different features of those texts: "In the case of Algerian women's autobiographies in France, the marketing strategies of publishers are inextricably linked to attempts to capitalize on the public's interest in the lives of North African women and on those cultural practices that are perceived to affirm their "exoticism" and their alterity." (175)

This example is characteristic of the great influence of the publishing world, whose agents might manipulate literary texts, often misrepresenting identity. At the same time, however, it is indicative of the plurality of meanings and identities inherent in literary texts. Probably more than any other literary practice, it is translation that has the potential to reveal them. To appreciate the crucial role of translation in not just representing and bridging cultures, but also its potential to highlight identities and difference in both national and transnational literary texts, one could turn to the work of Walter Benjamin ([1923] 2021) and Homi Bhabha (1990, 1994), as well as to Goethe's concept of *Weltliteratur* (world literature). All of them move beyond the notion of a 'single' original culture depicted in texts. Moreover, Goethe's appreciation of translators is well documented, as in his view "the merit of the translator is not just that he or she is interpolated into a hitherto inaccessible, alien culture, but rather that this transfer also creates a counter-movement of approach to the other culture by exciting 'an irresistible attraction for the original' that the translation creates." (Sturm-Trigonakis 2013, 9)

In line with these views, it is arguable that what is salient as difference, i.e. identity, (which is expected to attract the readers' interest) will be found in those elements articulated and living on through translation, securing the text's "afterlife," as Benjamin ([1923] 2021) famously states in "The Translator's Task." Undoubtedly, the way identity will be represented in translation will also depend on the dominant discourses, norms, tastes, and expectations of the target culture. Creating a metaphor with scientific investigation, translation will play the role of a microscope or a magnifying glass: difference will be highlighted and made evident, but depending largely on what the researcher is seeking.

Taking everything into account, what emerges as a significant parameter when discussing identity in both national and transnational texts is that the notion of singularity is futile. The idea that there is one singular identity, exclusive and vested with authenticity has long been contested (Bhabha 1994; Appiah 2006). The notion that cultural identities are not solid, pure, and monolithic is accompanied by the idea that a single story cannot be the only authentic representation of a culture, as all cultures, national and transnational foster hybridity. In a TED talk, the Nigerian novelist Chimamanda Ngozi Adichie (2009) warns against the perils of relying on a single story to perceive and appreciate cultural identity: "the single story creates stereotypes and the problem with stereotypes is not that they are untrue, but that they are incomplete. They make one story become the only story." (12:49)

The persistent existence of national literatures and canons which then largely feed the demand for foreign books translated in other countries, confirm that the nation still serves as a potent framework to approach identity in literary texts. Even in this case, however, translators have the potential and responsibility to bring forth the multiplicity of identities and stories found in national literatures. Alongside these literatures, runs an alternative stream of transnational texts which, thanks to their diasporic, migrant, or postcolonial character, reject national identity as primary and defy the clichés that might be attached to a single nation, a single location, or a single discourse.

Arguably, by being syncretic and unique in their combination of multiple identities, transnational texts bear a new type of "authenticity" that is difficult to replicate. It is then up to the translators to treat those elements of transnational texts that might be considered salient in expressing identity in a manner that will not obscure them, but will rather underscore their uniqueness. Ultimately, whether national or transnational, texts foster hybridity and contingency of meaning; these notions may broaden our perspective on how cultures come into contact through translation and how translators operate in the space between cultures.

References

Adichie, Chimamanda Ngozi. 2009. "The Danger of a Single Story." TED talk. TEDGlobal 2009, April. Video, 18 min., 32 sec. https://www. ted.com/talks/chimamanda_ngozi_adichie_the_danger_of_a_sin gle_story/transcript?subtitle=en.

Anderson, Benedict. 1991. *Imagined Communities: Reflections on the Origin and Spread of Nationalism.* Rev. ed. Verso.

Appiah, Kwame Anthony. 2006. *Cosmopolitanism: Ethics in a World of Strangers.* W. W. Norton.

Baldwin, Elaine, Brian Longhurst, Scott McCracken, Miles Ogborn, and Greg Smith. 1999. *Introducing Cultural Studies.* Prentice Hall.

Barstad, Guri E., Karen S. P. Knutsen, and Elin Nesje Vestli. 2019. *Exploring Identity in Literature and Life Stories.* Cambridge Scholars Publishing.

Bassel, Naftoli. 1991. "National Literature and Interliterary System." Translated by Ilana Gomel. In "National Literatures/Social Spaces." Special issue, *Poetics Today* 12 (4): 773-779. https://doi.org/10.2307 /1772716.

Bassnett, Susan. 2013. *Translation Studies.* 4th ed. Routledge.

Bassnett, Susan, and André Lefevere, eds. 1990. *Translation, History and Culture.* Pinter Publishers.

———, eds. 1998. *Constructing Cultures: Essays on Literary Translation.* Multilingual Matters.

Baucom, Ian. 1999. *Out of Place: Englishness, Empire and the Locations of Identity.* Princeton University Press.

Bhabha, Homi K. 1988. "The Commitment to Theory." *New Formations* 5 (Summer): 5-23.

———. 1990. "DissemiNation: Time, Narrative, and the Margins of the Modern Nation." In *Nation and Narration*, edited by Homi K. Bhabha, 291-322. Routledge.

———. 1994. *The Location of Culture*. London: Routledge.

Benjamin, Walter. (1923) 2021. "The Translator's Task." Translated by Steven Rendall. In Venuti 2021, 89-97.

Berman, Antoine. (1985) 2021. "Translation and the Trials of the Foreign." Translated by Lawrence Venuti. In Venuti 2021, 247-260.

Bourne, Randolph S. 1916. "Trans-national America." *Atlantic Monthly* 118 (July): 86–97. https://www.swarthmore.edu/SocSci/rbannis1/AIH1 9th/Bourne.html.

Brisset, Annie. 2003. "Alterity in Translation: An Overview of Theories and Practices." Translated by Donna Williams and Michelle Healey. In *Translation Translation*, edited by Susan Petrilli, 101-132. Rodopi.

Butler, Judith. 1993. *Bodies that Matter: On the Discursive Limits of "Sex"*. Routledge.

Cerulo, Karen A. 1997. "Identity Construction: New Issues, New Directions." *Annual Review of Sociology* 23:385-409. http://www.jstor.org/stable/2952557.

Childs, Peter. 1999. "Colonial History, National Identity and 'English Literature.'" Introduction to *Postcolonial Theory and English Literature: A Reader*, 1-31. Edited by Peter Childs. Edinburgh University Press.

Chrisman, Laura. 2003. *Postcolonial Contraventions: Cultural Readings of Race, Imperialism and Transnationalism*. Manchester University Press.

Clifford, James. 1992. "Traveling Cultures." In *Cultural Studies*, edited by Lawrence Grossberg, Cary Nelson, and Paula A. Treichler, 96-112. Routledge.

Clingman, Stephen. 2009. *The Grammar of Identity: Transnational Fiction and the Nature of the Boundary*. Oxford University Press.

Corrigan, Philip, and Derek Sayer. 1985. *The Great Arch: English State For-*

mation *as Cultural Revolution*. Blackwell.

Cohen, Robin. 1994. *Frontiers of Identity: The British and the Others.* Longman.

Corse, Sarah M. 1997. *Nationalism and Literature: The Politics of Culture in Canada and the United States.* Cambridge University Press.

Côté, James E. 2006. "Identity Studies: How Close Are We to Developing a Social Science of Identity?–An Appraisal of the Field." *Identity* 6 (1): 3-25. https://doi.org/10.1207/s1532706xid0601_2.

Côté, James E., and Charles G. Levine. 2002. *Identity Formation, Agency, and Culture: A Social Psychological Synthesis.* Lawrence Erlbaum Associates.

Cronin, Michael. 2006. *Translation and Identity.* Routledge.

Davies, Bronwyn, and Rom Harré. 1991. "Positioning: The Discursive Production of Selves." *Journal for the Theory of Social Behaviour* 20 (1): 43-63.

Derrida, Jacques. 1978. *Writing and Difference.* Translated by Alan Bass. Chicago University Press.

———. 1998. *Monolingualism of the Other; or, The Prosthesis of Origin.* Translated by Patrick Mensah. Stanford University Press.

Dirlik, Arif. 2002. "Literature/Identity: Transnationalism, Narrative and Representation." *Review of Education, Pedagogy, and Cultural Studies* 24 (3): 209-234. https://doi:10.1080/10714410213688.

Dodd, Philip. 1986. "Englishness and the National Culture." In *Englishness: Politics and Culture 1880-1920*, edited by Robert Colls, and Philip Dodd, 1-28. Croom Helm.

Eagleton, Terry, Fredric Jameson, and Edward W. Said. 1990. *Nationalism, Colonialism and Literature.* University of Minnesota Press.

Easthope, Antony. 1983. *Poetry as Discourse.* Methuen.

———. 1999. *Englishness and National Culture.* Routledge.

Ellis, Roder, and Liz Oakley-Brown, eds. 2001. *Translation and Nation: Towards a Cultural Politics of Englishness*. Multilingual Matters.

Erdal, Marta Bivand, and Ceri Oeppen. 2013. "Migrant Balancing Acts: Understanding the Interactions Between Integration and Transnationalism." *Journal of Ethnic and Migration Studies* 39 (6): 867–884. https://doi.org/10.1080/1369183X.2013.765647.

Fine, Robert. 2007. *Cosmopolitanism*. Routledge.

Geesey, Patricia. 2012. "Identity and Community in Autobiographies of Algerian Women in France." In *Going Global: The Transnational Reception of Third World Women Writers*, edited by Amal Amireh and Lisa Suhair Majaj, 173-205. Routledge.

Gellner, Ernest. 1964. *Thought and Change*. Weidenfeld and Nicolson.

———. 1983. *Nations and Nationalism*. Blackwell.

Genette, Gerard. 1997. *Paratexts: Thresholds of Interpretation*. Translated by Jane E. Lewin. Cambridge University Press.

Gilroy, Paul. 1993. *The Black Atlantic: Modernity and Double Consciousness*. Verso Books.

———. 1997. "Diaspora and the Detours of Identity." In *Identity and Difference*, edited by Kathryn Woodward, 299-343. Sage in association with Open University.

Glick Schiller, Nina, Linda Basch, and Christina Blanc-Szanton. 1992. "Transnationalism: A New Analytic Framework for Understanding Migration." *Annals of the New York Academy of Sciences* 645 (1): 1–24.

Green, Nancy L. 2019. *The Limits of Transnationalism*. University of Chicago Press.

Grossberg, Lawrence. 1996. "Identity and Cultural Studies: Is That All There Is?" In *Questions of Cultural Identity*, edited by Stuart Hall and Paul du Gay, 87-107. Sage.

Gruffudd, Pyrs. 1995. "Remaking Wales: Nation-Building and the Geographical Imagination, 1925-1950." *Political Geography* 14 (3): 219-39.

Hall, Jonathan. 2002. *Hellenicity: Between Ethnicity and Culture.* University of Chicago Press.

Hall, Stuart. 1991. "Old and New Identities, Old and New Ethnicities." In *Culture, Globalization and the World System: Contemporary Conditions for the Representation of Identity*, edited by Anthony King, 41-68. Macmillan, 1991.

———. 1996. "Who Needs 'Identity'?" Introduction to *Questions of Cultural Identity*, 1-17. Edited by Stuart Hall and Paul du Gay. Sage.

Hawley, John, C., ed. 1996. *Writing the Nation: Self and Country in Post-colonial Imagination.* Rodopi.

Hegel, Georg Wilhelm Friedrich. (1812) 1969. *Hegel's Science of Logic.* Translated by A. V. Miller. Allen and Unwin.

Hermans, Theo, ed. 1985. *The Manipulation of Literature: Studies in Literary Translation.* Croom Helm.

Hönig, Hans G., and Paul Kußmaul. 1984. *Strategie der Übersetzung. Ein Lehr- und Arbeitsbuch.* Narr.

House, Juliane, M. Rosario Martín Ruano, and Nicole Baumgarten, eds. 2005. *Translation and the Construction of Identity: IATIS Yearbook 2005.* IATIS.

Huntington, Samuel P. 2004. *Who Are We? America's Great Debate.* Free Press.

Hutchinson, John, and Anthony Smith. 1994. Introduction to *Nationalism*, 3-13. Edited by John Hutchinson and Anthony Smith. Oxford University Press.

International Organization for Migration. 2008. *World Migration Report 2008: Managing Labour Mobility in the Evolving Global Economy.* International Organization for Migration.

Innes, C. L. 1996. "'Forging the Conscience of Their Race': Nationalist Writers." In *New National and Post-Colonial Literatures: An Introduction*, edited by Bruce King, 120-39. Clarendon-Oxford University Press.

Jackson, Ronald L. II, and Thurmon Garner. 1999. "Tracing the Evolution of 'Race,' 'Ethnicity,' and 'Culture' in Communication Studies." *The Howard Journal of Communication* 9 (1): 41-45.

Jay, Paul. 2010. *Global Matters: The Transnational Turn in Literary Studies*. Cornell University Press.

———. 2021. *Transnational Literature: The Basics*. Routledge.

Kaldor, Mary. 1999. "Transnational Civil Society." In *Human Rights in Global Politics*, edited by Tim Dunne and Nicholas J. Wheeler, 195-213. Cambridge University Press.

Kant, Immanuel. (1781) 1855. *Critique of Pure Reason*. Translated by J. M. D. Meiklejohn. Bohn.

Kedourie, Elie. 2000. *Nationalism*. 4th ed. Blackwell.

Kroeber, A. L., and Clyde Kluckhohn. (1952) 1963. *Culture: A Critical Review of Concepts and Definitions*. Vintage.

Laclau, Ernesto. 1990. *New Reflections on the Revolution of Our Time*. Verso.

Lefevere, André. 1992. *Translation, Rewriting and the Manipulation of the Literary Fame*. Routledge.

Lefevere, André, and Susan, Bassnett. 1990. "Introduction: Proust's Grandmother and the Thousand and One Nights. The 'Cultural Turn" in Translation Studies." In Bassnett and Lefevere 1990, 1-13.

Levitt, Peggy, and Nina Glick Schiller. 2004. "Transnational Perspectives on Migration: Conceptualizing Simultaneity." *International Migration Review* 38 (3): 1002-39.

Locke, John. (1689) 1813. *An Essay Concerning Human Understanding*. Vol. 1. Cummings & Hilliard and J. T. Buckingham.

Lustig, Myron W., and Jolene Koester. 1999. *Intercultural Competence: Interpersonal Communication across Cultures*. Addison-Wesley.

Milner, Andrew, and Jeff Browitt. 2002. *Contemporary Cultural Theory: An Introduction*. Routledge.

Peck, Sarah. 2020. "Transnational Social Capital: The Socio-Spatialities of Civil Society." *Global Networks* 20 (1): 126–149. https://doi.org/10.1111/glob.12234.

Porter-Szücs, Brian. 2009. "Beyond the Study of Nationalism." In *Nationalisms Today*, edited by Krzysztof Jaskulowski and Tomasz Kamusella, 3-15. Peter Lang.

Portes, Alejandro. 2001. "Introduction: The Debates and Significance of Immigrant Transnationalism." *Global Networks* 1 (3): 181–194.

Reiss, Katharina, and Hans J. Vermeer. 1984. *Grundlegung einer allgemeinen Translationstheorie*. Niemeyer.

Reiss, Timothy J. 1992. "Mapping Identities: Literature, Nationalism, Colonialism." *American Literary History* 4 (4): 649-677. https://www.jstor.org/stable/i221327.

Robbins, Bruce. 1998. "Introduction Part I: Actually Existing Cosmopolitanism." In *Cosmopolitics: Thinking and Feeling beyond the Nation*, edited by Pheng Cheah and Bruce Robbins, 1-19. University of Minnesota Press.

Roudometof, Victor. 2005. "Transnationalism, Cosmopolitanism and Glocalization." *Current Sociology* 53 (1): 113–35. https://doi.org/10.1177/0011392105048291.

Rushdie, Salman. 1991. *Imaginary Homelands: Essays and Criticism, 1981-1991*. Granta Books.

Said, Edward W. 1994. *Culture and Imperialism*. Vintage.

———. 2003. *Orientalism*. Penguin.

Samuel, Raphael. 1989. "Exciting to Be English." Introduction to *Patriotism: The Making and Unmaking of British National Identity*. Vol. 1, xviii-lxvii. Edited by Raphael Samuel. Routledge.

Sidiropoulou, Maria, ed. 2005. *Identity and Difference: Translation Shaping Culture*. Lang.

Smith, Anthony D. 1991. *National Identity*. Penguin.

Snell-Hornby, Mary. 1990. "Linguistic Transcoding or Cultural Transfer? A Critique of Translation Theory in Germany." In Bassnett and Lefevere 1990, 79-86.

————. 1995. *Translation Studies: An Integrated Approach*. Rev. ed. John Benjamins.

Sommer, Elena. 2020. *Social Capital as a Resource for Migrant Entrepreneurship: Self Employed Migrants from the Former Soviet Union in Germany*. Springer.

Spivak, Gayatri Chakravorty. 2008. "More Thoughts on Cultural Translation." In "Borders, Nations, Translations." Special issue, *Transversal/ EIPCP multilingual webjournal* (April). https://transversal.at/trans versal/0608/spivak/en.

Sturge, Kate. 2009. "Cultural Translation." In *The Routledge Encyclopedia of Translation Studies*, 2nd ed., edited by Mona Baker and Gabriela Saldanha, 67-70. Routledge.

Sturm-Trigonakis, Elke. 2013. *Comparative Cultural Studies and the New Weltliteratur*. Translated by Athanasia Margoni and Maria Kaisar. Purdue University Press.

Szeman, Imre. 2003. *Zones of Instability: Literature, Postcolonialism and the Nation*. Johns Hopkins University Press.

Venuti, Lawrence. 1995. *The Translator's Invisibility: A History of Translation*. Routledge.

Venuti, Lawrence, ed. 2021. *The Translation Studies Reader*. 4th ed. Routledge.

Vertovec, Steven. 1999. "Conceiving and Researching Transnationalism." *Ethnic and Racial Studies* 22 (2): 447-62. https://doi.org/10.1080/ 014198799329558.

————. 2001. "Transnationalism and Identity." *Journal of Ethnic and Migration Studies* 27 (4): 573–82. https://doi:10.1080/136918301 20090386.

Wertsch, James V. 2021. *How Nations Remember: A Narrative Approach*.

Oxford University Press.

Wiegandt, Kai. 2020. "Transnational Migrant Fiction as World Literature: Identity, Translatability, and the Global Book Market." In *The Transnational in Literary Studies: Potential and Limitations of a Concept*, edited by Kai Wiegandt, 206-25. De Gruyter.

Wolf, Michaela. 2008. "Interference from the *Third Space*? The Construction of Cultural Identity through Translation." In *New Trends in Translation and Cultural Identity*, edited by Micaela Muñoz-Calvo, Carmen Buesa-Gómez and M. Ángeles Ruiz-Moneva, 11-20. Cambridge Scholars.

Woodward, Kath. 2000. Introduction to *Questioning Identity: Gender, Class, Nation*, 1-6. Edited by Kath Woodward. Routledge in association with Open University.

Yeoh, Brenda S.A., and Francis L. Collins. 2022. Introduction to *Handbook on Transnationalism*, 1-28. Edited by Brenda S.A. Yeoh and Francis L. Collins. Edward Elgar Publishing.

Identity and Settler-Colonial Recognition: Hegel, Fanon, Sartre and Coulthard in Conversation

Laxana Paskaran, MEd.

Abstract

Identity and Settler-Colonial Recognition: Hegel, Fanon, Sartre and Coulthard in Conversation This paper places W. G. Hegel, Frantz Fanon, Jean-Paul Sartre and Glen Coulthard in conversation on the issue of identity and recognition within the settler-colonial state. This paper uses an anti-colonial discursive framework to discuss "what is and what ought to be." (Dei 2001, 298) An anti-colonial discursive framework allows scholars to "work within a more flexible, transparent, and fluid language," (Dei and Asgaharzadeh 2001, 299). As such, this paper consists of two sections starting with a brief sketch of Hegel's master-slave dialectic and the complexification of the dialectic. The first section focuses on Hegel's master-slave dialectic. Next, this section provides a close reading of a passage from Black Skin, White Masks to show Fanon's interpretation of Hegel's master-slave dialectic to theorize colonized subjectivities and the trapping of colonized subjects into a domain absent of reciprocal recognition (1952). The second section of the paper is heavily shaped by Fanon's criticisms of mutual reciprocity under the colonial gaze. This section starts with an understanding of decolonization and what it means to resist the settler colonial state. Next, it explores Jean-Paul Sartre's argument of self-affirmation as symbolized by the Négritude movement as a moment in the dialectic, not an end (1964). Further, this paper engages with the essentialist view on the risks associated with using identity as the focal point for resisting the colonial gaze. The paper ends with Coulthard's argument that self-recognition extends past a mere transitional role and places itself firmly in creating anti-colonial, anti-capitalist, anti-racist and Indigenous futures. Ultimately, this paper attempts to question if the granted settler-colonial state's recognition stands as a true demarcation of freedom for marginalized groups. This paper compares Sartre, Fanon and Coulthard's arguments to discuss self-recognition as both a means and an end to colonial rule, domination and control.

Keywords: Master-Slave Dialectics, Colonial, Power, Resistance, Normativity

Introduction

This paper places Frantz Fanon, Jean-Paul Sartre and Glen Coulthard in conversation on identity and recognition within the settler-colonial state. While Sartre argues that a focus on identity results in "anti-racist racism," Coulthard reiterates that culture and Indigenous resurgence are part of a self-recognition strategy that works to resist the settler-colonial state. I use an anti-colonial discursive framework to discuss "what is and what ought to be." (Dei 2001, 298) I use this framework as a form of resistance to White supremacy and liberal politics by critically engaging with literature that questions and investigates the impact of the politics of recognition on colonized subjects. In other words, this paper engages not only with theorists who critique the politics of recognition and the functions of essentialized identities but also acknowledges where this line of thinking stems from.

An anti-colonial discursive framework allows scholars to "work within a more flexible, transparent, and fluid language." (Dei and Asgaharzadeh 2001, 299) As such, this paper consists of three sections starting with a brief sketch of Hegel's master-slave dialectic and the complexification of the dialectic. The first section, titled Theoretical Debates on Identity and Recognition, focuses on Hegel's master-slave dialectic. This prominent theory influenced many liberal theorists to think about recognition within the context of liberal politics and the liberal state. This section then provides a close reading of a passage from *Black Skin, White Masks* to show Fanon's interpretation of Hegel's master-slave dialectic to theorize colonized subjectivities and the trapping of colonized subjects into a domain absent of reciprocal recognition (1952).

The next section, shaped by Fanon's criticisms of mutual reciprocity under the colonial gaze, engages with the scholarship of George J. Sefa Dei, Walter D. Mignolo, Eve Tuck, Wayne Yang, Glen Sean Coulthard, and Leanne Simpson. I start with an understanding of decolonization and what it means to resist the settler-colonial state. In this section, I also explore Jean-Paul Sartre's argument of self-affirmation as symbolized by the Négritude movement as a moment in the dialectic, not an end (1964). This sub-section examines the essentialist view on the risks associated with using identity as the focal point for resisting the colonial gaze. I turn to Coulthard's argument that self-recognition is a necessary framework that extends past a mere transitional role and places itself firmly in creating anti-colonial, anti-capitalist, anti-racist and Indigenous futures.

This paper also engages with Coulthard's understanding of settler-colonial recognition as understood and posited by Indigenous people on Turtle Island, especially the relationship between recognition and land. Thus, I draw from Glen Sean Coulthard to show that self-recognition works in three main ways: 1) Indigenous culture, knowledge systems and ontology affirm and recognize colonized subjects (2014); 2) provides a means through which the liberal state's existence and legitimacy is called into question (2014) and; 3) reframes the struggle to provide a structure for a de/anti-colonial future (2014). Ultimately, this paper attempts to address the following question: is recognition granted by the settler-colonial state truly a demarcation of freedom for marginalized groups? I compare and contrast Sartre, Fanon and Coulthard's arguments to engage in a conversation around self-recognition as both a means and an end to colonial rule, domination and control.

1- Theoretical Debates on Identity and Recognition

1-1 Hegel's Master-Slave Dialectic

In *Phenomenology of the Spirit*, Hegel argues that for consciousness to develop into self-consciousness, it must encounter another consciousness (1807). Commonly referred to as the master-slave dialectic, Hegel's theory around a relationship of unequal interdependence forms the basis of continued discussion around identity politics and recognition (1807). The focal point of Hegel's argument is that a relationship of independence is a non-negotiable aspect of the dialectic (1807). According to Hegel, consciousness cannot obtain self-consciousness without meeting other beings (1807). In Hegel's master-slave dialectic, the two consciousnesses meet and engage in a struggle to death (1807). This struggle to death is a result of both consciousnesses feeling threatened. According to Hegel, the struggle must happen as one of the consciousnesses to adhere to the other consciousness (1807).

These consciousnesses attempts to overpower the other through a "struggle to the death." (Hegel 1807) It is important to note here that this "struggle to death" does not result in the elimination of one consciousness (1807). Further, Hegel's inclusion of a "struggle to death" implies that mutual recognition must be achieved and is not given freely (1807). The unequal relationship between the two consciousnesses that emerges after this struggle to death is a key proponent in the dialectic (1807). The inequality between the two consciousnesses interferes with mutual recognition (1807). In the Hegelian dialectic, the slave consciousness, or the Other, fails to obtain recognition as an independent self-consciousness and therefore becomes an object (1807). When this happens, the object is put to work by the master consciousness (Hegel, 1807). The object works to recognize the master consciousness and the master consciousness becomes dependent on the object (1807).

As previously mentioned, the nature of the relationship remains one of interdependence through the object's servitude to the master (Hegel 1807). However, according to Hegel, the master consciousness cannot obtain the recognition it needs from the object despite relying on the object for sustenance (1807). The recognition the master seeks can only be given by another subject (1807). During this time the object gains a sense of self through its servitude to the master consciousness (1807). As such, Hegel claims that the object must master subordination to reach full recognition. At this point, the object no longer needs the master to stay alive (1807). This is where Hegel argues that mutual recognition can be achieved (1807). Hegel argues that "self-consciousness seeks to obtain self-certainty [...] through being recognized." (McQueen 2015, 53) Thus, recognition according to theorists such as Charles Taylor and Axel Honneth, plays an important role in shaping social and political identities (McQueen 2015). Also, in the Hegelian dialectic, the positioning of the master and slave consciousness marks a continuum of binary opposition

(Haddour 2021). Fanon builds off this opposition in *Black Skin, White Masks*, further theorizing the interdependent relationship to understand the psyche of the colonized.

1-2 *The Hegelian Tradition and the Contemporary Debate of Identity Politics*

In this sub-section, I provide a brief breakdown of two theorists, Axel Honneth and Charles Taylor, who participated in a revived conversation on the politics of recognition in the 1990s and early 2000s. Following a Hegelian tradition, both theorists centered recognition by state structures in their arguments about society and multicultural nations. For Honneth, the pursuit of recognition is political and cultural, including legal, social and physiological (2003). In an exchange between theorists Axel Honneth and Nancy Fraser regarding recognition and redistribution, Honneth followed the Hegelian tradition and states that everyone primarily seeks recognition and that redistribution is a form of this recognition (2003). In this debate, while the concept of redistribution is outside the scope of this paper, it is important to note the impact of Hegel's master-slave dialectic continues to have on the contemporary debate around identity politics and recognition. Honneth, unlike Sartre and Fanon, has a much more optimistic view of the dialectic and builds on it to theorize more modern liberal iterations of mutual recognition (2003). In his debate with Fraser, Honneth stresses the interdependent relationship between identity and justice within the context of disproportionate power relations relating to (2003). For Fraser, her argument for redistribution is related to an analysis of socioeconomic (2003).

The politics of recognition concerns an intersubjective relationship. Likewise, Charles Taylor suggests, "due recognition is not just a courtesy we owe people. It is vital human need." (1994) Taylor's understanding of recognition follows "modern essentialist theories of identity." (Day 2000, 35) Referencing Hegel, Taylor posits that there are two planes on which recognition is understood (1994, 36). First, there is the individual plane through which individuals come to know themselves, or shape an identity, through their interactions with others (1994 36). Second, there is the social plane (Taylor 1994, 36). It is on this plane that we experience "a politics of equal recognition" and while the state may not exist on the same plane as the social, the social shapes the State and vice versa in many ways (Taylor 1994, 36).

Addressing the specifics of the latter plane, Taylor states that for cultures to survive there must be both recognition of equal value amongst different groups and cultures as well as an acknowledgement of their worth (1994, 64). However, how does this theory translate to practice? How does the State shape the consciousness of the social? Through an examination of the history of multiculturalism policies in Canada, types of group-specific rights, and national majorities, the ideas discussed by Hegel, Honneth and Taylor will become more evident in practice later in this paper. Though, before moving to a case study, this section ends with a close reading of a passage from Fanon's *Black Skin, White Masks* as an exploration of a major critique of the relationship between identity, recognition, and justice: essentialized identities and the colonizer's gaze.

1-3 Essentializing Identities

> I made up my mind, since it was impossible to rid myself of an *innate* complex, to assert myself as a BLACK MAN. Since the Other was reluctant to recognize me, there was only one answer: to make myself known. (Fanon 1952, 95)

In *Black Skin, White Masks*, Fanon traces the process of subordination by examining the psychological impact of colonization on the minds of colonized people. The passage above is crucial in the understanding of Fanon's main argument regarding the colonial gaze. Fanon draws from Sartre's concept of "the look" or "the gaze" (1943) to further theorize the impact of colonial domination and control on colonized people's consciousnesses. In *Being and Nothingness*, Sartre discusses the intersubjective nature of human consciousness through the concept of the gaze (1943). According to Sartre, humans are not beholden to a primordial existence that forever determines our identity, instead, our identity is a judgement of how we have acted throughout our lives (1943). In order words, Sartre states that the nature of our being as humans is open and radically free (1943). This should not be confused with the idea of humans as politically free, as we will discuss this throughout the paper in different contexts. According to Sartre, humans are beings who are free to alter their identity throughout their lives and cannot be "solid." (1943; 1946)

However, how do we know that other subjects exist and how do we come to learn about ourselves through our interaction with other subjects?

Here enters "the gaze." Sartre posits, drawing from Hegel, that there is a conflict when you first encounter another being (1943). Through this interaction, Sartre explains the process through which you become an object when met with the gaze of another being (1943). He describes two actions: 1) looking at another person and 2) the other person looking at me (1943). In the second action, Sartre describes his subjectivity's denial and objectification as a result of being looked at (1943). Sartre names this feeling: Shame (1943). For Fanon, this idea of being looked at and subsequently turned into an object involves an interpersonal relationship between the colonizer and the colonized.

In the passage above, Fanon's use of the phrase "*innate* complex" refers to 1) his race; an entity he is "*fixed*" (1952, 95) into, and 2) the White gaze that constantly posits him in this position (1952, 95). At the beginning of the chapter Fanon stresses, "the Other fixes [him] with his gaze, his gestures and attitude" (1952, 89) referring to the colonizer. Through the use of the word fix[ed], Fanon draws on Sartre's understanding of being radically free and how the colonizer's gaze attempts to and is successful in turning him into a "solid" being. This relationship between the Self and the Other is related to the Hegelian master-slave dialectic. Further, Hegel's conclusion is that the master facilitates his understanding of himself through the slave (190).

According to Fanon, the White man is the Other *and* the master consciousness (1952, 117) with the power to shape his being or in his words, "the Other was reluctant to recognize [him]." (1952, 95) The Other's reluctance to "recognize" him pushes Fanon to reclaim Blackness and Black Subjectivity. Fanon's reference to his "*innate* complex" speaks to this relationship, one that renders him an "object among other objects" (1952, 89) and "a slave [...] to his appearance." (1952, 95) In other words, the White gaze creates the Black subject and traps the Black Man in a constant struggle for recognition or freedom (1952, 191).

Secondly, through the proclamation "I made up my mind [...] to assert myself as a BLACK MAN," Fanon arrives in dialectic where he asserts his freedom to exist in this world as a BLACK MAN. Fanon decides to reclaim his identity, reaffirmed by his statement, "there was only one answer, to make myself known" in the world despite the White/colonizer's gaze. By essentializing Blackness, Fanon stands in the power of reclaiming a narrative on his terms. Fanon states that through this reclamation, he has "put the White man back in his place" (1952, 110) thus, forcing the White man to "accommodate [Fanon] as [he] am; [he is] not accommodating anyone." As such, the passage symbolizes the moment where the Self emphasizes its ability to be ontologically free. However, Fanon stresses that this does not translate to freedom for the Black Man in its true sense (1952, 194). Fanon is clear that while each being can assert his identity, the Black Man will be shaped by the Other, the colonizer, the White man and the White gaze.

Finally, revisiting Fanon's assertion that "since the Other was reluctant to recognize [him]" is essential in understanding the master-slave dialectic as it applies to Black subjugation and the question of whether the Black Man has achieved freedom. According to Fanon, "[the Black Man] did not fight for his freedom," (1952, 194) because the Black Man has yet to exercise or be the master consciousness (1952, 194). Fanon states that in the Hegelian dialectic, there is "absolute reciprocity," or in other words, there is a moment in the dialectic, as discussed in the previous section, that reaches self-consciousness through its servitude to the master. Fanon reiterates Hegel in stating, "man is human only to the extent to which he tries to impose himself on another man to be recognized by him," (1952, 191). As mentioned, this is different from political freedom granted by the ruling class or by White society. Mutual recognition in the Hegelian dialectic symbolizes a moment when both consciousness reach harmony; when the master and slave are equals. For Fanon, the Black Man "does not know the price of freedom," (1952, 195) and although the Black Man "from time to time … fights for liberty and justice, but it's […] for values secreted by his masters." (1952, 195)

Therefore, Fanon describes through his own assertion as a BLACK MAN the moment in the dialectic that keeps the colonized subject contained with a particular identity given to him by the White gaze. For Fanon, this stage in the Hegelian Dialectic represents when the Other consciousness is only dependent on his "labour" to keep itself content. In other words, the master consciousness or in this case, the colonial gaze, requires colonized people to be "objects" that work to sustain a Eurocentric world.

Fanon argues that the Black man will never achieve mutual recognition from the White man because he is "fixed" into his blackness (1952, 89).

The colonized gaze impacts the colonized consciousness even when it is not under the direct gaze of the colonizer (Fanon 1952). Even in the absence of the White man, as Fanon points out, the colonial subject works to seek recognition from the White man (1952). Fanon uses the colonial tongue to explain this process of being locked in. He argues that through the adoption of the colonizer's language, in this case French, the Black man gets "Whiter" (1952, 2) or in other words, "the closer he comes to becoming a true human being." (1952, 2) Through this example, we understand that subjection is two-fold. First, the Black man "rejects his blackness" (1952, 2) by learning the colonial language which symbolizes the process of subordination by power.

I draw from Fanon's theorization of colonized identities and his skepticism of Hegel's theory of mutual reciprocity to show how resistance to the colonial gaze cannot fall into the trap of essentializing identities as a tactic. However, before turning to Coulthard's argument for self-recognition following a discussion of Sartre and Fanon's critiques of the Négritude movement, I use a Fanonist understanding of the colonial gaze and all of its apparatuses to understand three key pillars of the settler-colonial state of Canada: Multicultural policies and Act, group-specific rights, and national majorities.

2- Coloniality and the Quest for Recognition

2-1 *The Colonial Matrix of Power and Decolonial Resistance*

It is safe to conclude that Fanon is "skeptical of the liberatory potential of a struggle for recognition that is directed at securing recognition from the colonial "master"." (Chari 2004, 110) An example of this includes the project of decolonization and the quest for recognition of decolonization in spaces such as academia results in often contradictory understandings of the term, notion and action (Pictou 2020). This skepticism remains an important reminder of the reasons behind the liberal strive for a multicultural society and a state apparatus that upholds "diversity." Both Sartre and Fanon understand the colonized subject's struggle for recognition as involving 1) the colonial gaze that fixes the colonized subject into an innate object as well as 2) a state-sanctioned agenda that "has its own interest in defining the terrain of the struggle for recognition." (Chari 2004, 116) The latter is especially significant, for example, within the context of Canadian multiculturalism.

It is within the state structure and interests that the multiculturalism policy was formed and promoted by Trudeau. As such, its legacy remains tied to the idea that it is only granted to those who fully reflect the Canadian image. A meaningful understanding of multiculturalism should be able to separate the ideology and what the practice claims to do vs what it actually does (Fleras 2013, 245). Fleras makes this distinction by stating that the belief that multiculturalism is an inclusive model overshadows the reality of it being a hegemonic model (2013, 245). As such the distinction between the two must be made in our analysis. Gramsci differentiated hegemony from dominance by positing that the former is a practice of power that rests considerably "on the consent of various strata achieved by groups possessing or seeking state power." (Ali 2015, 241) Dominance, according to Gramsci, "is a practice of power relying primarily on coercion." (Ali 2015, 241) This distinction by Gramsci is interesting, especially when considering the contradictory nature of multiculturalism. Sherene Razack notes, "White […] is the colour of domination." (1998, 11)

Fanon and Razack's use of what is seemingly skin deep is an assertion of how Whiteness operates to influence hegemonic discourse, especially regarding the idea of multiculturalism. Moreover, Razack recognizes the lack of choice for immigrants when seeking protection from oppression (1998, 28). Razack asks, "How much of a choice is it to flee poverty and starvation in lands ravaged by a global economy dominated by the First World? Who is ultimately responsible for such flight?" (1998, 28) This question highlights the dome of colonial dominance that manages the movement of colonized subjects within the realm of Whiteness and Eurocentrism. Importantly, the logic of White supremacy deeply intertwines with the politics of recognition and, as Dei posits, the dehumanization that results from this logic continues to be a thread that ties the experiences of Black and Indigenous populations in Canada (2017, 24). Further, White supremacy plays a larger role in constructing identities that benefit the nation-state-building project (Dei 2017).

Those studying and critiquing multiculturalism and colonial recognition, myself included, must ask: how can an ideology with its roots in promoting a largely European society and thus expanding Eurocentrism through a settler-colonial agenda be decolonized? How should the resistance to multicultural policies, ideologies, and values be shaped to avoid the risks

Fanon and Sartre caution against, regarding the essentialization of identities and remaining trapped within the state apparatus? Liberal forms of government, as Dei mentions, are an extension of White supremacy and must be considered as a conjunction that moves through the contemporary moment (2017, 24). Further, Dei also shares that while the liberal forms of governance may provide freedom to some, it simultaneously delegitimizes others as well as regions and ways of being (2017, 24).

According to Mignolo, we must "engag[e] in epistemic disobedience and delinking from the colonial matrix to open up decolonial options." (2011, 9) This will result in "a vision of life and society that requires decolonial subjects, decolonial knowledge, and decolonial institutions." (Mignolo 2011, 9) While I used the case study to show how colonial recognition is built into the settler-colonial state national building project, this paper wishes to critically engage with the critiques of colonial recognition and the proposed ways of resisting colonial recognition. First, it is imperative to understand what decolonization is. The word is often thrown around as a "metaphor" (Tuck and Yang 2012) or to fix colonial structures and processes; however, this is not the case. Tuck and Yang emphasize that decolonization is not a metaphor. They further posit that decolonization cannot be an add-on to existing frameworks and discourses (2012). Therefore, decolonization is the political and epistemological de-linking from Westernization (Mignolo 2021; 2011).

Mignolo mentions three ways in which this process happens, including "the work toward epistemic and aesthetic reconstitution." (2021, 321) Moreover, decolonization and anti-colonialism work in conjunction with one another (Dei and Jaimungal 2018). Decolonization concerns "the power of non-hegemonic thinking and the transformative ideas we seek to engage with." (Dei and Jaimungal 2018, 2) Anti-colonialism, on the other hand, pairs action with decolonial ideas, such that political practice and resistance can take place (Dei and Jaimungal 2018, 2). Coulthard further explores this pairing in his theorization of Indigenous self-recognition. However, before exploring the argument of Indigenous knowledge systems and political resistance rooted in Indigenous resurgence, I explore Sartre, and Fanon's arguments against resistance movements that center and essentialize identities, even marginalized identities.

2-2 Sartre, Fanon and the Risk of Essentialist Movements

The Négritude movement started in Paris in the 1930s by Aimé Césaire, Léon Gontran Damas, and Léopold Sédar Senghor. Inspired by literary circles during the Harlem Renaissance movement, the Négritude movement emphasized the "spiritual, intellectual, and cultural remembering of continental Africa…and its diaspora, (Diagne 2018, 13). Further, the Négritude movement centers on poetry as a vehicle for an antithesis to White supremacy or "a means" through which a Black consciousness may arise. As such, language remains a proponent of the Négritude movement, especially through poetry's emphasis. Fanon views this proponent of Négritude as a way to escape the colonial gaze (1952, 102). However, Sartre's assertion that Négritude is a necessary but "weak stage" (1952, 117) in the dialectic of decolonization shatters Fanon's view of the movement (1952, 118).

Sartre and Fanon provide their insights around solutions for mutual recognition noting that each consciousness "wants to be recognized as an essential value outside of life, as transformation of subjective certainty into objective truth." (1952, 192) However, the strategies used by the Négritude movement, for example, received different views from Sartre, Fanon and Coulthard. I believe that Sartre and Fanon's critique poses important questions, while Coulthard provides strong alternatives through his notion of self-recognition and Indigenous resurgence. I return to the differences in their arguments and views in the final sub-section of this paper. In all three viewpoints, culture and knowledge are key proponents of resistance to the colonial gaze.

In *Black Orpheus*, Sartre argues that Négritude is "a means" (1964, 49) in the journey of decolonization and "not an end." (1964, 49) Fully endorsing the movement, he describes Négritude as a "dialectical and mystical return to origins" (Sartre 1964, 29) and remains devoted to the notion that the movement is "preparing the synthesis or realization of the human being in a raceless society." (Sartre 1964, 49) Sartre describes the Négritude movement as a "weak moment in the dialectic;" he also mentions the "method" remains a significant tool in "reveal[ing] the Black soul." (1964, 20) The poetry of Négritude, according to Sartre, delivers a crucial message: "Blackness has been rediscovered." (1964, 20)

This notion of rediscovering Blackness defies the colonial gaze, as indicated by Fanon's internal responses to being "fixed" in his Blackness by the White child (1952, 91-102). Fanon's use of Négritude era poetry and prose indicates his faith in the movement in reclaiming his Blackness and as a refusal to end up an "object among other objects." (1952, 89) Fanon includes Senghor's poetry as a part of this process and revels in the weight of Black rhythm, art and sculpture (1952, 102) and asserts that "on the other side of White world there lies a magical black culture." (1952, 102)

However, Fanon poses an important question about the Négritude movement and its poetry: "is this our salvation?" (1952, 102) Here, it is important to revisit Sartre's understanding of Négritude "as nothing but a phase in the dialectic" (Fanon 1952, 111) and Fanon's argument that provides important insights about the risks of essentializing identities. Sartre's reading considers the movement to be an "essentialist response to the colonialism's essentialization and racialization of the colonized, because [he] has considered it within the context of a face-to-face between the colonizer and the colonized." (Diagne 2018, 16) While, Diagne goes on to contest that reading by claiming that Senghor and Césaire are global thinkers and should not be reduced to mere colonized theorists (2018, 16), theorists such as Coulthard also refute the claim that cultural self-affirmation is a mere return to the past (2014). Coulthard mentions that Black and Indigenous cultures offer a way of living antithetically to the current and ongoing capitalist system rooted in colonial legacy.

According to Sartre, "anti-racist racism" symbolizes the transition into a "raceless society" (1964, 49). In *Black Orpheus*, Sartre (1964) envisions a world where White and Black do not exist and instead, people gain mutual recognition on equal ground, thus racial identity for Sartre does not carry any weight or significance. As such, Sartre posits that the Négritude movement falls into an "anti-racist racism" by upholding one racial identity over another (1964). For Sartre, this is not the right approach to resist power (1964). Similarly, as Sartre points out in *Anti-Semite and Jew*, the authentic Jew's approach of self-affirmation, while acknowledging its power to "strip anti-Semitism of its discursive power and virulence," (Coulthard 2014,135) if brought into a classless society that no longer requires differences, it runs the risk of perpetuating the same kinds of subjectivities that existed previously (Sartre 1944).

Sartre's critique of the authentic Jew's self-affirmation in a classless society is crucial for understanding his interpretation of the Négritude movement. While he endorses Négritude as a similar form of self-affirmation for Black colonized people and categorizes it as a way to turn the gaze back onto the colonizer, he provides the same warning that, like White supremacy, Black self-affirmation will create differences that end in subjectivities among society (Sartre 1965). Sartre argues that Self-affirmation threatens the dominant or oppressive gaze that "fixes" Jewish and Black people into essentialized identities, but it cannot exist in the anti-colonial or anti-capitalist world.

In this proposed raceless classless society, everybody will receive mutual recognition on the same level of power, and power will cease to exist. As he mentions in *Anti-Semite and Jew* and *Black Orpheus*, self-affirmation works in two ways. Firstly, it pushes back against the gaze that locks them into a particular identity; secondly, it reaffirms the subject's relationship with themselves to decolonize or create an anti-racist view of themselves from within (Sartre 1944; 1965). However, for Sartre, this raceless, classless society cannot have dominant ideologies that essentialize identities (Sartre 1944). As such, his view of humans as radically free is threatened by any notion of bringing these movements into the anti-colonial space or end goal.

The existentialist critique of movements that use self-affirmation of subjugated people warns us about the possibilities of power in a society that continues to form itself around certain ideologies and dominant power structures. Sartre claims that the "method [of self-affirmation] is not presented as a set of rules to be used in directing the spirit" (Sartre 1965) or, in other words, does not shift the human consciousness into a higher or next level in the dialectic. In the contemporary sense, it can be understood as Sartre's way of warning us against supremacies that may arise if the strategies through which we arrive at an anti-colonial anti-capitalist stage continue into the final stage of the dialectic.

2-3 Self-Recognition

In *Red Skin, White Masks*, Coulthard argues that self-recognition rooted in Indigenous resurgence and theories of grounded normativity, in addition to being a method of resistance against settler colonialism and capitalism, it also offers a framework for an anti-colonial future and way of being (2014). Self-recognition, according to Coulthard, holds several fundamental differences from the self-affirmation discussed by Sartre in Anti-Semite and Jew and the goals of Négritude (2014).

While Coulthard recognizes what Sartre and Fanon are weary of regarding self-affirmation and can lead to reproducing the same kind of essentialized identities seen through White supremacist societies, he suggests "the means" is intertwined with "the end." (2014) Additionally, Coulthard responds to Taylor's ideas around recognition by stating "the logic undergirding this dimension- where 'recognition' is conceived as something that is ultimately 'granted' (Taylor 1994, 148) or 'accorded' (41) to a subaltern group or entity by a dominant group or entity- prefigures its failure to significantly modify, let alone transcend, the breadth of power at play in colonial relationships." (2007, 442-443)

Although, Taylor's theorization of misrecognition attempts to vocalize the harm done to marginalized communities by offering "recognition" as a solution, it does not engage in a critical understanding nor question the colonial state's power structures that prohibit colonized groups from expressing self-determining actions and beliefs (Coulthard 2007). Coulthard challenges Taylor's interpretation that "a liberal regime of mutual recognition" is a solution to the mis- or non-recognition of colonial subjects (2007, 433). Coulthard draws from Fanon's understanding that the existence of the colonial state is contingent upon the "internalization of the forms of racist recognition imposed or bestowed on" colonized subjects (2007, 443). Thus, by rendering racialized settler communities into colonial subjects (Coulthard 2007, 443), the colonial social formation of the Canadian state is granted longevity (Coulthard 2007, 433). This phenomenon continues to play out through the promise of Canadian multiculturalism, as this paper has discussed.

Coulthard strengthens this argument through the key distinction that Western and Indigenous knowledge systems center on two different aspects in achieving their narratives: the former centers on time and the latter centres on space (2014, 60). Coulthard's argument rests on the premise that Indigenous resurgence exists both as a method and an anti-colonial way of existence (2014). For Coulthard and many other Indigenous scholars, Indigenous ontologies provide a framework that does not depend, even through the negation of, on colonial thought, gaze, or knowledge systems to sustain itself (2014).

Indigenous knowledge systems can exist on their own, or in other words, recognize themselves and do not "require [Indigenous peoples] to dialectically transcend Indigenous practices of the past once the affirmation of these practices has served to re-establish [Indigenous peoples] as historical protagonists in the present." (Coulthard 2014, 158) Drawing from Fanon's anti-colonial critique of the Hegelian notion of mutual recognition, Coulthard posits that self-recognition dismantles the liberal state and its forms of recognition, re-affirms Indigenous ways of being, and provides an anti-colonial framework (2014).

Coulthard also mentions that similar to the theorization of the colonial gaze that fixes the Black man, the settler gaze places Indigenous communities in a state of constantly needing to attain recognition from the settler state in ways that only re-affirms and recognizes the settler state, including its structure of liberal governance (2014). Recognition and reconciliation from the liberal state "coopt[s] Indigenous people into becoming instruments of their own dispossession." (Coulthard 2014, 156) Thus, Coulthard makes an important conclusion about Marx's theory of primitive accumulation, asserting that it must shift into the present when understanding the violent dispossession of Indigenous land and people for capital (2014).

As stated previously, Coulthard provides two examples of anti-racist and anti-capitalist modes of resistance in Indigenous Resurgence and the theory of Grounded Normativity. First, Coulthard posits that resurgence "builds on the value and insights of our past in our efforts to secure a non-colonial present and future." (2014, 149) Similarly, Leanne Simpson (2016) emphasizes her lack of interest in colonial justice systems and formations of justice, stating that she would much rather focus on Indigenous resurgence and self-determination. For Simpson, justice is "the return of land, the regeneration of Indigenous political, educational, and knowledge systems, the rehabilitation of the natural world, and the destruction of White supremacy, capitalism, and heteropatriarchy." (2016, 21)

Resurgence works in opposition to colonial knowledge systems and understandings of the world (Coulthard 2014; Simpson 2016). For example, the notion of nation-state building, as explored through the idea of multiculturalism in this paper, does not exist within the realm of resurgence (Simpson, 2016). Rather, collective resurgence emphasizes nation-building in ways that emphasize the autonomy and agency of Indigenous communities (Simpson 2016, 23). Indigenous resurgence reimagines the future of society and is "fundamentally nonhierarchical, nonexploitative, nonextractivist, and nonauthoritarian." (Simpson 2016, 23) Indigenous resurgence does not depend on justice and rights granted by settler-colonial institutions (Simpson 2016), and so, the notion of self-recognition is both theory and praxis. In other words, self-recognition restores power and knowledge back to colonized peoples while resisting colonial power (Coulthard 2014; Simpson 2016).

While disrupted by colonialism, the natural progression of Indigenous knowledge systems finds new ways of existing in the settler-colonial present (Coulthard 2014). Indigenous knowledge systems by holding an anti-colonial and anti-capitalist understanding of the world exist as forms of resistance (Coulthard 2014). Efforts such as 'Idle No More' and 1492 Land Back Lane are direct actions by Indigenous communities as "economic disruptions" to capital and offer an important example of self-recognition as both a form of resistance, affirmation and anti-colonial present and futurity (Coulthard 2014, 170).

Coulthard mentions the direct action for example, the blockages of resources represent a resurgence of land-based Indigenous political thought (2014,170). It is important to note that for Indigenous communities purporting land-based ideologies as forms of resistance symbolizes a negation of both colonial land dispossession and capitalism (Coulthard 2014). Through this example, the land is understood as both being tied to Indigenous resistance and Indigenous existence; ss such negates the liberal state and its relationship to the land for both its recognition as a nation-state and its resources that are integral in upholding capitalism (Coulthard 2014).

This is further explained by the theory of grounded normativity (Coulthard 2014). Coulthard describes grounded normativity as "the modalities of Indigenous land-connected practices and longstanding experiential knowledge that inform and structure [Indigenous] ethical engagements with the world and [Indigenous] relationships with human and nonhuman others over time." (2014, 13) Implementing the scholarship of Indigenous scholars-activists Leanne Simpson and Taiaiake Alfred to continue his argument around land-based knowledge has three main anti-colonial and anti-capitalist ontological properties (2014, 172). First, he highlights education as a form of returning to and revitalizing Indigenous knowledge (2014, 172). Second, he posits Indigenous political-economic methods as a way of detaching from the capitalist mode of production and creating decentralized and community-based systems for resources (2014, 172). Third, he argues that using Indigenous knowledge and political-economic alternatives presents a way for Indigenous communities and workers to benefit from a non-exploitative economic system (2014, 172).

Coulthard makes a strong argument for a future that addresses the systems of oppression that result in the misrecognition or nonrecognition of colonized people without abandoning Indigenous identities and knowledge systems. Coulthard's notion of self-recognition remains an important intervention into the conversations around the assertion of Indigenous culture and knowledge as both modes of resistance and futurities.

Conclusion

Coulthard's argument provides an alternative view of culture as political and politics. As stated previously, I believe that Sartre, Fanon, and Coulthard provide discerning critiques of dominant ideologies and their ability to render subjectivities through the regulation of power. Learning from all three theorists, I conclude that collective movements that aim to resist and subvert the White/colonial/settler gaze must decentralize power in every stage of the dialectic, including the strategies we employ.

In the next stage of the dialectic, Sartre and Fanon's concerns about society forming itself around power structures should be regarded as a welcome critique in our quest toward an anti-racist, anti-colonial and anti-capitalist future. To reiterate, "each consciousness of self is seeking absoluteness" (Fanon 1952, 192) and our efforts in directing the spirit into the next stage of elevated consciousness benefit greatly from Sartre, Fanon and Coulthard's critiques of colonial recognition.

Fanon's suspicions regarding Hegel's understanding of recognition remain pertinent today, as we continue to explore how settler-colonial states package freedom as a guise to uphold White Supremacy. Further, Fanon's reading of Hegel emphasizes the dangers of essentialized identities, and with this analysis, we can pinpoint how the settler-colonial state essentializes identities to validate itself. As such, the resistance to settler colonialism must be cognizant of the impact of essentializing identities.

References

Abu-Laban, Yasmeen, and Christina Gabriel. 2002. *Selling Diversity: Immigration, Multiculturalism, Employment Equity, and Globalization*. Broadview Press.

Ali, Noaman G. 2015. "Reading Gramsci through Fanon: Hegemony before Dominance in Revolutionary Theory." *Rethinking Marxism* 27 (2): 241–57. https://doi.org/10.1080/08935696.2015.1007793.

Chari, Anita. 2004. "Exceeding Recognition." *Sartre Studies International* 10 (2): 110–22. https://doi.org/10.3167/135715504780955302.

Coulthard, Glen S. 2007. "Subjects of Empire: Indigenous Peoples and the 'Politics of Recognition' in Canada." *Contemporary Political Theory* 6 (4): 437–60. https://doi.org/10.1057/palgrave.cpt.9300307.

———. 2014. *Red Skin, White Masks: Rejecting the Colonial Politics of Recognition*. Indigenous Americas Series. University of Minnesota Press.

Coulthard, Glen S., and Leanne Betasamosake Simpson. 2016. "Grounded Normativity / Place-Based Solidarity." *American Quarterly* 68 (2): 249–55. https://doi.org/10.1353/aq.2016.0038.

Day, Richard J. F. 2000. *Multiculturalism and the History of Canadian Diversity*. University of Toronto Press. https://doi.org/10.3138/9781442677449.

Dei, George J. Sefa. 2017. *Reframing Blackness and Black Solidarities through Anti-Colonial and Decolonial Prisms.*Springer. https://doi.org/10.1007/978-3-319-53079-6.

Dei, George J. Sefa, and Alireza Asgharzadeh. n.d. "The Power of Social Theory: The Anti-Colonial Discursive Framework." York University. Accessed June 29, 2024.

Dei, George J. Sefa, and Cristina Jaimungal. 2018. *Indigeneity and Decolonial Resistance: Alternatives to Colonial Thinking and Practice*. Myers Education Press.

Diagne, Souleymane Bachir. 2018. "Négritude as Existence." *NKA* 42–43: 10–19. https://doi.org/10.1215/10757163-7185701.

Du Bois, W. E. B. 1899. *The Philadelphia Negro: A Social Study.* Publications of the University of Pennsylvania. Ginn & Co.

Du Bois, W. E. B., and Nahum Dimitri Chandler. 2014. *The Problem of the Color Line at the Turn of the Twentieth Century: The Essential Early Essays.* American Philosophy Series. Fordham University Press. https://doi.org/10.1515/9780823254576.

Fanon, Frantz, and Richard Philcox. 2008. *Black Skin, White Masks.* Revised edition. Grove Press.

Fleras, Augie. 2014. *Racisms in Multicultural Canada: Paradoxes, Politics, and Resistance.* Wilfrid Laurier University Press.

Fraser, Nancy, and Axel Honneth. 2004. *Redistribution or Recognition?: A Political-Philosophical Exchange.* Translated by Joel Golb, James Ingram, and Christiane Wilke. Verso.

Haddour, Azzedine. 2021. "Fanon and Hegel: The Dialectic, the Phenomenology of Race, and Decolonization." In *The Palgrave Handbook of German Idealism and Phenomenology,* edited by Cynthia D. Coe, 173–99. Palgrave Macmillan.

Hegel, G. W. F., and J. N. Findlay. 1979. *Phenomenology of Spirit.* Translated by A. V. Miller. Oxford University Press.

McQueen, Paddy. 2015. *Subjectivity, Gender and the Struggle for Recognition.* Palgrave Macmillan UK.

Mignolo, Walter D. 2011. *The Darker Side of Western Modernity: Global Futures, Decolonial Options.* Latin America Otherwise Series. Duke University Press.

———. 2007. "Introduction: Coloniality of Power and de-Colonial Thinking." *Cultural Studies* 21 (2–3): 155–67. https://doi.org/10.1080/09502380601162498.

Pictou, Sherry. 2020. "Decolonizing Decolonization: An Indigenous Feminist Perspective on the Recognition and Rights Framework." *South*

Atlantic Quarterly 119 (2): 371–91. https://doi.org/10.1215/00 382876-8177809.

Puwar, Nirmal. 2004. *Space Invaders: Race, Gender and Bodies Out of Place.* Bloomsbury Academic.

Razack, Sherene. 1998. *Looking White People in the Eye: Gender, Race, and Culture in Courtrooms and Classrooms.* University of Toronto Press. https://doi.org/10.3138/9781442670204.

Robinson, Cedric J. 2000. *Black Marxism: The Making of the Black Radical Tradition.* University of North Carolina Press.

Rosenberg, Rae. 2021. "Psychic Geographies of Queer Multiculturalism: Reading Fanon, Settler Colonialism and Race in Queer Space." *Environment and Planning D: Society & Space* 39 (6): 1129–46. https://doi.org/10.1177/02637758211035132.

Sartre, Jean-Paul. 1965. *Anti-Semite and Jew.* Translated by George J. Becker. Schocken Books.

———. 2001. *Being and Nothingness: An Essay in Phenomenological Ontology.* Citadel Press.

Sartre, Jean-Paul, and John MacCombie. 1964. "Black Orpheus." *The Massachusetts Review* 6 (1): 13–52.

Simpson, Leanne Betasamosake. 2016. "Indigenous Resurgence and Co-Resistance." *Critical Ethnic Studies* 2 (2): 19–34. https://doi.org/10.5749/jcritethnstud.2.2.0019.

Taylor, Charles, K. Anthony Appiah, Jürgen Habermas, Steven C. Rockefeller, Michael Walzer, Susan Wolf, and Amy Gutmann. 1994. *Multiculturalism: Examining the Politics of Recognition.* Princeton University Press.

Tuck, Eve, and K. Wayne Yang. 2012. "Decolonization Is Not a Metaphor." Decolonization: Indigeneity, Education & Society 1 (1).

Navigating Urban Identity: Symbols and Cultural Expressions in Migrant Hubs

Guadalupe Ciocoletto, PhD.

ABSTRACT

This paper explores the dynamic relationship between urban environments and their socio-cultural constructs, emphasizing the interplay of space, identity, and symbolism in global cities. It examines how human interaction transforms neutral urban spaces into meaningful places, weaving social identity and cultural symbolism into their fabric. The main target is to discuss globalization's impact on urban aesthetics, highlighting tensions between homogenization and distinction, and to investigate the visual elements that shape perceptions of urban spaces. The concept of cultural symbols is explored as a tool for fostering identity and belonging, particularly in diverse urban hubs like Buenos Aires and Milan. These cities serve as case studies to illustrate how diverse cultural identities manifest through urban practices, economic activities, and symbolic expressions. By focusing on visual semiotics and identity, the paper emphasises the importance of relational space in fostering community bonds and negotiating social diversity. Additionally, it criticises the risks of superficial visual consumption in urban branding. Ultimately, this study positions urban spaces as relational environments where identity and diversity converge, offering insights into urban design, planning, and social geography in the globalized era.

Keywords: Identity, Cultural Symbols, Globalization, Urban Space, Diversity

Introduction

In an era shaped by globalization, urban spaces have become key sites for understanding the complex interplay between cultural diversity, identity, and socio-spatial dynamics. Cities worldwide serve as living laboratories where local and global influences converge, resulting in unique socio-cultural phenomena. This work explores these dynamics through the lens of urban identity, examining how spaces transform into meaningful places enriched by human relationships, cultural symbols, and shared experiences. Anchored in interdisciplinary perspectives, it emphasizes the critical role of visual semiotics, public space, and symbolic expressions in shaping identity and fostering community bonds.

Drawing on case studies from Milan and Buenos Aires—two global cities with distinct migratory histories and cultural tapestries—the study investigates how cultural diversity manifests in urban practices, economic activities, and spatial transformations. By situating these cities within broader global trends, the paper addresses themes of homogenization, distinction, and the tensions between global branding and local authenticity. Ultimately, it advocates for a nuanced understanding of urban environments as relational spaces where identity, belonging, and diversity intersect, offering insights relevant to urban design, planning, and social geography.

The Urban Environment as a Relational Space

The urban environment, conceptualized as a relational space, facilitates the transformation of undifferentiated areas into meaningful places through human relationships and experiences. This process is fundamentally anchored in the dynamic interplay between sensory perceptions and cognitive processes. Through relationships and experiences, humans convert undifferentiated spaces into meaningful places. Tuan affirms "Places are centres of felt value" (1977, 4) and that value is born out of experience -sensations, perceptions, and conceptions in which all organs and senses are involved. Tuan adds that human environments mirror the nature of our sensory perceptions and mental processes, highlighting how thought processes often extend beyond the immediate information provided by senses, warranting the abilities of navigating our surroundings, identifying patterns, anticipating others' behaviour, and hence making decisions. This capability enables the people inhabiting a certain place not only to generate entirely new ideas, scenarios, and possibilities by combining existing information in novel ways, but also to manipulate that environment which has been perceived and acknowledged. Hence, "The human being, by his mere presence, imposes a schema on space," (Tuan 1977, 36) be it physical or mental.

This interrelation between humans and the built environment is also supported by Arendt, who affirms that "Things and men form the environment for each of man's activities, which would be pointless without such location, yet this environment, the world into which we are born, would not exist without the human activity which produced it. " (Arendt 2018, 22) In this quote the reciprocal relationship between human activities and the environments we inhabit are highlighted, stating clearly that the activities of individuals shape the world around them, creating environments that are essential for carrying out further actions. This symbiotic relationship implies that human actions are not isolated occurrences, but are moreover deeply intertwined with the spaces and contexts in which they occur. In this sense, also Lefevbre equals Humanity to social practice:

> What we are concerned with, then, is the long history of space, even though space is neither a 'subject' nor an 'object' but rather a social reality that is to say, a set of relations and forms. This history is to be distinguished from an inventory of things in space (or what has recently been called material culture or civilization), as also from ideas and discourse about space. It must account for both representational spaces and representations of space, but above all for their interrelationships and their links with social practice. (Lefebvre 1974, 116)

Moreover, Arendt adds: "Man working and fabricating and building a world inhabited only by himself would still be a fabricator, though not *homo faber*: he would have lost his specifically human quality and, rather, be a god." (Arendt 2018, 22) And is this aspect that calls for special attention when trying to study and understand the built environment: it is an intrinsic characteristic of humans in community to modify their environments in relation to the others with whom they share those spaces. The environments in which individuals operate are not just physical spaces but also encompass social structures and systems.

Going back to Lefevbre, the author states "(Social) space is not a thing among other things, nor a product among other products: rather, it subsumes things produced, and encompasses their interrelationships in their coexistence and simultaneity — their (relative) order and/or (relative) disorder." (Lefebvre 1974, 73) This line of thought sheds light when analyzing human-made spaces, and so we can consider that what we call 'public space' is consequently transformed into a 'shared place', a fraternal place where everyday relationships can be exercised, a place with greater potential value.

For urban psychology scholars Vidal Moranta & Urrútia (2005), the emotional experience we develop in *places* implies that the actions that are carried out in that *place* and the conceptions of the place that are generated are intertwined. That is to say, the ontological-experiential and perceptual aspects are related to what happens on the sensitive plane, and this has also repercussions on the image that is fabricated of the inhabited space. Therefore, attachment, urban social identity, and the symbolism of public space are essential concepts when dealing with the design and quality of shared places within the city. For the same authors, human praxis is both instrumental and social, and from its internalisation arises consciousness. To understand urban space only in its physical plane would be equal to thinking of it as a pure and empty abstraction.

Human beings will look for the right place to establish shared ties with some and to differentiate themselves from others, and so the fraternal relationships that arise will need a place for expressing otherness. If we accept that an accurate way to interpret society is through the web of relationships that are formed in it, then we must consider that these relationships exist in a given space. Tuan (1977) poses the question of how space and the experience of spaciousness are related to the human sense of competence and self-determination. If space is a symbol of openness and freedom, it may, in a way, affect the presence of others and concrete experiences could allow us to assign distinctive meanings to space and spatiality, to population density, to overcrowding.

Interpreting what Tuan presents, competence (understood as a set of skills to read, analyze and understand the surroundings) and freedom can condition the perception we have of spaces and also of *others*: both influence the ways in which we relate to otherness, and both, at the same time, can be the cause of conflicts. Together with this, the presence of *others* conditions our perception of space and the symbolic charge we attach to it, primarily because the *others* -those who share the same space- cannot be ignored, since doing so would equal to create a fiction of everyday life where the unplanned use of spaces might become a source of unease (Muxí 2009).

From a philosophical perspective, this topic delves into questions of agency, intentionality, and the transformative power of human activities on the surrounding world. It also raises questions about how individuals negotiate and adapt to the environments they help create. We, then, can only understand the human being as a relational being, who, from experimentation with his body and with other people, organizes space so that it accommodates their biological needs and reciprocity with other people (Vidal Moranta and Urrútia 2005). In this regard, Hannerz (2001) proposes the concept 'habitats of meaning': habitats that can expand and contract; that can match completely, partially or not at all, and thus can be identified either in individuals or in collectivities. In the global ecumene, many individuals may share several habitats of meaning.

However, our habitat of meaning depends not only on the extent to which we are physically exposed to it, but also on our ability to conform to it: our relationships with other symbolic forms. Attachment, urban social identity, and the symbolism of public space are essential concepts when dealing with the design and quality of shared places within the city.

Communication alongside Industrial Capitalism: Globalization and Urban Space

In the era of globalization, cultural symbols have extended beyond traditional boundaries, becoming global icons with diverse meanings across contexts. This shift is evident in urban spaces, where the tension between homogenization and distinction plays out. Global cities often exhibit a homogenized aesthetic, shaped by international brands, architectural styles, and cultural motifs that create uniformity. However, within this landscape, cities strive to preserve unique identities through localized expressions of culture, heritage, and innovation. This duality significantly influences urban dwellers' sense of belonging as they navigate global and local influences, forging a sense of place amidst this fluidity.

Modern urban landscapes are meticulously branded, using strategies that highlight both global allure and local charm. This has given rise to an era focused on the 'pure image' (Muxí 2006, 2009), where representation often overshadows tangible realities. In this visually driven context, aesthetics and symbols shape urban narratives that resonate with residents and visitors alike. The interplay between global and local symbolism, the balance of uniformity and distinction, and the strategic branding of spaces collectively shape the perceptions and experiences of modern city life.

In the process of globalization, cities serve as crucial hubs for the production and dissemination of services, especially those at the forefront of innovation and internationalization (Sassen 2005). This can be analyzed from different points of view: firstly, cities offer a concentration of human capital, fostering creativity, collaboration, and knowledge exchange among skilled professionals. Secondly, cities boast an extensive physical infrastructure essential for the operation of leading firms in information industries. These strategic nodes are often characterized by hyper-concentration, creating clusters of expertise and resources that amplify their impact on the global stage.

As the material conditions within cities play a vital role in facilitating these processes, including factors such as reliable power supply, efficient transportation networks, and secure real estate for hosting critical infrastructure, global cities call also for the attention to the dynamics of the newcomers who arrive, not only to satisfy the needs of the new modern environment but also their necessities, such as jobs, accommodation, visibility. Sassen affirms: "But the city is a strategic frontier zone not just for the powerful but also for the conventionally powerless: disadvantaged outsiders or minorities facing discrimination. Those who are traditionally excluded can gain presence in global cities- presence vis-à-vis both power and each other." (Sassen 2012, 86)

The emergence of urban capabilities signifies a paradigm shift in political dynamics, reflecting the evolution of both urban spaces and political actors. Traditionally, access to the city was predominantly determined by formal power structures, such as governmental authority or economic influence. However, contemporary urban landscapes have undergone profound transformations, becoming hybrid environments where traditional power dynamics coexist with increasingly legitimized forms of informal politics. Drawing from Appadurai (1996), this mobile and unforeseeable relationship between mass-mediated events and migratory audiences defines the core of the link between globalization and the modern.

Urban spaces now serve as fertile ground for a diverse array of political actors, transcending conventional boundaries of power and authority. These actors leverage their urban capabilities to navigate and influence sociopolitical processes, often operating outside traditional institutional frameworks. This shift announces the rise of a new type of politics, characterized by the empowerment of grassroots movements, community organizations, and other non-traditional actors. The concept of urban capabilities encapsulates this phenomenon, emphasizing the capacity of individuals and groups to enact change within the urban context. It recognizes that access to the city is no longer solely contingent on formal power structures but also on the ability to mobilize resources, build networks, and engage in collective action within urban spaces (Sandercock 2000).

By re-framing the notion of political agency, urban capabilities offer a lens through which to understand and analyze the complex interplay between formal and informal power dynamics in contemporary cities: they underscore the importance of recognizing and harnessing the trans-formative potential inherent within urban environments, shaping a new landscape of political possibility centered around diverse and dynamic political actors.

It is for this reason that understanding the interdependent relationship between the social and physical aspects of urban environments is crucial. Social transformations often lead to changes in the city's structure, impacting both design and planning, as well as social behaviors of space usage. Early in the 20th century, thinkers like Simmel (1903) observed the influence of urban life on its residents, noting the emotional challenges posed by large cities. This perspective remains relevant today, as seen in contemporary analyses like the ever-relevant writings of Jacobs (1961).

However, modern societal shifts -characterized by job instability, rapid mobility, fleeting relationships, and adaptable work environments- mirror a decreasing sense of attachment to everyday spaces. This trend towards short-term engagement threatens loyalty to work, people, and places, undermining communal bonds. The prevailing lack of commitment in relationships with places, objects, and individuals reflects this broader societal detachment. Flexible capitalism has fostered uniformity, indifference, and impermanence both in urban environments and workplaces, eroding the durable set of common interests essential for fraternity. This neutrality obscures diversity and otherness, and this often reflects on urban environments.

Seeing, Owning, Creating Space through Symbols

In the contemporary global landscape, visual representation plays a pivotal role in shaping societal perceptions and interactions. Understanding the significance of what is seen and shown is crucial for comprehending the dynamics of urban spaces and the human experiences within them.

Knowledge is the consequence of what is given by experience -the sensibility and the senses that provide us with the discovery of the world around us- plus what is determined by the perceiving subject -his understanding, his reasoning. Taking the definitions of the terms object and subject from Williams (2003): object, from the Latin *objectum*, from the root *ob*: towards and *jacere*, to throw; subject, from the Latin *subjectus* and *subjectum*, from the root sub: under. An object supposes then, a thing thrown before the mind, hence seen or observed; to be a subject implies to be under the dominion of, to be held by something else. Thus, the senses allow us to have an idea of things as they present themselves before us -objectively- and to grasp them, to hold them, to possess them. It can also be added that seeing is human, but looking is cultural: it responds to the rules of the culture incorporated in each individual; the meaning perceived will be determined by the context to which the beholder belongs and in which the objects contemplated are found.

Seeing, observing, looking at the other plays a crucial role in the experience of the urban environment: on the one hand, we understand looking at others in the sense of observing and creating a thought about the presence of that *other* -that one who is not like us, that one with a different origin, age, gender, abilities, beliefs- in shared areas; on the other hand, the act of looking has its role in the sense of perception, in the way of apprehending the surrounding signs and spaces. Both aspects are interrelated. Looking, by definition, implies reviewing, registering, thinking, judging, considering, and being informed about something. The action of looking is constituted by multiple procedures within the biology and reasoning of the human being, which end up in - and determine - the way the world is perceived. It is not possible to look without an intellectual process about what is seen.

Everything that surrounds us, every person, every space, is then processed in our thinking, intellectualised: the objective world passes through the filter of subjectification. This process gives us a certain security about what we perceive, and through this process, we construct a set of small securities and shape our understanding of our environment. It is only after rationalizing our surroundings that we can operate on them.

Being observed can feel intimidating or invasive, as Delgado Ruiz (2021) notes, but it also affirms our presence in a shared space. This mutual recognition transforms the city from an abstract, infinite concept into a tangible environment defined by connections between individuals. These exchanges of gazes act as mediators, transmitting sensory and mental experiences that shape our perception of space. This process actively alters the things observed, shifting them from insecurity to a sense of security and fostering a connection to the urban environment. As de Certau (1984) suggests, observing the city allows for control and influence over the spaces within our field of vision, creating a sense of ownership and definition of the urban landscape.

Through observation, urban spaces are not only created but also appropriated, as people develop a sense of belonging and attachment. Jacobs (1961) highlights that these interactions, whether planned, such as window placements, or spontaneous, like passing glances, define areas of influence that continuously evolve throughout the day. Even unconsciously, individuals contribute to and become part of the urban fabric through the act of seeing. In this context, what is visible, and what is intentionally displayed or concealed, becomes essential to urban life, influencing perceptions and interactions within the city.

Cultural Symbols and Sense of Belonging

One significant challenge posed by globalization is the tendency to equate it with cultural homogenization, a perspective echoed by Maaluf (2000), who also notes its conflation with Westernization. This perception underscores the importance of cultural symbols in preserving and articulating both individual and collective identities. Within this context, the value attributed to cultural symbols becomes paramount as they serve as markers of identity amidst the backdrop of globalization's sweeping influence. These symbols, put out to be observed, not only retain their intrinsic significance but also take on added importance as repositories of cultural heritage and expressions of distinct identities. In essence, the preservation and promotion of cultural symbols serve as a means of resisting the perceived tide of homogenization and safeguarding the diversity of individual and group identities in the face of globalizing forces. Thus, the discourse surrounding globalization extends beyond mere economic and political dimensions to encompass the complex interplay of cultural preservation, identity construction, and the negotiation of power dynamics on a global scale.

Furthermore, and in connection to the preceding arguments, in the realm of urban planning, there has been a prevalent acceptance of the modernist principle of "one law for all" (Sandercock 2000) wherein a uniform framework is applied across diverse socio-cultural contexts. This paradigm assumes that a singular set of regulations can effectively govern the complexities of urban spaces, disregarding the nuanced needs and identities of various communities. However, this one-law approach fails to acknowledge the diverse cultural, social, and economic dynamics inherent within cities. By adhering rigidly to this paradigm, those with the task of changing the city (administration, planners, designers) may overlook the importance of context-specific interventions and fail to address the unique challenges faced by marginalized or under-represented groups within urban environments.

An individual's feeling of belonging to a particular group is predominantly shaped by the influence exerted upon them by others in their social sphere. Whether it be family members, compatriots, or those who share their religious beliefs, these individuals actively strive to integrate the person into their collective identity. Conversely, there are opposing forces at play, seeking to exclude the individual from their group. This tug-of-war between inclusion and exclusion is a pivotal determinant of one's affiliation. In this dynamic social landscape, individuals navigate pressures to conform to group norms while simultaneously facing resistance from rival factions. This idea accentuates the intricate interplay of social dynamics in shaping individual identities within the broader societal context. It suggests that while personal agency plays a role, the collective influence of social networks heavily influences the formation of group affiliations and, consequently, individual identities (Maaluf 2000).

Globalization and the culture of visual imagery are closely connected (Muxí 2009, 2006). Since the rise of post-war industrial capitalism, the value of products has grown, and this idea has influenced urban design through terms like styling, branding, and marketing. Today, the iconic, the visual, and the power of imagery dominate communication. This shift is evident in tourism and landscape representation, which are often promoted through media and brochures (Arfuch 2009; Muxí 2009; Zukin 2009). Social and urban life has been deeply affected by this trend, where visual elements are central to cultural consumption.

Over the past decades, urban life has become increasingly centered around visual experiences. Cities are now often seen as landscapes of consumption, catering to leisure and cultural desires rather than production needs. Urban development strategies now focus on visual attractions to captivate visitors and increase city revenue. This trend has led to a shift from a logo-centric to an iconocentric society, where public spaces are designed to appeal visually, enhancing their aesthetic value for both residents and consumers.

The visual component in the repertoire of identity references not only reaffirms the presence of *otherness*, but also helps discovering new social practices of action together with many forms of relationships and of constructing reality, giving rise to new forms of connection and communication. On the other hand, as affirmed by Arfuch (2009), it may no longer be possible to speak of the traditional sender-message-receiver triad, because today it is possible to find a diversity of receivers and because it would be impossible to propose a standardised reading. Interpretations today are as variable as there are different kinds of receivers. By replacing the original triad with the set of client-product-target/market segment, we would then have come to refer to the components of communication in commercial terms. Arfuch adds a shift from interest in the content of the image to the modalities of its appearance, including the contexts and the orientation of attention towards the receiver; the latter is mostly linked to market scenarios. Being excluded from consumption might equate to being marginalized from society.

So, when referring to cultural symbology, a significant distinction can be highlighted between communication and information, suggesting that information is merely a component of the broader communication process (Devalle 2009). Communication encompasses various phenomena, including persuasion, argumentation, and the formation of social discourse. Thus, communication should be recognized as a multifaceted and intricate element. Furthermore, communication must be contextualized, arising from specific social situations. By examining enunciation and different statements as actions within socio-cultural dynamics, we can understand the social production of meaning, where statements possess unique, subjective qualities while also being historical, cultural, and social.

The present work seeks to develop an understanding of this multiplicity and its social significance, noting that visual elements remain social material, and collective historical representations continue to influence reception. Ideology and its discourse should be seen as a set of social practices that become naturalized, framing a particular view of phenomena. As it will be discussed in the following lines, in some Global Cities the characteristics of some proposed identitarian symbols prove the objectification of some of elements by the spaces of power in favor of the *city branding* assigning a characteristic charge to the perception -embodiment- of the landscape.

Modernity and the Other: the Example of Two Global Hubs

The importance of visual signs on culturally diverse urban spaces in global cities has also been pointed out and studied by Krase & Shortell (2011) who have kept for many years an online photographic archive of urban neighborhoods in global cities. One of the key concepts of their work has been studying vernacular environments -understood as informal, "outside the control of political decisions and produces unstable forms." (Krase, Ballesta, and Larminat 2020, 150) Krase and Shortell's research underscores the decisive role of visual signs in culturally diverse urban spaces, as highlighted in their comprehensive examination of global city neighborhoods.

In vernacular environments, culturally diverse communities assert their agency through visual cues, categorized by Krase and Shortell as expressive and pathic signs. Expressive signs, like multilingual signage, showcase immigrant agency and mark social spaces as contested territories, reflecting linguistic diversity and participation in urban landscapes. Pathic signs, seen on businesses catering to immigrants (e.g., travel agencies, telecommunications shops, money transfer services), delineate "immigrant neighbourhoods" and reinforce spatial boundaries. These signs not only serve practical purposes but also contribute to the distinct socio-cultural identity of these areas within the urban fabric.

Another point of view useful for the present study is Hannerz's hypotheses on diversity (2001). Hannerz suggests diversity as an expression of adaptability and resilience within urban environments, a sign of equity and self-determination, and a mitigation of economic dependence, further emphasizing its multifaceted nature and significance in urban contexts. Moreover, he posits diversity as intellectual provocation, challenging conventional narratives and fostering new understandings of urban life. From this point of view, diversity becomes also a reservoir of memories, recognizing the richness and complexity of cultural heritage within diverse urban communities. Additionally, diversity can be seen as a monument to creativity,

In this context, we will examine the cultural identity expressions in two global cities, Milan and Buenos Aires, both of which have been previously studied by the author. These cities provide unique insights into the dynamics of cultural diversity and migrant identity, making them ideal subjects for understanding how these phenomena play out in urban settings. Buenos Aires, known for its rich cultural diversity and history of immigration, offers a fascinating example. As the capital of Argentina, it has attracted migrants from various backgrounds. The latest census shows that 31% of the city's population was born elsewhere, with a significant portion coming from Latin American countries. This shift from a European-majority population has shaped Buenos Aires' cultural identity, with ongoing immigration continuing to influence the city's neighborhoods and cultural expressions.

Similarly, Milan presents another compelling case of cultural diversity, with 19% of its population consisting of foreign-born migrants. A significant portion of these migrants comes from non-European countries, including large communities from Egypt, the Philippines, and China. This diverse population has introduced a variety of traditions, languages, and perspectives, influencing Milan's urban landscape. Studying both Buenos Aires and Milan helps to understand how diverse identities manifest in everyday life and how cities with different socio-geographical dynamics navigate cultural integration and identity formation.

By focusing on Buenos Aires and Milan, we gain valuable insights into the complex interplay between migration, cultural diversity, and urban life. These cities serve as microcosms of broader global trends, highlighting the ongoing processes of globalization, cosmopolitanism, and cultural exchange. Exploring these two examples allows for an examination of how migrants navigate urban spaces, negotiate their identities, and contribute to the cities' cultural vibrancy.

Identity and Adaptability

Hannerz (2001) conceptualizes adaptability from an ecological perspective, viewing it as the achievement of a viable equilibrium with one's environment, an equilibrium with one's habitat. This notion is crucial for understanding balance within urban settings. Ethnically diverse trade and services operate within both intra- and inter-cultural contexts, addressing unique community needs while interacting with broader societal structures. Ecologically, immigrants often fill vacant labor niches within host societies. Limited opportunities, caused also but the intrinsic characteristics of globalization, may drive migrants toward self-employment as a viable strategy. Another pertinent aspect to mention is social embeddedness, which links consumer demand with a regulatory framework that fosters economic development. Ethnic economies, in this view, thrive not solely based on consumer demand but on what groups are permitted and able to offer within the regulatory constraints.

The extent to which an economy aligns with one theory over another depends on the specific characteristics of the migrant population and the contextual environment in which they integrate, highlighting the importance of understanding the particular needs of the context. Drawing on Krase and Shortell (2011), it can be posited that the sense of belonging is often reinforced by symbolic elements embedded within ethnic commerce. The accompanying images (Fig. 1) illustrate similar scenarios, emphasizing the role of pathic signs in fostering a sense of community among ethnic groups.

As an example, the *Mercado Andino*: a place that in practice is not a market but rather a neighbourhood-scale commercial center located in the area of Liniers, on the border between the Capital Federal and the province of Buenos Aires. The *Mercado Andino* is a case of how, based on a present structure -a pre-existing commercial area, proximity to the points of residence of the Bolivian community- the social fabric - a Bolivian collective with labor and visibility needs - has accepted and modified the public space, giving it a new identity while reaffirming its own through the use of national symbols and colors, and folk and religious elements. The presence of those symbols informally delimits the so-called 'mercado' area.

Similarly, identifying shops with signage in traditional Korean language, the Korean Neighborhood of Buenos Aires, also known as *Baek-Ku*, has gained prominence in recent years. It has become important not only for the Korean community but also as a tourist attraction promoted by the city's government[1].

Another example is Buenos Aires' *Chinatown*, which emerged during the last wave of Taiwanese immigration to the city in the 1980s. Although it is recognized as the city's *Chinatown*, the concentration of Chinese residents in this area is similar -or inferior- to other parts of Buenos Aires. This commercial area of the city, populated mostly with restaurants and supermarkets where to buy oriental goods that can hardly be found in other places of the city, serves not only as a tourist attraction but also as an effort to preserve cultural traditions and as an example of intercultural unity. The city of Milan also has its own *Chinatown*, located along Via Paolo Sarpi. This area has undergone various urban transformations, becoming a prominent hub for the Chinese community. It features a few cultural buildings and numerous shops adorned with Chinese symbols, not only along the main street but also on the intersecting streets.

The last images show a more diverse area of Milan, Via Padova, a context that has evolved to meet the integration needs of new populations over time, thanks to its unique structure and location. Its proximity to central urban areas, connectivity to the rest of the city, and abundance of affordable housing have historically attracted internal migrant workers and now draw international immigrants as well. The shops of the area and the pathic signs along Via Padova, belonging to different communities, prove the diversity of its population.

---

1   https://turismo.buenosaires.gob.ar/es/turismo-en-barrios/barrio-coreano-circuito-1

FIG.1

Identity and Provocation

Identitarian expression acts as an intellectual provocation (Hannerz 2001), challenging existing paradigms and stimulating innovative thought within urban environments. This intellectual challenge initiates a generative cultural process, where marginalized perspectives introduce new ways of seeing and understanding the city. From the margins, these perspectives propose new narratives that reshape the collective urban experience, highlighting the complexities and richness of multicultural interactions. The expression of multiform identities in urban spaces not only reflects the varied cultural landscapes but also emphasizes the importance of inclusivity and representation. Visibility of these diverse groups in the urban fabric underlines their contribution to the cultural vitality of the city, fostering a more integrated and dynamic urban community. By embracing and making space for this diversity, cities can develop a more nuanced and holistic narrative that captures the essence of contemporary urban life. Fig. 2 serves as an exemplary illustration of expressive signage, demonstrating the use of visual actions as a form of provocation within the public space.

Starting from two artistic works by the Equatorian Artist Boris Veliz, both located in the area of Via Padova in Milan. The first one, the *Dante Andino*, symbolically joins the great Italian writer together with Andean symbology, intentionally trying to transmit a cultural ibridization message[2]. The second, *Frammenti di identità* [Identity Fragments], finished in 2024, portrays research on diversity and the beauty of cultural multiplicity through the eyes of multicultural childhood. Created in the same area in 2023, Coquelicot Mafille's mural captures the diverse identities of the neighborhood through a collage. This contemporary 'frieze' is designed for the residents of Via Padova neighborhood, incorporating elements and everyday objects that represent the area, along with texts in over ten languages.

The last image shows a Wiphala—a flag of seven colours, originally used by the Andean peoples—depicted in the area of the *Andean Market* of Buenos Aires under the Liniers bridge, signaling one of the *Mercado Andino*'s virtual limits.

Diversity as Aesthetic Revaluation

Diversity can be seen as an opportunity for aesthetic revaluation, where different cultures are not just accepted but celebrated as valuable sources of enrichment. This view, as proposed by Hannerz, suggests that the global interconnectedness of cultures should be seen as a positive, offering new experiences that allow individuals to connect with others and their meanings. The "Other" becomes an essential part of our sensory and emotional landscape, providing fresh encounters that enhance our daily lives. People are naturally drawn to the unique cultural expressions they encounter, which offer new perspectives and deepen their understanding of the world. This engagement with cultural diversity fosters a more empathetic and interconnected global society.

---

2   Personal interview with the artist.

FIG.2

However, it's important to approach this celebration of diversity with caution. The line between appreciating other cultures and "exoticizing" them
is very fine. When diversity is viewed purely as an aesthetic experience,
it risks reducing cultures to stereotypes or exaggerated representations.
This can lead to the distortion of cultural differences for commercial gain
or to evoke fascination, without recognizing the underlying inequalities
or complexities of those cultures.

In this hypothesis, both pathic and expressive signs become crucial, as illustrated in Fig 3: in Buenos Aires' *Chinatown*, oriental symbolism is evident, particularly along Arribeños Street and its cross streets. This includes a grand arch marking the entrance, similar to other *Chinatowns* globally, as well as sculptures and red dragon posters on lampposts. The enhancement of this urban area has been a collaborative effort involving local institutions, the Chinese community, and government bodies. For instance, Chinese entities donated the entrance arch and sculptures, which were approved and inaugurated by local authorities. The arch serves as the central gathering point for every New Year's celebration. Analogously, a representative arch proposal has been erected in Milan's *Chinatown* during Milano Design Week 2024. In this instance, the temporary installation by artists Tommaso Lanciani and street artist Pao was created collaboratively with the involvement of workshops conducted with children from a Primary School and the Chinese Cultural Center of Via Paolo Sarpi[3].

FIG. 3

Diversity as a Reservoir of Memories

Diversity can also be seen as a reservoir of memories and ideas, serving as a rich source of initiatives, solutions to problems, and alternatives. This conceptualization emphasizes that diverse communities carry collective memories and experiences that inform innovative approaches to contemporary challenges. The management of otherness and the conflicts that arise from cultural differences is crucial in harnessing this potential. As

3   https://www.zonasarpi.com/via-sarpi

diverse identities interact, they exchange perspectives and develop hybrid solutions that might not emerge within more homogeneous settings. This collaborative dynamic fosters a more resilient and adaptive society, where the pooling of varied experiences and knowledge enhances collective problem-solving and drives social progress. Thus, diversity not only enriches the cultural tapestry but also strengthens societal capacity for innovation and conflict resolution.

Fig. 4 displays the *Urkupiña* celebrations in the *Mercado Andino* in 2020, a traditional Bolivian celebration that includes parades, dance, and music. Coupled with this, the image shows the *Chinese New Year's* celebrations, in Buenos Aires' *Chinatown* and Milano Design Week opening in Milan's *Paolo Sarpi*. These celebrations hold significant importance within urban environments as they often disrupt the intended use of specific public spaces due to their large attendance, temporarily transforming these spaces into sites imbued with diverse community identities and cultural significance. Such expressions of identity serve as conduits that foster cultural bridges between communities. Moreover, understanding these celebrations necessitates recognition of the important role played by ethnic entities or formal organizations in their orchestration. These celebrations convert spaces into locations infused with varied community identities and enduring cultural significance. These expressions of identity act as channels that promote cultural comprehension among communities, serving as a repository not just of collective cultural memories but also facilitating collaborative exchanges over time.

FIG. 4

Conclusion

The relationship between humans and their environment is a dynamic interplay where daily actions such as shopping, walking around, or celebrating shape and transform urban landscapes. These modifications are often driven by the practical needs and aspirations of the different communities. Urban environments serve not only as physical spaces but also as relational spaces where identity and cultural diversity are expressed and contested. As discussed, globalized urban landscapes frequently exhibit homogenized features, driven by economic and cultural forces that promote a standardized aesthetic. However, identity-related symbols act as powerful counterforces, challenging the notion of a uniform urban experience and asserting the uniqueness of local cultures. The examples shown are just a few; many more can be found on our daily experiences.

Visual communication emerges, then, as a crucial concept in modern globalized cities, facilitating the expression of otherness, identity, and differentiation. This visual dialogue is evident in the way cultural symbols, whether through murals, signage, or architectural elements, convey messages of belonging and diversity. The act of being observed and showing oneself is central to the interaction between and within culturally diverse groups, shaping both intra-community bonds and inter-community relationships. These symbols, in their myriad forms, address varied audiences and serve multiple purposes, from asserting community presence to fostering a sense of place and memory.

Urban capital condenses the inherited past, the living present, and the future as legacy. Identitarian symbols not only resist the homogenizing pressures of globalization but also enrich the urban fabric by adding depth through layers of historical and cultural significance. They become tools for communities to communicate their identities, resist marginalization, and contribute to the city's evolving narrative. In this way, cultural symbols and visual communication do more than *beautify* urban spaces; they foster a deeper understanding and appreciation of the diverse human experiences that inhabit them. This interplay between the global and the local, the homogenized and the unique, transforms urban environments into vibrant, living repositories of collective memory and identity, continually shaped by the actions and interactions of their inhabitants.

Acknowledgment

I, Guadalupe Ciocoletto, author of this article confirm that I own the rights to use all images included in the manuscript submitted for publication. I authorize the publishing house to reproduce and publish these images as part of the above mentioned article.

References

Appadurai, Arjun. 1996. *Modernity at Large: Cultural Dimensions of Globalization.* Public Worlds, vol. 1. University of Minnesota Press.

Arendt, Hannah. 2018. *The Human Condition.* 2nd ed. Chicago: University of Chicago Press.

Arfuch, Leonor. 2009. "Ver el mundo con otros ojos: Poderes y paradojas de la imagen en la sociedad global." In *Visualidades sin fin: Imagen y diseño en la sociedad global,* edited by Leonor Arfuch, 1st ed., xx–xx. Prometeo Libros.

De Certeau, Michel. 1984. *The Practice of Everyday Life.* Translated by Steven Rendall. University of California Press.

Delgado, Manuel. 2021. "La disolución de las identidades: Espacio público y derecho a la indiferencia." *Astrágalo: Cultura de la arquitectura y la ciudad* 18: 33–46. https://doi.org/10.12795/astragalo.2001.i18.04.

Devalle, Veronica. 2009. "El análisis cultural: Nuevas perspectivas para pensar el diseño." In *Visualidades sin fin: Imagen y diseño en la sociedad global*, edited by Leonor Arfuch, 1st ed., xx–xx. Prometeo Libros.

Hannerz, Ulf. 2001. *La Diversità Culturale.* Il Mulino.

Instituto Nacional de Estadística y Censos (INDEC). 2024. "Censo Nacional De Población, Hogares Y Viviendas 2022." Accessed May 21, 2025. https://censo.gob.ar/index.php/datos_definitivos_caba/.

Istat – Istituto Nazionale di Statistica. 2024. "Population and Households." Accessed May 21, 2025. https://www.istat.it/en/population-and-households?data-and-indicators.

Jacobs, Jane. 1961. *The Death and Life of Great American Cities.* Vintage Books.

Krase, Jerome, Jordi Ballesta, and Eliane De Larminat. 2020. "Visual Sociology of the Vernacular Urban Landscape: An Interview with Jerome Krase." *Interfaces* 44 (December): 145–67. https://doi.org/10.4000/interfaces.1856.

Krase, Jerome, and Timothy Shortell. 2011. "On the Spatial Semiotics of Vernacular Landscapes in Global Cities." *Visual Communication* 10 (3): 367–400. https://doi.org/10.1177/1470357211408821..

Lefebvre, Henri. 1974. *The Production of Space.* Translated by Donald Nicholson-Smith. Blackwell Publishing.

Maalouf, Amin. 2000. *On Identity.* Harvill Press.

Ministero del Lavoro e delle Politiche Sociali. 2020. "La Presenza dai Migranti nella Città Metropolitana di Milano." *Rapporti sulla Presenza Migrante nelle Città Metropolitane.* Accessed May 21, 2025. https://www.lavoro.gov.it/documenti-e-norme/studi-e-statistiche/Documents/RAM-2020-Milano.pdf..

Muxí, Zaida. 2006. "La Ciudad Dual o el Reto de la Globalización Sobre las Ciudades." *Ide@sostenible* 14 (March).

———. 2009. *La Arquitectura de la Ciudad Global.* Nobuko.

Sandercock, Leonie. 2000. "When Strangers Become Neighbours: Managing Cities of Difference." *Planning Theory & Practice* 1 (1): 13–30. https://doi.org/10.1080/14649350050135176..

Sassen, Saskia. 2012. "The Global City: Introducing a Concept." Accessed May 21, 2025.

———. "Urban Capabilities: An Essay on Our Challenges and Differences." *Journal of International Affairs* 65 (2): 85–95.

Simmel, Georg. 1903. "Las Grandes Ciudades y la Vida del Espíritu." *Cuadernos Políticos* (January–March): 5–10.

Tuan, Yi-Fu. 1977. *Space and Place: The Perspective of Experience.* 7th ed. University of Minnesota Press.

Vidal Moranta, Tomeu, and Enric Pol Urrútia. 2005. "La Apropiación del Espacio: Una Propuesta Teórica para Comprender la Vinculación entre las Personas y los Lugares." *Anuario de Psicología* 36: 281–97.

Williams, Raymond. 2003. *Palabras Clave: Un Vocabulario de la Cultura y la Sociedad.* 1st ed. Nueva Visión.

Zukin, Sharon. 2009. "Changing Landscapes of Power: Opulence and the Urge for Authenticity." *International Journal of Urban and Regional Research* 33 (2): 543–53. https://doi.org/10.1111/j.1468-2427.2009.00867.x..

Stephen Dedalus' Artistic Self-Creation: A Stoic Journey

Abdelhak Jebbar, PhD. & Najah Mahmi, PhD.

Abstract

In *A Portrait of The Artist as A Young Man* (1916), James Joyce questions the intrinsic nature of life, inspecting the complexity of human relationships amid a nonfinite series of chaotic inner and outer motions, and thus a machinery of apparatuses and power forces permanently generating psychological and mental struggles that shape human existence as both an action and a reaction towards empirical reality. Through Stephen Dedalus' stream of consciousness and epiphanies, human identity is shaken in different stages of the novel, in an attempt to reach self-revelation, self-assertion and self-mastery notwithstanding all social, cultural and political challenges as well as inner psychic turmoils. Stephen's rebellious attitudes towards socio-cultural conventions, resilience, intellectual autonomy, artistic liberation, and thus ataraxia and eudaimonia are paralleled in the novel with the Greek myth of Daedalus and his son Icarus. This mythological intertextuality fortifies the portrayal of the consciousness evolution of Dedalus as an artist and highlights the power of his inner agency. In this novel, the human being is portrayed as the primary subject and substance of life, whose system of ethics and morals is capable of reshaping fates and reproducing realities. This summarizes life in the right "to err, to fall, to triumph, to recreate life out of life!" (213) recognizing the supreme power of self-control, courage, endurance, strong will, and human dignity, and thus claiming James Joyce as one of the important modernist writers who implicitly revived stoic philosophy in their literary tradition.

Keywords: Stoic, Ataraxia, Eudaimonia, Myth, Truth

Introduction

> One by one they were all becoming shades. Better pass
> boldly into that other world, in the full glory of some
> passion, than fade and wither dismally with age.
>
> (Joyce 1914, 125)

In *Epiphanies*, written between 1901 and 1904 and first published in 1956, James Joyce accounts for revelations about life and existence through six-teen scenes and abrupt short conversations and six lyrical prose poems, recording epiphanies which he defines in *Stephen Hero* as "sudden spiritu-al manifestation[s], whether in the vulgarity of speech or of gesture or in a memorable phase of the mind itself. [...] They themselves are the most delicate and evanescent of moments." (1956, 211)

Joyce's concept of epiphany has not only established his great literary tra-dition but shaped the narrative structure of modern literature, and thus character development and thematic exploration. He pioneered with *Dubliners* (1914) and *A Portrait of The Artist as A Young Man* (1916) the stream-of-consciousness technique which allows a vast space for char-acters' internal realisation through nonlinear speculations, fragmented monologues, mythic intertextuality and linguistic and stylistic experi-mentation which have liberated the literary text from the conventions of dramatic narration. This Joycean tradition has influenced a great number of authors among whom are Virginia Woolf, William Faulkner, Don De-Lillo, Katherine Mansfield, Samuel Beckett, Ezra Pound, T.S. Eliot,[1] and Vladimir Nabokov, to name a few.

Joyce's central theme in his writings is the depiction of the name and nature of human existence, questioning humanity's limitations and con-demning conventional political, religious and societal constraints which abstract all possibilities of concretising personal identity outside the re-straints of social, national and collective identities. His writings vindicate the self through intellectual autonomy, self-governance and courage to question the sense and essence of truth and identify what the real thing

---

1   The influence in the case of T.S. Eliot's relationship with James Joyce was reciprocal. Eliot defended Joyce's *Ulysses* and expressed his admiration of the work, admitting it to be the most important literary expression of the modern age. He contributed to the promotion of the Joycean mythical method, praising his artistic talent in establishing parallelism be-tween classical mythology and experimental modernist writing techniques.

is: What? Why? When? How? Why not? And, what if?

Joyce's protagonists reflect external challenges through contemplation, endurance, resilience, silence, exile, and resignation, considering them as self-mastery, self-defence and self-assertion apparatuses through which they express their rejection of the status quo, and thus get regenerated and redefined in tranquillity. This implicitly resonates stoic philosophy with the author's existential and modernist tradition. Characters in *Epiphanies* are intellectually active, contemplating life and reality; Gabriel Conroy in "The Dead" (1914) and Eveline Hill in "Eveline" (1914) endure self-awareness and societal paralysis, yet they both opt for stoic resilience and escape within themselves; Stephen Dedalus detaches himself from political, social and religious orders and reaches liberty through artistic autonomy in *A Portrait of The Artist as A Young Man* (1916) and rational maturity in *Ulysses* (1922) all along with his paternal figure Leopold Bloom who symbolises resilience and rationality; Richard Rowan in *Exiles* (1918) epitomises unconventional absolute freedom and personal independence through artistic creativity; Humphrey Chimpden Earwicker in *Finnegans Wake* (1939) stands for historical recurrence through elastic processes of self-formation and reformation within a universal context. They all debate identity politics within inner and external controllable and uncontrollable life circumstances.

Stephen Dedalus' Journey of Self-Creation

A Portrait of The Artist as A Young Man (1916), developed by James Joyce from an earlier abandoned autobiographical novel titled *Stephen Hero* written between 1903 and 1905, is a bildungsroman that traces the inner growth and social development of the artist-figure named Stephen Dedalus, from childhood to manhood, through a continuous series of epiphanies and inner struggles and thus rebellion against socio-cultural apparatuses and religious norms, leading to his transformation from a controlled boy to a free autonomous self-governed artist.

While the novel has been acknowledged to be a Kunstlerroman, thus an aesthetic autobiography of an artist, recalling in this context Kenner's discussion of the artist's self-creation in the novel (1955) and the large debate in *The Cambridge Companion to James Joyce* (2004), led by Rabaté, Fordham, Caserio, and Mulligan, investigating Stephen's artistic journey within the realms of self-definition and artistic concretization, some critics, on the other hand, like Terry Eagleton (2004), see that the novel is a semi-autobiography, not fully based on Joycian real life and then not fully faithful to the typical structure of the Kunstlerroman genre, stressing the modernist structure of the novel as well as its ideological and socio-political implications.

Through Stephen Dedalus' stream of consciousness and epiphanies, human identity is scrutinized in different phases of the novel, via Stephen's continuous implicit and explicit questioning of the sense and essence of life as an epitome of existence and reality. He leads a constant journey of observing the real meaning of life, waving between reality and illusion, mortality and eternity, spiritual and secular, demon and angel, doubt and certainty, and darkness and light. The shaping features of his existence are keenly attributed to the conventions of religion, society and politics which stand for him as the 'other', and more critically to the 'self'. This suggests a pause to question the prospects of ultimate truth about human nature and reconsider the way external factors affect the human experience. What is truth? What is reality? And, what is the real thing? To what extent can humanity control outer reality? What are the limitations of human agency? And to what extent can they be challenged? And how?

As a child at Clongowes Wood College- though Stephen denies he "was ever a child," (296) he identifies himself based on family, geographical and institutional affiliations, accepting his ascribed social identity marked by his name, school, nationality and religion which were at this stage his world: his universe:

> Stephen Dedalus
> Class of Elements
> Clongowes Wood College
> Sallins
> County Kildare
> Ireland
> Europe
> The World
> The Universe
> [...]
> Stephen Dedalus is my name,

Ireland is my nation.

Clongowes is my dwelling place.

And heaven my expectation. (11-12)

However, this implies his early ability to observe and trespass societal borders, as locating himself within the universe broadens the scope of his existential questioning in further stages of his growth. For him, places "were all in different countries and the countries were in continents and the continents were in the world and the world was in the universe." (13)

Throughout the different stages of Stephen Dedalus' growth in the novel, he continuously questions reality, scrutinising human existence and his positioning within the universe. One of his early philosophical cogitations which reflects his curiosity about space and divinity, and thus explicitly expresses his youthful perception of the vast unlimited cosmos is:

> What was after the universe? Nothing. But was there anything round the universe to show where it stopped before the nothing place began? It could not be a wall but there could be a thin thin line there all round everything. It was very big to think about everything and everywhere. Only God could do that. [...] It made him very tired to think that way. It made him feel his head very big. (12)

This contemplation on the genuine nature of existence will be echoed six years later in *Ulysses*, questioning the spatiotemporal dimensions of the universe:

> [...] Of the universe of human serum constellated with red and white bodies, themselves universes of void space constellated with other bodies, each, in continuity, its universe of divisible component bodies of which each was again divisible in divisions of redivisible component bodies, dividends and divisors ever diminishing without actual division till, if the progress were carried far enough, nought nowhere was never reached. (820)

Then comes the existential question: 'Who was the first person in the universe before there was anybody that made it all." (931)

Since childhood, Stephen Dedalus has proven avant-gardist convictions and fastidious consciousness towards his environment shaped by sceptic stances towards reality, illusion and fantasy, acknowledging humanity's limitation within the frames of doctrinal truth, yet non-finite elastic re-generative nature within the shores of artistic imagination. This tension paves the way towards his future maturity through artistic autonomy.

The strained relations between Stephen and his outer reality are due to his different struggles with society, amid a series of chaotic inner and outer motions, and thus a machinery of apparatuses and power forces which generate psychological and mental struggles that shape his existence as both an action and a reaction towards his surrounding physical reality. His isolation at Clongowes Wood College due to physical weakness and longing for his family forged his feeling of alienation and estrangement, yet, paradoxically was a source of happiness and moral freedom, as he:

> Was happy only when he was far from them [his family, masters, and classmates who ridiculed him] beyond their call, alone or in the company of phantasmal comrades. [...] He was alone. He was unheeded, happy, and near to the wild heart of life. (93)

Besides, Stephen's religious scepticism stands as another cause of self-confinement and aspiration for a life beyond "The vastness and strangeness of the life suggested to him" (73) led by: "some instinct [...] stronger than education or piety quickened within him at every near approach to that life, an instinct subtle and hostile, and armed him against acquiescence. [...] What had come of the pride of his spirit which had always made him conceive himself as a being apart in every order?" (187) He was confused and "did not know well what politics meant and that he did not know where the universe ended. He felt small and weak." (13) As a young boy, Stephen questioned political and religious doctrines framed within the circle of sin and punishment which "made him very tired [...]. It made him feel his head very big." (13)

This is rooted in Stephen's family's debates on politics and religion, especially the Christmas dinner in which he witnessed a dispute between his governess Dante who defends the Catholic Church, Mr. Casey who criticizes its negative influence on Ireland and cries "No God for Ireland! [...] We have had too much God in Ireland. Away with God!" (40), and his father Simon Dedalus who moans the country's fate. This debate was the germinating seed of his future rejection of Catholic orthodoxy and resulted in one of his early epiphanies on personal and national identities. His mother Mary Dedalus embodies Irish Catholicism and functions as a mirror that reflects his inner psychological turmoils and conflicts, for he can neither please her and conform to the societal mode of life hence "serve" (281), nor enjoy spiritual freedom and being "an excitable bloody man," (281) as he feels guilty towards her.

Although Stephen expresses a sceptic attitude towards his outer reality, it has been impossible for him to be identified and affirmed as existent without reference to it, as it functions as his representative mirror through which his identity is referred; a mirror which puts him in tension with the idealized image forged in his artistic cognition. Thus, he is related to his context through a relation of differentiation rather than sameness, recalling in this context Emmanuel Levinas' theory of alterity and differentiation, explored in *Totality and Infinity* (1969) and elaborated in *Otherwise than Being or Beyond Essence* (1974).

Both Stephen's inner conception of self and the social structures within which he is positioned can be qualified as vivid agents in his journey of self-identification and self-creation. It is then the interaction between Stephen's cognitive self-processes and societal structures that creates his individual identity and then concretizes his agency, recalling in this context Mc Call & Simmons (1966).

Through his inner development, Stephen Dedalus suggests wisdom, courage, endurance, honour and dignity as the main motifs of human existence. His journey from uncertainty and loss to knowledge and liberation has been activated through rebellion against religious and socio-political conventions, thus through the assertion of his system of ethics and morals rather than those of Ireland. He rejects social and religious conventions and then escapes the imposed gloomy and foggy mode of life which sounds to him a weary of life even before entering upon it towards a simple and beautiful life of peace and virtue, formulating his sense of life as the right "to err, to fall, to triumph, to recreate life out of life!" (200)

He succeeds in tailoring his system of aesthetics in which meanings are permanently generated, errors are admitted and ups and downs are tolerated as part and parcel of human nature; a life which allows "all the ways of error and glory. On and on and on and on!" (200)

Stephen Dedalus as a Stoic Figure

In a dialogue with Cranly, his friend at University College in Dublin, Stephen asserts that he "do[es] not fear. [He] do[es] not fear to be alone or to be spurned for another or to leave whatever [he] ha[s] to leave. And [he is] not afraid to make a mistake, even a great mistake, a lifelong mistake and perhaps as long as eternity too. [... He] will take the risk." (292) This sense of self-contentment, flexible acceptance of erring, courage to face external reality, and acknowledgement that an individual cannot control the universe, goes hand in hand with the stoic philosophy of Epictetus based on resilience and control dichotomy.

In *Discourses* and *The Enchiridion*, compiled by Epictetus' pupil Arrian in the second century, Epictetus divides external reality into controlled and uncontrolled events, urging humanity to be wise and cautious towards controlled instances of reality and assume full responsibility for one's own opinions, judgements and decisions, and, on the other hand, calling people to be flexible towards things related to the divine powers of the cosmos and have enough courage to accept them in their most painful concretisations. His philosophy is that of emotional freedom, attitude, self-discipline, self-knowledge, self-governance, moderation and tranquillity: ataraxia. For him, freedom and happiness: eudaimonia are an inner construct rather than an outcome of external conditions, and thus pain is often a result of attempting to control what is beyond humanity's power. *The Enchiridion* opens with:

> There are things which are within our power, and there are things which are beyond our power. Within our power are opinion, aim, desire, aversion, and, in one word, whatever affairs are our own. Beyond our power are body, property, reputation, office, and, in one word, whatever are not properly our own affairs. Now the things within our power are by nature free, unrestricted, unhindered; but those beyond our power are weak, dependent, restricted, alien. [...] Seek at once, therefore, to be able to say to every unpleasing semblance, "You are but semblance and by no means the real thing." And then examine it [...] first and chiefly by this: whether it

concerns the things which are within our own power or
those which are not; and if it concerns anything beyond
our power, be prepared to say that it is nothing to you.
Remember that desire demands the attainment of that
of which you are desirous; and aversion demands the
avoidance of that to which you are averse; that he who
fails of the object of his desires is disappointed; and he
who incurs the object of his aversion is wretched. (I- II)

Epictetus is mentioned in the fifth chapter of Joyce's novel in a conversation between Stephen and the Dean of Studies on the lamp of Epictetus,
as part of a general discussion of the soul, literature, philosophy, art and
the artist's aesthetic responsibility of enlightenment. This implies a reviv-
al of stoic philosophy and highlights its influence on the literary tradition.

The conversation reveals the great knowledge gap between Stephen and
the Dean, depicting the Dean's limited knowledge and weakness in reasoning and synthesising, as he could not see the symbolic function of the
lamp which symbolizes the stoic philosopher's resilience, wisdom and
enlightening mission. In addition, the dean had no idea about Epictetus'
argument for the thief's unreasonable motif of stealing an iron lamp, as
he concludes that the thief paid a high price to become a thief, losing his
virtue. The iron lamp symbolizes Epictetus' self-sufficiency, while the
earthenware lamp with which Epictetus replaced the iron one epitomises
his acceptance of external reality as is, self-control, flexibility and virtue:

> Epictetus also had a lamp—said the dean—which was
> sold for a fancy price after his death. It was the lamp he
> wrote his philosophical dissertations by. You know Epic-
> tetus?
>
> —An old gentleman—said Stephen coarsely—who said
> that the soul is very like a bucketful of water.
>
> —He tells us in his homely way—the dean went on—
> that he put an iron lamp before a statue of one of the
> gods and that a thief stole the lamp. What did the phi-
> losopher do? He reflected that it was in the character of
> a thief to steal and determined to buy an earthen lamp
> next day instead of the iron lamp. (218)

For Stephen, the dean is a mere subject to whom he satirically refers as "a faithful serving man," (222) indoctrinated within himself and by allusive notions of religion, society, politics and nationalism, and so he felt towards his teachers, priests, his friends and fellow students, as well as his family including his mother and father, and then Ireland as a whole.

The characters with whom Stephen reacts in the novel function as foils through which he gradually dissociates himself from society and asserts personal artistic identity, as he verifies his intellectual speculations and validates the inefficiency of belonging to his environment. While Stephen Dedalus is all the time using logic in interpreting outer reality, the people of Ireland are conforming to the system.

In his conversation with his college friend Davin, Stephen refuses automated loyalty to Ireland and hence an imposed national identity, as he believes that "Ireland is the old sow that eats her farrow," (238) foregrounding thus rather self-governance and independent reasoning as a source of "serenity, freedom, and tranquillity." (*The Enchiridion*, XXIX) For Stephen, Ireland imprisons its citizens within alleged doctrines of nationalism which limits their existence within the frames of clerical mindsets; thus, blind obedience to the system. He says: "When the soul of a man is born in this country there are nets flung at it to hold it back from flight. You talk to me of nationality, language, religion. I shall try to fly by those nets." (238) Stephen Dedalus refuses to pay for his ancestors' faults as they "threw off their language and took another [...]. They allowed a handful of foreigners to subject them." (237) He decides rather be himself: "I shall express myself as I am," (237) challenging the borders of race and nationality.

Stephen's ancestors date back to Mesolithic Hunter-Gatherers, in 8000 BCE, who inhabited Ériu—Ireland's earliest name derived from the goddess Ériu in Irish mythology, to become later Éire and then Éire-land; then Ireland. In 4000 BCE, Neolithic Farmers settled in the land and created communities which were expanded later by the Celts in 500 BCE, the Vikings who settled in the period between the 9th and 11th centuries, the Normans who invaded in the 12th century, arriving to Gaelic Clans & Anglo-Irish Nobility in the medieval period, and then the modern and post-modern eras. These ancestors created Ireland's history and shaped its national identity through a machinery of control and resistance, among which is language, as asserted by Stephen.

> As a representational system, language stands as a rigorous tool of control and power. Every act of representation involves a perspective and correlates with power and hegemony epitomized in discourse "for which and by which there is struggle." (Foucault 1971, 8) This discourse shapes thus knowledge and power politics and gets activated through the representation's affiliations, knowing that meanings are constructed through language and cultural systems (Hall 1997), hence interaction, applying Bakhtin's Dialogism, and situational context, as argued by Paul Grice, John Searle, Dan Sperber, Deirdre Wilson, and others. This denies the referential theory of meaning which defends the inherently fixed correlative relationship between the linguistic system and outer reality, thus Kripke's argument that "a name designates the same object in all possible worlds in which that object exists." (1980, 48)

Stephen's conversation with the Dean of Studies about the meaning of words like art, artist, and philosophy expresses his rejection of the Dean's prescribed institutionalised meaning(s) of language which reflects his pragmatic and dogmatic frame of mind, and thus Stephen's emphasis on the philosophical implications of meta-discourse and rejection of being a man of *order*, as "speculation [cannot be] free thinking inasmuch as all thinking must be bound by its own laws." (218). His philosophical question about the relevance of the use of words according to the literary tradition or the tradition of the marketplace (219) is a key question about the real meaning of truth and existence and a condemnation of conventions.

This stand joins Michel Foucault's theory of discourse which emphasises institutions as a shaping power of discursive formations and then "a plethora of signifying elements in relation to [the] 'signified' [...] because each discourse contains the power to say something other than what it actually says, and thus to embrace a plurality of meanings," (1969, 88) knowing that "In every society the production of discourse is at once controlled, selected, organized, and redistributed according to a certain number of procedures." (1970, 216-217)

For Stephen, free thinking can only be attained through wisdom to consider the deepest philosophical assumptions of Aristotle and Aquinas, the courage to analyse them and self-reliance to come out with "something for [him]self by their light." (1916, 218) He draws analogy between intellectual autonomy and the light of a lamp brightened by disillusionment and disinterestedness in material restrictions, implying Epictetus' lamp of wisdom and affirming that "If the lamp smokes or smells [he] shall try to trim it. If it does not give light enough [he] shall sell it and buy another." (218) The light of the soul awakening lamp of wisdom will keep illuminating Stephen's journey of maturity and self-discovery in *Ulysses* (1922), cherishing his moments of silence and exile "with its faint voice." (3)

In his conversation with Cranly, Stephen interconnects the concept of freedom with autonomy and self-defence through silence, exile and cunning; applying stoic philosophy, though not explicitly. He affirms:

> You have asked me what I would do and what I would not do. I will tell you what I will do and what I will not do. I will not serve that in which I no longer believe, whether it calls itself my home, my fatherland or my church: and I will try to express myself in some mode of life or art as freely as I can and as wholly as I can, using for my defence the only arms I allow myself to use, silence, exile and cunning. (1916, 291)

In his further discussion of aesthetics with Lynch, Stephen defines art as a created image of beauty derived from trespassed contours of sound, shape and colour which restrict human existence. It is "the human disposition of sensible or intelligible matter for an esthetic end." (242) For him, beauty is an aesthetic apprehension, or, in Aquinas' words: "Pulcra sunt quæ visa placent- beautiful things are those that please when seen, emphasising their state of being which invites artistic contemplating and appreciation," (243) instead of state of becoming which would activate desire, action and emotions: "a stasis and not a kinesis." (243)

This establishes a keen relationship between truth, art and beauty, hence the representation of the object and artistic apprehension. According to Stephen, and based on his readings in Aristotle, Plato and Aquinas, beauty incorporates three constituents: wholeness (integritas), harmony (consonantia) and radiance (claritas); "Ad pulcritudinem tria requiruntur integritas, consonantia, claritas." (248) These components allow the observer to receive and perceive the represented object identified within the spatio-temporal real context and experience its essence: quidditas, yet as a unique subject entity with a unique aesthetic dimension that meets the artist's aesthetic image conceived in her/ his imagination: Haecceity, and then appreciate its artistic representation.

Art is thus both sensible and intelligible, considering that beauty is an ideal reflection of empirical reality which bridges truth and aesthetic imagination:

> In order to see that basket [...] your mind first of all separates the basket from the rest of the visible universe which is not the basket. The first phase of apprehension is a bounding line drawn about the object to be apprehended. An esthetic image is presented to us either in space or in time. [...] The esthetic image is first luminously apprehended as self-bounded and self-contained upon the immeasurable background of space or time which is not it. You apprehended it as one thing. You see it as one whole. You apprehend its wholeness. That is integritas. [...] Having first felt that it is one thing you feel now that it is a thing. You apprehend it as complex, multiple, divisible, separable, made up of its parts, the result of its parts and their sum, harmonious. That is consonantia.[...] Claritas[...] is rather vague [...] [It refers to] the artistic discovery and representation of the divine purpose in anything or a force of generalization which would make the esthetic image a universal one, make it outshine its proper conditions. I un-derstand it so. (248-249)

Stephen's surname Dedalus alludes to the myth of Daedalus and his son Icarus mentioned in the novel's epigraph. In Greek Mythology, Daedalus was a wise architect, inventor and master craftsman. King Minos of Crete asked him to invent and build an inescapable labyrinth to imprison a Minotaur, and then he imprisoned Daedalus and his son, but Daedalus could escape as he invented wings made of feathers and wax. Icarus flew too close to the sun, though his father warned him to be moderate in his flight and get away from high and low extremes foregrounding the virtue of temperance: sophrosyne. The wax melted and Icarus fell down and died. Daedalus did not give up on grief, and he flew to Sicily for a new life. This proves Daedalus' stoic resilience and acceptance of fate.

Daedalus symbolizes artistic creativity, autonomy and intellectual escape, and thus stands as Stephen Dedalus' inner consciousness and source of aspiration. Dedalus functions as the mirrored image of Daedalus which shapes and reshapes his ambitious personal identity and seeks escape from society's constraints through artistic liberation.

The novel is structured in the form of a labyrinth, as Stephen Dedalus experiences a transition from infantry innocence in the first chapter in which he is a young observer who still lives in happiness and peace, to adolescent doubt and uncertainty in the second chapter, as he starts questioning religious and societal orders, then a state of reasoning and truth verification in chapters three and four, to reach a state of certainty and disillusionment, as he decides to escape his reality for a new one, and then freedom through braking down with Christianity and attaining artistic liberation in the fifth chapter.

Stephen adopts his own faith: a faith in himself and art. It is his journey of rebellion against institutions and established law, and then his decision of self-exile and detachment from his environment that granted him freedom, while attachment sorrowed and humiliated him. One of his epiphanies which awakened his soul and paved the way towards his liberation is his exciting experience by the sea in which he was disconnected and then felt "a new wild life was singing in his veins," (198) establishing in him a vivid self-determined artist:

> He was alone and young and wilful and wild-hearted, alone amid a waste of wild air and brackish waters and the sea-harvest of shells and tangle and veiled grey sunlight and gay clad light clad figures of children and girls and voices childish and girlish in the air. (198- 199)

Stephen was anxious, sad and afraid when he was in Catholicism, lost with permanent concerns of sin and guilt, right and wrong, light and gloom. He was estranged and paralysed by the superficial and hypocritical teachings of bishops and priests who "must be obeyed" (31) and have minimised the very concept of religion in hell and punishment, by his father who has been degraded from a medical student, an actor and politician to a bankrupt who praises his past. His mother's conforming spirit and criticism for him "hav[ing] a queer mind and have [been] read[ing] too much," (294) his professors, his fellows, and the people of Ireland who could not embrace the artist in him. He could not survive the coercion of conformity. He created and pursued "intangible phantoms" to escape the hollow sounds "urging him to be a gentleman above all things and urging him to be a good Catholic above all things." (93)

He reaches an intense state of belief through religious scepticism experiencing life in death, as the young in him dies when attached to society, religion and politics, and resurrects when self-exiled from all established apparatuses, flying in liberty towards himself, his own established stoic world, in which he reaches the maximum of agency within the limitations of allowed agency.

He admits that truth is a mere perception the meanings of which differ from one human being to another, applying Epictetus' philosophy that a human being is but an impression and that a person needs to listen to her/ his inner reality which shapes outer reality through self-processes of reception and perception. Thus, he decides to "take the risk" (292) and escape from the status-quo labyrinth, and establish his truth: a free artistic truth, asserting that he "will not serve that in which [he] no longer believe[s]." (291)

This decision is energised by Epictetus' invocation of intellectual autonomy and self-satisfaction:

> If you ever happen to turn your attention to externals, for
> the pleasure of anyone, be assured that you have ruined
> your scheme of life. Be content, then, in everything, with
> being a philosopher; and if you wish to seem so likewise
> to anyone, appear so to yourself, and it will suffice you.
> (*The Enchiridion* XXIV)

The end of the novel marks Stephen Dedalus' artistic liberation and fresh will to establish his "own life [...] away from home and friends [to rediscover] what the heart is and what it feels." (299) With courage, he inaugurates a new life through the gate of experiment and discovery, aspiring for an uncreated identity which would allow him the joys of being HimSelf, chanting:

> O life! I go to encounter for the millionth time the reality
> of experience and to forge in the smithy of my soul the
> uncreated conscience of my race. (299)

Conclusion

In his different stages of self-creation, Stephen Dedalus refuses *serviam* as he criticises concepts of obedience and servitude which bind humanity, void their souls and deny their genuine right to ask and doubt, calling for intellectual and spiritual freedom and courage for self-knowledge and self-governance to reach ataraxia. For him, thinking is a major part of human beings' fate, the acceptance of which necessitates a perpetual reconsideration of "buil[t] order [... and] the sordid tide of life [...thus] rules of conduct [...] active interests and [...] filial relations." (110) Stephen Dedalus refuses to be part of the system and upholds scepticism and self-exile as a primary sketch for his portrait as an artist and a young man, who exists beyond all recognized dimensions of time and place, questioning the most unquestionable questions, among which is Lucifer's "cast out of heaven into hell for ever [for] non serviam: I will not serve," (134) through which he puts into question the very legitimacy of the human experience on earth and not in heaven; if there has ever been a heaven.

References

Eagleton, Terry. 2004. *The English Novel: An Introduction*. Blackwell Publishing.

Epictetus. 108 CE. *Discourses*. Translated by Elizabeth Carter. Edited by Arrian.

———. 1948 [125CE]. *The Enchiridion*. Translated by Thomas Wentworth Higginson. Edited by Arrian. Introduction by Albert Salomon. The Liberal Arts Press.

Foucault, Michel. 1969. *The Archaeology of Knowledge*. Translated by A.M. Sheridan Smith. Routledge.

———. 1971. *The Order of Discourse*. Translated by Ian McLeod. Gallimard.

Hall, Stuart, ed. 1997. *Representation: Cultural Representations and Signifying Practices.* Sage Publications & Open University.

Joyce, James. 1914. *"The Dead."* In *Dubliners.* Grant Richards.

———. 1914. *Dubliners.* Grant Richards.

———. 1914. "Eveline." In *Dubliners.* Grant Richards.

———. 1916. *A Portrait of The Artist as A Young Man.* B.W. Huebsch.

———. 1918. *Exiles: A Play in Three Acts.* B. W. Huebsch

———. 1922. *Ulysses.* Shakespeare and Company.

———. 1939. *Finnegans Wake.* Faber and Faber

———. 1956. *Epiphanies.* University of Buffalo.

Kenner, Hugh. 1955. *Dublin's Joyce.* Chatto & Windus.

Kripke, Saul. 1980. *Naming and Necessity.* Harvard University Press.

Levinas, Emmanuel. 1969. *Totality and Infinity: An Essay on Exteriority.* Translated by Alphonso Lingis. Duquesne University Press.

———. 1974. *Otherwise than Being or Beyond Essence.* Translated by Alphonso Lingis. Duquesne University Press.

McCall, George J., and J.L. Simmons. 1966. *Identities and Interactions: An Examination of Human Associations in Everyday Life.* Free Press.

Rabaté, Jean-Michel, Finn Fordham, Cesario Caserio, and Peter Mulligan, eds. 2004. *The Cambridge Companion to James Joyce.* Cambridge University Press.

J.M. Coetzee's Doctoring of Painful Identarian Truths in *Summertime*

Sheila Collingwood-Whittick, PhD.

ABSTRACT

Summertime, the third volume in J M Coetzee's life-writing trilogy, is to a large extent concerned with the *modus operandi* of 'Vincent', a young English researcher who is said to be gathering material for a biography of the author, J. M. Coetzee, shortly after the latter's death. Culled from a series of interviews with individuals who played a variety of roles in Coetzee's life during the crucial threshold period when he was "finding his feet as a writer," the material Vincent assembles contains many verifiable facts about the real J. M. Coetzee. Yet, premised, as it is, on a number of manifest falsehoods and monumental omissions, the biographical narrative that ultimately emerges offers an image of J.M. Coetzee's life that, in certain key respects, radically differs from that of the real author. On one level, then, *Summertime* works to *deconstruct* biography, both by exposing the flaws inherent in the genre and by interrogating the questionable relationship the finished biographical work bears to the truth of its subject's identity. At the same time, Coetzee's final memoir is not, I contend, simply concerned with making an *academic* point. Focusing on the specific life-defining events (and the profound emotional repercussions they produced) that are deliberately deleted from the narrative *Summertime* offers of Coetzee's adult existence, I seek to explain why, apparently abandoning the truth-seeking mission unflinchingly pursued in *Boyhood* and *Youth,* the author opts instead for a lighter, doctored and thus inevitably falsified account of his identity during his early adult life.

Keywords: Biography, Autobiography, Memoir, Life-Narrative, Identity, Confession, Oral Testimony, Facts, Truth, Quest, Inner Self, Personal History, Self-Interest, Pain Avoidance

"All versions of the *I* are fictions of the *I*."
(Attwell 1992, 75)

Autobiographical Truths on which *Summertime* is Based

Published in 2009, *Summertime,* is described on the book's dustcover as completing J.M. Coetzee's "majestic trilogy of fictionalised memoir begun with *Boyhood* [1997] and *Youth* [2002]." Thus, while it goes no further than the fourth decade of the author's life, *Summertime* must, if we are to believe the paratext, be regarded as constituting the final instalment in the author's project of self-exploration.[1]

As in the two previous *autre*biographical narratives which describe the tenor of Coetzee's existence between the ages of ten and twenty-three, the author of *Summertime* observes the subsequent phase of his evolving self from the hyperfocal distance afforded by third person narration. Where *Summertime* diverges from the pattern established in the earlier memoirs, however, is in its departure from the *auto*biographical mode. Abandoning the hegemonic, monological narration used in *Boyhood* and *Youth*, Coetzee opts for a polyvocal narrative, the aggregate of diverse testimonies solicited by 'Vincent', a young English researcher, whose declared aim is to produce a "serious book, a seriously intended *biography*" (Coetzee 2009, 225.[2] My italics.) of Coetzee in his thirties.

The notebook fragments attributed to a certain J.M. Coetzee with which the text begins and ends are, Coetzee scholar David Attwell informs us, only "lightly fictionalized" (Attwell 2016, 58). The first set of notes dated 1972-1975 record, in the third person, Coetzee's observations on life in the South Africa of the 1970s. Some journal entries record the outrageous

---

1   Brian Macaskill raises the interesting point of the differences between the paratexts accompanying respectively the UK and US editions of *Summertime*. The title-page of the London imprint appends "Scenes from Provincial Life" to [...] *Summertime,* thereby intimately (from the inside) linking it to the dust cover and title pages of *Boyhood [:] Scenes from Provincial Life* and to the dust cover, at least, of *Youth [:] SCENES FROM PROVINCIAL LIFE* (which omits the subtitle on its inner title page). [...] On both its dust cover and again on its title page, the New York edition more directly and more explicitly stipulates the genre to which it belongs: "Fiction by the author of DISGRACE" (dust cover); "Summertime [:] FICTION (title page)." (Macaskill 2014, 129) There are also significant differences between the photographs of Coetzee used in these two editions." (Macaskill 2014, 127) Such discrepancies clearly demonstrate the generic ambiguity of the work.

2   All further references to *Summertime* will be confined to page numbers.

quotidian violence of an apartheid regime that is finally spinning out of control. Others offer a glimpse of the author's humdrum existence, note his views on diverse aspects of South African culture or, occasionally, analyse his reaction to some minor occurrence that has destabilized his seemingly precarious psychological equilibrium. By contrast, the somewhat longer section of *undated* notebook extracts with which the novel closes, focuses almost exclusively on Coetzee's problematical and profoundly distressing relationship with his elderly father.

Framed by reflections whose truth status the reader has, unlike Attwell who has accessed the Coetzee archive, no means of determining, is Vincent's biographical portrait of John Coetzee at the outset of his writing career, or, more accurately, a representation of the raw source material from which that portrait will ultimately be fashioned. This 'raw material', which is the main body of *Summertime*, consists of a series of five interviews with people who knew Coetzee during the "threshold period" (Powers 2016, 325) in which, Vincent contends, he was "finding his feet as a writer." (225)[3]

Of the four female interviewees, two, Julia a white South African psychotherapist and Sophie a French academic, are divorcees who had an adulterous affair with the subject before he became a celebrated author. One, Adriana, a Brazilian dancer, is a widow, who was not only immune to but totally incensed by "Mr Coetzee's" amorous pursuit of her while her husband lay dying in hospital. And one is, unmistakably, the real-life author's favourite cousin—referred to by her real name, Agnes, in *Boyhood* and introduced as Margot in *Summertime*. The sole male interviewee, Martin, is described as a former colleague and one-time friend of the author during the latter's teaching career at the University of Cape Town in the 1970s.

Those most prepared to divulge anecdotal evidence about the private man are Julia, Margot and Adriana. Martin and Sophie by contrast, refuse to engage in discussions of Coetzee's personality, confining their testimony to observations on his pedagogy, his politics and his public persona as writer and intellectual. Both these academics may be regarded as ventriloquial conduits for Coetzee, each rehearsing the latter's well-known view

---

3   It is worth noting that, speaking of that period in one of the interviews with Attwell, Coetzee remarks "I cannot stress how directionless I was in those days. I was thirty years old and had published nothing." (*Doubling the Point* 337)

that the reader's understanding of a literary oeuvre should not be filtered through knowledge of the writer's personal experience.

Martin, for example, warns Vincent against the risk of producing "an account that is slanted towards the personal and the intimate at the expense of the man's actual achievements as a writer." (218) "Who can say," he asks, "what goes on in people's inner lives?" (216) Sophie, for her part, rejects Vincent's appeal to "comment on the human side of Coetzee," or recount "personal stories from [their] time together." (235) Such stories, she jokes, will be saved for her own memoirs." (236) Considering the number and pertinence of the critical questions the book poses about the validity of the biographical project, *Summertime*, may then be legitimately considered as functioning in part to undermine the credibility of any future biography of Coetzee himself.

Most of the data yielded by all five informants conform nonetheless to the biographical facts of the author's life. Like the real J.M. Coetzee, the subject of Vincent's biography is, for example, a South African writer of Afrikaner descent who "decamped" to Australia late on in his life (209). He is the author of such novels as *Dusklands* (55), *In the Heart of the Country* (234), *Foe* (200), *Boyhood* (240) and *Disgrace* (242). He is also a Nobel Laureate (242), the son of parents named Vera and Jack (130), the grandson of a "gentleman horse-breeder and sheep-farmer" (107) who founded the family farm named Voëlfontein (87), and the brother of Vera and Jack's only other son who lived overseas in the 1970s. Despite his Afrikaner origins, he is said to have spoken English from an early age (161) and, after spending the 1960s working and studying first in Britain and then in America (209), he eventually returned to South Africa where he accepted a post in the English Department at the University of Cape Town (221).

All these details can be easily cross-checked against information provided by the author in his two previous memoirs, his non-fictional writing and in a number of key interviews he gave at various points in his career. They are also corroborated by J. C. Kannemeyer's *J.M. Coetzee: A Life in Writing*,[4] the first biography of the author to be published and a project

---

4   It is, I think, significant that the author of the first of what will doubtless become a deluge of Coetzee biographies, was, unlike Vincent, Coetzee's fictional *English* biographer, an *Afrikaner*. Equally significantly, Kannemeyer was, as one reviewer underlines, "a dominant voice in South African letters: [...] the author of the weighty, two-volume Geskiedenis van die Afrikaanse literatuur (History of Afrikaans Literature), and the acclaimed biographer

on which, according to the author, Coetzee cooperated "unstintingly and even enthusiastically." (7)

Crucial Omissions from and Misrepresentations of Coetzee's Identity in *Summertime*

Yet, disconcertingly embedded in the veridical and verifiable evidence offered by the interviewees are several major *untruths* on which the entire narrative is premised. These include the fictions that J.M. Coetzee is dead,[5] that in the 1970s, the period of the author's life which Vincent is most interested in investigating, Coetzee was a single man who had "no family in the conventional sense. [...] No wife, no children," (31) that his mother (who in reality died in 1985) was already dead by the 1970s, and that, following his mother's death, he co-habited with his widowed and ailing father.[6] Though comparatively few in number, these *contre-vérités*[7] deform the story of the real John Coetzee's life to the point where, as Kannemeyer remarks "The relation between events and distortions, facts and fiction, truth and lies becomes a central factor in the structure of the novel." (606)

In the following analysis I focus on two of the main questions that *Summertime* provokes. Why, after publishing two widely acclaimed autobiographical works, does Coetzee switch to a *fictionalised biography* to complete his trilogy of personal memoirs? And what reason can be adduced to account for the author's subversive introduction of conspicuous *untruths* into a biographical portrait dealing with the period of his life leading up to his emergence as an author? Since both of the answers I propose involve a transgressive disregard for Coetzee's frequent strictures on the practice of referencing a writer's personal experience to explain aspects of his/her literary production,[8] I will begin with a few self-justificatory remarks.

---

of Afrikaans literary giants" (Clarkson 264).

5   Ironically, Kannemeyer who began research for his 700+page biography while *Summertime* was still being written, died in 2012 shortly before the final editing of this major work was completed.

6   On a more playful level is Vincent's manifestly untrue observation to Martin that the third volume of Coetzee's memoirs "never saw the light of day" (205).

7   Untruths, falsehoods (Collins Robert, French-English, English-French Dictionary).

8   As Neuman underlines, "Coetzee remains consistent in his belief that the private life of a writer could and probably should be dismissed as irrelevant information." (Neuman 2011, 32) Kannemeyer further points out that two major Coetzee scholars, Teresa Dovey and David Attwell endorse the author's view on this question (Kannemeyer 2013, 8).

Trying to comprehend his undeflectable search for the *man* who produced the literary oeuvre he reveres, the narrator of *Flaubert's Parrot* asks:
"Why does the writing make us chase the writer? [...] Why aren't the
books enough? Flaubert wanted them to be: few writers believed more
in the objectivity of the written text and the insignificance of the writer's
personality; *yet still we disobediently pursue.*" (Barnes 12, my italics)

I confess that my own 'disobedient' pursuit both stems from and is emboldened by the numerous inconsistencies I find in Coetzee's position
vis à vis the issue Barnes evokes in the previous quotation. In the essays
that comprise the collections *Stranger Shores* and *Inner Workings* (literary reviews in which Coetzee repeatedly references biographical data to
support his interpretation of the work of novelists he is reviewing), the
disconnect between his critical praxis and the edict he seeks to impose
on scholars of his work is flagrant. Referring to Coetzee's MA thesis on
Ford Madox Ford, Kannemeyer observes for instance that: "The dissertation is notable for its meticulous style, confident use of sources and *the
biographical emphasis that would also characterise Coetzee's later essays on
literature* and his reviews in the *New York Review of Books.*" (Kannemeyer
2013, 126. My italics)

More striking still is the cognitive dissonance that exists between, on the
one hand, the repugnance Coetzee has expressed for "the violation of private space" (Attwell 1992, 65) and on the other, both the surprising act of
self-exposure to which the author commits himself in his autobiographical trilogy and his reportedly "unstinting" and "enthusiastic" cooperation
with his South African biographer.

It is, however, Coetzee's observations on Philip Roth's intentions in *The
Plot against America* that have most comforted my approach to *Summertime.* "If," says Coetzee in his review of Roth's novel, "the author [...] had
meant to write about a fictive child whose sole existence is between the
pages of a novel, *he would not have called that child Philip Roth, born in the
same year as himself and of parents with the same names as his.*" (Coetzee
1997, 233)

To understand Coetzee's recourse to the genre of biography (albeit fictional) in the last volume of his autobiographical trilogy, it is salutary, I
think, to remind ourselves first of the forensic investigation into confession and autobiography the author carried out in his essay "Confession

and Double Thoughts." (Attwell 1992) For, as he has since affirmed, this was no mere abstract, academic enquiry into life-writing genres. The questions he was asking in that pivotal essay had a very *personal* resonance for him (Attwell 1992, 391-395). Finding a way through the dense thickets of self-deception that obstructed such illustrious would-be confessants as Tolstoy, Rousseau and Dostoevsky has always, in fact, been one of the main driving forces behind Coetzee's writing both autobiographical and fictional. Yet, as he points out in his discussion with Attwell, alongside the truth-teller he ardently aspires to be, there exists a second self, subversively insisting that:

> ... there is no ultimate truth about oneself, there is no point in trying to reach it [...] Autobiography is dominated by self-interest [...]. The only sure truth in autobiography is that one's self interest will be located at one's blind spot (Attwell 1992, 392).

On the face of it, like his much-discussed use of third person narration in *Boyhood*, the biographical format Coetzee adopts in *Summertime* can be construed as another authorial stratagem by means of which he can elude the clamorous demands of self-interest that, he believes, constantly threaten to undermine the truth-seeking vocation of autobiography. Interestingly, support for this view can be found in one of the published 'exchanges' between Coetzee and psycho-therapist, Arabella Kurtz who sees *Summertime* as expressing an intention on the author's part to "know and understand [himself] through others." (Kurtz and Coetzee 11. My italics)

If, however, a straightforward intellectual/ethical commitment to truthtelling remains to some extent a driving force in this final volume of his three-part memoir, an equally compelling reason for Coetzee's turn to fictionalised biography consists of those crucial aspects of the author's personal experience that are omitted from *Summertime*.

Two years before the book's publication, Coetzee was diagnosed as suffering from prostate cancer (Kannemeyer 2013, 603). Suddenly confronted with the looming reality—as opposed to the abstract notion—of his mortality, propelled henceforth into "the shadow of last things,"[9] the

---

9   This is the phrase Coetzee uses to refer to the situation in which the dying Ippolit makes his confession in *Notes from Underground* (Attwell 1992, 284).

author's perspective on life generally and, on his life history in particular, had, necessarily, undergone a significant re-adjustment.

The certain knowledge that, in the wake of his death, "the booming 'critical industry' of Coetzee scholarship" (Coghlan 2021, n.p.) would indubitably zero in on all the previously unexcavated details of the author's private life must have further darkened the latter's already bleak outlook. For a man who has never concealed his craving for privacy, the proleptic contemplation of unknown biographers of dubious integrity probing and picking over the intimate details of his private life, of prurient or merely inaccurate versions of his personal history being released into the world, could only be anathema. Viewed from this perspective, Coetzee's deconstructive biography can be understood as stemming from the same kind of defence mechanism that Doris Lessing describes when explaining her motivation for embarking on an autobiography:

> Why an autobiography at all? Self-defence: biographies are being written. It is a jumpy business, as if you were walking along a flat and often tedious road in an agreeable half-dark but you know a searchlight may be switched on at any minute [...] less and less do facts matter, partly because writers are like pegs to hang peoples' fantasies on. [...] Writers may protest as much as they like but our lives do not belong to us. (Lessing 1995, 14-15)

Paradoxically, then, one of *Summertime*'s objectives is precisely to undermine the claim that biography is capable of un/dis/covering the true history of the subject's life. For, interwoven into the narration of Vincent's uneasy and often conflictual exchanges with his informants, is a subversive metafictional commentary highlighting the many flaws and shortcomings inherent in the genre.

Exemplifying the casual, unprofessional interviewer of whom Coetzee speaks with such evident disdain in "The Poetics of Reciprocity," (Attwell 1992, 65) Vincent argues perversely that, the fact that "he never met [Coetzee] in the flesh." (34) is an advantage Having no "sense of obligation" toward the author will, he points out, "leave [him] free to write what [he] wish[es]." (35) The shameless *mauvaise foi*[10] behind Vincent's

---

10   Bad faith (Collins Robert, French-English, English-French Dictionary).

posture, the fatuousness of such reasoning, are immediately exposed by Julia's incredulity that, though he has gone to the trouble of meeting *her*, a mere bit player in Coetzee's life, he *chose* not to meet the actual subject of his biography (35).

As will become clear through subsequent interviews, the questions Vincent asks about Coetzee don't just produce information about Coetzee, they also prompt the interviewees to interrogate the biographer about the integrity of his project or about the weaknesses of the *modus operandi* he has elected to pursue. What, he is asked, are the criteria that have determined his selection of sources? (216) Why is the number of interviewees so small? (216) Exactly what kind of biography is he intending to write? Will it, for example, be a prurient, gossipy, blowing-the-lid-off exposé of Coetzee, the famous author? wonders Adriana. (170) What justification can he offer for intending to concentrate on such a short period of the subject's life? (225). How can he defend his exclusive focus on the oral testimony of informants when there is an entire archive of Coetzee's diaries, letters and notebooks waiting to be explored? (225). What authorization does he have for the memoir he proposes to publish? (227).

Indications of the tenuousness, the dubious veracity of the biographical narrative can also be found in a variety of textual references signalling the distorted picture that inevitably results from the ego-centric perspective of the informant. For, if Vincent imagines that this issue is one that can be solved by a bit of "quick manipulation" or "some clever editing," (44) he is, as Julia stresses, making a big mistake (44). As she underlines, there is only one story of Coetzee that she is able to tell: "the story of *my* life and *his* part in it, which is quite different, quite another matter, from the story of *his* life and *my* part in it" (43 my italics).

Glimpses of the egocentricity of the informant's vision can also be observed in Julia's desire to have a copy of the photo Vincent claims John kept of her (36) and in Adriana's request to be sent a copy of *Foe*, whose female protagonist is, Vincent suggests, modelled on her (201). The question of how to assess the truth-value of information provided by an informant with an "axe to grind" (217) is also raised, as well as that of how much credence can be placed in testimony (as is the case for Adriana) that has transited unchecked through the linguistic filter of a translator. And what can be done to remediate the loss or destruction of documents with the potential to illuminate unexplored areas of the subject's life (170, 194).

Finally, Vincent's shamelessly sexed-up version of the unsophisticated account Margot gives of her cousin's life illuminates the problem of the denaturing impact that unauthorized editing can have on testimony provided by biographical sources. "I said nothing remotely like that. You are putting words of your own in my mouth," (119) protests Margot on hearing what Vincent has written, "You are just making things up." (137) Minimising the transformative impact he has had in his retelling of a story he found too dull and artless, the smooth-talking Vincent, explains that all he has done is to "fix[..] up the prose." (87) "Changing the form," he assures her, "should have no effect on the content." (91)

Influenced by this ambiance of doubt and mistrust, the reader, too, is prompted to ask questions about 1. the trustworthiness of testimony based on recollections that are not only decades old but are almost certain to be impinged upon, corrupted even, by a retrospective awareness of Coetzee's later celebrity and/or 'death'; and 2. the likelihood of producing a balanced, coherent, biographical account from the kind of discontinuous, fragmentary, and self-centred narratives that Vincent collects.

One thing is certain: given the essentially negative impression of Coetzee that emerges from the interviews Vincent conducts, it could hardly be argued that the final volume of Coetzee's autobiographical trilogy springs from an authorial intention to leave behind a more complaisant image of himself. The John Coetzee recalled by the five informants is not only lacking in relational skills, self-awareness, empathy and common sense, he is also physically unattractive, eccentric, and despite his often-obsessional behaviour and outlandish sexual impulses, ultimately unremarkable. In Kannemeyer's opinion: "Literature has seldom known such an example of authorial self-disgust as this embodiment of the person of J M Coetzee." (2013, 608) At the same time, emphasises Coetzee's first authorised biographer, *Summertime* conveys "an unambiguous warning to any real-life biographer who might want to trace the life of J M Coetzee." (Kannemeyer 2013, 608)

One crucial question that can be seen to arise from *Summertime*'s "metafictional pre-empting of interpretation"[11] is, thus, precisely that posed by the narrator of *Flaubert's Parrot* "What chance would the craftiest biographer stand against the subject who saw him coming and decided to amuse himself?" (Barnes 1985, 38)

Though widely commented on, the changes Coetzee makes to key elements of his life history has not, to my knowledge, given rise to close analysis. Thomas Jones, for example, simply warns that "readers have no grounds for believing that anything else they are told about the character John Coetzee necessarily holds true for his eponymous creator." (Jones 2009). Frank Kermode similarly fails to probe the question he raises of "why should we believe this and not that, especially when the tricks are made so easy to spot?" (Kermode 2009, 10) And in an article otherwise brimming with psychological insights into Coetzee's work, James Meek nevertheless balks at discussing the author's disfiguring obliteration of the life he led as husband and father, observing merely that: "Of these stories, there are no traces in *Summertime*." (Meek 2009)

Contesting the proscription imposed both by Coetzee and some Coetzee scholars on using non-literary elements of the writer's life to illuminate aspects of his writing, I wish to argue that *Summertime* only becomes fully comprehensible when considered in the light of Coetzee's personal experience. For while this enigmatic memoir can be taken, on one level, as a mildly satirical narrative in which is staged the unedifying life of the both eccentric and egocentric, would-be author in the pre-dawn of his Nobel prize-winning career, *Summertime* is, above all, I contend, a kind of dumb show, gesturing with the power of which only the most deeply repressed emotion is capable, towards the author's grief.

The erasure of John's identity as husband and father, the reduction of his adult life to an experience of child-like, semi-celibate co-existence with his widowed father are, I suggest, strategies of pain avoidance. They are the psychological defences the author has erected against the agonising and/or traumatogenic experiences that, Kannemeyer's biography reveals, tore apart his life in the 70s and 80s.

For it was during this period that, in addition to the gradual disintegration of Coetzee's marriage to his first wife, Philippa Jubber, the author

---

11   The expression is that which Coetzee himself uses in an interview with Attwell (1992, 204).

was, within the space of a mere five years, confronted with the death of four of the most important people in his life. His mother, Vera, described in *Boyhood* as "the firmest thing in his life, the rock on which he stands" (35) died of a heart attack. His father Jack, against whom he had waged an unresolved war of attrition since childhood, succumbed to cancer of the larynx. Less than a year later, Nicholas, his twenty-two-year-old only son, plunged to his death from the balcony of a flat on the eleventh floor of an apartment building. And, in 1990, his former wife, Philippa, aged 51, died from an aggressive form of breast cancer.

Other painful details of Coetzee's private life revealed (with the author's consent) in Kannemeyer's biography include the essentially dysfunctional nature of his relationships with his children, his chronic inability to exercise parental authority, the inexorable estrangement between himself and Nicholas, whose turbulent youth was marred by episodes of substance abuse and petty criminality, and the profound distress of his daughter Gisela whose serial struggles with anorexia, alcoholism and epilepsy have taken a terrible toll on both her own health and her father's peace of mind.

Such a relentless succession of tragic events would unquestionably wreak emotional damage on any sentient human being. As *Boyhood* testifies, however, Coetzee is not simply a person of normal sensibility. He is an inordinately sensitive being who suffered in his childhood from the hyperalgesic sense that "he is damaged [...] that something is slowly tearing inside him all the time: a wall, a membrane." (Coetzee 1997, 9) Tormented by the feeling that "[e]veryone is staring at him, judging him, finding him wanting." (Coetzee 1997, 150), the image young John has of himself is that of "a crab pulled out of its shell, pink and wounded and obscene." (150) In order to prevent this dangerous vulnerability from being exposed, he must, he decides "be more prudent," when talking about himself to others, "always tell[ing] less rather than more." (Coetzee 1997, 29)

Significantly, despite his robust assertion that his book is not intended as "a psychological study of the man," (Kannemeyer 2013, 14) Kannemeyer's observations about the adult Coetzee depict him as a man who does not differ essentially from the younger version of himself portrayed in *Boyhood* and *Youth*. He is a sensitive and psychologically complex being, deeply affected by the emotional blows life has dealt him yet loath to speak about the injuries from which he continues to suffer. Most importantly, Kannemeyer's portrait shows him to be both a heartbroken father for whom the death of his son remains, *"a constant corrosive pain from which there is no deliverance,"* (Kannemeyer 2013, 457. My italics) and an author whose bottled-up feelings and "obsessive temperament" (Kannemeyer 2013, 578) seek release in the compulsive writing habit he has maintained since the 1970s.

Yet, if writing affords Coetzee some relief from his demons, the respite it offers is, as he explained in an interview with the South African writer, Allister Sparks, only partial and temporary: "It's bad if I write but worse if I don't." (Kannemeyer 2013, 429)

Hypothesising Coetzee's Censoring of Important Identarian Truths

Why is it, then, that critical commentary on *Summertime* remains mute on the text's surprising omission of the compound emotional injuries from which the biographical subject is known to have suffered? Why do Coetzee specialists consistently interpret the blanks and distortions in his fictionalised biography as mere demonstrations of postmodern, literary high jinks rather than a reflexive avoidance of the suffering generated by the multiple existential wounds that have scarred the author's life? Why does analysis of the biographical portrait *Summertime* presents tend to be limited to what it tells us about Coetzee's writerly practice? What is it in the literary critic's formation that makes them shy away from discussion of the pain to which *all* Coetzee's work gestures?

In one of the discussions with Attwell, Coetzee tellingly suggests to his interviewer that even "the subject may not know the whole truth because *the resistances and repressions involved are too strong.*" (Attwell 1992, 105. My italics) Similarly, at the outset of his fascinating dialogue with psycho-therapist Arabella Kurtz, (sub-titled, *Exchanges on Truth, Fiction and Psychotherapy*), Coetzee's scepticism about the (in)capacity of life-narratives to yield the truth about the self is articulated once again, though for a different reason. The narrative imagination is, he asserts, "a faculty we use to elaborate for ourselves and our circle *the story that suits us best,* a story that justifies the way we have behaved in the past and behave in the present, a story in which we are generally right and other people are generally wrong." (Kurtz and Coetzee 2016, 4)

Returning to this idea in a subsequent exchange, however, his position is less theoretical, less distanced; "we" has become "one." Rather than focusing on the self-serving strategies most people consciously deploy for avoiding the truth, he foregrounds the emotional barriers the psyche constructs to prevent human beings from accessing truths about themselves that are too painful to bear (Kurtz and Coetzee 2016, 52).

And yet, "the longing or nostalgia for the one and only truth" is, Coetzee eventually confesses to Kurtz, "a longing that I myself happen to feel strongly." (Kurtz and Coetzee 2016, 68) As I see it then, this unusually frank admission is an expression of the author's yearning to recover the spontaneous, feeling self that 'John' sequestered in his childhood; the self to which the analysand is denied access by the analytical, cerebral Coetzee, the aloof and impenetrable intellectual who insists that "All versions of the *I* are fictions of the *I*. The primal *I*, is not recoverable." (Attwell 1992, 75)

The formidable intellect that lends such power and, paradoxically, passion to all of Coetzee's writing should perhaps be seen therefore not so much as a tool that serves to uncover the truth in Summertime but as a sophisticated instrument the author wields for the purpose of concealing pain, or, more specifically, the pain that, in his experience, the truth represents. Indeed, the kind of literary, linguistic and narratological game-playing in which Coetzee continually engages, not just in *Summertime* but, to some extent, in his oeuvre as a whole, can, I suggest, be regarded as a mask the author uses to disguise existential truths that are too painful to expose.

In his elegant analysis of the phenomenon of *"larvatus prodeo,"*[12] French philosopher, writer, literary critic and semiotician, Roland Barthes, stresses that:

> [I]l faut que cacher se voie : sachez que je suis en train de vous cacher quelque chose, tel est le paradoxe actif que je dois résoudre: il faut en même temps que ça se cache et que ça ne se sache pas : que l'on sache que je ne veux pas le montrer : voilà le message que j'adresse à l'autre. *Larvatus prodeo* : je m'avance en montrant mon masque du doigt : je mets un masque sur ma passion, mais d'un

---

12   I go forward masked.

doigt discret (et retors) je désigne ce masque. (Barthes 1977, 52-3).[13]

This, then, it seems to me, accurately represents what *Summertime* is designed to achieve. By omitting all reference to his identity as a husband and as a father during the time period covered in this supposedly biographical work, the author is able to mask the suffering that exposing such painful elements of his lived reality would necessarily entail. At the same time, the flagrant distortion of the truth incurred by covering up these primal identarian elements is the means by which the author signals to the reader the emotional torment that the mask is used to hide.

Significantly, in his discussion with Kurtz some six years later the grief that the mask conceals in *Summertime* unexpectedly erupts in an epiphanic moment when Coetzee, responding to a question posed by his interlocutor, suddenly declares: "I am looking for someone before whom I can cry, or in a metaphor that might cover both words and tears, before whom I can pour myself out." (57)

My point is, then, that while, in the first two volumes of his autobiographical trilogy, Coetzee is able to offer a 'bare-faced' account of the pain and shame he suffered during his childhood and youth, the realities of his later experience are felt by him as being "simply too painful" to expose. Representing the subject of this final volume of his memoir as an unattached, childless, directionless, neanimorphic being is the fictive device the author chooses as a means of simultaneously concealing and silently gesturing towards an inexpressible distress. To that extent, *Summertime* can, I suggest, be seen as the site where the savage, ravaging grief arising from the multiple losses Coetzee sustained throughout his thirties, the very basis, in other words, of his adult identity, lies buried.

---

13 Hiding has to be seen. Be aware that I'm hiding something from you, *this* is the paradox that I have to resolve. It has to be both hidden and unknown; people need to know that I don't want to show it. That's the message I'm communicating to the other. *Larvatus prodeo*, I go forth pointing to my mask. I cover my passion with a mask but, discreetly and slyly, I draw attention to this mask by pointing to it. (My translation. It is to Rita Barnard, who presents part of the above quotation as an epigraph to her investigation of Coetzee's complex relationship with Afrikaans (84), that I owe this insight.)

References

Attwell, David, ed. 1992. *Doubling the Point: Essays and Interviews*. Cambridge, MA: Harvard University Press.

Attwell, David. 2016. *J.M. Coetzee and the Life of Writing: Face to Face with Time*. New York: Penguin.

Barnard, Rita. 2009. "Coetzee in/and Afrikaans." *Journal of Literary Studies* 25 (4): 84–105.

Barnes, Julian. 1985. *Flaubert's Parrot*. London: Picador.

Barthes, Roland. 1977. *Fragments d'un Discours Amoureux*. Paris: Editions du Seuil.

Clarkson, Carrol. 2014. "J. M. Coetzee: 'n Geskryfde Lewe / J. M. Coetzee: A Life in Writing." *Life-Writing* 11 (2): 263–270.

Coetzee, J. M. 1997. *Inner Workings: Essays 2000–2005*. London: Harvill Secker.

———. 2009. *Summertime*. London: Harvill Secker.

Coetzee, J. M., and Arabella Kurtz. 2016. *The Good Story: Exchanges on Truth, Fiction and Psychotherapy*. London: Vintage.

Coghlan, Alexandra. 2012. "On His Terms, J. C. Kannemeyer's *JM Coetzee: A Life in Writing*." *The Monthly*, December. Accessed April 10, 2021. https://www.themonthly.com.au/issue/2012/december/135 8291432/alexandra-coghlan/his-terms#mtr.

Jones, Thomas. 2009. "Summertime by JM Coetzee." *The Guardian*, September 6. Accessed July 9, 2017. https://www.theguardian.com/ books/2009/sep/06/jm-coetzee-summertime.

Kannemeyer, J. C. 2013. *J.M. Coetzee: A Life in Writing*. London: Scribe Publications.

Kermode, Frank. 2009. "Fictioneering." *London Review of Books* 31 (19): 8–10.

Kurtz, Arabella, and J. M. Coetzee. 2016. *The Good Story: Exchanges on*

Truth, Fiction and Psychotherapy. London: Vintage.

Lessing, Doris. 1995. *Under My Skin.* London: Flamingo.

Macaskill, Brian. 2014. "Titular Space in J M Coetzee's *Summertime*: A Maquette for a Portrait, or a Self-Portrait, of the Artist Finding His Feet." *MediaTropes* 4 (2).

Meek, James. 2009. "All about John." *The Guardian*, September 5. Accessed July 9, 2017. https://www.theguardian.com/books/2009/sep /05/jm-coetzee-books1.

Neuman, Justin. 2011. "Unexpected Cosmopolitans: Media and Diaspora in J. M. Coetzee's *Summertime.*" *Criticism* 53 (1). Accessed July 13, 2021. https://digitalcommons.wayne.edu/cgi/viewcontent.cgi?arti cle=1831&context=criticism.

Powers, Donald. 2016. "Beyond the Death of the Author: *Summertime* and J. M. Coetzee's Afterlives." *Life Writing* 13 (3).

We Are What We Experience: Identity Performance During British Black Lives Matter Protests

Isabel Ekua-Thompson, MA.

Abstract

How do individual identities make themselves heard in the collective environment of a demonstration? What do we select from our identities, and what parts of ourselves do we offer to others and why? This article seeks to add to the growing body of research surrounding protest identity through an investigation of the particularity of the British Black Lives Matter protest wave in the summer of 2020. An analysis will be undertaken to understand if protest attendees of colour foreground identity labels other than race, and how this could be accomplished outside of the national context of the USA. Through empirical research, focus will be paid to how protest attendees understand their own identity and that of others, however particular attention will be continually paid to the significance of the nationally defined context of this protest identity in a bid to explicate the centrality of this to individual protest identity performance. The decision to focus on the UK pertains to its historical trajectories of protest and the entanglement of anti-state sentiment in Black British protesting history. This is of crucial interest as we can track a legacy of protest rhetoric that has pushed for anti-state, over racial justice, narratives during moments of protest. Does this legacy carry through to the contemporary period? If so, is it more important to attend a Black Lives Matter protest as a Black person, or as someone that self-identifies as anti-state? Through the following research paper, these questions will be tackled to track a specific British rhetoric when it comes to protest identity performance, and to understand in what ways and why identities are *foregrounded* during socio-political demonstrations.

Keywords: Black Lives Matter, United Kingdom, Identity, Intersectionality

Introduction

I want to start with a brief anecdote. After attending many LGBTQ+ pride marches in the UK and Netherlands I started to become aware of the similarities in character between the events: happiness, freedom, and a lot of dancing (and drinking). There is an absence of aims and desires as such, but a celebration of queer life and love. That's not to say there are not solidarity marches for LGBTQ+ populations in the West for those that continue to face national and socio-political oppression, but these protests seem to run apart from the main pride walks. Then, in the summer of 2021, I attended the first pride march in Vilnius, Lithuania. The character of the march was visibly and emotionally disparate from Western iterations. Here, in a country where LGBTQ+ marriage has yet to be legalised, the rhetoric of the march was more about rights, anti-violence and acceptance. It was sullen. I felt a deeper sense of emotional awareness from the crowd. It felt as though we were marching for something rather than celebrating something. Although both in the West and the East marches and demonstrations are occurring in the same temporal moment, the identity of each protest was markedly different. The national and socio-political boundaries of these protests shaped the aims, motivations, and emotionality of protest attendees. It is this perception of the way in which context frames the nature of protest that informs this project.

In this article, I want to explore the implications of this insight for thinking about the transnational character of the BLM protests that spread globally from the US following the murder of a black man, George Floyd in Spring 2020 while under restraint by a white police officer. More specifically, I want to consider specifically how the take up of the BLM protests in the UK in the Summer of 2020, afforded different possibilities for the articulation both of the focus of the protest—anti-capitalist—anti-government, and the possibilities of identity performance in the context of those protests. To explore this latter phenomena I began my inquiry by formulating the concept of intersectional foregrounding, which will be defined and explained shortly.

The summer of 2020 saw global protests mobilized under the banner of Black Lives Matter (BLM), which took on its transnational character following the murder of a Black man, George Floyd, whilst under restraint by a white American police officer. What ensued became a myriad of different protests across the world in support of the larger and more historical racial justice movement. It is the ways in which that originally US American protest was changed by its uptake in the global racial justice movement that concerns me in my research. I am interested in the ways in which the character of the protest changed to reflect local conditions outside the US, and the ways that this, in turn, had an effect on protest identity construction. Put another way, I am concerned with the ways in which racial identification becomes supplemented with other forms of identification once the protest moves outside the US – and, at another level, how we might theorise the performance of differentiated identities who may have, at the outset, attended BLM protests with entirely anti-racist motivations?

Although I will be concerned primarily with the performance of identity within British BLM protests, I want to point to the importance to my analysis of the words of the Black American Combahee River Collective Statement. In their statement from 1983, the writers conclude with the following: "We are not convinced that a socialist revolution that is also not… anti-racist… will guarantee our liberation" (Combahee River Collective 1983)

What is striking is that from a Black feminist perspective, we can still see other identity labels acting concurrently. The individual members of the Combahee River Collective maintain their socialist positionality as well as their racial one. They propose, in other words, that a socialist revolution can never fully liberate people of colour without being inherently anti-racist as well, because in their view the ideology of socialism has also been developed with the supremacy of whiteness at the foreground – and socialism's racist narratives cannot be ignored through revolution.

The 'Statement' raises the question 'what intersections stand out subjectively to the individual in their imaginary for a better world?' 'Why, here, would an individual's race be foregrounded over other identity labels?'.

These questions lead directly into my initially proposed working concept for this research. Namely: *intersectional foregrounding*. Intersectional foregrounding, in my configuration, entails a subjective move that underlines and describes the active process of identity performance during times of protest and discursive change. This process is entirely dependent on an individual's conceptualisation of what identity marker they feel most strongly ties in with a specific protest narrative, and what they choose to make visible on the public stage of protest. Thus, in the context of BLM, is it possible find evidence of people of colour *intersectionally foregrounding* their socialist[1] identity over their racial one?[2]

Exploring the existence of a binary between race and political opinion triggers the question: is being Black, [at a given time] synonymous with being politically left leaning? I can reason that the answer is no, as there is social evidence of conservative Black people. However, if we understand that during BLM we have individuals that were at once Black, and at once left-leaning, I want to consider if the latter can be seen as a natural extension of the former to the individual *in construction*. In-construction being the moment in which an individual during times of protest might understand how different marginalised identity labels come together – and how they subjectively build their own puzzle of internal labels.

Jennifer Nash claims that female POCs will always be subjects of intersectional analysis because of their marginalisation as women. Extending this further, we can also contend that all POCs who live in a structurally racist system are also subjected to discriminatory forces that warrant intersectional analysis because of the disadvantage race will already play in their lived realities. Intersectionality, in this research specifically, then, will focus on those individuals that possess marginal and oppressed labels dependent on the contextual boundaries in which they are subjectively imagined.

With attention paid to the contextual, the imagining of Black bodies across space and time can create differently marginal Black experiences.

---

1   When socialist/socialism is referred to in terms of individual sentiment throughout this paper, I am exclusively looking at anti-state and anti-capitalist rhetoric or expression. I do not want to use socialist as a term that calls to an entire ideology of practice, but more so what socialist means in Western democratic sphere – i.e., socially democratic principles.

2   Foregrounding a socialist identity, for the purposes of my current research, involve the voicing of anti-capitalist, anti-government, and anti-individualist sentiment.

Adding to Nash's interrogation, an attempt will be made to understand intersectional identity performance - noted when Nash asks, "what determines which identity is foregrounded in a particular moment?" (Nash 2008, 11) - and not to unpack the complexities of a life-long experience of an intersectional individual.

It suffices to say that the majority of the primary and empirical evidence in academic surveys conducted around BLM were undertaken in the US —where George Floyd's murder, the catalyst of widespread protest, took place. However, I propose to gather data from other Western cultural epicentres. This paper will, as an alternative to virtually all primary data regarding BLM and identity, conduct analysis in the context of the United Kingdom.

Theorizing Protest Identity

Pieter Klandermans offers his understanding of the relationship between nation-state and protest identity, explaining that individual identification with the nation-state and its wrong-doings comes "as a consequence of the process of politicization." (Klandermans 2014, 7). What I intend to make clear through primary research is in fact the opposite. That politicization, especially of the individual during protest, is in fact nationally defined. National boundaries allow for particular political identities to thrive. Hence, allowing for varied processes of intersectional foregrounding. However, he continues to position national identity and subgroup identity as distinctly different categories. I ask instead, what if we looked at them together? Through understanding how protests are nationally specific – should we not turn our attention to how subgroup identities perform in the nation? As a result of my consciousness of the difference in the nature of protest in different LGBTQ+ marches, I maintain that subgroup identities do not always have an immediately visible rejection of, or support for, a national identity but are continuously influenced by the national context in which they are bred.

How an individual understands the ideology that shapes their lives, has equal or more importance than the external ideological narrative. Thus, revealing that all motivations to protest are rooted in individual agency. This agency, this inclination to protest for a specific reason, will be analysed for its nationally defined character in an attempt to answer the question: is agency to protest nationally specific?

David Meyer in his opening statements to *Protest and Political Opportunities* understands that contextual and external factors are key to internal protest processes, most specifically the advancement of "particular claims rather than others." (Meyer 2004, 126) This makes a case for contextually and nationally specific practices of intersectional foregrounding – thus meaning, when analysing this concept scholars should place the action within contextually specific boundaries. Meyer understands that the issue with protest analysis at present concerns the way in which researchers analyse the outcomes of individual protest behaviour – instead of assuming that seemingly disparate protest performances may actually work towards the same ends. Protestors may actually be there for a myriad of different reasons, but working under the same banner. Thus, intersectional foregrounding may not be a lone activity, but help shape a collective protest character as well.

A Non-American (British) Perspective on Black Power

A quick search online reveals the triggering nature that anti-state or anti-capitalist protest sentiment may have in the American context. Currently, and for the past few decades, there has been a drive away from the term 'socialism' in American public and governmental discourse due to all the associations it brings with it. This term is usually reflected back into the context of the Cold War, and highlights the contemporary maintenance of anti-communist narratives in American governance. Catherine Westall, when writing on the topic, explains that "there has always been a strong individualist tradition in the US, based on the idea that every person is free to control their destiny" (Westall 2021). In such a way, then, this explains why socialists have been portrayed as "radical, lazy, America-hating communists," (Francis and Wright-Rigueur 2021, 443) because they go against the ideology of the American 'way of life' and thus, as a term, 'socialist' is less popular in use within communities that are aiming for recognition and respect in the American public sphere.

I want to turn now to an American article, entitled *Black Lives Matter in Historical Perspective*, where, at the beginning, the authors outline the situation in which Ida B. Wells found herself in at the end of the Nineteenth Century. They begin with crediting the activism of Ida B. Wells as laying "the groundwork for all future campaigns against lynching and racial violence in the United States." (Francis and Wright-Rigueur

2021, 442) They place the contours of her situation within an economic setting; Wells began to campaign more openly for racial equality when she realised that white grocery store owners were attacking more successful Black owned businesses. Thus, their argument seems to rest on the understanding that there were economic origins for racial justice movements in the US: in order for Black lives to equal white ones, they need equal access to capital, control, and economic freedoms. This isn't a mission to overthrow or create an alternative political system; but an attempt to change the contours of pre-existing capitalist structures.

British racial justice movements began from the same economic vantage point, but the origins of the British Black Power (BBP) movement slowly fabricated a more socialist (i.e. anti-capitalist) character in their contextual environment in the 1970s. John Narayan reveals the distinct British character of the BBP, as they placed their socio-political critique on the boundaries of British conceptions of race and class. He underlines the foundation of the re-emergence of British Black Power sentiment to the end of the 1960s/ beginning of the 70s regarding the government's racist approach to New Commonwealth Immigration Policy. Narayan theorizes that BBP's grievances "were specifically located at the historical juncture between the fall of the British social democracy and the rise of British neoliberalism." (Narayan 2019, 946) Hence, it wasn't just a cause fighting for Black existence but they intertwined critiques on the hierarchy of British class structure and neoliberalism at large with racial justice opinions.

What's more, 'political blackness' was used by the BBP as an identifying tool to unite peoples across different racial and national distinctions to unite their trauma into an undeniable existence – so that the state would have to respond to them all as a whole; a whole of 'Black peoples' fighting under the same banner. This meant building solidarity with Indian and Asian communities living in Britain at the time. Even in more Afro-centric circles, the term Black was extended to all those continually facing oppression under post-colonial racist British policy. Reflecting upon Britain's colonial conquest and subsequent global empire, the aims of the BBP, thus, concerned national and global manifestations of oppressive capitalist systems.

Racism, in the eyes of the BBP, "[was] the result of the 'system' and 'that system is capitalism.'" (Narayan 2019, 952) Due to their immediate national context; race, class and capitalism were intrinsically linked and had to be critiqued together. In other words, the perceived 'enemy' for the BBP initiative was the post-imperialist sentiment of the British government, and class disparities for communities of colour—so they rooted their solution within an anti-capitalist and anti-state position. Thus, they effectively foregrounded other markers of oppression, rather than purely their race, to create an organising protest public. This protest public did not have a clear racial configuration, but all had similar anti-state sentiments because of their classification in British society.

Using the BBP movement as a contextual backdrop for contemporary British BLM protests has, therefore, been an academic necessity in recent years. Alfie Hancox writes of a mirroring of emotionality between British Black Power movements in the 60s and 70s and the contemporary British BLM movement (Hancox 2020). He underlines the core narrative of anti-imperialism and its critique of global neo-capitalist racist structures as still being embedded into the contemporary narrative of British BLM protests. This is important in understanding differing contexts of BLM protests across the Atlantic, as he discerns anti-imperial and anti-capitalist sentiment at the forefront of British BLM protest character.

After a contextual reading of BLM in the British locality, what I've been able to immediately deduce is, again, the importance of understanding protests as nationally specific. It remains important that US-based racial justice movements and events are understood—however, it seems limiting that BLM, in its contemporary dimension, should continue to be geographically limited in academic research.

Reconsidering Intersectionality

Before beginning the analysis and discussion of the performance of *intersectional* foregrounding within British BLM protest attendees in 2020, I want to comment on one important conceptual conclusion of the empirical data collected here, namely, the ways in which the interviews have called for a reconceptualization of intersectional foregrounding.

By *intersectional* foregrounding I mean the individual and selective process of foregrounding identity labels other than a racial one, to thicken BLM protest narrative away from purely racialised discussions and into more anti-capitalist or socialist ones. It shouldn't be necessary to say that (intersectional) foregrounding as a working concept, is not to be conflated with an 'All Lives Matter' rhetoric. Intersectional foregrounding is not intended to suggest that other identities are more prevalent or should go beyond the 'black' in Black Lives Matter, but rather to echo and build upon the argument put forward by Judith Butler in which they ascertain that "it is necessary to realize that we are but one population who has been and can be exposed to conditions of precarity," (Butler 2015, 62) and that "the condition of precarity is differentially distributed." (Butler 2015, 63) Thus, rewording the concept to simply *foregrounding*, better helps explain experiences of oppression within identities that are viewed externally as essentialist (such as race).

As Sarah Hansen in *Bodies on the Line* explains: "while vulnerability can expose us to systems of violence and control, it is also a condition that allows us to connect and engage in political life." (Hansen 2018, 158) Thus, instead of foregrounding an identity label, the primary research gathered here encourages me to conclude that is more useful to focus on the foregrounding of experiences rather than identities insofar as experiences provide the basis for connection with other marginalised communities in their suffering.

Initially, I was not considering the possibility that race is more than an essential identity category. I had concluded that everyone could experience life intersectionally because they were already living under a racial label that marked them as 'other.' What I found, in contrast to this, is that the visibility of Blackness in protest spaces, acted as a precondition of motivation. Thus, I suppose that while *intersectional* foregrounding could definitely be used and applied to protest spaces and narratives concerned with issues beyond individual identity, it is more useful to analyse *foregrounding* by focusing on differentiated experiences within racialised communities than intersectional identities, given that BLM as a movement places racial identities at the core of the issue.

Foregrounding Experience, Foregrounding Difference

The diversity within the interlocutors interviewed can be described as follows: 11 interlocutors were people of colour, and responses were gathered from five persons that identified as female and six that identified as male.[3]

---

3   All interlocutors wished to remain anonymous, therefore they have been given a letter corresponding to the order in which I conducted the interviews.

Almost everyone interviewed constructed their motivations to protest around their existence as a person of colour, which, as I have said, is one of the main reasons I have chosen to abandon the 'intersectional' in intersectional foregrounding. Even those who did admit to having an intersectional identity (understood as female *and* Black from the two interlocutors who mentioned this) believed that intersectionality didn't inform their motivations to attend a protest. Instead, their blackness acted as a silent marker of their affinity and closeness with the BLM narrative.

Interviewee K, a Black activist and radio host from Greater London, insisted upon the power of fighting against Black oppression as a key to opening up conversations about other marginal communities. She felt the power of institutional racism was an obvious target to tackle first and foremost. She admitted to attending as a Black person, attributing this to her and her family's experience with racism in the UK. She felt that attending, intersectionally, as a Black woman, wasn't going to help in this case. "It actually wasn't about splitting, splitting that identity up, it was just all of us as a community fighting against racism" (Interview with Respondent K, Zoom, April 20, 2023), she added.

It seems as though for many of the interlocutors, foregrounding different parts of their identity other than their racial identity felt like a betrayal to the core message of BLM. Hence, it could be that the rigidness of the movement itself, restricted the identity performance of its protestors to limit them to creating solidarity solely along racial lines. This means racial identity performance had as much to say about the individual as well as the general protest space that BLM allowed for. Appreciably, this mirrors Klandermans' argumentation that follows that ideology and individuality work in tandem.

I want to firstly recognise Anthony Appiah's understanding of racial labels as stemming from ascription and identification, from there deducing that in cases of racism, racial identification is thus simultaneously the disease and the remedy. Ascription, as understood by Appiah, entails ascribing an identity label to an individual externally, and without involving the individual in this process—such labels as male and female, White and Black, gay, and straight. Thus, again, foregrounding tells us as much about the identification of the individual as it does about the ascription of their identity in their contextual environment. He maintains that "people act 'under descriptions' [...] it follows, of course, that what people can do depends on what concepts they have available to them." (Appiah 1996, 106) Here, what can be read from this is the fact that under a common understanding through interlocutor response that BLM ascribes 'black' as a marker of identity to those effected by global systems of oppression —protestors and supporters are only able to act and perform identities within this 'language'. Thus, blackness is at once the disease (the subject of oppression) and the remedy (the overcomer of said oppression).

Having established that my interlocutors were all coming from a place of attendance as a person of colour, once I began to probe into their understanding of BLM as more than just an anti-racist movement, some interlocutors did in fact highlight their anti-state positionality but illustrated it more as a natural offshoot of anti-racist sentiment. Thus, anti-state, anti-establishment, and left-wing dispositions were continually framed as a departing thread from the racist nucleus of the BLM movement.

When discussing BLM as more than just an anti-racist movement, Interviewee K pointed to the fact that she had always aligned with different 'anti-' movements, and these experiences had informed her mindset as an activist. She characterised this by characterising her mindset as stemming from the "idea that you need to fight against all forms of oppression." (Interview with Respondent K, Zoom, April 20, 2023) Although you'll recall Interviewee K's rejection of intersectionality as a basis of identity performance. Her individual identity construction, thus, premised off of her rejection of all oppressions, but the situatedness of BLM saw her championing for racial justice at the forefront of other injustices she was also strongly against.

From this, I can untangle a deeper understanding of identity and its performance in the context of BLM. This understanding now departs from an intersectional focus on identity but rather can be found in individual motivations to protest and their attachment and depiction of the Black British community as a multi-cultural and multi-marginal space in which foregrounding acts as a tool for solidarity and emphatic recognition.

One of the most important revelations I had unearthed through the primary evidence of the interviews was the weight attributed to personal experiences over identity labels. Although every interviewee attested to their presence as a person of colour during a BLM protest as vital to their conception of a protest identity, many recognised the heterogeneity of the POC community. Instead suggesting that through revealing experiences (be that in the workplace, at home, within family, within friendship groups) in which racism or oppression was felt was more important in establishing solidarity than ascribing to an alternative identity label (such as a working-class person, woman, LGBTQ+ member and so on).

Interviewee F, an activist for Black and Muslim rights living in Leeds, continued on this vein to recognise the heterogeneity within the Black community, explaining that "there's different values, and people sort of come in with different ideas and I think they all matter. It's about sharing our experience." (Interview with Respondent F, Zoom, April 7, 2023) Here, obviously, she places herself within this varied community. She further said "[as] Black people we are all different... we come from different places; we have different experiences." (Interview with Respondent F, Zoom, April 7, 2023) Hence, for her, it wasn't sufficient to attend only as a Black person but a Black person with a specific set of experiences that could hopefully be widely understood. She admitted to attending, and speaking, at the protest in Leeds Hyde Park to share her story of racism in the workplace.

For background, in the summer of 2020, she was undergoing a personal experience with racism in the workplace. She'd made an online post about it that went viral and was dealing with the support and scrutiny from her community during the times of protest. From this, she'd realised that a lot more people had gone through similar experiences and was shocked by the number of similarities. Interviewee F sees pure heterogeneity, however, as easily contested. With the immense similarities between her experience and her communities' that she recognised, she saw everyone's experiences as different, however, weaved into the same narrative. From that, she realised "[people] are not so different... they might just have a tiny little different view and opinion." (Interview with Respondent F, Zoom, April 7, 2023) Hence, from her understanding about society, there's more of a need to exist in all your multiplicity than foreground identity properties. Her foregrounding 'experience' during BLM is testament to this. Instead of attending the protest, and speaking there to that extent, as a 'label'—Interviewee F had already rejected homogeneity in the Black community so went to foreground an experience in solidarity with the wider narrative.

Johny Pitts, in *Afropean*, puts forward the compelling argument that Black communities within Europe (away from America) have a distinct identity that needs to be separately investigated. The interesting point is that an *afropean* identity largely stems from experiencing blackness in the locality and context of the individual: accordingly, Pitts divides his book into chapters covering different cities. Pitts claims that an identity like "*afropean* had to be more than… an obsession with an authentic self, and something more like a contribution to a community." (Pitts 2022, 5)

This, again, aids the research at hand if we read foregrounding into his argument. Taking the 'authentic self' described here as a static identity (by static I mean an identity in which there is assumed homogeneity within essentialist conceptions of race/gender/class etc.), and 'contribution' as experience—this sentiment here definitely echoes the explanations of some of my interlocutor response concerning foregrounding. Many felt as though the foregrounding of experience over the foregrounding of an identity label felt more appropriate in cementing solidarity within the Black community, and with other marginal communities to that extent.

Another way in which I found that foregrounding experience was framed from interlocutor response was in its power to reach other marginalised communities. Many interviewees made me aware of existing bridges to other oppressed peoples, especially the LGBTQ+ community. Hence, the foregrounding of experience was also seen as a way in which individuals viewed their place within a larger global illustration of general oppressions – that they believed could be unmasked by the narrative offshoots of the BLM conversation.

Interviewee C, instead of picking up on intersectional foregrounding as a useful protest tool, enthusiastically viewed the multiplicity of marginal identities in protests as a key important factor in the BLM narrative. He said, "these protests—they don't have to be about black, black, black" (Interview with Respondent C, Zoom, March 21, 2023). Interviewee E additionally touched upon the multi-racial attendance of BLM protests in a positive light. He felt like it soothed feelings of isolation within the Black community. He also reflected upon the cross-group solidarity in oppression, commenting that "I feel we were able to unite [with other minorities] they understand the struggle minorities go through." (Interview with Respondent E, Zoom, April 5, 2023).

What I intend to take from this is that, even though intersectional subjects are no longer the focus of this current research, intersectional *forms* of solidarity can be located through interlocutor response. The intention is to take the sentiment of intersectional solidarity to explain the reasoning for protest motivation in the first place—framing it as a tool for further protest instead of a blueprint for protest itself. In what has been understood through interview, protestors located their position as Black people as a way to signal solidarity with other marginalised communities, through an imaginary of shared struggle. Thus, using the essentialist identity labels ascribed unto them as a way of expressing solidarity with a wider movement against all global oppression.

In the BLM context, this could mean that intersectionality is surpassed altogether to unite all those who fall victim to discrimination based on the colour of one's skin. This would then mean that although a certain level of awareness of one's intersectional identity (take for example a Black woman) is always present, in times where solidarity against a larger perceived evil is existent, expressing coalition under shared social oppression becomes more important in the fight. This can be explained more clearly as so: "successful race-based mobilizations have in reality been less concerned with shared bloodlines than with shared histories of blood spilled." (Kelley 1999, 7)

For some, however, anti-state sentiment was expressed *through* acceptance of a racial ascription. Not directly as a pronounced and foregrounded identity label, but through experiences that were conceived of as racialised. Anti- state sentiment seemed to be a future wish for some that held such views—but there was optimism felt about such sentiment slowly garnering more attraction. Hence, 'Black' worked as an ascriptive identity label that was able to become nuanced and more individually distinct through foregrounding experiences that they hoped to would lead to deeper and more overarching solidarity within the Black community. The assumption of heterogeneity meant protestors didn't feel the need to foreground additional labels for themselves, but instead focus on experience within a racialised identity that could lead to exploring commonalities.

Yet, there is something to be said about the particularity when it comes to understanding the nationalities that fell into 'Black' as a marker of race. The interlocutors I was able to speak to had similar illustrations of a Black community that was not 'African' per se, but 'of colour'—which certainly reflects a specifically British understanding, that I could argue relates back to the British phenomenon of political blackness. Narayan's conceptualisation of political blackness as a distinctly British phenomenon, addresses the reality that blackness in the UK can apply to many non-white communities. This could further sustain the fact that many of the interlocutors saw BLM as a movement that could be translated to a solidarity with other marginalised communities.

The De-Globalization of Protest Identity

Those that felt protest critique as directed towards the government and the state placed their positionality within a British continuum, whereas those looking past the state to the global visualised themselves as members of an international community. Whilst discussing the localisation of protest, I made sure to prompt interlocutor's understanding of the contextual situatedness of protest, and 30% of them attested to a global character of BLM and that nationally specific grievances were not felt as much as gesturing to a wider transnational community.

Predictably, almost all interlocutors pointed to the closeness of the event of George Flloyd's death to its national context in North America. Although not every interlocutor felt a particularly strong American narrative present at protests they had attended, they did all mention the centrality of North America in location to views surrounding solidarity. What's interesting is that when they reflected upon the British situation, they used the US as an example or tool in constructing their perception of a British BLM character.

Interviewee H reflected upon the difference between the UK and US and pointed to the fact that in the UK many were still getting to grips with the British system of institutionalised racism. So they felt as though the US's more visible institutional racism, unfortunately, tainted the national character of protest once it was translated over into European BLM protest narratives. Interviewee L attested to the fact that the leading power in the movement originated in the US; but that "there was an attempt to look at the particular case of institutional racism in Britain." (Interview with Respondent L, Zoom, May 4, 2023) Thus, for those interlocutors that saw the American context as leading the way in conversations about different national racisms, it was apprehended in a positive light. Centring the US context in different countries, for them, aided the national fight for racial equality.

Through the centralisation of the American context, however, interlocutors were able to point to the beginnings of a British public turn to the domestic realities of racism. Interviewee G felt as though as time passed during the summer of 2020, more and more British situated racist experiences and historical injustices surfaced—and more attention was paid to the UK government and police system. He felt because things were more blatant in the US, that "[in the UK] we were more of a community when it came to discovering everything that had gone wrong within the UK system and government system" (Interview with Respondent G, Zoom, April 7, 2023). Interviewee L discussed the cost-of-living crisis, and how specifically the British BLM protests had shaped the way that the UK experienced cultural and social crises. He also noted that "very quickly the protests here raised the questions of [Britain's history of colonialism]." (Interview with Respondent L, Zoom, May 4, 2023) Therefore, although there was placement of America as a contextual cornerstone in individual understandings of the locality of protest, there was a concerted feeling that in the future protests would slowly begin to be centred around the specific British experience within this.

One of the main social communities that interlocutors did discuss having strong affinity to was actually on a much smaller scale than that of the nation of the United Kingdom: it was the local community in which they lived or where they attended protests. When discussing the difference between attending a protest in Watford versus Brighton, Interviewee H disclosed the fact that different parts of herself were probably more valued at one over the other. Attesting to Watford's multicultural character, Interviewee H felt more of a community feeling, in which her blackness didn't centralise her motivation to attend. Instead, she was more able to connect based on experiences to other members of the same community.

On the other hand, the majorly white protest public in Brighton meant that her identity as a person of colour felt more pronounced. However, other parts of her identity were also more acceptable to be performed in Brighton because of the city's history of affinity to the LGBTQ+ community. She admitted that [referring to her queerness) "knowing the cohort of Watford, maybe there was a part of myself that I parked to be able to take part in that space." (Interview with Respondent H, Zoom, April 7, 2023) Hence, here, I can see how at the level of a direct localised community, understandings of self begin to change and morph when the diversity and locality of the protest crowd changes.

One contextual anchor that was brought up organically by almost every interlocutor without my questioning, was the specific context of BLM taking place within the Covid-19 pandemic. Many felt at that particular contextual moment, the character of BLM morphed to this situation and had the murder of George Floyd taken place outside of it, the construction of protest identities would have been markedly different. Thus, we can begin to understand the entanglement of identity and context – and how the pandemic acted as an environment in which the two interacted to an ever-larger scale.

The localised understanding of protest, effectively in every response that attested to this, followed that their protest identity was more based in experience and in their blackness. This seems logical if the imagined protest community is downsized to the level of their direct community; less homogeneity is felt within smaller and more intimate circles as a thicker understanding of each individual is expected. In a larger global and transnationally conceptualised community, imaginaries of sameness pervaded interlocutor response. And when reflected in their foregrounding experience, blackness was always seen as a common signal of solidarity.

Conclusion

What I've been able to map out in this project is the entanglement of identity and context, however it could be said that both concepts act in synergy. It seems somewhat obvious that identity is informed by context if I take the revised concept of foregrounding to be true. If one can construct and offer a protest identity reliant on personal experience with the larger issue at hand, then personal experience will have to always be placed within the locality in which the event occurred. Individual affinity to the imagined locality of protest undoubtedly had an effect of subjective understandings of personal protest identity. What's more, intersectional foregrounding perhaps falls into this logic as well.

The majority of interlocutors constructed their understanding of the Black community as heterogenous, that being multi-faceted and made up of different ascriptions to blackness. There seemed to be a totalising understanding that blackness was at the core of BLM, but this didn't have to mean that the core could not produce peripheries that needed to be taken into account. Once heterogeneity was assumed by the individual, there seemed to be a dismissal of foregrounding intersectionally (through specific identity labels) as a way to unite difference, and more of an insistence upon experiential foregrounding. Yes, this foregrounding of experience was under a racialised banner, but it also sought to establish connection with other marginalised communities.

This is most heavily exampled through the response of Interviewee F, who we recall is a Black and Muslim activist located in Leeds. Interviewee F understands differentiated experiences as integral to the prosperity of protests that rely on essentialist identity categories. To me, she had shared how she had spoken at Leeds Hyde Park about an instance of racism at her workplace, in which she was shocked that others so closely had experienced similar things. Following this revelation, Interviewee F had shared that she felt as though listening to so many different 'experiences' of racism had allowed her to introspectively reflect on similar situations she'd encountered. In hearing the varied lived realities of individuals living under the ascription of Black, she was able to clearly see heterogeneity in her direct community. Interviewee F's understanding of solidarity in heterogeneity, therefore, places identity on the backburner in place of real experiences and stories that can lead to an expansive solidarity with her local community.

On the other hand, when higher levels of homogeneity were assumed, racialised identity markers were understood as an all-encompassing catch-all for all protest attendees—at the cost of leaving other marginalised existences out of the picture. When interlocuters turned their attention away from the local to the global, understandings of foregrounding dramatically shifted. When conceptions of BLM are escalated to an international level, it becomes harder to see individual uniqueness within the Black community. Hence, more homogeneity is imagined as it is the only thing to imagine.

Therefore, there seems to be a relationship between individual conceptions of the 'Britishness' of BLM and their use of foregrounding. The majority of responses discerning British racism as discreet, comparing that with the more overt racism in the US, turned their grievances specifically to the discreet ways that racism penetrated their day-to-day existence. This could be a possible explanation of the lack of intersectional foregrounding and a focus on solidarity and exposing experiences.

Massimo De Angelis' argumentation, when describing the issue of globalisation under Zapatismo's approach to social relations, draws striking similarities with my conception of foregrounding in the British context. What he understands from Zapatista circles is that "globalisation... leads to a reflection of what is common between the indigenous communities they are part of, and other world 'minorities' they are interdependent with." (De Angelis 2005, 191) He goes on to discuss this interdependence as contributing to feelings of 'wholeness' despite fragmentation and heterogeneity across the landscape of minority existence.

There is also something to be said about the 'perceived evils', if we recall the BBP movement's angle, of particular protest narratives. It seems to follow that this idea plays a much larger part in identity construction and foregrounding than I first anticipated. The assumed evil that an individual constructs to protest against, shapes their whole understanding of who they are in comparison to it. Akin to the academic theorization of othering as a very real tool in social and global relationships, POCs in attendance of BLM protests across the UK in 2020, very much relied upon their very biological sense of blackness as a visible marker of protest. However, the nuance lies within the fact that if this 'blackness' is a given as an oppositional positionality, experience is what creates the protestor.

Identity seems to remain on the back burner here, visible identity markers (such as skin colour) are already doing the work to situate an individual as *other*, to the perceived evil, and *same*, to the protest public. Foregrounding, then, cannot be intersectional because it does not rest on static identity labels. It rests on the very fragmented existence of the individual. Similar to Nash's rethinking of intersectionality as a concept that should illustrate more than the entanglement of race and gender, foregrounding should be understood as a concept that looks beyond essential identity categories to the heterogeneity of experience within marginalised communities.

Looking back to my introductory remarks, when I posited that the British nature of protest could be viewed as more anti-state in sentiment than purely anti-racist, there are a few reflections I can now make. Firstly, and most importantly, is that although anti-state rhetoric underlined the majority of interlocutor response, it was seen as mainly a periphery grievance. What was at the centre, thus, was the impact of state racism onto the day-to-day lives of the British public, which is why foregrounding seemed to occur within localised protests. Therefore, foregrounding was used by protest attendees to begin the conversation around the state's policies that effected banal areas of life at the local and community level.

What my conclusions can add to contemporary social and protest theory lies in how foregrounding is understood. Foregrounding as a concept and a tool used by protestors can illustrate, then, the effect of an essentialising protest movement on individual protest identity as well as giving us insight into the particular locality in which foregrounding occurs. Foregrounding allows us to visualise the interdependency of protest narrative and context, whilst retaining the agency of the individual.

References

Appiah, Anthony K. 1996. "Race, Culture, Identity: Misunderstood Connections, Part II." In *Color Conscious,* edited by Anthony K. Appiah and Amy Guttman, Princeton: Princeton University Press. https://doi-org.proxy.uba.uva.nl/10.1515/9781400822096-002.

Butler, Judith. 2015. "Bodies in Alliance and the Politics of the Street." In *Notes Toward a Performative Theory of Assembly.* Cambridge, MA: Harvard University Press. https://doi-org.proxy.uba.uva.nl/10.4159/9780674495548-003.

Combahee River Collective. 1983. "The Combahee River Collective Statement." In *Home Girls: A Black Feminist Anthology.*

De Angelis, Massimo. 2005. "'Zapatismo' and Globalisation as Social Relations." *Humboldt Journal of Social Relations* 29 (1): 179–203. https://www.jstor.org/stable/23263129.

Hancox, Alfie. 2020. "Black Lives Matter UK Revives the Anti-Imperialist Spirit of British Black Power." *Hampton Think.* https://www.hamptonthink.org/read/black-lives-matter-uk-revives-the-anti-imperialist-spirit-of-british-black-power.

Hansen, Sarah. 2018. "Bodies on the Line: The Performativity of Protest." *GLQ: A Journal of Lesbian and Gay Studies* 24 (1): 156–158. https://muse.jhu.edu/pub/4/article/686240/pdf.

Kelley, Robin. 1999. "People in Me." In *ColorLines Magazine.*

Klandermans, Pieter G. 2014. "Identity Politics and Politicized Identities: Identity Processes and the Dynamics of Protest." *Political Psychology* 35 (1): 1–22. https://www.jstor.org/stable/43785856.

Meyer, David S. 2004. "Protest and Political Opportunities." *Annual Review of Sociology* 30: 125–145. https://doi-org.proxy.uba.uva.nl/10.1146/annurev.soc.30.012703.110545.

Narayan, John. 2019. "British Black Power: The Anti-Imperialism of Political Blackness and the Problem of Nativist Socialism." *The Sociological Review* 67 (5): 945–967. https://doi-org.proxy.uba.uva.nl/10.1177/00380261198455.

Nash, Jennifer C. 2008. "Re-thinking Intersectionality." *Feminist Review* 89 (1): 1–15. https://doi-org.proxy.uba.uva.nl/10.1057/fr.2008.4.

Pitts, Johny. 2022. *Afropean.* Madrid: Capitán Swing Libros.

Westall, Catherine. 2021. "Why Is 'Socialism' a Dirty Word in US Politics?" *A News Education.* https://www.anewseducation.com/post/socialism-and-us-politics.

Postcolonial Subjectivities and Meera Syal's *Anita and Me*

Gary Forster, Ph.D

Abstract

Postcolonial studies have moved from "dismantling the centre / margin binarism" (Ashcroft 1995, 117) to a transcultural approach encompassing the "local and the global," and "differences and commonalities," without "Western-centric uniformisation or the denial of particularisms." (Pereira-Ares 2018, xiv) Meera Syal's landmark semi-autobiographical debut novel *Anita and Me* (1996) exemplifies this cultural evolution and a movement from rejecting to tentatively accepting and finally celebrating a hybridised British Indian identity. Homi K. Bhabha's theoretical third space of enunciation is a key model for conceptualising the multifaceted-ness of the fluid identity (and subjectiv*ies*) of the character Meena Kumar because third spaces (interstitial contact zones that disseminate culture) mediate unequal social groups and engender an indefinable, self-questioning hybrid subjectivity that criticises itself and culture to gain a new perspective, and thereby become "neither One nor the Other but something else besides." (Bhabha 2004, 41) As Mary Louise Pratt theorises, this mutual encounter transforms the metropolitan centre and colonial periphery to produce estrangement and a new identity (Pratt 1992, 144). Neither group is the same, following the exchange, as the third space moves beyond binary oppositions (race, gender, politics) to a process of becoming. This chapter extends this scholarship by drawing on the (Sartre-inspired) tripartite model of identity proposed by Sura P. Rath: "being for itself, being-for-others, and being-in-the-world."

Keywords: Adaptations, Critical Theory, Diaspora, England, Hybridity, Identity, India, Meera Syal, Postcolonialism, Postculturalism

"I never think of you as, you know, foreign. You're just like one of us."

(Syal 1996, 29)

Introduction

Meera Syal's *Anita and Me* has contributed to a change in the British cultural landscape whereby Asian identities are celebrated and racial stereotypes are laughed at and thus deflated. Almost thirty years have passed since the novel's publication, which inspired Syal's radio show *Goodness Gracious Me* (1996-1998), adapted into a TV series (1998-2015), and her comedy chat show *The Kumars at No. 42* (2001-2006). Sanjeev Bhaskar (Syal's husband) plays Sanjeev Kumar and likewise plays Shyam Kumar in Metin Hüseyin's film adaptation of *Anita and Me* (2002). The normalisation of British Indian talent in British media is in part why postcolonial criticism often optimistically envisions the West replacing "*given* cultures" with cultures that are open to "reconstruction" and which "draw on the multiplicity of cultural experiences [and] voices that have been marginalised." (Brinker-Gabler 1995, 8) To achieve this requires "listening to and speaking to each other [...] without reducing differences." (Brinker-Gabler 1995, 8) It is through *hearing* that new, hybridised, subjectivities can emerge from the third space. In an interview, Meera Syal advertises *Anita and Me* as a tale that teaches readers about the "value of connecting with people who are different to yourself. What's more important is the stuff we share, our humanity, rather than the stuff that makes us different." (Social 2017)

Anita and Me, a linear first-person narrative, recounts the harmonisation of Meena's diasporic identity, from ages 9~13, in a house, within a village, within a landmass: England. Postcolonial theorists such as Bhabha and Rath refer to these external spatial territories as a geographical identity or "Identity-as-Place," and see being English as a VIP backstage pass (Rath 2002). Meena encounters difficulties because her pass is partly written in Indian. She internalises local customs and ideas, but the village never absorbs *her* Indian traditions. Although a national identity cannot encompass *all* of who Meena is as a person, she feels hurt and at a remove because the Indian jokes she repeats at school "lost a lot in translation." (Syal 2002, 56)

Home is the starting point within a place, if not where we belong. Meena lets her guard down at home: a safe space among people she knows and to whom she need not explain herself or justify her presence. It stands for community, mutual connections, and recognition; and home can mean many places. Meena is a global citizen where multiple countries have different holds, pulls, meanings, and influences on her and her family. She inhabits an increasingly globalised world where borders disappear or encroach on other borders. Uniting her geographical identity is a repository of collective memories built up over thousands of years. Sura P. Rath (2002) refers to the "reservoir of public myths and private memories" that inform cultures. Jung calls these the Collective Cultural Unconscious and Personal Unconscious, respectively.

Stuart Hall aptly examines "memory, fantasy, narrative, and myth" that are used as a "*positioning*" to locate us (Hall 1990, 225). This positioning explains why Meena tells stories. Given that Meena is on a quest to locate and anchor herself in the world, she creates fiction about her life to fill in the gaps in her identity, asserting that: "those of us deprived of history sometimes need to turn to mythology to feel complete, to belong." (Syal 2002, 10) Meena speaks of a need for mythology, but she defines mythology as "double entendre." (9) Meena prefaces her tale by evoking a gap analysed below: "I've always been a sucker for a good double entendre; the gap between what is said and what is thought, what is stated and what is implied." (10)

Cultural identities are "positionalities," as are the many histories that inform identity and locate us. British and Indian Meena are in constant dialogue. She has a dialogic identity. Meena is identified as one thing (brown and Indian) and not the other (white and English). *The Incredible Hulk* cartoon, as one example, depicts identity as a battlefield. Viewers enter the Incredible Hulk's mind and see his divided identity, where Green Hulk and Grey Hulk fight to control his consciousness. *Anita and Me* has similar psychological contests. It calls the conscience an "irritating other me that sat on my brain and kept confusing me," (94) and it explores the competing identities that constitute characters. Meena Kumar negotiates with 'British Meena' and 'Indian Meena' until they are harmonised, and cultivates an open-ended identity that resists labels. She keeps her "options open" (328) and sees identity pluralistically: British Meena, Indian Meena, and British Indian Meena.

Postcolonial theory often describes a homeland identity, a settled identity, and a hyphenated identity. The heart of Meena's mother, Daljit, is in her homeland, India. She finds a settled identity in England. Her hyphenated identity is the combination of her British and Indian lives. However, the presence of a hyphen is problematic because it denotes a break and/ or a barrier. It is more accurate to say that Daljit has a 'British-Indian', 'Indian-British', or 'English' identity. Meena traces a complicated journey towards an expansive identity. Although she is English, England is initially external to her, given its history of exclusion and expropriation. Meena calls herself "too Indian to be a real Tollington wench [...] living in the grey area between all categories felt [...] like home." (Syal 2002, 150) Meena develops her hybridised identity in this "grey area" or third space of enunciation.

Rath's Theoretical Model of Identity

Sura P. Rath likens the third space to a "twilight zone" (or the collective unconscious) that holds all pieces of identity and "bits of potential" from which consciousness is assembled (Rath 2002). Meena has never been to India. It speaks to her from elsewhere, in dreams; she assimilates content fed by her unconscious. Her identity is like a palimpsest onto which Indian and British cultures have been overlaid. By the end, she is aware of all that she can be and faces the world. Sartre might say that her "circuit of selfness" is a "synthesis" of her "Being-in-Itself, Being-for-Itself, and Being-in-the-World." (Sartre 1957,102) Meena's body is a being in and of itself. Meena has a consciousness that thinks for itself: a mind in the body, through which she is seen and exists in the world.

To unpack these categories further: "Being-in-Itself" means noun. It is the word characters use to name an object or being they see. The object, like Meena's inanimate house, is defined by its function. It is being (as a verb) and exists in this world. Its meaning is fixed. Humans can *choose* what they want to do and be, unlike a tree, which is self-aware, but can only be a tree. It lacks the self-determining capacity for transcendence, like software that runs but cannot upgrade itself, at least not *consciously*.

When Meena is bullied, she never allows it to defeat her; she elects to move beyond it and becomes stronger; she transcends the abuse.

While Meena is defined in terms of lack and the way she exists via the others' I(s), Sartre calls this the consciousness that simply is: content, at peace with itself, and "never revealing itself completely to consciousness." (Sartre 1957, xiii) The "Being-for-Itself" component of Rath's model updates Sartre's model. It is the ghost in the machine, ego, 'I' that witnesses the world through the subject's own eyes. This conscious being thinks for itself, aware of being in the world and of being an individual: "I know I am not that other person."

Re-Evaluating Allegiances and Overcoming Cultural Stereotypes

Meena is aware that she has a historical past, present, and future potential. However, much of the world exists outside Meena's complete comprehension, as it does for the villagers who subject the Kumars to worn-out racial stereotypes. Meena begins her story as a nine-year-old British Indian girl in a labyrinth of meanings and cultures. Meena's misbehaving is a rebellion against an inscrutable world and a way of working towards individuation. Equally, Daljit's desire to be accepted by Tollington (the host culture) whilst maintaining her heritage and language is experienced as 'unhomeliness' and as 'bothness', and a psychological vacillation between integration and segregation. Salient is that diasporas enable us to examine unstable and forever-changing cultural identities, because they create third spaces that enable transgressive subjectivities to emerge. Identity is repositioned as ever-evolving, even in a community that denies the intellectual capacity of British Indian immigrants.

Patronising views of Indians as vapid subalterns plague the Kumars; their assimilation is treated like a promotion or rise from Indian to English: "I never think of you as [...] foreign. You're just like one of us" (Syal 2002, 29). Daljit is furious because, as Gisela Brinker-Gabler argues, migrant "culture should not be interpreted based on an orientation towards one's *own* culture, nor [...] experienced in terms of 'similar to' or 'just like'" (Brinker-Gabler 1995, 2). It is as if locals only accept the Kumars as neighbours because they "don't think we are Indian. 'Oh you're so English, Mrs K!' Like it is a [...] compliment!" (Syal 2002, 172) This accords with the colonial idea that English means white, and that an immigrant "becomes whiter as he renounces his blackness, his jungle." (Fanon 1986, 18) That is, the villagers educate the Kumars (Others) and show they are benevolent by letting colonised resemble coloniser via mimicry; yet they must maintain *some* differences or else they become equals.

Heaven forbid the Kumars have too many similarities and become subversive. Although the English language has already reached India, it is seen as a sign of racial purity and the preservation of natives. Using English further dilutes colour, assuming that language belongs to British culture. The Kumars interact and think in English, another language, fluently. The host culture's Other tongue thus supplants and becomes the Mother tongue. Language marks the border between the internal- he subject's mind and body, and the outside world- everything external to the human body. The Kumars threaten the fault lines separating white and brown, England and India, and familiar and unfamiliar, by literally crossing from one nation into another, and vice versa. Meena is a second-generation British Indian whose Indian family and English community act as coordinates as she locates herself within their interlinked cultures. Meena performs Indian songs to please Aunties and Uncles, yet she is identifiably English: "She sings Punjabi with a Birmingham accent!" (114) Their reaction reinforces ideas of racial and cultural sanctity. English may be sung in 'Brummie', but not Punjabi, which is unexpected and unacceptable.

Meena's Tollington identity is just one personal identity that merges with her identity as an Indian daughter. Meena cannot change her visible racial identity, her brown skin sets her apart from the whites, but she *can* adapt her dialect to suit specific membership groups and adopt "proper" speech (53) to appear more 'English' at school and home, and only use slang with friends because *Daljit* chastises her: "You take the best from their culture, not the worst." (53) Culture is thus treated like a menu from which options are selected. The Aunties criticise Meena's supposedly British mannerisms (her menu choices) as if she is wearing clothes that do not fit. She tries to satisfy this extended family that expects her to be Indian, *and* answer competing (contradictory) calls to fit in with Britons who look with derision at her Indian ways. As the saying goes, it takes a village to raise a family. Unfortunately, Meena inhabits many 'villages' or little communities simultaneously.

The Aunties (her Indian 'village') see the English as promiscuous and immoral. Even Daljit critiques "the habits of her English friends" (29) and criticises their garden ornaments as "an English thing [...] They have to mark out their territory," (33) like a colonial overhang. She stops herself from saying "like dogs" (33), but it is implied. Mocking the host culture is a common self-defence mechanism for minorities because they attempt to demolish but have unwittingly "internalised [...] the false" and "mutually generative" stereotypes "within which [they have] been entrapped." (Deane 1990, 12) Meanwhile, Meena speaks lovingly of her mother and aunts and how "I could not imagine existing without them, although I hated the way they continually interfered in my upbringing." (Syal 2002, 30) They subject her to "a moral marathon," (Syal 2002, 30) each taking up "the baton" (30) and offering their opinion of how she should behave. Even so, "they were a formidable mafia," (33) and their exercising demands and unwritten social rules come from a place of love.

Anita Rutter and Meena's Multiple Subjectivities

Queen Bee Anita Rutter is Meena's defining childhood figure and first platonic love. Meena calls her "my passport to acceptance" (148) in England: white, blonde, and beautiful. She has a "brown birthmark under one eye," (39) hence there is a tiny amount of brown in her (a little bit of Meena), but not enough melatonin to be othered. It is tempting to over-interpret the white eye above brown skin as a colonial symbol. A more plausible symbolic reading is that Anita is Meena's identity made flesh: "she gave voice to all the wicked things I had often thought." (138) Anita helps her to "shed inhibitions" (139) and her sense of inferiority, embrace her burgeoning sexuality, and negotiate childhood by learning local customs. While Anita thinks Meena is a lesbian, she is simply infatuated because of Anita's popularity. The Being-in(side)-Itself category of Rath's model is applicable here since it relates to Meena's actions, thoughts, and will. Meena lacks complete self-knowledge and fills in the gaps in her self-image by constructing Anita as her soul mate: the impossible "ideal Other against which [a subject] can articulate its identity [and] see its own mirror image." (Rath 2002)

As Meena lacks the full picture, it takes her two years to realise that Anita is a "Bad Influence" (Syal 2002, 133) and "needed me [...] more than I needed her." (242) Meena befriends and impresses Anita by stealing sweets from Mr. Ormerod's shop, even though her father "was going to kill me" (16). Meena calculates that it is worth being "told off by a white person", which means "letting down the whole Indian nation" (45) and defying its demand for honesty, for she "physically aches" for Anita's company (39) and to join her "Wenches Brigade." (138)

It is as if they are one character or one soul in two bodies: Yin and Yang. Meena puts Anita before herself in the title of her book. Meena is the 'and me'. Although it suggests they come as a pair, Meena is secondary and like an afterthought. Sartre states that "The Ego with the double grammatical form of 'I' and 'Me' represents our person as a transcendent psychic unity." (Sartre 1957, 162) The idea of consciousness (a) reaching towards totality and (b) being transcendent and thus ever-evolving has key applications for postcolonial scholarship, and the third space in particular. The paradox is that Anita and Meena appear to be two people and one person at the same time, both entirely white and English, and both entirely brown and Indian. The act of Meena naming Anita confirms her existence independent of her: "to affirm this object is to simultaneously deny that I am this object [and] make oneself other." (155) Meena makes herself the Other of Anita, but in the title of the book, she is Anita's other half. Alternatively, they are just in alphabetical order, and the English language typically refers to another person before the first person, such as "Mum and I will be going." One other possibility, among many, is that the title is "and me" rather than "I," because this is how Meena speaks, *and* because we see more than one "I."

We see a multiplicity of Meenas, informed by cultural hybridity, that never exist in stasis but grow in knowledge and evolve. Indeed, the book proves that there are various ways of being when the older Meena habitually intrudes on younger Meena's narratives (we hear both voices at once) to pass on her wisdom.

Several English characters feel a duty to pass their customs on to the Kumars, as in 'The Beach of Falesá', where John Wiltshire civilises his native cat-faced 'wife' Uma, with her primitive dress and dances: "I'm a white man, and a British subject [...] and I've come to [...] bring them civilisation." (Stevenson 1892, 23) However, morals are often askew, as in Joseph Conrad's 'An Outpost of Progress', with its "tall cross much out of the perpendicular." (Conrad 1897, 610) In *Anita and Me*, villagers have questionable motives. Meena speaks of being "invaded by [...] visiting Indian families [...] every weekend" (Syal 2002, 29), and "I could see our neighbours shift uncomfortably, contemplating the apparent size of my family and the fact we had somehow managed to bring every one of them over here." (29)

The horrified neighbours act as if they have an allergy to anything Other. Outsiders—and especially *Indian* outsiders—are perceived as a threat whose intention is to replace the locals. Villagers also speak slowly, believing Daljit cannot rise to the level of Standard English. Yet Daljit 'civilises' *them* and is driven by an educative desire: "looking glamorous in saris and formal Indian suits was part of the English people's education. It was her duty to show them that we could wear discreet gold jewellery, dress in tasteful silks and speak English without an accent." (25) Daljit wears her clothing and, as a teacher, proves that her family are 'good enough' for the village.

Costume as an Extension of Identity

Clothing underpins *Anita and Me* because it is a "visual metaphor for identity [...] registering the culturally anchored ambivalences that resonate within and among identities." (Davis 1992, 95) To this day, it draws a line "between what is Western and what is Indian. Fashion [...] has been crucial [...] in debates before and after Indian Independence in 1947 about the tastes and outward appearance of the 'authentic Indian.'" (Bruzzi 2013, 44) It is a way of 'positioning' (to borrow from Stuart Hall) and revealing or concealing our identity. Noemí Pereira-Ares unpacks this further: "Through dress, we project our identity [...] real or contrived, transmitting information [about] gender, ethnicity, class [...] religion, culture or collective affiliation." (Pereira-Ares 2018, xvii) Daljit's saris, as examined above, mark a revised view of Britain's Asian presence. Seen as "royalty" (Syal 2002, 28), and a stylish goddess, Daljit defies conformity, and is a reminder of how saris became *the* "anti-colonialist" symbol of the "Indian woman [as] guardian of hearth, home, and traditional values" (Bruzzi 2013, 45) *and*, paradoxically, the new, liberated, fashion-forward modern woman. Meena's clothes likewise give her space for agency and to carve out and express her own identity because they are a "site of identity inscription, negotiation, and *reinvention*." (Pereira-Ares 2018, xii)

Meena has a complicated relationship with clothing as a vehicle for expressing her British and Indian identities. Meena attempts to convince Anita "silently" (Syal 2002, 17) through facial expressions alone—"a haunted look" (17)—that her frilly, pleated, floral Indian dresses are "not me," (17) and uses non-verbal cues to say she is *forced* to wear them like skins and be an advertisement for India. All markers of India are confined to her indoors/private/home life to make her outside/public/England life easier. Meena even swaps a "*salwar kameez* suit" (107) for "trousers and a jumper" (116) when going out. Because she feels out of place, inadequate, and unfashionable, Meena writes a letter to Cathy and Claire, the *Jackie* magazine columnists: "I am brown [...] Will this stop me getting a guy?" (145) They give vital life advice after she broadcasts her anxieties to the world: "BE YOURSELF!" (146), yet Meena is ashamed of her colour, and now feels overburdened by her saris' hallmark styles and cultural baggage: "I wanted to shed my body like a snake slithering out of its skin and emerge reborn, pink and unrecognisable [...] I refused to put on the Indian suits my mother laid out for me." (146)

Meena loves her Indian heritage (the ornate saris at *gurudwara* comfort her and evoke home) yet her acts of defiance stem from a fear that she will be rejected (unloved) by boys because she is brown and an outsider in foreign attire, and thus must adopt the guise of English people, even though she *is* native-born. Although Anita offers encouragement by praising Meena's wardrobe full of Indian dresses- Daljit catches Anita sneaking them out of Meena's house, Meena "began avoiding mirrors;" (146) yet, sees her reflection, "disappointed it was still there." (146)

Meena resists identification with the Meena looking back at her: "I knew what it was like to live inside a body you did not feel was yours." (189) These words typify diaspora and ideas of noble savages: "almost the same, but not quite" and "almost the same, but not white." (Bhabha 1984, 89) Added to this, Meena is aware that she *must* behave, having been taught not to "give [the English] a chance to say we're worse than they already think we are." (45) Consequently, one strand of Meena's journey concerns learning how to combine her 'outfits', her Indian and British identities, just as she interchanges Indian clothes and European outfits. Fittingly, Tania in *Life Isn't All Ha Ha Hee Hee* rejects all claims of "ethnic denial" that arise from adopting Western attire because "the roots go deeper than that, honey." (146) Tania never subscribes to the notion that her identity is signposted exclusively by clothing. Asians, she adds, are "force-fed [...] language and rituals as a matter of survival, our defence against the corruption outside our front door." (146) Although she embraces hybridity, Asian history is vouchsafed, and the preservation of cultural 'purity' occurs through storytelling.

Disseminating Culture through Storytelling

India is preserved and passed on through Oral Tradition: "exchanging anecdotes [...] reinforced their shared histories." (31) The British Indian community "all have these stories [...] What was happening to you was also happening to us." (73) Meena connects to the past through Shyam's haunting Punjabi singing and discovers how "a single line [...] somehow captured life, death and the unknown." (72) Memory fills the *mehfils* and mournful *ghazals*, during which her relatives "in these moments [...] were all far, far away." (72) Music takes them beyond themselves, elsewhere, back to India and back to the past. The word *"Wah"* (72) shows the inadequacy of orthodox language systems in encapsulating their human emotions. The word "had no literal meaning," but then "what word would there be for these feelings that Papa's songs awoke in everyone?" (72) Papa's singing "unleashed [...] emotions [...] in a language I could not recognise but felt I could speak in my sleep, in my dreams, evocative of a country I had never visited but which sounded like the only home I had ever known." (112)

The unconscious, in Freudian terms, communicates with the conscious mind and makes sense of and makes accessible otherwise unknowable content. The ineffable becomes effable and comprehensible and seeks expression through art, such as Shyam's music: "The songs made me realise that there was a corner of me that would be forever not England." (112) To have a "corner" that is exclusively hers means something that England cannot claim is theirs. It also alludes to and cleverly reworks Rupert Brooke's "The Soldier" (1915): "If I should die, think only this of me: / That there's some corner of a foreign field / That is for ever England." (ll.1-3)

Shyam and Daljit replace 'The Boy who Cried Wolf' with 'The Boy who Cried Tiger' to discourage Meena from stealing. They try to create a space for Meena (who is resistant) to open up and help them finally understand what would motivate her to commit petty crimes. As Shyam narrates this tale, Meena feels insulted: "Did he think I would swallow an old story dressed up in Indian clothes?" (70) Meena considers the English (wolf) version the legitimate hypotext and the Indian version a derivative adaptation: an old tale in a new skin. Her reaction parallels her fear that

Tollington (based on Syal's childhood mining village Essington) will not "swallow" an Indian girl dressed up in English clothes (like the Big Bad Wolf). This also explains why she 'zones out', and imagines inhabiting a new body with "blonde" hair (70). She retreats to a conceptualisation of herself as white and singing "Let's Go Fly a Kite" (70) from the quintessentially British film adaptation *Mary Poppins* (1964). In her fantasy world, she is Anita and therefore concludes that she is 'missing' something: whiteness.

Meena also dreams of appearing on *Opportunity Knocks* to propel her into stardom, but is fearful that being Asian "might count against me", having "never seen anyone who wasn't white on the show." (65) As a sign of the times, Meena writes that "If a brown or black face ever did appear on TV, it stopped us all in our tracks" (165) and the whole family is called into the room to watch. The redefinition of Meena's identity, examined below, calls into question racial hierarchies, *and* Meena recognises that they are not stereotypical Asians or the "helpless idiots" (216) caricatured on TV. Positive representations include Dr. Reita Faria (Miss India), who won a Miss World title. She becomes Meena's idol because she has beauty *and* intelligence.

Popular Culture and Friendships as Vehicles for Identity Formation

Meena navigates her awkward early teenage years by reading style magazines along with Anita, Sherrie, and Fat Sally, and models her identity on its *helpful* examples of how to act, dress fashionably, and attract boys. Meena projects her self-image onto the gang and finds belonging and acceptance in an entirely white friendship group. She uses magazine advice columns and expert opinions as a frame of reference that informs her views, just as she internalises her neighbours talking about which male is most attractive and why: "I now knew what a sex symbol was supposed to look like." (42) At the same time, as Meena bases her style on (and connects with) Anita to complete herself, she is defined through this Other, and what she feels she cannot truly be. For Sartre, "diaspora" causes "cohesion and dispersion" (136). Looking to Anita for validation is problematic. While a reflection is united to that which it reflects, Anita and Meena stop being friends. If they *are* one person, we see a "turning back on itself" and "a wrenching away from self" (Sartre 1957,154) to find recovery.

Much of the novel concerns Meena transforming her perspective, having "fought for this friendship [...] measured myself against it, lost myself inside it." (Syal 2002, 277) Her identity is subsumed by a desire to please Anita: "the world reversed like a negative and I found myself inside [Anita's] head, looking out of her eyes." (186) This corresponds with Sura P. Rath's Being-for-Others, by which he means the 'I' that exists for others and which receives itself through how "it is observed by everybody beyond the borders of itself." (Rath 2002) It has a flawed and incomplete view of itself because knowing what someone else truly thinks calls for the operation of their mind. Meena can only *imagine* how Anita thinks, yet everything that Anita teaches her "tilt[s] my small world slightly off its axis so I saw the familiar and the mundane through new eyes, Anita's eyes." (Syal 2002, 139)

As a final example, Meena listens to a tale of a rickshaw driver being killed in India, "and heard huge boulders moving somewhere, my centre of gravity shifted [...] Terrible things could happen, even to ordinary people like me, and they were always unplanned." (36) It is interesting that Meena sees herself as normal here *and* that the "boulders moving" represent Meena's estrangement, as she realises that she is at the mercy of the unsafe universe and is exposed to danger. Equally, she discovers that "those you called friends could suddenly become tormentors." (142) They punish anyone exhibiting "difference" (142) because being non-standard, "an outsider, an individual even, was somehow [considered] infectious." (142) Conformity to cultural norms is mandatory.

Confronting Racism and the Destabilisation of a Secure 'Home' Identity

Sam Lowbridge expresses a hyper-masculine identity by shaving his head and joining the anti-immigrant skinhead gangs: a resentful white subculture in 1960s Britain engendered by a fear of being replaced and outdone by immigrants. Rocking up on a moped at Tollington's Spring Fête, his new style confirms he has been ideologically captured. Sam's racism appears to be a reaction to lack and abandonment. Raised without a father, his gang provides a sense of membership. He is taught to see outsiders as the cause of all his pain. He repeatedly voices fears of characters leaving him and of having no future. Perhaps, rather than genuinely hating immigrants, he is just performing the "Tollington stance [...] attack [first] and never ever show [...] pain." (52) His conflicts are projected onto outsiders who lack particularity. This is one reason why he objects to sending charity money abroad: "This is our patch. Not some wogs' handout!" (193) His racial slur universalises all non-whites as parasitic, and devastates Meena: "I felt as if I had been punched in the stomach" and the "crowd had turned into one huge eyeball [that] swivelled slowly between me and papa." (193) Meena feels exposed to the gaze of the crowd as if they look in unison, as one white England, judge her, and associate her with this dehumanising term. Sam's racist remark "had taken away my innocence;" (227) hence, Meena is always on guard in case there are more racist outbursts.

Just as demolishing the primary school marks the end of Meena's child-hood, Sam shatters the foundations of Meena's identity and, in a single moment, takes England away from her. While Meena enjoys making pos-itive contributions to and connections with her community by helping the Reverend with humanitarian causes (as do all of the local children), her "illusion of coherence and safety" (Kayışçı 2010, 47) is broken by Sam, who later attacks the enterprising motorway builder, "Rajesh Bhatra from Rettenhall." (Syal 2002, 275) Meena wonders "if Tollington would ever truly be home again." (275) Meena treats people as individuals and avoids homogenisation; "Not *all* the English are selfish." (67) Yet, Sam makes her question her right to be in England *twice* by collectivising out-siders. He turns Rajesh into a 'bogeyman' that stands for all immigrants that Sam believes thwart his life chances; and yet Sam's life never improves after he assaults him (Rajesh never fights back), because immigrants are not responsible for his life choices: *he* is.

Experiencing racism threatens Meena's identity during her first trip to the *gurudwara*. Daljit cannot drive in reverse down a hill, wearing san-dals. Meena asks the drivers behind them to give her space. A bus driver reverses because Meena calls him "Uncle". Meena's aunts and uncles are not biological relatives but are all linked by something deeper: India. She uses words like cultural currency or a secret password that communicates shared values and makes him think of other contexts in which he, as an In-dian, has used it. And it creates an affinity and an understanding by imply-ing that they are the same. Meanwhile, Meena speaks of her "deliberately exaggerated Tollington accent proving that I was [...] one of [the English] [...] I belonged." (97) She sees her bicultural identity positively here.

However, an elderly white woman calls Meena a "stupid wog." (97) Mee-na believes her accent lets her 'pass' as white and opens doors that her brown skin shuts, yet she is reduced to a gollywog and racial stereotypes that support the woman's negative conceptions of immigrants. Bhabha writes of how "skin" is used as a "sign" of "identity" *and* "inferiority or degeneracy." (Bhabha 1984, 83) Although they have identical accents, the elderly woman's voice and white skin have primacy. She uses skin colour as an index of intelligence to call Meena stupid. She repeats her insult, has the final word, and cannot see the English identity Meena projects. She therefore reasons that Meena can speak the language but never belong. Meena brackets herself and her mother off from the English and worries about how they see "people like us." (Syal 2002, 97) She almost tells Shyam, but keeps her hurt a secret because of an epiphany: "what had happened to me must have happened to papa countless times." (98) Meena disengages from Tollington, the only home she has ever known, oscillating between public and private displays of her bicultural identity. As Berthold Schoene-Harwood puts it, "In Meena's case, hybridity signifies a state of not [belonging or] being able to meet the standards of either culture." (Harwood 1999, 46)

Diaspora and Nanima as a Bridge between England and India

Daljit has a mental collapse, torn by competing impulses to be Indian and English. She believes England "through squinted eyes, could almost look something like home," (Syal 2002, 35) but Daljit longs for her "Punjabi village [near] Chandigarh" (34) where she "milked goats, stroked peacocks, [and] pulled sugar cane from the earth as a mid-morning snack." (36) Shyam's plans for a trip to India excite Daljit. He pronounces the word "home" so "naturally" that Meena wonders if "everything surrounding us was merely our temporary lodgings." (263) Intriguingly, Meena says that Daljit is "a country girl lost in the big city." (35) If Daljit *is* a country girl, then that country is India.

An Indian psychic tells Meena that her family needs "help from over the seas." (184) Right on cue, after birthing Meena's brother, Daljit despairs: "Back home I would have sisters [...] I can't do this any more. I can't." (196) Her mother (Meena's Nanima) arrives from India and is a symbol of family and the past. Her presence revivifies Daljit: "daughter, mother and grandmother, all of us the product of each other" (201) and "linked like Russian dolls." (202) Meena has always felt "excluded" from the Daljit that existed in India and her "past" and her earlier "incarnations." (36) Nanima brings that upbeat child back to life—the girl that grew up to be

"All Delhi College Champion" and "lecturer" (35) and "actress, athlete, teacher." (36) *Everyone* wants to meet Nanima because she is "one of the generation they had left behind" and they can "catch up on the latest news from the Motherland." (201) Vitally, Meena admits that "my two worlds had collided and mingled so easily." (204) And this foreshadows her reconciling her diasporic subjectivity.

Meena sees British and Indian as immutable and oppositional categories of being until Nanima puts everything into "context for me." (211) This flesh-and-blood individual's real memories of India's aromas, sights and people are an antidote to the racist woman and Meena's history books, whose biased Grand Narratives venerate the British Empire and Imperialism. Tollington's pre-Internet age has limited access to India. All students "'did' India at school" (211) and find it a boring topic. Meena believes that colonised Indians (after the British leave) have "nothing to do with me," (212) but they have *everything* to do with her because of her family's colonial scars and life in Britain's dominating culture; the textbooks are like photo albums of ancestors, yet compel Meena to prove that she is unlike the 'savages' on display: "'modern' images, culled from newspaper and television clips, where hollow-eyed skeletons, barely recognisable as human beings squatted listlessly [...] and machete-wielding thugs tore into each other in messy streets, under the benevolent gaze of a statue of Queen Victoria." (211) Meena cannot identify with an England that treats India (and her) this way; this is why she is astonished to hear Mr. Topsy/Turvey, a lone voice, mirror her private thoughts: "We should never have been there. Criminal it was!" (222) Her family's accounts also fragment truth claims; Meena's maternal grandfather is arrested for *refusing* to fight for colonial Britain, in "their army." (209)

Meena cannot control how others see her, but she can question historical representations of subjugated Indians (her 'relatives') and resist the version of Indian-ness imposed on her by England. Meena's "urge to reinvent myself" was "driven [...] by shame" (211) of her dual cultural heritage. Nanima brings healing and allows Meena to see India anew. Meena celebrates rather than hides the Indian identity she enjoys at home because Nanima expands the definition of Indian to include hyperactivity and rebelliousness. Meena adds that she "desperately wanted to visit India and claim some of this magic as mine." (211) And when her family loudly and unashamedly celebrates Nanima staying with them, they show Meena how affirming her Punjabi heritage is. Hearing Punjabi, an "indoor language," (203) being spoken outdoors is freeing and exhilarating. It is normally reserved for whispering and saying "something intimate, personal, about feelings;" (203) otherwise, the family shouts in English. Meena confesses that she speaks Punjabi in her dreams. It is the language of her unconscious and (in Jungian terms) of the *collective* unconscious, or inherited cultural memories of India.

Meena reconstructs Nanima's memories in her imagination, and she 're-lives' Partition second-hand through stories she was denied for so long. Integrated into her identity, they give her important historical context. Her deepening admiration of her family leads to a realisation that "In the silence that followed, a hundred other memories were being briefly relived." (74) This is the double entendre Meena defines: "the gap between what is said and what is thought." (10) They remember to try to move on, but never forget. As Nanima recounts her life, she ends by saying she is "reborn in Delhi." (231) After "the fields were given over to English soldiers [...] nothing was ours anymore, not even our names, our breath." (231) These words wash over and resonate with Meena: "I knew this feeling, I had felt it too, but did not know why." (231) Meena relates to these memories, which echo hers. They articulate her deep-seated fears of alienation and death. Nanima answers her concerns by questioning "What is there to fear when you have already lived two lives?" (231) Meena finds her fearlessness inspirational, and thus "re-views" her mother (to use Adrienne Rich's feminist terminology), because *this* is what Daljit is living.

India and England are experienced as two lives. As Nanima puts it: "Your mama is on her second one, here, over here." (232) The repetition of 'here' is central because Nanima reminds herself that she is currently in England. India is her usual 'here' but is presently a 'there'. Her daughter, Daljit, inherits her tremendous psychological fortitude. She starts a new life in another country, and reconciles 'here' and 'there' with her biculturality.

Hani Zubida revisits the idea of 'options' to argue that first and second generation migrants form "their personal identity" by confronting "conflicting ethnic, personal and national identity options" alongside "host and origin social constructs, contradicting expectations, traditions and norms." (Zubida 2013, 2) Belonging and alienation, here and there, are in flux. Meena's perspectives and identity as English and Indian during her formative years are also seen "against the backdrop of racial diversity and cultural hybridity." (Dunphy 2004, 637)

Meena (a second-generation immigrant) encounters representational instability and finds that her bicultural languages are needed to clarify the concept of a 'homeland'. Her identity shows commonness with that of Daljit, here, who carries many traumatic memories with her, such as seeing "someone stabbed to death [in] Delhi [during] partition riots." (Syal 2002, 36) Daljit's arrival in England in the 1960s is a fresh start that coincides with the rise of second-wave feminist calls for female solidarity and sisterhood, which Nanima's historical narratives answer and nurture: "Never did I think I was less than a man. More than a man sometimes [...] To cook and clean and carry and fetch and soothe." (231) Her role as carer and primary caregiver throws into sharp relief the attitude of the nurse who (echoing Nanima's trauma) is seizing Meena's name.

Meena's Hospitalisation and the Symbolic Order— New Expressions of Identity

The hospitalisation of Meena (she breaks her leg when she rides Trixie the horse) is an "enforced separation" needed to "erase [Anita] like a child's pencil drawing." (282) She must break her leg to break contact (a physical rift). She realises, on her hospital bed, "Anita and I had never been meant for each other," (282) and creates a space to concentrate on recovery. Meena's leg is in a plaster cast, and she enters a metaphorical chrysalis: "I decided [...] to heal [...] in body and mind. It was time." (284) Throughout her stay, a nurse never asks how to pronounce "Meena". Colonising and Westernising her name, she calls her "Mary." (280) Meena cannot object given the power imbalance. Given her nascent knowledge of language that is "spoken" versus language that is "understood", when the nurse says she cannot utter the two syllables "Mee-na", Meena understands she *will not*. Here we find a subtle allusion to an earlier question: how could Marina the mermaid in the TV show *Stingray* "emit bubbles" instead of speaking to the enamoured Troy? (80) Her full name, Aquamarina, is also changed. The gap between them is caused by Marina's inability to use human language and be heard.

Meena can only communicate with a patient, Robert, by writing messages and holding them up to the glass. He is being isolated, and she becomes like Marina: "words were secondary, unnecessary [...] my first [...] relationship with a boy was conducted via scribbled messages on scrap paper through a pane of glass blend where you could look but not touch, understand but not hear." (286) Meena and Robert play with and make up their language. Just as Derrida's term *differance* disrupts settled meaning—and how we look at the word *difference*—and shows how words cannot fully capture all meanings, Meena adds letters to words and constructs "unpronounceable sentences." (286)

For Derrida, language is often over-determined and given to excesses. The similarity between Meera/Meena is one such example of something "left over", as if the 'n' is an extended 'r' and is a form of *differance*, simultaneously telling us that we are and are not hearing the story of Meera Syal's childhood, and that meaning in language always unfolds in new ways. Beyond the addition of letters, where "How are you?" becomes "Haobw Acrde Yeofu?" (286) Robert is anticipating queries, or else moves beyond speech and communicates telepathically; often he had already written "the answer to something I had been about to ask him." (287)

This recalls *The Bone People*'s Simon recovering in hospital, deaf: "absorbed in rediscovery" and recovery (Hulme 2001, 469), communication turns into a game of Simon Says, where "lips don't shape themselves in the shape of words" (469) and messages are written in "felt-tip" on "a square of plastic with a transparent sheet [...] you lift the transparency [and] the words vanish." (476) And just as characters use "finger-fashion" gestures (473), Meena gestures towards the unsayable when admiring Daljit and "The way her fingers say what her mouth cannot." (Syal 2002, 32) On 20 December, the day Meena leaves the hospital, Robert Oakes holds her hand to say that they are in a relationship. When they finally hear each other speak, neither expects the other to have a Black Country accent, just as Meena never imagines she will find out by letter that "Robert died" (299) on 31 December.

The Symbolic Finale Revelation and Integration of Meena's Hybrid Subjectivities

A showdown with Meena, Anita, Sam, Tracey, and the owner of the Big House invites psychoanalytic postcolonial readings *and* evokes *To Kill A Mockingbird* (1960). Harper Lee's text permeates Meena's tale because it is a "great learning experience" (296) and taught Meera Syal "racism wasn't about me [but rather] the people that were exponents of it." (Lawson

2017) Meena gives Robert a copy, but he dies before reading it. Meena never finishes it but *lives* it. She trespasses in the garden of the Big House at night, is knocked unconscious by a fence, and drops her Mother's diamond pendant. It is returned by the elusive Harinder P. Singh. Harper Lee's Jem explores the old house garden at night; his trousers are caught on a fence and left behind. Boo Radley returns them.

The combinatory framework signposted above *moves beyond* identifying these allusions by examining how the narrative deals with racism and violence, ties everything together, and liberates and celebrates Meena's fluid identity. Signally, Meena discovers the Big House's statue of "our [...] elephant god, Ganesha." (127) She releases it "from the jungle" (127) of ivy and moss and frees the religious identity she once thought embarrassing. Bhabha theorises that "intersubjective and collective experiences of nationness, community [...] or cultural values are negotiated" in "interstices" that unsettle "domains of difference." (Bhabha 1984, 2) A gap appears at the novel's climax, in the form of a literal pool of water, where Meena reconciles her history. Meena's ultimate confrontation with Sam opens up a symbolic rift or liminal contact zone that they both enter. Having heard her family's vivid memories of racism and war, "the past" stops being a "sentimental journey." (Syal 2002, 75) History is "a murky bottomless pool full of monsters and the odd shining coin, with a deceptively still surface and a deadly undercurrent [...] how could I jump in before I had learned to swim?" (75)

The Hollow Pond in the garden of the Big House answers her question. It is a mineshaft now filled with water and connected to "a labyrinth of other shafts." (125) This labyrinth *is* the unconscious: hidden, "bottomless, unforgiving." (125) Meena warns that "if you fell in, you were lost forever." (310) Meena encounters Sam Lowbridge over troubled waters here, along with Hollow Pond's reclusive "child-eating monster:" (124) a Boo Radley "figure, huge and shaggy as a bear." (206) Besides half-remembered visits with her father as an infant, and a handful of excursions with Anita, she only returns to Hollow Pond, under a Full Moon, because Tracey bangs on her door, thinking Anita is being killed. It transpires that Anita and Sam are simply teasing Tracey by having (or simulating) sexual intercourse.

If identity *is* a constant becoming, as Meena discovers at Hollow Pond, then we need to *keep* entering third spaces to negotiate, probe, contemplate, and emerge mutually transformed: "I still live here [...] you haven't driven me out yet." (312) Meena's words certify her sense of belonging in England, her affinity with India, and expose Sam as an oppressor bent on expelling foreigners from his village. She makes him verbalise a rationale for his racism: "Sam grabbed me by the wrist" and reasons that when he made racist remarks "I never meant you, Meena! It was all the others, not yow!" (313) Her response "like the Bank Manager?" (313) reveals her knowledge of his "Paki bashing." (277) He grabs her to distract her, and never apologises, just as he admits sending Meena hate mail and makes excuses: he only let Anita write insulting notes as he wrote "nice ones". He is childish, narcissistic, and the archetypal male that bullies a girl he secretly likes; yet he is *so* much older than Meena; and there is an unspoken suspicion that young Tracey is raped by Sam or her father: "the row of bruises around Tracey's thighs [...] mimicking the imprint of ten cruel angry fingers." (142) Purple marks aside, Tracey hates anyone touching Anita, is uncontrollably violent to Sam, and says: "you let him touch yow too." (276) It is unconfirmed if this "him" is Sam or Roberto. Indeed, Anita "clamped [...] her hand over [Tracey's] mouth" and vows: "one more word [and] I'll kill you." (276)

Sam putting his lips on Meena's mouth signifies a double silencing. Having just 'conquered' Anita, he tries to silence Meena with his lips and body. Sam categorises Meena not as a foreigner but as a lover. She is a guilty exotic pleasure, and he consciously moves her out of his line of fire. He directs his abuse at all other Others. She is the "best wench [...] anywhere." (313) As Tania puts it in *Life Isn't All Ha Ha Hee Hee*: "brown was indeed the new black." (Syal 2000, 109) Meena is acceptable as a girlfriend because she stands out in a 'good way'. Her wit and beauty override Sam's hatred of non-whites, *and* she is light enough not to be a "darky". However, Meena *is* taboo in that she is too young to be desirable; while Sam says Anita is "jealous" (313) of them, Meena's first kiss is forbidden. It is a romantic and a colonial encounter. Sam (the centre) seeks to dominate Meena (the outsider); yet, they osculate on *her* terms: "I let him, feeling mighty and huge, knowing I had won and that every time he saw another Meena on a street corner he would remember this and feel totally powerless." (313)

Meena reclaims her power and finds female unity. She is every woman Sam will see, and he will consider her every Asian enchanting, conquering, and rejecting him after they kiss. Indeed, when Sam says "You're not like the others", Meena utters four powerful words: "I *am* the others." (314) This revelation of a mighty female subjectivity is the direct result of a third-space encounter.

Tracey becomes another Meena when wearing Meena's sweatshirt and "flying" over Hollow Pond's "edge" (313) and falling into the pool. The retelling of this event is disjointed. Meena's memories are mere "frames" (313) and "poses caught in the pop of a flashbulb." (245) Tracey, Anita, and Sam all begin fighting. Tracey seeks justice but, amid the frenzy, plunges into the water. Sura. P Rath's postcolonial model of identity and discussion of *Ramayana* are apt here because Tracey's fall mirrors King Trishanku encountering "an intermediate virtual space between Heaven and Earth" that signifies the "dichotomy between the body and spirit." (Rath 2000) That is, the King tries to enter Heaven in his flesh-and-blood body, but Indra (ruler of the gods) sends him down to Earth. *Anita and Me* echoes his overreaching when Tracey plummets- "arms outstretched like wings," (313) with a "terrible splash which sucked in half the night with it- and silence." (313)

As King Trishanku falls, he is suspended in silent "ethereal space" and "remains in that third space. Indeed, he *is* that third space." (Rath 2002) Tracey, like Trishanku, is kept in stasis, given that she is "pronounced clinically dead." (Syal 2002, 320) She becomes or switches places with Meena (in Meena's clothes) as a sacrifice. She 'dies' to produce the shock of strangeness that jolts the characters out of normality and sets Meena free from Anita and Sam. Crucially, hybrid identities that emerge from third spaces derive from "a long history of confrontations [...] in which the stronger culture struggles to control, remake, or eliminate the subordinate partner." (Lavie 2001, 9) Sam, the aggressor, fights with and eliminates the weaker Tracey.

In the 2002 film adaptation, it is *Meena* who falls into the pool, the ethereal space, and "prayed for help. The only thing that could save us. And he came." The arrival of Harry Singh, the novel's mythical "yeti" (Syal 2002, 47) monster, in a wolf-skin coat hints at cosmic intervention: "The yeti plunged into the bottomless pool. The water murky with memories and betrayal to save the girl who broke hearts." As he dives in after Meena and Anita, who collide in the water, this cleansing third space brings healing and a rebirth. Unconscious Anita is reawakened, and the monster is de-mythologised: "Not sucking her blood as I'd always feared but forcing the life back into her." He roars as he rises from the water and the audience is informed: "If he hadn't have come, I wouldn't have believed anything. He saved both of us: Anita and Me." Singh is thus the reason for the title of the film. The novel's Tracey goes a stage further than the film—and Tr-ishanku—as she hovers in between life and death, by being resuscitated with a defibrillator. Resurrected and re-emerging from the third space, she is named on TV as the Tollington Angel, and inspires Meena to move on with her life.

Conclusion

Pointing beyond geography to healing, Meera Syal's postculturalist text ends with the revelation of self-confidence and clarity: "The place in which I belonged was wherever I stood [...] nothing stopp[ed] me simply moving forward and claiming each resting place as home. This sense of displacement I had always carried [...] shrivelled into insignificance." (Syal 2002, 303) By treating her hybridised, diasporic subjectivity in an affirming, celebratory way, Meena is emancipated from the confines of representation in terms of a single ethnicity. Belonging in multiple cultures without rejecting her particularism (Meena-ness), she develops identification with her Indian community and dual heritage.

Meena calls it a "miracle" that "The Big House boss was an Indian." (317) Harinder P. Singh is the ultimate validation, for "he spoke Punjabi with a village twang," (317) just like Meena, and is the best example of a unified British Indian identity: a Cambridge law graduate who (along with his chemist wife, Mireille) calls Tollington "paradise." (319) Unlike much of diasporic fiction, Meena loves her village also, seen idyllically: "miles of flat green fields" (11) where houses form "a gap-toothed smile." (11) Shyam also forms an instant rapport with Singh: "All this time we have had a brother round the corner... All this time." (323) The ellipsis hints at how better their lives might have been had they met sooner. *Singh* "found Nanima's diamond necklace." (327) The restoration of a prized family heirloom brings the Kumars closure.

Singh represents an "expansion" of a "scope of options" (Stein 2004, 40) and a "furthering of subject positions" (Stein 2004, 38) for Meena because he is affluent, resembles her Indian father, and owns property, which she expects only of white Britons. The girl who accepts everything finally questions everything, and Meena's fluid identity embraces heterogeneities and commonalities. Everywhere and nowhere can be called home, and the Kumars' generations of pain and sacrifice are all worth it. The big reveal is that Meena is the first village resident in "a decade" to pass "the Eleven-Plus exam." (136) The family have "justification for their departure from India" (306) and "five thousand mile journey." (213) Her Auntie Shaila's final act is to give Meena "a beautiful ink pen with my name engraved on the side." (328) She uses it to write Anita a goodbye note: "I'm going to the grammar school." (328) Although Anita never replies, Meena's words effect catharsis. She has the power of the pen, and she uses it to heal and move on. Meena ultimately wins because she finds self-reliance and psychic totality. Instead of Anita and me, now it is just me.

References

Aunty Social. 2017. "Interview: Meera Syal." Accessed March 24, 2024. https://www.blackpoolsocial.club/24664-interview-meera-syal/.

Bhabha, Homi K. 1984. "Of Mimicry and Man: The Ambivalence of Colonial Discourse." *Discipleship* 28: 125–33.

———. 2004 [1984]. *The Location of Culture.* Routledge.

Brinker-Gabler, Gisela, ed. 1995. *Encountering the Other(s): Studies in Literature, History, and Culture.* State University of New York Press.

Bruzzi, Stella, and Pamela Church Gibson, eds. 2013. *Fashion Cultures Revisited: Theories, Explorations and Analysis.* Routledge.

Conrad, Joseph. 1897. "An Outpost of Progress." *Cosmopolis* 6: 609–20.

Deane, Seamus, ed. 1990. *Nationalism, Colonialism and Literature.* University of Minnesota Press.

Dunphy, Graeme. 2004. "Meena's Mockingbird: From Harper Lee to Meera Syal." *Neophilologus* 88: 637–59.

Fanon, Frantz. 1986. *Black Faces, White Masks.* Routledge.

Hall, Stuart. 1990. "Cultural Identity and Diaspora." In *Identity: Commu-*

nity, Culture, Difference, edited by Jonathan Rutherford, 222–37. Lawrence & Wishart.

Hulme, Keri. 2001 [1984]. *The Bone People.* Macmillan.

Kayışçı, Burcu. 2010. "Where Is Home? Where Are Roots? The Politics of Multiculturalism in *Anita and Me* and *White Teeth.*" *Interactions* 19: 41–52.

Lavie, Smadar, and Ted Swedenburg, eds. 2001 [1996]. *Displacement, Diaspora, and Geographies of Identity.* Duke University Press.

Lawson, Mark. 2017. "Front Row's Cultural Exchange: Meera Syal." Accessed March 24, 2024. https://www.bbc.co.uk/programmes/profiles/26T9Y1xc9GQHdqQNZ1fcXNV/meera-syal.

Neti, Leila. 2008. "Siting Speech: The Politics of Imagining the Other in Meera Syal's *Anita and Me.*" In *British Asian Fiction: Framing the Contemporary,* edited by Neil Murphy, 97–116. Cambria Press.

Pereira-Ares, Noemí. 2018. *Fashion, Dress and Identity in South Asian Diaspora Narratives: From the Eighteenth Century to Monica Ali.* Palgrave Macmillan.

Pratt, Mary Louise. 2002. *Imperial Eyes: Travel Writing and Transculturation.* Routledge.

Rath, Sura P. 2002. "Home(s) Abroad: Diasporic Identities in Third Spaces." Accessed March 24, 2024. https://legacy.chass.ncsu.edu/jouvert/v4i3/rath1.htm

———. 2000. "Three Homes." Accessed March 24, 2024. https://www.postcolonialweb.org/diasporas/rath1e.html.

Sartre, Jean-Paul. 1957. *Being and Nothingness: An Essay On Phenomenological Ontology.* Translated by Hazel Estella Barnes. University of Colorado Press.

Schoene-Harwood, Berthold. 1999. "Beyond (T)race: Bildung and Proprioception in Meera Syal's *Anita and Me.*" *Journal of Commonwealth Literature* 34: 159–68.

Stein, Mark. 2004. *Black British Literature: Novels of Transformation.* Ohio State University Press.

Stevenson, Robert Louis. 1999. *South Sea Tales.* Edited by Roslyn Nelly. Oxford University Press.

Syal, Meera. 2002. *Anita and Me.* Harper Perennial.

———. 2000. *Life Isn't All Ha Ha Hee Hee.* Harper Perennial.

Zubida, Hani, Liron Lavi, Robin A. Harper, Ora Nakash, and Anat Shoshani. 2013. "Home and Away: Hybrid Perspective on Identity Formation in 1.5 and 2nd Generation Adolescent Immigrants in Israel." *Glocalism: Journal of Culture, Politics and Innovation* 1: 1–28.

"Divided We Stand, Together We Fall": Identity, Biopolitics & Indian Minorities

Nishant Upadhyay, PhD.

Abstract

The rise of neo-nationalist political power and its impact on the social fabric of India has been a subject of ongoing discussions in both academic literature and the public sphere. One of the main pillars of Hindu nationalism has been its effort to devise political discourse for constituting a Hindu majority while marginalising other religious minorities. The fact that Hindu nationalism repeatedly has 'Other-ed' Indian Muslims has been focused on in literature. However, it is equally important to see how this 'Othering' shapes a 'Self.' The proposed chapter assesses how the Indian right-wing discourses have aimed to produce a monolith, political Hindu identity, subsuming its internal contradictions by instrumentalizing divides along the lines of sectarian identity and gender to divide Muslims first and then reconstitute them as a single 'Other.' This chapter argues that by instrumentalizing the internal divisions of Indian Muslims, the state has actively sought to use particular cases for making a stereotyped, universal 'Other' out of Indian Muslims, and through this, constituted Muslims as the 'Other' while constituting a Hindu 'Self.' This chapter demonstrates this by considering the case against Instant Triple Talaq— also known as Shayara Bano v. Union of India—to subsume religious authority, interpretation, and identity differences into a single 'frame.' Triple Talaq, or uttering a divorce thrice to divorce, is a valid form of divorce in Islam and constitutes a central practice of granting a divorce. However, a practice not-so-prevalent and banned in other Islamic countries, named *talaq-i-biddat* (instant divorce), became a subject of scrutiny, applied further by right-wing discourses in two major ways. First, it is a *problem* of all Muslims and, by extension, evidence of their incompatibility in the secular-democratic structure. Second, it became a way to fracture Muslim identity initially by 'saving Muslim women' through legislation and putting Muslims in a singular, undifferentiated category, and by default, defining Hindu men and women as 'free' and 'democratic.'

Keywords: Triple Talaq, Biopolitics, Hindu Nationalism, Indian Muslims, Identity Politics

Introduction

Since 2014, the rise of the Bhartiya Janta Party (BJP), India's right-wing Hindu nationalist party, has marked an unprecedented surge in the discourses vilifying Muslims. Neither Hindu-Muslim religious tensions nor the rise of the BJP is new to Indian politics is new to Indian politics. The rise of Modi and his brand of strongman politics in the parliament renewed the discourse of Hindu nationalism to a more aggressive position. Dubbed in the discourse of a Hindu majority, with some currents within the BJP arguing for a Hindu nation, the neo-nationalist discourse has targeted the Indian Muslim communities on multiple fronts. From the raging controversies on *hijab to* declaring Muslims as *outsiders and invaders to* physical violence in organised riots, the Hindu nationalist ideology has demonstrated the use of state and organised violence to legitimise its standing and othering of Muslims (Assadi 2024). Moreover, the discourses which emerge from the democratic participation of Muslims, such as through their interaction with juridical apparatuses and the courts, have also been appropriated by the right-wing to legitimise their standing and further their agenda, evident even during the COVID-19 Pandemic crisis (Tieri and Ranjan 2023, Amanullah, Nadaf and Neyazi 2023, Assadi 2024). The case of Shayara Bano v. The Union of India & Others (2017), also known commonly as the Triple Talaq case, is one of the best examples of such appropriation.

India, as a secular Republic, guarantees fundamental rights to all minorities, including Muslims. One of these rights, enshrined in Article 25(1) of the Indian constitution, guarantees a right "to freedom of conscience and the right freely to profess, practise and propagate religion." (The Constitution of India 1950). This guarantee is maintained through applying personal laws, another term for the Family Laws, which provide the right to religious freedom in one's personal and domestic life. In India, for Muslims, the laws on marriage, inheritance, and succession are stipulated in the Muslim Personal Law (Shariat) Application Act of 1937, while the issue of divorce and marriage dissolution are stipulated in the Dissolution of Muslim Marriages Act of 1939 (Kidwai and Engineer 2019). However, the Shayara Bano v. The Union of India & Others (2017) and the Supreme Court's judgment on the case highlights tensions between India's constitutional framework and personal laws and is also used by the Hindu nationalists to appropriate this tension in their discourse to further the marginalisation of Muslims.

While the construction of the *other in* these discourses is evident, this chapter aims to highlight how the *self* is produced in the context of Triple Talaq discourses. In constituting this *self*, Indian right-wing discourses produce a monolith, political Hindu identity, by subsuming its internal contradictions, such as gender and caste. In producing the Muslim *other*, the right-wing discourses instrumentally use the divides along the sectarian identity and gender issues by subsuming the diversity of opinions and approaches into a single category. In the case of Shayara Bano v. Union of India (2017), this chapter demonstrates that the right-wing discourses appropriated the court's judgments to subsume the cultural and religious authority of Indian Muslims to the Indian law, while using this issue as a tool to construct them as the *other* to invent a *self*.

Thus, in framing this issue as a *problem of* all Muslims, the right-wing discourses employed different tropes to fracture the community along the lines of gender, where it represents all Muslim men in a singularised category of *oppressors against* Muslim women who *need to be saved*. Through this, the Hindu right-wing produced a Hindu *self* which is characteristically opposite of the monolithic Muslim *other*. In this regard, this chapter aims to answer these questions: how does the Hindu nationalist agenda use these appropriate discourses and to what ends? What are the characteristics of the Muslim *other* and the Hindu *self*? How does it contribute to the legitimacy of the discourses of the BJP and its associates and its ideology and authority to construct the Hindu *Self*? This chapter assesses the Hindu communal discourses on Muslims on the issue of Triple Talaq through the lenses of Critical Discourse Analysis (CDA) and aims to understand how *the 'Self'* is constructed with regard to the *other*.

1. Background and Context

1.1. The Narratives of Othering

Communalism in the Indian context is defined by a strong sense of connection or allegiance to one's identity group (Malviya 2021). These identity groups in a communal context refer to religious identities, primarily Hindu and Muslim, where the Hindus are a numerical majority, while Muslims constitute a sizable minority. The communal issues in the context of India are not new and date back to the 1880s (Noorani 1990, Bakker 1991, Lal 2005). However, the emergence of the Hindu nationalist movement in the 1920s and the demand for a separate nation, Pakistan, in the 1930s led to communal riots, clashes, and pogroms, ultimately culminating in the Partition of India in 1947. However, the communal politics sustained in newly-formed and independent India at a different pace since the partition, leading to confrontation, riots, and violence in a more contained area around specific issues till the 1980s (Shani 2007, 3).

Other challenges, including the demands for linguistic reorganisation of the states in India, conflict and insurgencies, and other issues of identity, such as socio-cultural and cinematic representation vis-à-vis changing spectres of security post-9/11, furthered the divide, intensifying of communal differences (Sherman 2015, Drabu 2018, Jana 2022, Ahmd 2022, Karmakar and Caterall 2024, Kolås 2023a, Kolås 2023b, Ali 2025). The rise of a political party as the more cohesive right-wing movement in the 1980s, organised around the demand for the Rama Temple in the northern Indian small-town of Ayodhya, transformed *how* communalism is represented in national politics (Bakker 1991, Lal 2005, Mehta 2015, Jha and Jha 2016, Kishore 2016, Khurshid 2020, Mishra 2024). As a political discourse and an ideology, communalism constructs new binaries along the lines of religious identities while subsuming any internal contradictions in the name of facing the *other* (Engineer 1997, Upadhyay and Robinson 2012, Bhattacharya 2019, Sinha and Priyam 2023).

The Hindu nationalist narrative is built on the core idea that Muslims are *outsiders* on two grounds. First, it reappropriates the historical narratives of Islamic rule in India and represents the dynasties as *outsiders*. Second, in a more modern sense, it reappropriates the discourses from the partition of India and argues that Muslims belong to Pakistan, an Islamic country, which was made for them, and India should be the land for Hindus (Badri 2015, Å. Kolås 2023a, Assadi 2024). At the same time, the first narrative is built on the idea of erasing the Muslim cultural and historical existence in favour of presenting the Hindus as subalterns, manufacturing victimhood. The scholarship on Islamicate India denies any validity to such claims. Through the second narrative, Hindu nationalists aim to construct Muslim *otherness in* terms of the nation while constructing their *self* in similar terms. In other words, if all the Muslims belong to Pakistan, ergo, India belongs to Hindus. These narratives have been at the centre of *othering* Muslims in different parts of India, also acquiring a violent form targeting Indian Muslims. This framework of exteriorising and *othering* Muslims is reconstituted in other discourses that Hindu nationalist groups and institutions either produce or appropriate against Muslims. One such avenue exists in the appropriation of discourses on gender rights.

1.2. Gender, Gender Justice, and Appropriating Discourses

In Indian law and personal laws, gender justice and equality have been a significant debate. On the one hand, the Indian Constitution guarantees the rights of equality to all, notwithstanding gender, caste, race or other markers of identity (Baxi 2007, Srikantan 2017, Sindhu 2021). On the other hand, Personal Laws are alleged to protect certain traditional norms, primarily in terms of inheritance, and appear to be biased against women. However, personal laws cannot be challenged or read about the Articles in the Constitution guaranteeing the rights of equality, as the former preserves and guarantees religious and cultural rights (Khurshid 2018, Agnes 2017, Agnes 2019). Gender stands at a complicated intersection where Indian women, and more particularly, Indian women from marginalised backgrounds and categories of caste and minority religions, face a bind comparable to the Black and Indigenous American women in the United States concerning race (Ceserani 2020, Sindhu 2021). The discourse on gender, when entering the orbit of Personal Laws, therefore, becomes charged with debates around religiosity, religious existence, and preserving cultural rights (Engineer 1992, Engineer 2011). This has been the case with the issue of a particular divorce practice, *talaq-i-biddat* or *talaq-i-bida*, more commonly known as instant Triple Talaq. This practice entailed a man reciting *talaq* or divorce thrice, through any medium i.e., written, oral, and in some cases, electronic, leading to an instant divorce without any mediation (Saxena and Sen 2021, 53).

Shayara Bano, the appellant in this case, approached the Supreme Court after being divorced from a marriage of fifteen years, challenging the practice of instant triple talaq, polygamy, and *niqah halala* violating several fundamental rights. In the petition, Bano's representative argued that such practices, protected by the personal laws, violated Article 14's provision of equality before law, Article 15's provision of non-discrimination, Article 21's provision of right to life with dignity, and Article 25's provisions of right to freedom of conscience and religion (The Constitution of India 1950).

The defendants, which included several Ministries but also, the All India Muslim Personal Law Board (AIMPLB)—a non-governmental body which represents the interests of Indian Muslims with regard to the Personal Law. In response to the petition, the AIMPLB argued that uncodified Muslim Personal Law is beyond the court's jurisdiction as it is not subject to the constitutional judicial review and challenges the "essential practices" of Islam and Islamic faith which are protected under Article 25 of the Constitution. One of the core issues in front of the Supreme Court was, therefore, to establish whether the practice of talaq-i-biddat was an essential practice to Islam and whether it violates the fundamental rights as laid out in the Constitution. Based on these points, the issue of gender justice for the court was secondary to establishing whether the practice qualifies as an essential, and therefore, a protected practice.

In this context, Indian and global media largely echoed the simplified narratives and represented this case regarding *gender justice,* continuing in line with Indian judiciary and media's pitching of minority rights discourses against gender rights discourses, as Agnes (2007) and Baxi (2007) note in the instances of evoking "Uniform Civil Code" debate before the Triple Talaq controversy (Agnes 2007, Baxi 2007, Wu 2017, Safi 2017, Agnes 2017, Agnes 2018b, Piedalue, Gilbertson and Raturi 2021). While the issues of equality and inequality—primarily about gender—are not rooted in a particular religion, as patriarchic norms and practices pervade through most societies and their religious practices, the singling out of talaq-i-biddat represented a contradictory norm by the Hindu right, in particular, and Indian media, in general (Piedalue, Gilbertson and Raturi 2021, Zainab 2021, Parveen 2022). Besides the selective approach of championing gender justice for Muslim women while employing oppressive norms, discourses, and symbolics against Hindu women, Hindu majoritarianism aimed to exert control and authority over the discourses of gender justice rather than committing to the welfare and equality of women (Agnes 2019).

This also remains starkly evident in three simple facts that constitute the fallacy of Hindu nationalism and the popular reading of this case. Firstly, while the Hindu nationalists were posing themselves as a champion of gender justice on the grounds of defending abandoned Muslim women, out of 2.3 million abandoned women in India, 2 million are Hindu (Agnes 2019). This notion of gender justice was weaponised as a tool of othering and a distraction from addressing the depth of the issue (Agnes 2017, Agnes 2018a, 277). Secondly, the court's judgment, with a divided opinion 3:2, was not passing a judgment on the Muslims but on the fact whether the practice is essential to Islam. In addition, the court's judgment did not favour Hindu nationalists; however, through their discourses, they aligned and juxtaposed their positions with the judgment. Thirdly, in appropriating the discourse of gender justice and furthering it by bringing legislation to the Parliament with the majority, the Hindu nationalist position also opened the personal laws, including the Hindu code, to the scrutiny of law, which undermines their authority as representatives of Hindus or other religious communities, such as the Buddhists, Jains or Sikhs who are classified in the broader term 'Hindu' in the Indian constitution (Mahmood 2014).

In addition, the court's judgment—and the case in particular—only questioned the specific practice of *instant* Triple Talaq. Whereas the procedure of giving a divorce in Islamic law, where the marriages are contractual, remains in the form of uttering the word divorce thrice. The standard practice only differs among the Shi'i and Sunni (and other denominations within them) with the different interpretations throughout *iddat*, i.e., whether it is three months or two months where it is recited twice again after the first utterance (Kidwai and Engineer 2019). In the context of this case's facts and issues along with the fallacies of appropriation, this chapter aims to interrogate the public and political discourses around this case. In appropriating the court's judgment to their end—along with the plight of women and gender justice organisations—the

165

BJP and its functionaries produced an image of their leadership of gender justice. Through this *self*—which is more political than ontological—the BJP employed discourses which directly fed their core agenda of marginalising Muslims and exerted further control of the state in the spheres of personal law. To investigate a range of themes, symbolics, and imageries in these discourses, which are unique to the Indian political context, this chapter will use Critical Discourse Analysis (CDA) to focus on discourse structure, symbolism, ideology, and intent to give detailed consideration to the construction of the *self* by framing the *other*.

2. Theoretical Framework and Methodology

In the Indian context, the multitude of identities, e.g., religious, linguistic, and sectarian, to name a few, play an essential role in producing political discourses and determining the audience. Moreover, identity politics has played a significant role in sustaining India's democratic institutions and representation of various identities, acting as checks and balances against majoritarianism (Badri 2015). This is evident in India's linguistic diversity and representation, caste-based representations, and their role in sustaining local politics. However, since 2014, there has been a polarisation of identities—especially along the communal lines—leading to other identities, such as caste, sectarian, and gender identities, to be subsumed into the larger religious *Hindu* and Muslim binaries. This does not mean that the issues and grievances within these identities have ended; instead, the Hindu nationalist discourses have successfully produced a substratum of discourse which appeals to other identities, such as caste, and allows them space to participate in the Hindu nationalist political vision. Since the production of such *new* categories functions in discursive representations of the *Other*, assessing discourses, particularly their promulgation in the public and political spheres, is essential. In this context, Othering refers to "the process of distinguishing a person or a group as fundamentally different from, and often inferior to, another." (Å. Kolås 2023a) Such analysis requires to account for the sociocultural contexts within which these discourses emerge, articulate, and function.

Critical Discourse Analysis (CDA) is essential for investigating identity discourses. The discourses promulgated around identity imbibe culturally specific epistemological, ideological, and ontological imagery, which is critical for their legitimisation and acceptance. In such a context, assessing the binaries' elements that correspond to the identities, including the imageries, symbolics, historical contexts, and localised representations that construct and reinforce power dynamics, is crucial. Moreover, the CDA highlights the modes in which "social-power abuse and inequality are enacted, reproduced, legitimated and resisted." (van Dijk 2015, 466) Rather than merely describing the identities, the CDA assesses how discourse structures enact, confirm, and legitimise power dynamics and structures (van Dijk 2015, 467–468). While the other methods to assess discourses, such as Discourse Analysis (DA), merely focus on discourse structures, the CDA brings discourse structures into a dialogue with socio-political and cultural issues that provide a broader interpretive licence (Fairclough and Wodak 1997). When assessing binaries—as demonstrated in Said's *opus* Orientalism – the discursive control of representation is apparent in constructing the Orient as the *Other* and simultaneously the *Self* in the form of the Occident.

This also represents the power of inclusion and exclusion of an institution. In understanding identities, the role of an institution in promulgating a *truth*—which Said (1975) noted as just another form of representation —occurs even in a context where the *Other* is either silent/incapable or vocal/capable of representing itself (Said 1978). Moreover, the power of inclusion and exclusion is neither asserted arbitrarily nor in a pre-devised manner. Instead, it is aligned with political and ideological paradigms. Therefore, the creation of the *other* occurs in a spatial context framed within the cultural, ideological, historical, and political currents (Vujačić 2015). In the context of the Triple Talaq case, the discourses from the government and the ruling party were promulgated with an ideological bias of exclusion, framing Muslims, their cultural practices, and religiosity by overriding the internal differences along the lines of sectarian affiliation, socio-economic standings, and ethnolinguistic identities. In doing so, these discourses implicitly constructed a *self* which represented different values, however, like the *Other's* misrepresentation, represented the *self* as sustained by the lack of internal contradictions.

This chapter relies on media discourses in India to access the public and political narratives and meanings. The rise of electronic media in India, with widespread circulation, has made such discourses accessible to households, strengthening the role these discourses play in creating a narrative and garnering legitimacy. Besides, the BJP has relied extensively on media for public outreach, including fake news and distortion of facts, and this makes the role of media more potent than in conventional contexts. In other words, the role of media—equally with the emergence of uncritical and ideologically pro-BJP media—has evolved as a promulgator of public and political discourses, colluded as one. However, this chapter accounts for various media sources, including the electronic formats of the newspapers, such as the Hindu, Times of India, Hindustan Times, and popular media channels, such as NDTV and Aaj Tak, to name a few. In using these sources to acquire data on how the BJP and Hindu nationalist ideologues and politicians have constructed and framed the Muslim *other*, this chapter accesses the subtle references to the *self*. This *self*, defined in communal terms, is similar to Muslim *others in* how comprehensive and united it is; however, quality-wise, it is the polar opposite of the Muslim *other*.

The selected discourses are from 2016 onwards since the writ petition was filed in the Supreme Court this year, and a majority of the political discourses have been promulgated since then. However, despite the end of the case with the Supreme Court's final judgment in 2017 and the passing of the Muslim Women (Protection of Rights on Marriage) Bill 2019 in the Indian parliament, the issue has re-emerged time again in the context of electoral speeches in both the national elections of 2019 and 2024 and numerous other state elections in this period. In using the CDA on the discourses, this chapter will look at how the conception of *the other* and the *self* are created, the structural differences in representation and misrepresentations, and the interpretation of the symbolics and context of these discourses.

For example, Prime Minister Narendra Modi gave this speech during the 2024 electoral campaign, where he remarked that "we have saved the entire Muslim family" by bringing the legislation against the Triple Talaq (Press Trust of India 2024). Moreover, in comparing the practice with "the fear of the sword hanging over," Modi asserts that he has "liberated" Muslim women (Press Trust of India 2024). In using the first person plural pronoun of "we" along with liberation, Modi's speech leaves the category open-ended, i.e., whether this "we" refers to Hindus, the BJP, or the people in that context. Similarly, in underlining this *achievement*, Modi involves himself by suggesting that "for centuries to come, Muslim daughters will continue to bless Modi." (*Press Trust of India* 2024) From framing the relationship with Muslim women in terms of "father-daughter," Modi asserts his authority in paternalistic terms while also subtly alienating the "saved" Muslim women from the *other*, i.e., Muslim men.

3. "What Is Bad in Theology is Bad in Law," But Is it Bad in Public Too?

3.1. Media Discourse Between Identities and their Intersection

In the Supreme Court's judgment, in siding with the majority opinion, Justice Kurian remarked that "what is held to be bad in the Holy Quran cannot be good in Shariat and, what is bad in theology is bad in law as well." (The Supreme Court of India 2017) Remarking on the point that provided such a practice—which is arbitrary—even if followed by a majority of the people, cannot constitute an essential element of faith. Justice Kurian's reasoning does not seem applicable in the growing environment of majoritarianism in Indian politics. The discourses from the BJP on the Triple Talaq during the hearing evoked controversial statements. In shaping the Muslim *other*, the statements from the BJP reflected an active effort to vilify and frame Islamic divorce procedure and religious values while drawing an apparent rift along the lines of gender. While Muslim men were painted in the Orientalist tropes of being violent, sexually aggressive, unjust, and barbaric against vulnerable Muslim women – both in terms of justice from the Muslim society and sexually insofar they are represented as objects of Muslim men – need protection, and saving (Simons 2003, 24-25, Muslim Public Affairs Committee 2023). Such construction of the identity serves towards garnering—if not realistic, then at least discursive—polarisation in the identity of Muslims, further isolating Muslim men and women.

This is evident in the remarks from one of the BJP ministers from the Indian state of Uttar Pradesh, where he suggested that "[they] abandon their children, wives to beg on the roads." (Press Trust of India 2017c) On the one hand, such imagery reflects the vulnerability of Muslim women. On the other hand, it serves as a justification for both the BJP's political purpose and to marginalise Muslim men as unfit, unjust, and impulsive. In the same statement, this minister added that "without a rhyme or reason, they divorce their wives, and constantly change their wives to satiate their lust." (Press Trust of India 2017c) In a direct tone, such a statement frames Muslim divorces in a light where Muslim men's authority over women is ultimate, unilateral, and unjust. This statement also raises a question about Muslim marriage and family structure. It contributes to another debate which was going on over the case of *love jihad*, where Muslim men were accused of targeting, grooming, and converting non-Muslim women to leave them ultimately.

Adding to this, another BJP central minister, Swamy, supported Maurya's remarks and argued that "Islam permits men to commit atrocities against women" further adding that "Maulana's may disguise the fact but this is the reality of Muslim religion." (Associate News of India 2017) The narrative of patriarchal oppression associated explicitly with Islam has been borne out of Orientalist and neo-Orientalist representations of Islam, with the Hindu right's discourses contributing further to it. The idea to problematise Islam, as Swamy brings it, has been a central theme of Hindu right-wing discourses both to exteriorise and marginalise Muslims. Moreover, such claims also fuel an existing stereotype, mainly borne out of the Western discourses towards Muslims since the colonial period. In constructing a Muslim *other*, the Hindu *self* aimed to identify itself with values such as democratic, free, and just. However, the construction of the Hindu *self* has not always been that implicit. Instead, the discourse against Triple Talaq was also constructed by bringing Hindu cultural and religious idioms and images into its construction. Evidently, through such comparison, the aim was to reach a broader non-Muslim audience, to bring the religious idiom of the Hindu *self* for legitimacy, and finally, to construct a framework of moral and value judgments to impose externally.

This is evident in another BJP leader and Chief Minister of Uttar Pradesh, Yogi Adityanath's statement. In comparing the silence of certain sections of Indian politics, he was referring to the opposition party and the Muslim leaders, with the silence of people in the Hindu epic Mahabharata's scene of robbing Draupadi's clothes in a king's court (Press Trust of India 2017f). In equating the need for justice and dignity of Muslim women with Draupadi, Adityanath openly framed the opposition in terms of "the accomplices," bringing an ideological element of framing the opposition in negative terms (Press Trust of India 2017f).

In addition, his statement appeals to an open polarisation of religious identity and politics in framing BJP and the Hindu *self* in explicit opposition to the opposition parties and the Muslim *other*. In the cultural context, the story of Draupadi's cloth-robbing represents an evident injustice

kept silent by those in power, along with the start of the war of righteousness, as it is represented in the Mahabharata. Implicitly, Yogi's statement
reflected a division within the Muslim *other*, where Muslim women require saving and external intervention while representing Muslim men
as oppressors in terms of both Triple Talaq and Hindu mythology's reli-
gio-cultural imagery.

Similar to Yogi's speech, which draws upon cultural and religious elements
for the more explicit construction of the Hindu *self*, other discourses incorporated similar elements, albeit towards a different end. In the case
of the All India Shia Personal Law Board (AISPLB), the discourses from
the board primarily contested the AIMPLB, which arguably represented
Sunni interests. The sectarian fracture within the Muslim *self*, however,
employed a different discourse, which, on the one hand, appears to confirm a majoritarian position. However, on the other hand, it can be seen
as a struggle for authority to represent the Muslims and their political and
religious interests. In his statement, the Shia Board's Chairman Abbas argued that a mere boycott of those who practice Triple Talaq would not be
enough and that there must be "to enact a strict law against triple talaq in
one go that is similar to the anti-sati law to prevent any Muslim woman
from getting victimised and ensure that the culprit is punished." (Press
Trust of India 2017a, Press Trust of India 2017c)

Comparing Triple Talaq with *sati*, a practice of immolating a woman
on her husband's pyre, reflects a twofold construction. Firstly, it brings
Triple Talaq into a morally apprehensible fold of Sati, a practice that has
been banned and condemned morally. While reflecting a difference in
the Muslim *self*, such demand subtly plays a role in claiming authority to
construct a moral and political framework in the eyes of the Hindu other.
Secondly, it more explicitly shows a Muslim *self*, which is divided along
the lines of the issue of Triple Talaq against a unified Hindu *other*, united
against the issue of Triple Talaq.

While comparing two different practices, the Shia position tries to bring
it into a moral framework at the intersection of law and religiosity. Moreover, using the equivalence of Sati for Triple Talaq in public discourse
can be read as a strategy for pitching the sectarian *self* against the *other* in
terms of authority. This is evident in Abbas' statement again, suggesting
that in the Shia community, "there has been no place for triple talaq in

one go." (Press Trust of India 2017a) In constructing a Shia *self* against a Sunni *other*, Maulana Abbas—as the chairman of AISPLB—is using his authority to produce an alternative definition within the Muslim *self*, challenging the interpretations of the Hindu *other* at large. However, rather than understanding this in terms of a sectarian split, this should be seen in the context of an institutional split equally, where two Boards, i.e., the AIMPLB and the AISPLB, are contesting for the authority of representing Islam in an interpretive sense and Muslims in the institutional sense. Moreover, Abbas' statement does not emerge in a vacuum and should be interpreted in two interconnected discursive contexts.

A similar equivalence was raised in the Supreme Court hearing by the appellant side, i.e., the Union of India, arguing that if religious practices, such as Untouchability and Sati, could be outlawed and banned, why should instantaneous Triple Talaq be an exception (Scroll News Staff 2017). Moreover, in countering the argument about the Triple Talaq having customary status, the appellant side also argued that given that human sacrifice is older, does it allow validity to the practice as a custom (Press Trust of India 2017d)? The use of equivalence, from the courtroom to the public discourse, reflects how these discourses, particularly equivalences and tropes, are appropriated in constructing the *self* and the *other*. However, using such analogies, while provocative and attention-grabbing, constitutes a slippery slope fallacy. Moreover, fallaciously situating these different practices into a single category also produces new problems. For example, untouchability was an act against different types of identities, i.e., social and ethnic groups of people, that were targeted towards an individual. The Triple Talaq is an issue of personal law, i.e., a matter between two people in the marriage contract. The demands of criminalisation, vocal from both the Union of India and AISPLB, also serve as an avenue to transform the discourse back into the juridico-political fold.

The second interconnected discursive context of Maulana Abbas' statement comes from Narendra Modi's media-released statements at the BJP's national executive committee meeting. Modi emphasised "delivering justice to our Muslim sisters" while not willing to cause "any conflicts in Muslim society" over the Triple Talaq issue (Indo-Asian News Service 2017). In framing Triple Talaq as a "bad practice," Modi argued for resolving it through "awakening the society." (Indo-Asian News Service 2017) However, with the Supreme Court already considering the case, such social resolutions were neither possible nor approached. In addition, Modi's speech hints at a turn towards a more amicable resolution, in contrast to the statements made by the party members. This change in tone is not a product of an ideological change. Instead, such an approach allows the BJP leadership to raise a stake in claiming the outcomes of the democratic process, along with building a narrative for change or criminalisation outside the institutional frameworks. Maulana Abbas' statement representing the Shia Waqf Board highlights the trope of criminalisation in a new light. This further produces dissension in the Muslim *other* for the Hindu *self*, producing a binary within the Muslim *other*, where one section respects democratic norms, reasonable, and just against those who are not.

3.2. Constructing the Other and the Self

In the 2017 Independence Day speech, Modi reinforced the narrative of the Muslim *other*, with a particular focus on the role of Muslim women. In his speech, Modi emphasised the role of Muslim women "who had to lead miserable lives due to Triple Talaq" in starting a movement which "created an environment in the whole nation against the practice." (Press Trust of India 2017e) In addition to praising Muslim women, he said their success is inevitable as "the whole country supports them in this significant step towards women's empowerment." (Press Trust of India 2017e) Through embedding values, Modi's speech played a role in constructing an imaginary narrative emphasising values. Modi's speech uses the phrase "the whole nation" to produce a tripartite effect. On the first level, it constructs a form of *national* narrative. In this narrative, anyone who opposes the idea is naturally excluded from the narrative.

On the second level, through "the whole nation" and its relation with other positive elements, such as the end of miserable life and women empowerment, Modi constructed a value judgment. Any opposition to such values, whether on an ideological or religious basis, naturally posits the individual or group against other associated values. With the narrative of the whole nation, Modi also aimed to construct a Hindu *self*, reflecting his ideological proclivities. This is also evident in the fact that by producing a rift in the Muslim *other*—both in terms of gender and in terms of the stand towards the Triple Talaq—a Hindu *self* fills the category of "the whole nation." On the final level, Modi's assertion of "the whole nation" in the above terms also reflects his call for authority and legitimacy as a Prime Minister with the majority in the parliament and the ability to speak for "the whole nation." Narratives with value judgments produce a discursive structure that is inclusive and exclusive by the values associated with them, not the context or diversity of opinions or perspectives. Such narratives, while based on assumptions, e.g., the whole nation, can reinforce values as the site of judgment. Modi's speech, while including Muslim women who are victims of Triple Talaq, excludes those who are in the opposition, both from a democratic and inclusive narrative of Triple Talaq and from the imagination of the "whole nation."

Supreme Court's judgment on the case on August 22, 2017, played a significant role in the political discourses in the public sphere. In the judgment, the five judges of the Constitutional bench had a divided mandate of 3:2, with the majority siding for declaring the practice unconstitutional (Saxena and Sen 2021, 54-55). Two Justices held the practice unconstitutional on the grounds of its arbitrariness and found it to be regulated by the Shariat Act of 1937 (The Supreme Court of India 2017). Another Justice in the majority opinion suggested that the practice of instantaneous Triple Talaq is against theology and law, and mere religious sanctions by the masses cannot validate it. In remarking, "what is held to be bad in the Holy Qur'an cannot be good in Shariat and, what is bad in theology is bad in law as well," the justice argued that the lack of textual authority becomes the ground for a practice's rejection as an essential religious practice (The Supreme Court of India 2017).

In contrast, the dissenting opinion argued that this is a matter of personal law and, therefore, no constitutional intervention is possible. Moreover, Chief Justice Khehar and Justice Nazeer—two of the dissenting justices —remarked that the practice should be considered an essential part of Islam, provided it is an article of belief among several Muslims. In addition, the practice did not violate any exceptions mentioned in Article 25(1) of the Constitution, given that Shariat or Muslim Personal Law is not based on any state legislative action (The Supreme Court of India 2017). Supreme Court's judgment had a few critical implications on the political discourses around this case.

One of the grounds for declaring the Triple Talaq was its arbitrariness. This aspect validated partial aspects of the BJP's discourse against the practice. In the BJP's discourse, arbitrariness was associated with tropes like injustice, the sword hanging on the head, and other similar claims in the statements. While these discourses first emerged as ideological-ly motivated, the judicial outcome was appropriated politically towards strengthening the legitimacy of BJP's discourses. Secondly, this provided the BJP—in the majority—with the means to draft legislation to ban this practice. In doing so, the BJP brought versions of the Muslim Women (The Protection of Rights in Marriage) Bill in 2018, passed as a law in 2019 (S. Sinha 2019, The Government of India 2019). This act voided and criminalised the utterance of Triple Talaq and the practice of instan-taneous Talaq in all forms, be it written, spoken, or via electronic means. Despite the limits of criminalisation in making any social change, this was one of the first incidences of criminalisation of any aspect of Personal Law. It allows the state to extend its control in the interpersonal sphere, rendering already vulnerable Muslim minorities further subject to the scrutiny of the state (Agnes 2018b).

This also provides disproportionate power to the discourses, especially targeting Muslim men, and opens the door for criminalising other aspects of Personal Law and interpersonal relationships, which transitioned from being a part of civil disputes to criminal jurisdiction. Criminalising this practice also opened the doors for attaching value judgments and pro-ducing new discourses of marginalisation, along with validating the BJP's discourse of championing gender justice and saving Muslim women. This is evident in how the BJP used the issue of Triple Talaq in constructing the Hindu *self* in the coming elections through sustaining aggressive dis-courses at the Muslim *other*. In the Independence Day speech of 2019, during his second term, Modi framed Triple Talaq discourse in terms of tropes like suffering, fear, and evil. Suggesting that the Muslim women "had been suffering under this custom," and "were scared as they suffered due to the practice of Triple Talaq." (Indo-Asian News Service 2019) In bringing back the equivalence of the divorce custom, Modi argued that "when we can ban Sati." strong steps against female infanticide, child mar-riage, then why not this (Indo-Asian News Service 2019) In bringing dis-parate practices into equivalence, Modi's speech aimed to draw—even if based on faulty comparison—the justification for criminalisation. In ad-dition, Modi's statement and its general outlook portray Muslim women as individuals without any agency, and therefore, justify this intervention on their behalf.

In constructing the Muslim *other*, Modi's speech sows a divide along the lines of gender again. On the one hand, Muslim men are represented as aggressive, tyrants, arbitrary, and lacking respect towards women, whereas Muslim women live on their mercy and under their fear. On the other hand, representing Muslim women as subalterns, oppressed, subject to tyranny, and unable to act on their behalf, Modi's speech further appropriated the judicial outcome in favour of his political agenda. With Modi's agency in framing this discourse, he implicitly constructs the Hindu *self* in reference to the Muslim *other* vis-a-vis in appropriating the judicial outcome as his achievement. In this context, Modi's projected Hindu *self* reflects itself in binary opposition to the Muslim *other* as democratic, assertive, just, respectful of women, and gender just. While the two Independence Day speeches considered here show how Modi framed these issues with political authority and legitimacy as the Prime Minister, his speech during an election rally frames a similar picture, albeit with slightly more volatile categories.

In addressing an election rally in the northern Indian province of Uttar Pradesh, Modi framed the practice of instantaneous Triple Talaq as "an evil practice" while re-affirming the appropriate discourse of being a saviour of Muslim women (Press Trust of India 2024). In reaching the Muslim populated constituencies, Modi presented the legislation as "a strong law in the interest of millions of Muslim sisters" but also for "their parents and brothers who were always worried" about their daughter and sisters getting divorced (Press Trust of India 2024). Modi's discourse aimed to frame the discourse on Triple Talaq in terms of values, i.e., bad practice and good abolition, to a larger audience of Muslims. It is evident in Modi's speech to lure Muslim men into the fold of benefit, even if that is in apparent contradiction with the idea that it targeted Muslim men through criminalisation. Modi further argued that by ending the practice of Triple Talaq, he has "saved the entire Muslim family and liberated it from the fear of the sword hanging over" their heads (Press Trust of India 2024).

In contrast to the speech from Independence Day, a significant difference in this speech emerges in the form of Modi's extension of the *other* to include Muslim men. Through this, Modi aimed to appeal for votes and appear as the saviour of Muslim socio-cultural life. In appropriating Muslim men in the fold of this discourse, Modi aimed to draw a clear line, demarcating a broader conception of the *other in* terms similar to good Muslim bad Muslim. In contrast to this new Muslim *other*, the Hindu *self* is mediated by Modi's authority and legitimacy for the welfare of Hindus and Muslims, even if such welfare comes by opening a new door for meddling in Personal Laws. In the electoral context, Modi's efforts to keep a more open and inclusive discourse show ideology's malleability. In reconstituting the *other*, Modi's discourse frames the Muslim *other* in the sense of victims, where the Hindu *self* emerges as a saviour for all Muslims, including the Muslim family and family values. Another possible interpretation of this change rests in the ability of the BJP to exert control and power to reorganise identities and the limits of inclusion and exclusion to assert further control over Muslims. In other words, by including Muslim men as the beneficiaries of the Act against Triple Talaq, Modi's speech aims to reconstitute and redefine the boundaries of the one who is progressive and, therefore, a good Muslim against those who oppose and, therefore, a bad Muslim.

Conclusion

Muslims remain one of the most underdeveloped and backward communities in India in terms of their socio-economic growth, educational levels, and access to the benefits of India's growth since the 1990s. In this context, the BJP's focus on the issue of instantaneous Triple Talaq as that of "national importance" in explicit terms, while as a tool of propaganda which defines the existence of Muslims in India as the *other* in implicit terms is nothing short of a gimmick. From the negative constructions of the Muslim *other to* the demands of criminalisation, the discourses from Hindu right on Triple Talaq employ the religious and political tropes specific to the Indian context.

Whether Draupadi's cloth-robbing or negative portrayals of Islam as unjust towards women, the construction of a Muslim *other* is undertaken by giving positive attributes to the Hindu *self*. In this light, the negative association of qualities with the Muslim other—which includes a reuse of the Orientalist portrayals—the Hindu *self* is constructed in an idiom which upholds democratic values, gender-just, and inclusive. At the same time, the efforts to redraw the boundaries of the Muslim *other* were instrumental to the BJP's efforts to appropriate the instantaneous Triple Talaq discourse from the judiciary into politics and from Muslim women to the ambit of communal politics.

Moreover, the political appropriation of this issue also invigorated another divide within the Muslim *other*, which can be defined in terms of the struggle for religious authority and representation rather than in sectarian terms. The statement by the AISPLB's chairman, Maulana Abbas, represents the rift, especially how the existing differences in religious interpretation and practices appear sectarian and dissident discourses. At the same time, they are merely assertions of different interpretations. However, in the case of the AISPLB, the equivalence of the instantaneous Triple Talaq with Sati and demands criminalisation support the narratives of the Hindu *self* while negotiating the reconstitution of the Muslim *self* along the lines of a Shia interpretation and representation. Moreover, the stance of AISPLB challenges the Hindu *self*'s construction of the Muslim *other* in an absolute sense, as such rifts highlight generalisation and also challenge the unified, monolith representation of the Hindu *self*.

In the post-judgment period, the right-wing discourse on the instantaneous Triple Talaq revolved around its criminalisation and has been framed in terms of value judgments. In other words, the BJP—through its targeted discourses—aimed to produce an image of the Muslim *other* which vilified Muslim men at the cost of depicting Muslim women as victims and oppressed. This distinction allowed the BJP to appropriate the court's judgment to an extent to its end. At the same time, they also use the legislative power to bring the interpersonal into the ambit of criminal. Through criminalisation, the BJP aimed to push the Muslim *other to* the margins of both constitutional democracy and national imagination. Within democracy, the BJP's ability to appropriate the Supreme Court's judgment to set a precedent for intervening in Personal Laws also inaugurated the spectre of further intervention. This also sets a precedent to highlight certain practices of Muslims in a negative light. In terms of national imagination, political and religious elements used in the framing of the Muslim *other* depict this *other* in terms incompatible with the democratic values, partly by rooting those values in the description of the Hindu *self*.

Hindu nationalist agenda, with its blatant Islamophobia, has been built around the facets of challenging and controlling the Muslim religious and cultural existence in India, based on the view of India as a Hindu land. The use of majoritarianism to devise and renegotiate the constitutional provisions, along with appropriating discourses for justice emerging from the community's participation in democratic institutions, has characterised the BJP's strategy to marginalise Muslims. Constructing a Muslim *other*, which is vilified to construct a Hindu*self* emerges as one of the avenues in which the BJP and its associates claim the authority of representing the Hindu majority. However, this majority, divided by linguistic, ethnic, caste-based, gendered, and other differences, is as artificial and instrumental as the Muslim *other*. In contrast to the Indian state's vision of 'Unity in Diversity' and 'Together We Stand, Divided We Fall' to deal with a plethora of complex identities, BJP's opportunistic and reductive approach boils down to creating new categories which are mutually exclusive. Therefore, the new mantra for this vision could best be 'Divided We Stand, Together We Fall.'

References

Agnes, Flavia. 2019. "Aggressive Hindu Nationalism: Contextualising the Triple Talaq Controversy." In *Majoritarian State: How Hindu Nationalism is Changing India*, edited by Anagana P. Chatterji, Thomas Blom Hansen and Christopher Jaffrelot, 335-352. New Delhi: Oxford University Press.

Agnes, Flavia. 2007. "The Supreme Court, the Media, and the Uniform Civil Code Debate in India." In *The Crisis of Secularism in India*, edited by Anuradha Dingwaney Needham and Rajeswari Sunder Rajan, 294-315. New York: Duke University Press. doi:https://doi.org/10.1 515/9780822388418-017.

Agnes, Flavia, interview by Anupama Katakam. 2018b. *There Is a Misconception about Triple Talaq* Frontline Magazine. https://frontline.the-hindu.com/the-nation/there-is-a-misconception-about-triple-talaq/article10036300.ece.

Agnes, Flavia. 2018a. "Triple Talaq Controversy: Gender Concerns and Minority Safeguards." In *Discourses on Rights in India: Debates and Dilemmas*, edited by Bijaylaxmi Nanda and Nupur Ray, 273-296. Delhi: Routledge India.

Agnes, Flavia. 2017. "Triple Talaq: Gender Concerns and Minority Safeguards within a Communalised Polity, Can Conditional Nikahnama Offer a Solution." *National University of Juridical Sciences (NUJS) Law*

Review 427-450. https://nujslawreview.org/wp-content/uploads/20 17/07/10-%E2%80%93-3-%E2%80%93-Flavia-Agnes.pdf.

Ahmed, Saeed. 2022. "Muslim Pasts and Presents: Displacement and City-Making in a Delhi Neighbourhood." *Modern Asian Studies* 56 (6): 1872-1900. doi:https://doi.org/10.1017/S0026749X21000512.

Ali, Sagik. 2025. "The Changing Dynamics and Othering of Muslims in Bollywood Films: Rereading Sarfarosh (1999) and New York (2009)." *National Identities* 1-14. doi:https://doi.org/10.1080/14608944.202 5.2460499.

Amanullah, Arshad, Arif Hussain Nadaf, and Taberez Ahmed Neyazi. 2023. "Constructing the Muslim 'Other': A Critical Discourse Analysis of Indian News Coverage of the Tablighi Jamaat Congregation During the COVID-19 Pandemic." *Journalism.* doi:https://doi.org/10.1177/146 48849231188260.

Assadi, Muzaffar. 2024. *The 'Othering' of Muslims.* 14 05. https://www. deccanherald.com/opinion/the-othering-of-muslims-3023121.

Associate News of India. 2017. *Muslim Women Have 'Third Class Status' in Islam, Says Subramanian Swamy.* 29 04. ttps://www.business-standard.com/article/politics/muslim-women-have-third-class-status-in-islam-says-subramanian-swamy-117042900198_1.html.

Badri, Narayan. 2015. "Democracy and Identity Politics in India: Is It a Snake or a Rope?" *Economic and Political Weekly* 50 (16): 61-65. http://www.jstor.org/stable/24482067.

Bakker, Hans. 1991. "Ayodhya—a Hindu Jerusalem." *Numen* 38 (1): 80-109. doi:https://doi.org/10.1163/156852791X00051.

Baxi, Upendra. 2007. "Secularism in the Uniform Civil Code." In *The Crisis of Secularism in India*, edited by Anuradha Dingway Needham and Rajeswari Sundar Rajan, 267-293. Oberlin: Duke University Press.

Bhattacharya, Abhik. 2019. *Debate: It is Islamophobia—Not Only Communalism—We Encounter Everyday in India.* 17 05. https://thewire.in/communalism/debate-india-islamophobia-communalism-india.

Ceserani, Francesca. 2020. *Evaluating India's Supreme Court Judgment on* the Instant Divorce *"Triple Talaq"*. *Did the Verdict Build a Real Momentum for Gender Equality?* Berlin: GRIN Verlag.

Drabu, Onaiza. 2018. "Who Is the Muslim? Discursive Representations of the Muslims and Islam in Indian Prime-Time News." *Religions* 9 (9): 283-294. https://doi.org/10.3390/rel9090283.

Engineer, Asghar Ali. 2011. "Rights of Women and Muslim Societies." *Socio-Legal Review* 45 (1): 45-71. doi:https://doi.org/10.55496/YQ TQ4505.

Engineer, Ashgar Ali. 1997. "Communalism and Communal Violence, 1996." *Economic and Political Weekly* 32 (7): 323-326. https://www.jstor.org/stable/4405088.

———. 1992. *The Rights of Women in Islam.* Mumbai: Sterling Publishers.

Fairclough, Norman, and Ruth Wodak. 1997. "Critical Discourse Analysis." In *Discourse as Social Interaction: Discourse Studies: A Multidisciplinary Introduction*, edited by Tuen van Dijk, 258 - 284. Los Angeles: Thousand Oaks; Sage Publishers.

Indo-Asian News Service. 2017. *Don't Want Conflict in Muslim Society over Triple Talaq: PM Modi.* 16 04. https://www.indiatoday.in/india/sto ry/triple-talaq-modi-muslims-bjp-nitin-gadkari-971769-2017-04-16.

———. 2019. *If We Can Abolish Sati, Why Not Triple Talaq: PM Narendra Modi in Independence Day Speech.* 15 08. https://www.indiatoday.in/ india/story/abolish-sati-triple-talag-pm-modi-independence-day-spe ech-1580995-2019-08-15.

Jana, Sanyatani. 2022. "Decolonization and Genocide: Re-Examining Indian Partition, 1946–1947." *Holocaust and Genocide Studies* 36 (3): 354-352. doi:https://doi.org/10.1093/hgs/dcac035.

Jha, Krishna, and Dhirendra K. Jha. 2016. *Ayodhya: The Dark Night - The Secret History of Rama's Appearance In Babri Masjid.* Delhi: Harper Collins.

Karmakar, Goutam, and Pippa Caterall. 2024. "Nation, Nationalism and Indian Hindi cinema." *National Identities* 1-11. doi:https://doi.org/10

.1080/14608944.2024.2440753.

Khurshid, Salman. 2020. *Sunrise over Ayodhya: Nationhood in Our Times.* New Delhi: Penguin Randomhouse.

———. 2018. *Triple Talaq: Examining Faith.* New Delhi: Oxford University Press.

Kidwai, Qutub Jahan, and Ashgar Ali Engineer. 2019. *Codification of Muslim Personal Law.* Mumbai: Kalpaz Publication.

Kishore, Kunal. 2016. *Ayodhya Revisited.* New Delhi: Prabhat Publishers.

Kolås, Åshild. 2023a. *Exploring Identity and Politics: Northeast India's Muslim 'Othering'.* 05 12. https://perspectivesblog.sagepub.com/blog/research/exploring-identity-and-politics-northeast-indias-muslim-othering.

Kolås, Åshlid. 2023b. "This World and the "Other": Muslim Identity and Politics on the Indo-Bangladesh Border." *Alternatives* 48 (4): 223-241. doi:https://doi.org/10.1177/03043754231196587.

Lal, Vinay. 2005. "History as Holocaust: Ayodhya and the Historians." In *The History of History: Politics and Scholarship in Modern India,* by Vinay Lal, 141-185. Delhi: Oxford University Press.

Mahmood, Tahir. 2014. *Principles of Hindu Law : Personal Law of Hindus, Buddhists, Jains & Sikhs.* Second Edition. New Delhi: Universal Law Publishing Company.

Malviya, Shashank. 2021. *Communalism in India.* 14 09. https://timesofindia.indiatimes.com/readersblog/know-your-rights/communalism-in-india-37421/.

Mehta, Deepak. 2015. "The Ayodhya Dispute: The Absent Mosque, State of Emergency, and the Jural Deity." *Journal of Material Culture* 20 (4): 397-414. doi:DOI: 10.1177/1359183515607093.

Mishra, Anand. 2024. *How the Ramjanmabhoomi Movement Fuelled BJP's Rise and Reshaped India's Political Landscape.* 22 01. Accessed 12 23, 2024. https://frontline.thehindu.com/the-nation/project-temple-ayodhya-ram-mandir-birth-growth-of-idea-that-changed-india-politi cal-landscape/article67755692.ece.

Muslim Public Affairs Committee. 2023. *Orientalism: Violent Arab Muslim Men*. Muslim Public Affairs Committee (MPAC) UK. 26 11. https://mpacuk.org/2023/11/26/orientalism-violent-arab-muslim-men/.

Noorani, Abdul Ghafoor Majeed. 1990. "The Babri Masjid-Ramjanmabhoomi Question." In *The Babri Masjid-Ramjanmabhoomi Controversy*, edited by Ashgar Ali Engineer, 56-78. New Delhi: Ajanta Publishers.

Parveen, Nazima. 2022. "Muslim Personal Law and Triple Talaq: Claims, Counterclaims, and the Media Discourse." In *Rethinking Muslim Personal Law: Issues, Debates, and Reforms*, edited by Hilal Ahmed, R. K. Mishra and K. N. Jehangir, 80-109. Delhi: Taylor and Francis.

Piedalue, Amy, Amanda Gilbertson, and Manas Raturi. 2021. "A Majoritarian View of 'Gender Justice' in Contemporary India: Examining Media Coverage of 'Triple Talaq' and 'Love Jihad.'" *South Asian Journal of South Asian Studies* 44 (4): 739-755. doi:DOI:10.1080/00856401.2021.1951477.

Press Trust of India. 2017f. *Adityanath Slams Rivals' Silence on Triple Talaq*. 17 08. https://www.thehindu.com/news/national/adityanath-targets-politicians-silent-on-triple-talaq/article61794956.ece.

———. 2017b. *BJP Stands in Support of Adityanath's Statement on Triple Talaq*. 18 04. https://www.newindianexpress.com/nation/2017/Apr/18/bjp-stands-in-support-of-adityanaths-statement-on-triple-talaq-1594881.html.

———. 2017d. *Human Sacrifice Years Old Too, Center Tells Court, Opposing Triple Talaq*. 17 05. https://www.ndtv.com/india-news/triple-talaq-not-case-of-majority-vs-minority-centre-to-supreme-court-after-kapil-sibals-all-india-m-1694770.

———. 2017c. *Men Use Triple Talaq to Satiate Lust, Says U.P. Minister Swami Prasad Maurya*. 29 04. https://timesofindia.indiatimes.com/city/lucknow/men-use-triple-talaq-to-satiate-lust-says-up-minister-swami-prasad-maurya/articleshow/58439605.cms?utm_source=contentofinterest&utm_medium=text&utm_campaign=cppst+%252528.

———. 2024. *Muslim Daughters Will Bless Modi for Centuries: PM Modi on Triple Talaq Law.* 06 04. https://www.ndtv.com/india-news/pm-narendra-modi-triple-talaq-2024-lok-sabha-elections-muslim-daughters-will-bless-modi-for-centuries-pm-on-triple-talaq-law-5387886.

———. 2017e. *PM Narendra Modi Commends Muslim Women Fighting Triple Talaq.* 15 08. https://www.indiatoday.in/india/story/pm-modi-independence-day-speech-triple-talaq-muslim-women-1029674-2017-08-15.

———. 2017a. *Shia Board Compares Triple Talaq to Sati, Demands Strict Law.* 17 04. https://www.ndtv.com/india-news/shia-board-compares-triple-talaq-to-sati-demands-strict-law-1682510.

Safi, Micheal. 2017. *India Court Bans Islamic Instant Divorce in Huge Win for Women's Rights.* 22 08. https://www.theguardian.com/world/2017/aug/22/india-supreme-court-bans-islamic-instant-divorce-triple-talaq.

Said, Edward. 1978. *Orientalism: Western Conceptualisations of the Orient.* London: Penguin Publishers.

Saxena, Radhika, and Rajarshi Sen. 2021. "The Instant Triple Talaq Judgment - Its Contents and Discontents." *University of Pennsylvania Journal of Law and Social Change* 25 (1): 53-75. https://scholarship.law.upenn.edu/jlasc/vol25/iss1/4.

Saxena, Saumya. 2021. "Nikah Halala: The Petition, the Promise and the Politics of Personal Law." In *Mutinies for Equality: Contemporary Developments in Law and Gender in India,* edited by Tanja Herklotz and Siddhartha Peter D'Souza, 133-154. New Delhi: Cambridge University Press.

Scroll News Staff. 2017. *If Sati and Untouchability Were Outlawed, Why Not Triple Talaq, Asks Center in Supreme Court.* 17 05. https://scroll.in/latest/837934/if-sati-and-untouchability-were-outlawed-why-not-triple-talaq-asks-centre-in-supreme-court.

Shani, Ornit. 2007. "Introduction." In *Communalism, Caste, and Hindu Nationalism: The Violence in Gujarat,* by Ornit Shani, 1-22. Cambridge: Cambridge University Press.

Shayara Bano v. the Union of India & Others. The Constitutional Bench of the Supreme Court of India - Civil Jurisdiction. 2017. Suo Motu Writ (C) No. 2 of 2015 (The Supreme Court of India).

Sherman, Taylor C. 2015. *Muslim Belonging in Secular India: Negotiating Citizenship in Postcolonial India.* Cambridge: Cambridge University Press.

Simons, Hazel. 2003. "Orientalism and Representation of Muslim Women as 'Sexual Objects.'" *al-Raida* 20 (99): 23-32.

Sindhu, Seema. 2021. *The Journey from S.R. Bommai vs. Union of India to Javed vs. State of UP.* 15 09. https://theleaflet.in/the-journey-from-s-r-bommai-vs-union-of-india-to-javed-vs-state-of-up/.

Sinha, Aseem, and Manisha Priyam. 2023. "'Willing' Ethnic-Nationalists, Diffusion, and Resentment in India: A Micro-Foundational Account." *Modern Asian Studies* 57 (3): 1027-1058. doi:https://doi.org/10.1017/S0026749X22000208.

Sinha, Shubham. 2019. *The Muslim Women (Protection of Rights on Marriage) Bill, 2018—Triple Talaq Bill or Triple Talaq Law of India.* New Delhi: Independently Published; the Supreme Court of India.

Srikantan, Geetanjali. 2017. "Reexamining Secularism: The Ayodhya Dispute and the Equal Treatment of Religions." *Journal of Law, Religion, and State* 5: 117-147. https://brill.com/view/journals/jlrs/5/2/article-p117_2.xml?ebody=pdf-130820.

The Constitution of India. 1950. *Article 25: Freedom of Conscience and Free Profession, Practice, and Propagation of Religion.* 26 01. https://www.constitutionofindia.net/articles/article-25-freedom-of-conscience-and-free-profession-practice-and-propagation-of-religion/#:~:text=Article%2025%2C%20Constitution%20of%20India.

The Government of India. 2019. *The Muslim Women (Protection of Rights on Marriage) Act, 2019, or an Act to Protect the Rights of Married Muslim Women and to Prohibit Divorce by Pronouncing Talaq by Their Husbands and to Provide for Matters Connected There with or Incidental Thereto.* Vers. Volume Act Number 20 of 2019. http://egazette.nic.in/WriteReadData/2019/209473.pdf.

Tieri, Silvia, and Amit Ranjan. 2023. "Covid-19, Communalism, and Islamophobia: India Facing the Disease." *Social Identities: Journal for the Study of Race, Nation, and Culture* 29 (1): 62-78. doi:https://doi.org/10.1080/13504630.2023.2207460.

Upadhyay, Surya Prakash, and Rowena Robinson. 2012. "Revisiting Communalism and Fundamentalism in India." *Economic and Political Weekly* 47 (36): 35-57. https://www.jstor.org/stable/41720111.

van Dijk, Tuen. 2015. "Critical Discourse Analysis." In *The Handbook of Discourse Analysis*, edited by Deborah Tannen, Heidi E. Hamilton and Deborah Schiffrin, 466 - 485. West Sussex: Wiley-Blackwell.

Vujačić, Veljko. 2015. "Nationalism, Sociology of." In *International Encyclopedia of the Social and Behavourial Sciences*, edited by James Wright, 290-296. London: Elsevier Books.

Wu, Huizhong. 2017. *Triple Talaq: India's Top Court Bans Islamic Practice of Instant Divorce.* 18 05. https://edition.cnn.com/2017/05/18/asia/triple-talaq-supreme-court/index.html.

Zainab, Sikander. 2021. "Islamophobia in Indian Media." *Islamophobia Studies Journal* 6 (2): 120-129.

Raqs Sharqi "رقص شرقي" and Mental Sovereignty: The Psychology of Aesthetic Self-Representation and Performative META Identity

Maryam Farahani, PhD. & Ian Schermbrucker, PhD.

ABSTRACT

This study examines multidimensional aesthetics in *Raqs Sharqi*, identifying historical, mental, and cultural sovereignty in the wider META region (Middle East, Türkiye, and Africa). In so doing, we explore several theoretical domains to highlight scholarly knowledge gap about identity and exoticism. We discuss how theorists —and their readerly practices around colonial Orientalism—paint an image of the East as a co-dependent, conquered, sexualized, and feminine identity. We outline how Western feminists' attempt to capture misogynist exoticism has failed to successfully challenge colonial ideologies that deliberate belly dancing as a globalised identity. We dispute the theory of entrainment that proposes potential for humanity's collective and empirical empathy by eliciting human intimacy via musicality.[1] Throughout this study, therefore, we assert that scholars have so far failed to offer tangible evidence to address the sovereignty transpiring in *Raqs Sharqi*. The methodology utilised by current Western scholars is dubious, i.e. some claim to the Western position of masculine logic and independence, bringing religious inferences. In this direction, we probe concepts such as emotional efficacy, which in Christian congregational song and practice are theorized to "generate relational strength, as well as

---

1   Clayton, Martin. 2013. "Entrainment, Ethnography, and Musical Interaction." In *Experience and Meaning in Music Performance*, edited by Martin Clayton, Byron Dueck, and Laura Leante, 19–37. New York: Oxford University Press.

communal and individual religious identity." (Myrick 2017, 78) Reflecting on previous work,[2] We argue that contrary to historical Western othering of META, negative affect paradigms can hardly be read about embodied identities in the wider geography of nineteenth-century colonial pan-Arabism or thereafter.

Keywords: Aesthetics, Assimilation, Body, Dance, Identity, META, Performative, Psychology, Raqs Sharqi, Sovereignty, Women

Today, in the Western English-speaking world, belly dancing is known as a feminine, sexual, and sensual performance originating in the Middle East (Moe 2012, 17). While this is now part of Western general knowledge, such stereotyping draws on psycho-historical implications inherent in a form of cognitive bias known, in psychology, as "anchoring" (Tversky & Kahneman 1974, Wegener et al. 2001, Hardt and Pohl 2003, Furnham and Boo 2011, Teovanović 2019). We propose that this type of persistent bias, categorically in the case of belly dancing, is routed in eighteenth- and nineteenth-century Western travellers' auditory and visual perceptions as they moved through the wider Middle East in pursuit of new surroundings, missionary work, medical retreats, intellectual stimulation, or political gain (Nash 2009, xii). We explore the Western belly-dance style as a sub-category, rather than the main one.

Attending to multidisciplinary representation, this work illustrates belly dancing as a multidimensional performative act (rather than artistic performance) with physical features sporadically brought together from around the world while screening its borrowed cultural segments for identity affirmation. To this end, in this chapter, Farahani examines the multidimensional aesthetics of *Raqs Sharqi* "رقص شرقي" to demonstrate variations by historical, cultural, and mental sovereignty, all of which digress from belly dancing. Schermbrucker offers the psychological nuances that underpin bias, reading through Farahani's elaboration on Oriental dance variations and historical relevances.

---

2   Farahani, Maryam. 2015. "Sufism and Pain: Poetic Procrastination of Unity in Classical Persian Verse Narratives." In *Reading the Abrahamic Faith: Rethinking Religion and Literature*, 205–17. London: Bloomsbury.

Cross-field research in belly dancing and its precise origins is sparse. We have a knowledge gap which, due to anchoring bias built up over centuries, has been exacerbated by regular Western deviation from the originality in native and ethnically diverse dance styles. From rituals, body movement aesthetics, musicality, and artistry in costumes to regional and tribal narrative and lyrical variations, *Raqs Sharqi* "رقص شرقي" with its colossal diversity in the META region (Middle East, Türkiye, and Africa) is fundamentally different from Western belly dancing. This is more palpable for those who have been trained as authentic native dancers, learning tradition, imagery, narratives, familial and linguistic livelihood of dance varieties from childhood; continuously passing it from one generation to another with their ancestry belonging in the META region. With historical and lived-experience prominence, therefore, this work emphasizes that introducing dance differentiations holds significance in defining concepts such as identity and belonging particularly among those who practice cultural, religious, and national rituals rather than indulging in Westernized performative aesthetics (Weedon 2004, 74).

Examples in this direction are many, diverse, and multifaceted since each META dance style can be reflected upon from a different incline configuring national and geographical identities, each of which requires comprehensive elaboration beyond the scope of this chapter. For one instance, however, Farahani refers to adaptive models of Westernized Sufi dances, and the elimination of original elements such as the removal of female dress codes and gender segregation during rituals, separating identity from belonging specifically when we contemplate authentic versus forged performance (Dominguez Diaz 2011, 230). Positing identity relevances through Durkheim's theory of ritual in his prominent work, *The Elementary Forms of Religious Life* (1912), we see Western belly dancing as a neo-Orientalist entertainment. This type of adaptive and performative dance of exotic bodily movement, we expand, indicates individual and collective yearning for power in forging women's sexual identities and belonging in the controversial realm of contemporary Western gender politics (Shay and Sellers 2003, 17).

While gender debates and gender identity recognition, in the West, have seen considerable change over the past 50 years, women (assigned female at birth) are yet viewed as somewhat emotionally weak. For example, studies suggest that hegemonic masculinity and andronormativity versus femininity are ascribed accordingly to high versus low physical and emotional strength levels regarding chronic pain assessed in healthcare (Samulowitz et al. 2018, 2-3); yet again, another form of stereotyping which ironically drives gender construction in current Western societies despite efforts for equity, equality, and inclusion for gender identities.

According to a latest *Lancet* article (2024), entitled "Gendered Pain: a Call for Recognition and Health Equity," women's pain is not taken seriously and if women suffer various diseases (including painful conditions such as endometriosis and adenomyosis), they face lack of timely healthcare recognition for diagnosis and treatment. In this medical model, which we suggest, is a continuation of Western Romantic-era aesthetics of femininity, women are seen as fragile, sensitive, and emotional; neither able to tolerate bodily pain nor able to express their precise level of pain; thereby, being dismissed and their suffering downplayed in modern Western medicine.

Interestingly, while research in physical and bodily pain is abundant, progress on the mind-body connection for pain sensation and cognition is slow (Hoffmann and Tarzian 2001, 15). This lack of agility intertwined with historical identity imagery, mainly that of the weak and beautiful femininity, poses well-being problems for Western women. A study at the University of York (2021-22) demonstrates that women often feel invisible, fobbed off, embarrassed, and brushed off about their health, specifically concerning reproductive health which is a sensitive topic for many women. While traditional conceptions of beauty and femininity are eroding in current Western gender debates, social expectation presents itself with double standards. For example, while Western women are active participants in all areas of life, especially in leadership roles within tough corporate cultures, there is still some discrepancy in (men versus women) wages as well as expectations as to motherhood and home-making; thereby, a crisis of dual identities (Bueskens, 2018 13-14).

Contemporary Western belly-dance style, in our view, feeds off this identity duality. On the one hand, the juxtaposition of identity confusion and belonging crisis may enforce the search for meaning in the physicality of one's bodily movement as it has potential to connect humans with a meaning-making process. The University of South-Eastern Norway, for example, offers relevant research and theoretical framework on the body, movement awareness, and meaningfulness. As such, non-normative bodily movements, alien to that of Western styles of dancing (e.g., in ballet as an official Western dance form) may connect women with new meaning-making opportunities not radically afforded in purely Western standards of dance and body movement.

Alien to the Western technicality of performance also, we argue, is the sense that verbal communication and body language (in addition to cultural, familial, and regional native nuances) are not precisely captured by Western dancers who try to learn and perform belly dancing. We believe that accurate performance is not possible even with long periods of living and learning belly dancing in the META region. This proposition goes as far as to suggest that such narrative, metanarrative, and lyrical nuances are only possible to manifest in the body if one's parental lineage is directly placed in the META region for several centuries.

On the other hand, while the objectification theory (Fredrickson & Roberts 1997, 174) proposes the risks to girls and women facing sexual objectification, the practice of professional dancing in so-called modern societies also poses specific risks to mental and physical well-being due to aggravating self-objectification, self-esteem evaluation, and self-monitoring, such as in the case of eating disorders, (Tiggemann & Slater 2001, 57). This is how we see the Western belly dancing practice as a gratifying, but risk-prone, process based on excessive use of technology and social media to play with imagery, enhance body shape, and costume aesthetics. This process may help women to build a new image of themselves by incorporating non-Western features, as a result of which they may remove (even though momentarily) themselves from societies' definitions of feminine identity. As a retreat to a meaning-making process, the modern belly dance style offers Western women a respite for new identities or an adventurous pathway towards self-recognition in Western societies where women's pain and suffering are undermined and inequality to access healthcare has been researched broadly (Marmot Review 2010). Scholars suggest that,

> The relationship between meaning and storytelling is something neither determined by innate biological drives nor solely created in the individual mind. Rather, to speak of meaning in storytelling and poetry, one must

include the concepts of culture, politics, history, and living in the world with others. No matter how we feel and act, our environment affects our ability to act and express our subjective feelings, through narrative (Joranger 2023, 1).

In Western adaptations of native META nuances, for belly dancing, cultural, political, historical, and lived experiences of native dancers have little to no place. Belly dancing, performed by Western imitation, emulates technicality without lyrical and metanarrative relevance. Skills-based models of learning create dancers who can move certain muscle groups to specific tunes, yet not communicating authentic messages of META lyricality and META narrative spectrum. Belly dancing, for the most part in the English-speaking communities in Farahani's experience, is devoid of story-telling in the way that one finds in the wider META region. A further gap in learning and research is, therefore, what we note in forced performative action versus purely authentic performance; or Western copying methodology without referencing META story-telling capabilities of dance, META politics, colonialism, Orientalism, and history of ancient empires. As a process, the contemporary belly-dance style is an identity forging assimilation via technicality beyond the mainstream cultural appropriation and its relevant gaps.

Belly Dancing as Identity Affirmation

So far, the Western belly dance landscape with its flaws, still seems like a positive performance for assimilating identity at least for Western women, explicitly if it offers formation of new and enabled identities despite dismissive social norms that define women's strengths less favourable than men's. However, a fairly elementary knowledge of the psychology of aesthetics helps to clarify why belly dancing is not a positive process to fulfil well-being, let alone establishing why it is fundamentally different from *Raqs Sharqi* "رقص شرقي." When humans process information, our cognitive progression of facts may be encountered by a gap in misinformation; for example, there may be a disengagement between myth and correction due to memory shortfalls (and fact connection not being integrated) or myth retrieval happening alone during information processing (Ecker et al. 2022, 17).

This scientific fact is crucial to the process of identity affirmation. Essential to cross-field examination of belly dancing, we need to understand what science suggests regarding identity as when positivity is verified, even out of myth and due to misinformation, it is less taxing for the brain to overlook reality. In this direction, researchers propose that,

> Identity affirmations involve a message or task (for example, writing a brief essay about one's strengths and values) that highlights important sources of self-worth. These exercises are assumed to protect and strengthen the correction recipient's self-esteem and the value of their identity, thereby reducing the threat associated with the correction and associated processing biases (Ecker et al. 2022, 22).

Belly dancing, as a message or task, involves building confidence through bodily movement which is a source of improved self-esteem and self-worth. It protects the dancer from their and their societies' associated biases while strengthening their sense of well-being and livelihood. In the process, however, the dancer may face a disconnect between myth, misinformation, and reality of META region dance nuances. This may be one way to explain why Western dancers' performance is not to be taken as authentic in the META region and around the world. A comparative example is necessary to visually showcase the difference. For this reason, we refer readers to watch contemporary belly dance variations by leading international dancer Oxana Bazaeva of Russia (B. 1987) in comparison with similar variations performed by Fifi Abdou of Egypt (B. 1945). Thankfully, one needs not ravelling to watch these performers as YouTube, an active and interactive platform, offers many opportunities to watch and compare dancers across the world.

On a different level, identity affirmation from regular belly dancing is significantly empowering for women in Western societies, where "aging" is understood as a negative and anxiety-prone process in one's lifespan (Calasanti et al. 2006, Baird et al. 2010, Abrams et al. 2011, Sargent-Cox et al. 2014; Killen and Makasgil 2020). For women, aging can present particular challenges with physical and hormonal changes that occur with menopause. As explained earlier, lack of pain recognition in healthcare settings may also worsen women's lived experiences of aging. Being able to move one's body in non-normative ways would potentially help build better confidence, yet again we have the dilemma of research gaps (both historical and geographical) and want of cross-field studies in this area. In relation to aging and meaning-making, Steger et al. (2009) have examined the concept of happiness, suggesting that,

> Meaning in life appears important to overall well-being at many life stages and is somewhat predictable from developmental theories (Arnett 2000, Erikson 1968). Additional evidence [in their research findings] was presented that global feelings of the presence of meaning in life are higher in later life, suggesting that in the face of changing roles, declining physical capacity, and accumulating interpersonal losses, people are able to make sense of their experiences and their purpose in life. Efforts should be made to incorporate meaning in life and related constructs into future work on identity development and successful aging.

While researchers need more empirical work relating to multifactorial and multidimensional corelations, for women, engaging in meaning-making processes, story-telling, bodily movement, and all-women group communication can all be hypothesized as potential key factors for successful aging in relation to belly dancing.

Adding identity correction by means of enhancing self-esteem and meaning-making processes, as part of practicing belly dancing, may protect women's well-being from the anxiety arising in new challenges such as current societal strengths definitions and expectations. As a bodily source of identity affirmation in the face of hegemonic masculine performative tropes in Western-style workplaces, belly dancing empowers women to enforce sexual difference through their physical capability of movement. However, the disconnect between Western identity affirmation versus historical and national realities of dance forms in the META region has reduced Western belly dancing to a leisurely and self-exhibiting manifestation. For those of us (such as Farahani) who understand regional META narratology, lyricism, and semantics by national, historical, and local diversions, Western belly dancing appears no more meaningful than a conglomeration of muscle movement in human form.

At its best, Western belly dance happens in some restaurants and local dance shows and, at worst, it can harass one's senses at office parties, Christmas gatherings, and by someone showcasing their belly dance skills at the gym. Not every dance-learner is technically adept and, even in the case of internationally renowned competitions and festivals, native dancers can differentiate between good and ill-performing Western dancers with intermediate technicality. Another problem is that the average Western citizen would not be able to identify any of the muscle movements in belly dancing in association with any national features of the META dance forms, song variations, and musical instrument specifications-of course except well-qualified researchers in this field. The other, and perhaps more contentious, side of belly dancing for identity affirmation, is that it protects Western women from the dark legacies of colonialism. It can be exercised, for instance, to showcase diversity and inclusion in workplaces, but it remains at the trivial level of mingling cultures but without debating the life and soul of META lyricism.

Not surprisingly, this is simply another tick-box exercise for the very reason that Western dancers and learners do not attempt to showcase the intersectionality of dance in the META region in terms of culture, stories, history, politics, and so forth. Misinformation about associating belly dancing with a global dance form, moreover, helps to establish the notion that European pagans invented this activity. Currently, a huge knowledge gap can be identified for primary sources of any combination of the Western belly dance style. Not only defining belly dancing as a historically pagan European affirmation may help Western women establish their version of identity, but it also reinforces misconceptions such as originality. This is all the more cause for concern and categorisations, specifically for lyrical and timebound additions to physical movements, forming a consistent thread throughout this chapter. By identifying variations, in the following sections, we discuss how neo-Orientalism is extrapolated through segmented cultural assimilation that capitalizes on historical Western aesthetics rather than delineating three overlooked areas of native authenticity, autonomy, and agency.

Multidimensional Discrepancies and Belly Dance Stagnation

Many dancers are eager, not only to apply identity affirmation by cultural assimilation, but also keen to teach belly dancing by which they indicate expertise. After all, why would they teach a particular dance, if they do not see themselves as professional specialists? The contemporary belly-dance style, informed by Western geographies can be deciphered as a physical stagnation of emotions and discounted meanings due to excessive collation of physique-obsession and bodily techniques with no attention to Eastern poetics, body language, familial relations, and narrative skills. Moreover, it draws on teaching the proliferation of muscle movements rather than readerly associations to dance moves. The main point is that Western belly-dance modulation is more like an exercise regime than consistent poetic deliberation.

By evidence-based observation, in this work, Farahani proposes a new theory termed as *dormant dance didactics*. By identifying gaps in contemporary belly dance style, driven by a value system predominantly relying on historical biases, Farahani contends that Western interpretation of Oriental dance, in general, masks performers in misinformation and ideological discrepancies which result in a lack of meaningfulness and stagnation. While being able to incorporate varieties of physical skills may sound like a positive move for dancers, being emboldened by outdated ideas about the East coupled with an unwarranted sense of expertise, conceals dancers in a shadow of colonialism.[3]

There are three major dimensions (with sub-categories) in the discourse of Western discrepancies and belly-dance practice, which feed off one another: principally, misinformed literary histories; secondly, the struggling state of feminism and; thirdly, double standards in theoretical entertainment frameworks for identity formation and maintenance. In the case of misinformed literary histories based on colonialism and Orientalism, theorists and readerly practices have, for centuries, sketched the East as co-dependent, co-conquered, sexual, irrationally sensual, lawless, and erotic geography. Not an enthralling illustration of literary analytics, but one of the best summaries of such account, we believe is explained by

---

3   In the UK and the US, for instance, there are different dance classes and academies with orientation on the generic Western belly-dance style, mainly teaching, but never quite thoroughly attempting to grasp Eastern authenticity, lyrical base, geographical meta-narratology, and philosophic body of dance in varieties of *Raqs Sharqi* "رقص شرقي". I see this excessive cultural appropriation as a persistent problem since it is not a showcase of belly dance, but a didactic approach, expanding teaching in so far as to publishing content, showcasing gaudy costumes, and selling such products at considerable cost variations without specifying what makes one costume more expensive than another. Websites are categorically tedious to search through and historical deliberations, if any at all, provide merely surface-level popular culture information rather than detailed or profound observation of geographical agency as to why the dance matters to people of native regions.

Joseph Boone as he notes,

> Perhaps nowhere else are the sexual politics of colonial
> narrative so explicitly thematized as in those voyages to
> the Near East recorded or imagined by Western men.
> "Since the time of the Prophet," one of these records
> proclaims, "fabulous Araby has reeked of aphrodisiac
> excitement." (Edwardes and Masters 175) With various
> shades of prurience and sophistication, similar senti-
> ments echo throughout the writings of novelists, poets,
> journalists, travel writers, sociologists, and ethnogra-
> phers whose pursuit of eros has brought them, in Rana
> Kabbani's phrase, "to the Orient on the flying carpet of
> Orientalism" (Passionate Nomad x). For such men, the
> geopolitical realities of the Arabic Orient become a psy-
> chic screen on which to project fantasies of illicit sexual-
> ity and unbridled excess-including, as Malek Alloula has
> observed, visions of "generalized perversion" (95) and,
> as Edward Said puts it, "sexual experience unobtainable
> in Europe," that is, "a different type of sexuality." (190)
> This appropriation of the so-called East to project onto
> it an otherness that mirrors Western psychosexual needs
> only confirms the phenomenon that Said calls "Orien-
> talism" in his book of that name. [...] Many heterosex-
> ually identified men have travelled to the Arabic Orient
> in pursuit of erotic fulfilment as well, but even these ad-
> venturers have had to confront the spectre of male-male
> sex that lurks in their fantasies of a decadent and lawless
> East; such encounters put into crisis assumptions about
> male sexual desire, masculinity, and heterosexuality that
> are specific to Western culture (Boone 1995, 89-90).

Not only a proportionate outline, showcasing a major dimension of Western discrepancy in Orientalist exoticism, this passage reiterates so much
about Western sub-categories of literary otherness. While Occidental
travellers engaged in sexual fantasies in the East, at least by way of their
writing practices, they ironically missed implementing their self-pro-
fessed Western reasoning and rationality in a methodical approach to
read perceptions of Oriental men's dancing. Narrative perversion seated

at the crux of sexual fantasy which, through the Western male gaze and pen, misses recounting male dancers' roles in Eastern familial spheres, also overlooks lyrical and metanarrative purposefulness of Eastern lives and livelihoods in dance.

While Boone relates omissions in Edward Said's *Orientalism* (1979) for topics around homosexuality, his evident lack of knowledge about Western belly dancing versus the discipline of *Raqs Sharqi* "رقص شرقي" is an inescapable aspect of his analytical terrain. While he attends to John Hindley's English translation of *Persian Lyrics* (1800), Edward Lane's classic study of modern Egyptian life (1833-35), and Gustave Flaubert (1821-1880) gazing at Oriental male dancers, researchers such as Boone categorically miss an opportunity to apply empirical methodologies to detangle cross-specialism findings about dance and narratological meaning-making. Though seemingly less of a provocation for ideological reinforcement of misinformation, such Western portrayal of low interest in reality versus myth, of certain life dimensions in the META region, elicits conflicting impact on proposed hypotheses about gender roles in general and in the West, specifically.

The continuation of Western biases via the male gaze can be read as a misinformation trend prevailing literary histories and historiographies. Lack of humility is also prevalent as inferred by not admitting that one cannot, for certain in any matter, know all aspects of a discipline more so with a loci in a linguistic domain alien to one's own. Dance-related literature, for one, is not about textuality alone, but the context wherein belly dancing otherwise occurs via the senses, thereafter observed and written as memory of an experience.

In recent years, this type of Western bias has been negatively tangible for women who are successfully engaging in intellectual debates. Juxtaposing emotionality, rationality, and geography (as Jordan Peterson asserts via social media platforms), exposes multidimensional discrepancies such as in the literary realm and sexual behaviour. Even his initially publicly successful work, *12 Rules for Life* (2018), borrows and assimilates some nuances regarding life rules from the East, a geography which he denounces as he highlights Western Christianity and rationality. Segmented adaptation and partial assimilation are real problems, rather than perceived, in historical Western debates that persist on the rationality of the West against the emotionality of the East.

On a secondary level, Western feminists' attempt to criticize misogynistic exoticism has failed to successfully challenge the legacies of colonial ideologies that incite belly dancing as a global dance or a way to build new multicultural identities. To rectify the complexity in this inference, we need to backtrack in the direction of debates upon masculine West versus feminine East, markedly rationality and orderliness proposed to be a crucial feature in the life of the Western world. Inconsistencies in methodology refute the credibility of such generalizations by scholars such as Jordan Peterson, for instance, since Western studies do not seem to simply consolidate disagreements around masculinity and femininity in the current psychological deliberation.

On a different note, Peterson's proposal of the rational West is limited, advancing only so far as he is concerned about Western masculinity as he generally speaks to and targets male audiences on YouTube, which he sees as a male-dominant platform; a *fallacy of composition* or hasty generalization, here Farahani argues, as media representation of the sexes varies possibly day by day. His claim to Western rationality necessitates part as whole, meaning men as the West, rather than Western human multidimensionality comprising also women, children, both White Westerners and migrants called ethnic minorities.

This type of bias may work its way through Western justification of part being identical to whole; nevertheless, it exposes intense discrepancy in rhetorical defence. Here, Farahani suggests that she would not, for instance, imagine that Jordan Peterson and similar like-minded scholars would dare publicly denounce women and migrants (including refugees) by defining the West as home only to white, English-speaking men alone; nevertheless, he takes the defensive stage, addressing mostly white men, thereby excluding *the other(s)* and failing to showcase absolute rationality. Western feminists have categorically failed to address such discrepancies in (un)intentional misogynoir-style rhetoric.

Here, again, Farahani suggests that the Western discourse of superiority is prone to a certain level of multidimensional preponderance to haste in its fallacy-indulgent approach to rhetorical claim to rational identity and belonging. In Western Christian debates, this haste and chaotic justification becomes even more tangible, as we can see in the case of Jordan Peterson.

By contrast, the Islamic discourse benefits from reflexive justification and procrastination in ritual processes such as those unifying the human soul with the superior spiritual domain. Evidence to this religious realm could be seen in conceptions of emotional efficacy which, in Christian congregational song and practice, are theorized to "generate relational strength" and communal and individual religious identity (Myrick 2017). Yet, another discrepancy which identifies religious belonging via relationality, not rationality, and relational emotions. Western religious theoreticians propose that, unlike hymnody in Christianity and Judaism, for example, there is no adoration aesthetics in some Islamic poetics (Lewis 2001, 26). However, other scholars note discrepancies, conferring that

> This is a neglected area in the study of Abrahamic faiths and literature. [...] in hypothesizing Sufi poetry as non-liturgical, these scholars presume want of therapeutic features in Sufi versification as a problem, against the depth and wealth of healing qualities in Christian and Judaic texts [...] According to William Chittick, it may well be that in their encounter with Persian Sufi poets such as Rūmi, the 'Western reader faces several obstacles', including 'drawbacks of translation in general', 'constant reference to Islamic teachings', and understanding each poet's versification based on comprehending his schooling system [...] Stylistics and aesthetic divergences, in my view, are among the greatest obstacles a contemporary Western non-Muslim reader may face in comprehending Sufi poetry (Farahani 2015, 206).

Corresponding to these obstacles for Western comprehension regarding Islamic-style poetics is Western misunderstandings or overlooking when we think of Islamic variations of rituals such as the Sema dance. Parallel to these analogies, belly dancing as a Western construct lacks in META stylistics and emotional physicality compared with *Raqs Sharqi* "رقص شرقي." On the one hand, we note claims of non-emotional and rational superiority of the West, while we are told that Western Christianity is full of emotional and relational therapeutics. One wonders then, if Islamic poetics are seen as non-emotional and non-therapeutic, how can the Middle Eastern geographies with their diversity of Islamic belonging be the loci of emotional identities? With such discrepancy, moreover, why would

Western women adopt and adapt Middle Eastern dance moves to collate their Western belly dance style, if they cannot find any benefit for their therapeutic health objectives via assimilating so-called Oriental dances? Multidimensional discrepancies expose a lack of detailed philosophical META knowledge in the Western domain aggravated by stubborn biases over centuries, essentially stamping out any prejudiced reasoning to prove Western superiority of thought or emotions.

With male-dominated discourses of Western superiority, "chaos" is forefront beyond multidimensional discrepancies. For example, scholars have proposed that masculine chaos and disorderliness are associated with libidinal investment in the monetary route of Western Capitalism (Cremin 2020, Fotaki and Pollen 2024). Others, by contrast, argue that disorderliness is a female trope and weakness is a male characteristic, both holding significance in divorce and romantic relationships and due to separation rates (Nock and Brinig 2002). If we read these studies, mainly with Western ideological bearing, again particular challenge exists in grouping the rationale in literature review and referencing methodologies in addition to inconsistencies in connectivity of rationale-building approaches. If we adopt these inconsistencies to formulate any hypothesis, we are bound to question many ideological gaps. For instance, let us, for a moment, reflect on the facts so far discussed in this chapter.

By contemporary indication, Western men are known as being rational in judgement and disorderly in investment. Why, then, did such men travel to the META region in the first place? Why would a rational man travel to a so-called loci of lawlessness, rigid non-emotional or concealed affections and sexual perversions with little monetary privileges to entice Romantic-era hardships of journeying in hot clime? Western men are known as being physically stronger than women, taken more seriously by healthcare professionals than women for accounting for their pain levels and hardships. And, if Western men are weak and, that reasoning compelling for divorce rates, why would contemporary feminists continuously choose them as life partners while also advertising powerful feminine identities by assuming Oriental dances for body politics of belonging?

It seems that misinformed rationalisations in contemporary debates around gender roles are, at least in rhetorical principle, chaotic and disorderly. Enforcing discrepancy in identity definition and gender roles may call for chaos responses. The belly-dance style is one such chaotic response, as previously noted here; a conglomeration of muscle movements, jumping about from side to side, taking up end-to-end space similar to gymnastics floor routine, neither relating to Oriental dance varieties nor adhering to META *Raqs Sharqi* "رقص شرقي" variations. Furthermore, rather than transpiring as a sporting event, it is a form of public entertainment, scaffolding sexual promiscuity by bodily & sensual exposure in grouped audiences while engaging them in auditory and visual perception. Neither of these features composes authenticity which is the individual and native agency in *Raqs Sharqi* "رقص شرقي" and its diversity of comprehensive non-sensual, but communal, characteristics. However, it is all entertaining and entraining, specifically for the non-trained spectator, unfamiliar with *Raqs Sharqi* "رقص شرقي" pedagogies & performance characteristics. It is argued that group entertainment promotes belonging and elevation of emotion to the level of entertaining abstraction, act, object, element, or human as we read,

Dynamical or complex systems theory describes and models the behaviour of interacting systems comprising autonomous agents. Entrainment theory is a part of this wider field concerned with the interaction between independent rhythmic systems. Entrainment has proved a powerful tool in explaining how, through processes of self-organisation, the behaviour of a dynamical system amounts to more than the sum of its parts (Clayton 2013, 17-18).

Self-organized and self-exhibited, the belly-dance style drives such analogous notion of a dynamical system, which singularly comprises powerful inferences for fitness, rhythmic association, and random excitation among onlookers.

However, while, as a bodily system, it can live up to group entrainment and, thereby entraining individual systems with space, more than the sum of its singular or partial components, it presents its value as that of a globalised and group identity. The dynamics between beautiful, colourful, rhythmic sexuality and expectant audience appropriates a transactional stage where complexity bias explains why people are entrained and entertained by the belly-dance style. Here, Schermbrucker suggests that a chaotic, all-encompassing activity combined with music and jollity may be seen as a welcome prospect for collective self-organisation against what

Farahani described as the multidimensionality of contemporary Western discrepancies in defining identity and belonging.

When discussing disorderliness and chaos related to discrepancies, we both emphasize that Western thinkers are quick to use geography as a standpoint; typifying the most mundane instances of everyday physical movement such as placing London commuters and crowds against the rest of the world. Instead of showcasing the simplicity of bodily movement nuances in the East, for example, walking mannerisms in Japan or China, they magnify misconceptions of disordered complexity in a usual colonial fashion. Such distinctions are made, unsurprisingly as cognitive biases endure, by pernicious use of degrading language to exaggerate self-perceived Western superiority. They instruct readers in a didactic manner, with expertise-assumed and self-declared authority,

> Travel around the world and you will find the differences are striking: orderly queues of patient people in London; disorderly mobs clamoring for train tickets in Beijing and Casablanca. In much of Asia, people will crowd around counters, each person demanding the attention of the service providers. Although many Westerners are appalled, the system works well (Norman 2010, 193).

The bizarrely antagonistic and passive-aggressive yet merely observational comparison goes on to also project righteousness onto Western territories by attesting that "a Chinese friend explained" in chaos, you can better get the attention of counter staff. Now, we can not certainly surmise whether such a friend really exists or is perhaps just a figment of imagination in the neo-Oriental mindset of some Westerners when they imply *otherness* with a phrasing process. In racial debates, these phrase constructions are long established as a common attempt by racists, who utilize such typical wording in "the infamous 'some of my best friends are black ...' expression" (Jackman and Crane 1986, 460).

Embarrassment aside, such level of ignorance about physical movement is another exposure to multidimensional discrepancies. In Farahani's opinion here, some Western comedians are the best advocates for proving such gaps in knowledge. In a TV series, entitled *Little Britain* (2002-2006), Western public-facing employees working in a healthcare setting were portrayed as impolite and disorderly even though seemingly working in a well-structured system. At the start of one sketch which is available on Youtube, uploaded some 15 years ago as *Little Britain USA – Rude British Receptionist*, the narrator jokes, "The British pride themselves on being the rudest, most unhelpful people in the world." (@TheRebelAlliant, 2008)

What follows afterwards is a show of incompetence at the service provider's counter intertwined with lack of emotional awareness on the part of both counter employee and the public. In these examples, Western critics not only mock misconstrued disorderliness in the East by taking on centre-stage as the (dis)orderly West, they also make fun of their own presumed orderliness. Neither of these concepts of order and chaos holds truth when we look at such life situations by analysing underlying characteristics of life narratives and metanarratives. Nonetheless, one conjecture is inevitable: the ever-pressing obsession with geographies and *othering* processes which, instead of enabling global debate, reduce physical movement rhetoric to discrepancies.

Despite multidimensional discrepancies in the Western ideologies in/directly espousing the belly-dance style, *Raqs Sharqi* "رقص شرقي" portrays multimodal and multidimensional aesthetics enhancing Eastern value-driven approaches to dance segments related to communal objectives by individual rhetoric and communication rather than endorsing chaotic and globalised rationalisations. Independence and sovereignty, as demonstrated in the next section, in *Raqs Sharqi* "رقص شرقي" are multifaceted, regulating agency, authenticity, and autonomy for the dancer and observer.

Raqs Sharqi "رقص شرقي" and META Dance Multimodality

Geographically, Western placement of belly dancing is currently in the Nile region which is demonstrated in rock carvings illustrating dancers in predynastic Egypt (Garfinkel 2003). These ancient portrayals (Fig. 1) entrain a multifunctional value system that, to this day, celebrates the complexity, triumph, and, immensity of life through dance aesthetics, self- and other-representation, and meaning-making in early art modalities. Such multimodal depiction in various art forms delineates independence of intellectual entrainment rather than entertaining society with a physical gymnastic or acrobatic activity.

Figure 1. Musicians and Dancers: Tomb of Nebamun,
British Museum, room 61

Exciting leisurely shows are beside the point as these modalities communicate a performative identity denoting times and places of belonging. While rock carvings provide such evidence, there are other artistic modalities mainly in pottery, mosaics, and lyricism, complementing the multifunctionality of dance aesthetics. These objects, on a more intrinsic abstraction, successfully convey the observational approach and psychology of ancient artists in how they saw dancers, their body movements, and the space afforded to performance.

Further to aesthetic dance abstraction in designed objects and rock remnants, we can read the multimodality of Oriental dances in various life spectacles and processes, such as in agricultural activities.

> In ancient agricultural societies, dance was invested with special importance on several parallel levels, and this was the secret of its success. On an individual level, it enabled self-expression and active participation in ritual. It enabled entry into trance states, which are the core of religious-mystical activity, and the creation of a relationship with divine powers. It was utilized as a method of creating social solidarity. Religious ceremonies were also a means of coordinating agricultural activities. The need for timely plowing, sowing and harvesting to prevent

the agricultural community from facing starvation and death was a central existential requisite and consequently dance was a dominant element of human society for thousands of years. In periods before schools and writing, community rituals, symbolized by dance, were the basic mechanisms for conveying education and knowledge to the adult members of the community and from one generation to the next (Garfinkel 2003).

Ancient Oriental femininity-in its contemporary misconception of sexually-charged sensuality-held little, if any at all, functional implication for the centrality of dance as an individual and socio-communal identity-building ritual (Garfinkel 2003). It was agriculture and ecosystems, their by-products in survival and maintenance of life, and funeral commemorations, which called people to dance as intrapersonal and interpersonal rituals often inspired by ancient divinity. Predominantly, it was hardship, tough and rough lived experience of daily struggles, hunger, malnutrition, disease, and death, which prompted community practices.

Wars and migrations were secondary and there were centuries of intersectional junctures in Eastern geographies before femininity even became a point of debate in belly dancing in the Western-defined eighteenth century onwards. Farahani's argument here isolates the dominance of this tertiary phenomenon (beauty-femininity binary) by advancing beyond continental European and Anglo-Irish philosophies following Edmund Burke (1729-1797), generally known as Burkean ideologies. Farahani notes that identity and belonging are on a disparaging expressive route in today's Western interpretation of belly dancing in international shows, competitions, and festivals. It is not the global assimilation of native dance characteristics, but the continuity and ingenuity of collective ethnic rituals that reflect mental sovereignty in the META region. Not the bourgeois escapades and imaginary mannerisms to evade realities of life and suffering, but the genuine dance moves that correspond to Eastern autonomy in dance.

Instead of repeating sensualism with gender-sexual bias binaries, which already occupy Western popular cultures about belly dancing, readers are invited to discover Eastern dances as powerhouses for artistic modalities which are long borrowed by Western rivalry through centuries of invasion and cultural appropriation.[4] Farahani's interest (over decades) in *Raqs Sharqi* "رقص شرقي" multimodality develops beyond national characteristics but, for want of space, we refer readers to only a few major dance varieties which she hereby categorises into celebratory life-death segmentation in a cyclical model, corroborating life remembrance modalities, the significance of which Western ideological discrepancies often overlook by exaggerating globalisation (see Fig. 2).

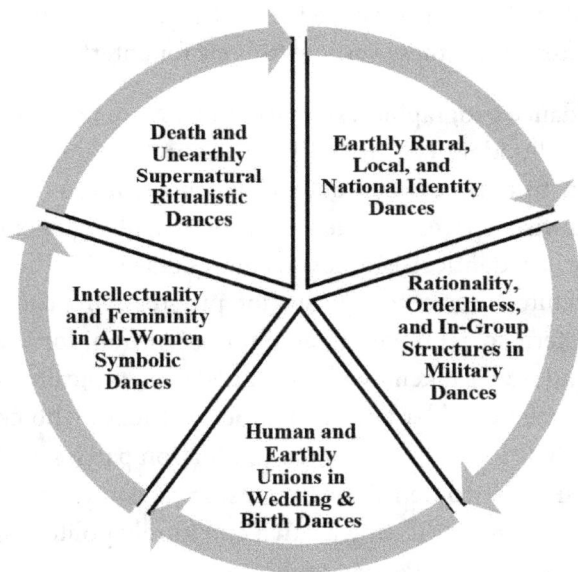

Figure 2. Raqs Sharqi "رقص شرقي" Celebrations of the Life Cycle

Each celebratory variation in *Raqs Sharqi* "رقص شرقي" has a mental and physical identity by its merit in specific bodily movements, musical instruments, spatial setting, and timebound rhythms. While through Western improvisions, critics of belly dancing define *Raqs Sharqi* "رقص شرقي" as a singular Egyptian-style performance by one individual for a group of peoples, varieties indicate otherwise. *Raqs Sharqi* "رقص شرقي" is interpreted as Oriental dance and, even in transliteration, we note identity

---

4   The long centuries of war be it regional, colonial, and international are beyond the scope of this chapter. Elaboration on the current history of Western powers' means of entrance into and presence in the Middle East region is multifaceted and expansive; thereby, such length is not central to this chapter for relevant methodology, remaining only a referential framework. So, is the debate of Western competition over the Middle East during previous centuries.

risks posed by this terminology. Arising from the fantasies of the eighteenth-century Western male gaze, the belly-dance style is a chaotic conglomeration of various META dances.

By contrast, *Raqs Sharqi* "رقص شرقي" is a wide-ranging and multidimensional ritual with precise geographical characteristics in bodily movement. Orientation on torso agility is as diverse across the region as waist- and hip-concentration, when shaking and undulations are involved. The miscellany which is nowadays called belly dancing lacks identity and belonging as it juxtaposes these varieties merely for entertainment.

Speaking of dance geographies, spatial platforms are not to be confused as architecturally identical. In the East, we argue, taking up space in dance is akin to a sacred step beyond language, imagery, music, and rhythm. Likewise, spaces afforded to ancient and eighteenth-century dancers were not identical. Moreover, neither resembled the technological dance architectures of today's staging progression, pageantry, lighting, and Western social media interventions. In Iran, for example, the sacred dancing step is taken by familial invitation, typically offered by a more experienced or older family member or friend, who commences dancing in rituals for birth, weddings, graduation parties, and other life ceremonies. Iranian women abide by a historical compassion definition called *Taarof* "تعارف" indicating a ritual and kindly politeness encapsulating all spheres of Arab-Persian multimodality.

When a dance offer is made, the invited dancer does not immediately jump about the scene broadly laughing and smiling, but they take time and poise with reservation while awaiting encouragement. This does not mean they lack confidence, but they merely comply with sacred processing to respect elders, identity, and belonging to Eastern rituals of life. Reserved manners also extend to clothing and accessories (Fig. 3). However, today, belly dance psycho-aesthetics has evolved into the realm of non-authentic. The rest of the META region is not much different in how women step into dance performance. This psycho-aesthetic realm is far from performativity defined by the sleazy Western male gaze of the eighteenth- and nineteenth-century narcissistic phantasmagoria of Orientalism.

In Morrocco, both Arabs and Amazigh "أمازيغ" women exercise reserved and polite rituals in community activities, which is again a far cry from

Western belly dance exhibitions. *Berber Exploitation* (1997) is an example of Western media intervention in the cultural and ritual practices of Eastern and African territories. Farahani again here suggests that this type of interpretation may have more political nuances than real value for research. While the documentary criticizes the Moroccan government as an exploitative and opportunistic body, relying on Western tourism cash splash, it is inevitable to note how this documentary is more politically oriented than artistically. We wanted to see dance variations in Moroccan cultures, yet we observed ironical political rhetoric as the title distinctly reads. Producing fragmented interviews neither semantically nor semiotically detailed and structured, they discuss how the term *Berber* "بربر" is itself an exploitation of non-Arab peoples. One wonders, therefore, why such title is applied to the documentary. "*Berber Exploitation* by who" we may enquire.

French is noticeably a dominant language when criticizing the Arab influence in this documentary, so why would critics, anthropologists, or any researcher for that matter, see this type of media intervention as anything less than a Western political exploitation? Double standards, misconceptions, and misinformation are prevalent as the documentary does not hold any space for real artistic exploration of Moroccan dance varieties, poetry, rituals, and life of the Amazigh people. It also engages only with limited numbers of community members; therefore, eliminating any empirical and evidence-based value in the production.

In Egypt, multidimensional variations come together forming *Raqs Sharqi* "رقص شرقي" and its multimodality. The most revered aspect of Egyptian dance, in Farahani's opinion, is its ancient and Arab multimodal inter-connectedness and variance. Unlike, modern Western interest in the scoping of multimodality, the META region has a long history of interrelated communicating modalities beyond language (Jewitt 2009, 3-16). Egyptian dance is itself an ensemble of various modalities ranging from local to national, and on to META identities. The Baladī "بلدي" is, for instance, the rural country dance mainly to the *Masmoudi Sogheir* rhythm, sometimes confused with Sa'idi dance "صعيدى." The multimodality equivalent of this dance can be found in the Khaleegy dance "خليجي," reciprocating rural parts of several Middle Eastern countries, Iraq, Oman, Bahrain, Iran, Saudi Arabia, Qatar, and Kuwait.

167 EGYPTIAN TYPES AND SCENES.
Arab Dancing Girl — I.L.

Figure 3. Postcard photograph of two Egyptian Ghawazi dancers

The Sa'idi dance "صعیدی" embodies Eastern military belonging against foreign invasion, involving sticks (for men) and canes/assayas (for women) by variation, each with different meanings, yet fighting foreign entities such as disease, enemies, ghosts, conflicts, famine, and so forth. While a show of military strength, it also celebrates gender equality and equity as both men and women actively dance with their symbols to match body rhythms. Farahani argues that the multimodality entrained in the Sa'idi dance "s," while historically significant, refutes all types of Western interpretation as to the suppression of women in the East. In these dances, both men and women are invited and included with specifications for each group in the form of stick or cane. These props are more than merely dance decorations; they are narrative enablers as the physicality afforded to this dance expands beyond the spatial limitations of a room or platform. While all of these three dances take up space, the boundary allowed to bodily and dance-prop movement remains distinctly unique, similar to the personal zone required when facing enemies or friends. The Khaleegy dance "خليجي" takes up space in the rhythm, of natural elements, corresponding to its local adherence to META eco-systems.

Figure 4. La danse de l'almée (The Dance of the Almeh)
by Jean-Léon Gérôme, 1863

The Levant region has its own identities in dance, mainly conveyed via Dabkeh "دبكة" multimodality, establishing multiple forms of orderliness, community belonging, and communal objectives. Dabkeh does not exhibit singularity in performance, but in-group identity in the form of mental sovereignty in leadership and well-managed pacing with precise mathematics to stepping actions. The torso and legs engaged, this type of dance is also a manifestation of gender equality as both men and women are immersed in the entirety of the dance from start to finish. Varying forms incorporate Al-Shamaliyya, Al-Sha'rawiyya, Al-Taiyyara, Al-Farah, and Al-Ghazal. Each one of these variations interrelates with one another in semantics and semiotics, yet, all together, displays acts of unity in identity and belonging to the Levant region.

Other in-group celebrations such as META region weddings are diverse and yet multimodally interconnected. The Zaffah Al-Arousa "العروسة

"زفـّة" dance variations unify in modalities to denote identity descriptions for each local and national region with bodily movement that cannot be seen precisely as similar as in other celebratory dances. Another group modality, the Zār "زار" dance is enthralling as its history stretches to ancient times in the Semitic region when strange life experiences with unfamiliar elements were seen as the spirits' intrusion; therefore, a dance was created with rituals to drive away disease, ill-willed spirits, and absurdity against celebrating life and livelihood. Similar to Zaffah Al-Arousa, this dance is geographically practiced across the entire META region, mostly in rural areas, with local, cultural, and lyrical variations relating to the language of each region. The narrative characteristics of the Zār "زار" dance intrinsically reflect the customs, metanarrative memory, historical relevance, and habits of each particular region in such a way that Zār "زار" performed in Iran is significantly different from that in Sudan or Egypt. The interpersonal and collective objective remains the same, however, assuring people that any threat or risk can be handled by the individuality of rituals.

Western Orientalisation of the East, as a process of *othering* non-Western peoples, we conclude, is a mis-informed by-product of Romantic male travellers' pervert desires to see naked women among men (Fig. 4). These men had no understanding of psycho-aesthetic multimodality which forever endures in Eastern geographies due to ancient and religious legacies. They were likely never invited to intellectual-religious all-women ceremonies in the East due to Islamic doctrines that give prominence to privacy for women. If they happened to watch any at all, it was merely witnessing a non-authentic entertaining re-creation.

In Farahani's lived experience of dance diversity in the Middle East, all-female ceremonies distinguish body language compared with mixed dance rituals. Facial, particularly eye gestures, bodily movements, proximity to the audience, and post-dance rest and respite are dance-style unique. Romantic Western men, therefore, failed to capture the psycho-aesthetic realities, for instance, in all-female Awālim "عوالم" dance variations (Fig 4). Authenticity in Egyptian Awālim "عوالم" draws on its women-plurality of belonging by assembling singularly educated women but, in Western perception, they are imagined as concubines.

In reality, Awālim "عوالم" is the plural of Almah "عالمة" which means the "learned woman." (Karayanni, 2006, 28-29) Such dances celebrate women's agency both individually and in belonging to communities of in-group women. The agency-authenticity binary in such dances is thoroughly overlooked not only by Romantic-era, but also by contemporary Western critics including white liberal Western feminists. In conclusion, negative or oppressed emotions and weakness mis-attributed to so-called subjugated Eastern women have no place in *Raqs Sharqi* "شرقي رقص". Contrary to Western *othering* of Africa and the wider East, negative emotional paradigms can hardly be read in relation to authentic dance identities in the broad geography of nineteenth-century colonial pan-Arabism or thereafter.

References

Abrams, Dominic, Christin-Melonie Vauclair, and Hannah Swift. 2011. *"Predictors of Attitude to Age Across Europe."* Department for Work and Pensions Research Report (735).

Baird, Brendan M., Richard E. Lucas, and M. Brent Donnellan. 2010. "Life Satisfaction Across the Lifespan: Findings from Two Nationally Representative Panel Studies." *Social Indicators Research* 99(183-203). https://doi.org/10.1007/s11205-010-9584-9.

Berber Exploitation, 1 Nov 1997, ABC Australia. https://www.youtube.com/watch?v=ymfAxe_XcH8 and https://www.journeyman.tv/film/397.

"Body, Movement, Meaning." https://www.usn.no/english/research/our-research-centres-and-groups/humanities/body-movement-meaning/.

Boone, Joseph A. 1995. "Vacation Cruises; Or, the Homoerotics of Orientalism." *PMLA : Publications of the Modern Language Association of America* 110 (1). https://doi.org/10.2307/463197.

Bueskens, Petra. 2018. *Modern Motherhood and Women's Dual Identities: Rewriting the Sexual Contract.* Routledge.

Calasanti, Toni M, Kathleen F. Slevin, and Neal King. 2006. "Ageism and Feminism: From "Et Cetera" to Center." *NWSA Journal* 18(1): 13-

30. muse.jhu.edu/article/195212.

Clayton, Martin. 2013. "Entrainment, Ethnography, and Musical Interaction." In *Experience and Meaning in Music Performance*, edited by Martin Clayton, Byron Dueck, and Laura Leante. Oxford University Press.

Cremin, Ciara. 2020. *The Future is Feminine: Capitalism and the Masculine Disorder*. Bloomsbury.

Dominguez Diaz, Marta. 2011. "Performance, Belonging and Identity: Ritual Variations in the British Qadiriyya." *Religion, State and Society* 39(2-3). https://doi:10.1080/09637494.2011.577200.

Durkheim, Emile. 1912/1995. *The Elementary Forms of Religious Life*, translated by Karen E. Fields. Free Press.

Ecker, Ullrich K. H., Stephan Lewandowsky, John Cook, and Philip Schmid. 2022. "The Psychological Drivers of Misinformation Belief and Its Resistance to Correction." *Nature Reviews Psychology* 1(1):13–29. https://doi.org/10.1038/s44159-021-00006-y.

Elmarsafy, Ziad, Anna Bernard, and David Attwell, eds. 2013. *Debating Orientalism.*, Palgrave Macmillan.

Fotaki, Marianna, & Alison Pullen. 2024. "Feminist Theories and Activist Practices in Organization Studies." *Organization Studies* 45(4): 593-616. https://doi.org/10.1177/01708406231209861.

Garfinkel, Yosef. 2003. "The Earliest Dancing Scenes in the Near East." *Near Eastern Archaeology* 66(3): 84–95, https://doi.org/10.2307/3210910.

Hardt, Oliver, and Rüdiger F. Pohl. 2003. "Hindsight Bias as A Function of Anchor Distance and Anchor Plausibility." *Memory* 11(4-5):379-94. https://doi: 10.1080/09658210244000504.

Hoffmann, Diane E, and Anita J. Tarzian. 2001. "The Girl Who Cried Pain: A Bias Against Women in the Treatment of Pain." *Journal of Law, Medicine, and Ethics* 29(1):13-27. https://doi: 10.1111/j.1748-720x.2001.tb00037.x.

Jackman, Mary R., and Marie Crane. 1986. "'Some of My Best Friends Are

Black…': Interracial Friendship and Whites' Racial Attitudes." *Public Opinion Quarterly* 50(4): 459–86. https://doi.org/10.1086/268998.

Jewitt, Carey, ed. 2009. *The Routledge Handbook of Multimodal Analysis.* Routledge.

Joranger, Line. 2023. "Healing and Meaning Making Through Storytelling and Poetry." *Human Arenas.* https://doi.org/10.1007/s42087-023-00375-1.

Karayanni, Stavros Stavrou. 2006. *Dancing Fear and Desire: Race, Sexuality, and Imperial Politics in Middle Eastern Dance.* Wilfrid Laurier University Press.

Killen, Alison, and Ann Macaskill. 2020. "Positive Ageing: to What Extent can Current Models of Wellbeing Categorise the Life Events Perceived as Positive by Older Adults?" *International Journal of Applied Positive Psychology* 5. https://doi.org/10.1007/s41042-020-00028-6.

Lewis, Bernard. *Music of a Distant Drum : Classical Arabic, Persian, Turkish and Hebrew Poems / Translated and Introduced by Bernard Lewis.* Princeton University Press, 2011, https://doi.org/10.1515/9781400837908.

Moe, Angela M. 2012. "Beyond the Belly: An Appraisal of Middle Eastern Dance (Aka Belly Dance) as Leisure." *Journal of Leisure Research* 44(2): 201–33. doi:10.1080/00222216.2012.11950262.

Myrick, Nathan. 2017. "Relational Power, Music, and Identity: The Emotional Efficacy of Congregational Song," *Yale Journal of Music & Religion* 3(1). https://doi.org/10.17132/2377-231X.1060.

Nash, Geoffrey, ed. 2009. "INTRODUCTION." In *Travellers to the Middle East from Burckhardt to Thesiger: An Anthology* xi–xx. Anthem Press.

Nock, Steven L., and Margaret F. Brinig. 2002. "Weak Men and Disorderly Women: Divorce and the Division of Labor." In *The Law and Economics of Marriage and Divorce,* edited by Anthony W. Dnes. Cambridge University Press.

Norman, Donald A. 2010. *Living with Complexity Donald A. Norman.* MIT Press. Postcard photograph of two Egyptian Ghawazi dancers. Accessed July 12, 2020. https://commons.wikimedia.org/wiki/

File:167_Egyptian_types_and_scenes_-_Arab_Dancing_Girls.jpg.

Said, Edward. 1979. *Orientalism*. Vintage.

Samulowitz, Anke, Ida Gremyr, Erik Eriksson, and Gunnel Hensing. 2018. "Brave Men" and "Emotional Women": A Theory-Guided Literature Review on Gender Bias in Health Care and Gendered Norms Towards Patients with Chronic Pain." *Pain Research & Management: The Journal of the Canadian Pain Society* 14. https://doi:https://doi.org/10.1155/2018/6358624.

Sargent-Cox, Kerry A., Masori Rippon, and Richard A. Burns. 2014. "Measuring Anxiety about Aging Across the Adult Lifespan." *International Psychogeriatrics* 26. https://doi.org/10.1017/S1041610213001798.

Shay, Anthony, and Barbara Sellers. 2003. "Belly Dance: Orientalism-Exoticism-Self-Exoticism." *Dance Research Journal* 35(1): 13-37.

Steger, Michael F., Shigehiro Oishi, and Todd B. Kashdan. 2009. "Meaning in Life across the Life Span: Levels and Correlates of Meaning in Life from Emerging Adulthood to Older Adulthood." *The Journal of Positive Psychology* 4(1): 43–52. https://doi:10.1080/17439760802303127.

Teovanović, Predrag. 2019. "Individual Differences in Anchoring Effect: Evidence for the Role of Insufficient Adjustment." *Europe's Journal of Psychology* 15(1):8-24. https://doi: 10.5964/ejop.v15i1.1691.

Tiggemann, Marika, and Amy Slater. 2001. A Test of Objectification Theory in Former Dancers and Non-Dancers. *Psychology of Women Quarterly* 25(1): 57-64. https://doi-org.liverpool.idm.oclc.org/10.1111/1471-6402.00007.

Tversky, Amos and Daniel Kahneman. 1974. "Judgment under Uncertainty: Heuristics and Biases." *Science*. 185(4157):1124-31. https://doi: 10.1126/science.185.4157.1124.

Weedon, Chris. 2004. *Identity and Culture Narratives of Difference and Belonging*. McGraw-Hill Education.

Wegener, Duane T., Richard E. Petty, Brain T. Detweiler-Bedell, and W. Blair G. Jarvis. 2001. "Implications of Attitude Change Theories for Numerical Anchoring: Anchor Plausibility and the Limits of Anchor

Effectiveness." *Journal of Experimental Social Psychology* 37(1): 62–69. https://doi:. 10.1006/jesp.2000.1431.

York Research Outcomes, Accessed June 26, 2024. https://www.york. ac.uk/news-and-events/news/2022/research/women-healthcare-system/

Colonial Space and the Contour of Spatial Difference: Fez through the Lens of French Colonial Postcards

Abdelali Jebbar, PhD.

ABSTRACT

This paper delves into the depiction of colonial space through the lens of French colonial postcards, particularly focusing on the Moroccan city of Fez. The analysis scrutinizes how these postcards construct and perpetuate Orientalist tropes, portraying Fez as a space of exotic difference juxtaposed against the perceived modernity of the West. Through a detailed examination of visual representations, the study reveals how architecture, particularly the monumental gates and ramparts of Fez, serves as symbols of resistance and cultural identity, exposing colonial narratives of stagnation and decay. Furthermore, the study explores the portrayal of mosques and shrines in these postcards, highlighting the Western gaze's tendency to exoticize Islamic religious spaces. Despite attempts to capture the essence of these spaces, the inherent closure and sanctity of mosques and shrines often defy colonial attempts tovisually represent them. Ultimately, these colonial visual narratives were supposed to reinforce Western hegemony and justify the exploitation of non-Western cultures, perpetuating a constructed spatial identity that aligns with Western notions of progress and superiority. Thus, the paper engages critically with theoretical frameworks such as Orientalism and postcolonial theory to analyze these visual representations and lay bare the power dynamics and ideological underpinnings embedded within them.

Keywords: Colonial Postcards, Fez, Orientalist Tropes, Spatial Representation, Cultural Identity, Postcolonial Theory

Introduction

Throughout colonial history, the visual medium, like its linguistic predecessor, has served as a powerful tool for shaping perceptions and reinforcing narratives of dominance. French colonial postcards, in particular, offer a fascinating window into the construction of colonial space and the delineation of spatial difference. This study focuses on a variety of visual discourses communicated in these postcards, focusing on their portrayal of the Moroccan city of Fez. Through a content analysis of visual imagery and textual discourse, we embark on a journey to examine the layers of meaning embedded within these frozen glimpses of colonial gaze.Fez, with its rich mosaic of culture, architecture, and history, emerges as a focal point in the colonial imagination. The city's labyrinthine streets, towering gates, and majestic mosques serve as canvases upon which colonial fantasies are painted. Through the lens of French photographers, Fez is transformed into a fair of exoticism, a space frozen in time, perpetually contrasted against the dynamism and progress of the West.

Central to this study is an investigation into the visual tropesemployed in portraying Fez. The monumental gates and ramparts, symbols of the city's resilience and cultural identity, are analyzed to reveal the colonial gaze's fixation on notions of decay and stagnation. Through a careful examination of these architectural sites, we reveal the subtle methods by which colonial power asserts its dominance, relegating Fez to the category of the 'Other', continuously positioned in opposition to the supposed superiority of the West.

Moreover, this study also explores the portrayal of religious spaces within these postcards. Mosques and shrines, sacred sites imbued with centuries of spiritual significance, become subjects of colonial scrutiny, their sanctity commodified for the consumption of Western audiences. Yet, despite the colonial desire to capture and possess these spaces, their inherent closure and resistance challenge colonial representation, leaving gaps in the colonial narrative.

Through a content analysis of French colonial postcards, this study seeks to investigate the complex interplay of power, representation, and identity in the colonial gaze. By examining the underlying elements of visual discourse, we aim to illuminate the ways in which colonial discourse shapes perceptions of space, perpetuating hierarchies of difference and reinforcing narratives of Western supremacy.

The Shielding Gates and Ramparts

The Orient as a social and cultural geography is depicted in a number of Western ethnographic works. Its depiction varies according to the mode of representation deployed. However, its overall image is mostly tainted with stigmatizing stereotypes, which go beyond mere depictions of landscapes and spatial characteristics to the cooptation of people's identities onto colonial 'exhibitionary' practices. In addition, there are other predominant angles of vision which need deliberate attention and which embed traces of equal confrontation between the West and the Orient. As a mode of representation, colonial postcards also preach "the rhetoric of colonial grandeur"[1] (Said 1993, 74) as well as celebrate imperial achievements overseas.

The Moroccan city of Fez was part of the target territories that French colonial postcards visually reproduced according to a welter of Orientalistic axioms. In the following section, I show how the image of Fez in these postcards touches upon major segments of its national identity in an unspoken attempt to bring forth an 'exotic' Other who is meant to function as a foil for the Western Self. The focus is on the colonial deployment of architecture as a tool of demarcating the city's cultural identity, a demarcation which exceeds the plain documentation of spatial distinctions to make the Western viewer experience exotic visions about non-Westerners. Significantly enough, the reading of the selected postcards takes into consideration the photographers' awareness of the existing distinctions between the European architecture, that acts as a method of comparison, and Fez's spatial morphology which is played out as an indefinite referential of difference.

The gigantic gates of Fez along with their tawny thick walls that surround the city are deemed historical spatial evidence of the city's resistance to the test of time. They also acted as shields against foreign military threats. The gates apparently allude to the era of Islamic grandeur when the country was bathing in the reflected glory of its military power known worldwide. The city still looks medieval in its buildings, arches, streets and

---

1   Said explains how the Empire of France suffered insecurity during the Revolution and the Napoleonic era, and how it was the role of writers, painters and artists to secure its presence within the French culture.

in all its architectural designs. From a Western mirror, these two spatial segments of Fez, gates and ramparts, are represented as a form of Oriental space lagging behind the architectural development witnessed by the Western counterpart. I have chosen them to head this colonial visual catalogue because of their political significance and conspicuous influence on the photographer's gaze, as they both demonstrate the city's spatial mechanisms of defense, in a deplorable site signaling the decay of the Orient's civilization.

The protective role of Fez's gates is among the salient features of Islamic civilization. For this reason, a large number of postcards tend to exhibit the outside layout of the big doors punctuating the city's ramparts. The pictured architectural structure is most often about an apparent state of dilapidation. Another marginal angle resides in the distant ramparts that stretch along the North side of the city. This visual content may be deployed to show how this huge spatial extension has been made within the colonial eye's range, an idea which is highly symbolic of colonial containment. Other scattered pieces of the overall visual message may include other pictured types, like women or men entering the gate, either on foot or riding donkeys or horses. They may even include small crowdswhere beggars and merchants dwell together, wearing clothes that are as old and shabby as the 'tumble-down' gate.

There are other predominant discourses that are in conflict. On the one hand, the colonial postcard respects the conceptual framework of Orientalist studies in that it selects forms of visual knowledge that can be deployed as a ground for comparing the past, which refers to the 'Orient' as static and anachronistic, and the present, which refers to the West as highly developed. On the other hand, it exhibits an ephemeral visual instance that is bound to vanish within its social context[2] (Lidchi1997, 164).In other words, the pictured instance, in its genuine time and space, cannot exist after the birth (which practically marks the death of the pictured) of its copy which is the photograph[3] (Price and Wells 1996, 22).

---

2   Here, the pictured gate, as a piece of visual information, is received as the other artefacts displayed in ethnographic exhibitions. However, it is not as immortal as the other objects, to use Henrietta Lidchi's argument, because photography accords a temporary presence to the picture image that is "*destroyed in their proper social context.*"

3   The picture image is seen as a 'simulacrum', a copy for which there is no original, by the French philosopher, Jean Baudrillard. Unlike Roland Barthes, who sees that a photograph does have a referent, he argues that photographs have no referents and what they picture

Figure 1.1: Porte Bab Guissa

The gate of 'Bab Guissa', in figure 1.1, is made as one of the most spectacular entrances of Fez because of the selected viewpoint from which the photograph was shot, which allowed the depiction of an extended field of vision. The gate is located in the Northeast of the city. Its entrance leads to a network of streets and neighbourhoods. Just above the arched gate stands a colossal mosque. Despite the picturesque view that extends to reach the mosque of Moulay Idriss' shrine, the postcard seems to locate the pictured space in a time that bears a 'forced' resemblance[4] (Lidchi1997, 186) to a medieval architectural morphology. Its visual message may insinuate the Orient's 'timelessness', the existence of a stagnant 'other', which evokes both 'fascination' and 'pity' among the French audience.

The gate was built by Ajeessa, and it was named after him, to function as an entrance to the bank of Al-Karaouine. He was the son of one of the kings of Znata tribes, Dounass Ibn Hamama, and was in conflict with his

---

have autonomous existence outside the pictorial frame (Price and Wells 1996, 22).

4   This 'forced' resemblance is created by the photographic representation which aims at forging distinctions rather than reflecting them. The argument is defended by Lidchi who employs the Foucauldian model to recast "the field of anthropology as a discursive formation...which does not simply reflect 'real' distinctions between people, but creates them" (186).

brother, El-Foutouh, who was ruling the bank of Al-Andalous, for which he built the Gate of Bab Ftouh. During their time, the City was split into two parts that were separated by walls, which were demolished later by Lamtouna who built several bridges to connect the two banks[5] (Al-Jazaani1991, 40-41).

The presence of *Arabian Nights* is felt in most visual messages communicated in the pictured space of Fez. Its representation as a set of indistinguishable geographical sites is not dissimilar to Scheherazade's depictions of faraway geographies. The gate depicted in the following postcard, figure 1.2, is known as the gate of "Bab Ftouh." Historically, it functioned as Fez' Southeast gate, and was built by El-Foutouh. The 'exotic' presence of the Oriental difference, as wished by the French viewer, is forged via the 'intended' inclusion of both people and animals before a gigantic gate. The mechanical reproduction does not authenticate the real nature of the social space in question as its prime function is to provide the viewer with a resort of fantasy, creating more dimensions of the Orient's imaginary existence. This recurrent scene made the Western viewer develop a 'uniform' perception of non-Western cultures. Even romance and travel writers were deeply influenced with the image of the Orient as being 'unvaried'.

In his essay, "Marrakech," George Orwell sees that in a country like Morocco, which he describes as a tropical landscape, the European's eye "takes in everything except the human beings," because they are "the same colour as the earth, and a great deal less interesting to look at." (Spurr 1993, 192) In Figure 1.2, the glimpses that are deemed responsible for internalizing this uniform reception are having a far reaching influence on the viewer. The view of turbaned men dressed in shabby djellabas and cloaks (though pictured from a distance) is a familiar imagery in the *Arabian Nights'* representation of types. However, their forced indefiniteness is coincidentally sustained by the tawny ramparts which provide an overriding shape subjecting the wane grey colour of their clothes. This renders Orwell's description more alluding to the natives' right to preserve what really belongs to them, their very land, since they share the same colour with it.

---

5   Dounass Ibn Hamama was interested in the construction and renovation of Fez and his reign was marked by stability and prosperity, unlike his two son, El-Foutouh and Ajeessa, who were in armed conflict that ended by the killing of Ajeessa.

Figure 1.2: FEZ- Bab- Fetouh

Ramparts are also depicted in certain visual fragments reproducing different instances of their 'status-quo'. Their representation is also subjected to some inherited Western traditions. The recurrent way in which these ramparts are pictured gives the impression that the photographer put the social space under surveillance. The camera creates "an all seeing power," a sort of a "totalizing eye"[6] (De Certeau1984, 92) that caters for the Western desire to cover as many visual segments as possible, a kind of panorama that is highly satisfactory for an eye with an authoritarian scopic drive. In addition, there is a prevailed tendency, in almost all postcard depictions of ramparts, to spectacularize the Oriental space. This is done through creating a larger field of vision, a whole sight range including a huge amount of space, appropriating bulky details about the referent.

The following figures illustrate how photographs of ramparts deal with distance. They display 'exotic' ordering of Fez's outside shape. The inner side is hardly made visible, which questions the photographer's desire to present visible artefacts. The apparent purpose is to picture a dim shape

---

6   De Certeau refers to Renaissance painters whose representation of the city made of "the medieval spectator…a celestial eye." He affirms that the same scopic drive haunts nowadays architectural productions. In the context of photography, the manipulation of distance along with the selection of a technically ideal observing position allow the lens of the camera to maintain the role of this 'celestial eye' that seek a total visual containment of the seen.

of the Orient to authenticate its abstract presence within the shared imagination of the Western audience. Therefore, the postcard becomes an instrument of a colonial propaganda, like its predecessors (the travel narrative and paintings), which aims at ranking "peoples and societies on the path of progress towards the most elaborate (Western) civilization" (Staszak 2004, 358) as colonial pre-task to legitimize 'dominion' over the Orient[7] (Hodge 2007, 194).

The high ramparts were built to protect the city against intruders, but for the Western eye, they are there to veil the city's exotic side. The term exotic invokes paradoxical impulses in the viewer's psyche towards the city; therefore, the viewer, allured by endless images of Oriental pleasures, may desire to trespass those ramparts.

The spatial imagery enacted in the colonial way of seeing the Orient is appropriated from Western "spatial practices of mapping and naming."[8] (Jacobs 1996, 19) For example, the role of the map within the imperial enterprise is not dissimilar from that of visual representation since they both provide faulty versions of the approached geographical spaces[9] (19).

Another focal metaphor recurrent in French colonial postcards is the image of a 'disordered' human environment. The depiction of quasi-destroyed ramparts launches an assault on the city's cultural and religious values, as a vanishing civilisation before the grandeur of the West. This way of seeing induces the colonial false sentiment to rescue the Orient from dilapidation and decay, on the ground of 'moral obligation'. In such a visual construction, the visual presence of the city is partial and not outstanding as about three fourth of the picture image is occupied by the apparent presence of the tawny tumble-down ramparts. The overall vision renders the city as a half veiled woman whose unveiled part may count as a real challenge for Western imagination and curiosity to guess its hidden

---

7   The word *dominion* has religious connotation. It is derived from the Latin *dominus*, meaning 'Lord'. The word roughly refers to domination, and it was deployed in this sense to name the seventeenth century Dominion of New England (America).

8   This phrase is used by Jane M. Jacobs to refer to the Western cartographic practices. Jacobs sees that these practices do not "replicate" the environment.

9   Here I find the role of the postcards, as a mode of representation, and particularly postcards depicting both human and social landscapes in colonial Fez, part of what Jacobs terms "territorial imperatives," in the context of this paper, of Imperialism.

extensions[10]. Here, the photographing eye might have maintained similar roles as the colonial journalistic eye, which David Spurr describes as "mobile and selective, constantly filtering the visible for the sign…that when transformed into the verbal or photographic image, can alone have meaning for a Western audience by entering a familiar web of signification" (Spurr 1993, 21)The selection of specific landscapes aims at establishing a type of knowledge that allows virtual accessibility of the Orient, where the eye is meant to probe to experience deeper 'truths' of romantic accounts. Like the former role played by travel narrative, the picture image further enhanced the Western thinking by opening an emergent scope for more colonial determiners of otherness.

When photographers and postcard collectors and users were engaged in the circulation of manipulated forms of visual information about Morocco, parallel actions were taking place to rival these rhetorical modes, including other forms of colonial presence, of reproduction. This historical fact destabilizes the visual reception of the city as a static, passive and motionless Orient. The postcard, in this respect, is unable to comprehensively contain the colonial reality as it is subjected to a whole range of ideological strategies that determine for the photographer what, where and how to shoot.

The ultimate goal of such colonial configurations of dilapidated ramparts and historical edifices is to celebrate a long-awaited historical moment of the West's liberation from its sole past nightmare, the Islamic civilization. This view casts doubt on the West's expressed admiration of cultural difference, which leads to the conception that the postcard may serve to express a profound case of *schadenfreude* towards a defeated 'Other'.

The intricate plot of the colonial statement, which frames and maps the dual process of including and excluding certain elements of discourse within the photograph, tends to valorize certain meanings for the purpose to distance the West not only from its traditional adversary, the Orient, but also from its past confrontations with it which were marked with crushing forms of defeat. There is a deliberate attempt to resituate the signification of the city's mechanisms of defence made available by the nature of the Islamic architectural designs to a form of 'conception' which

---

10   The presence of the Oriental woman is scented even in the depiction of spatial entities, be
     it a linguistic or a picture image text.

aims at reading these collapsing ramparts in relation to the ongoing progress and prosperity lived by Europe. The past role of the pictured space
remains neglected by viewers who see such historic sites as evidencing
the city's inability to grow 'modern' in a fashion that is commensurate
with European architecture.[11]

a. Mosques, Shrines and the Colonial Dream of Trespass

The connotation of religious places in the visual reproduction of space
is nurtured by the Western tendency to identify and locate forms of 'difference' that would overtly stand as adversaries to Christian faith. Islam,
in this respect, received most of these prejudiced attitudes in that it has
been, since The Middle Ages, seen as a real threat to Europe (Barthelemy
1987, 10).By the twelfth century, Morocco was already having a firm grip
on Spain. Parallel to this, were Europe's repeated attempts, that were unsuccessful, to defeat the Muslims of the Middle East (fairly known as the
Arabian Island). These historical confrontations, which left "far-reaching
wounds in the psyche of Europe"[12] (Bekkaoui 1998, 1), were behind Europe's development of a whole tradition of stereotypical demarcation of
the non-Christians.

The representation of mosques and shrines, throughout the postcards
presented in this paper, is subjected to the Western "question of establishing authority through the demarcation of identity and difference" (Spurr
1993, 7). The reading of this visual representation finds greater support
in certain travel narratives descriptive of the religious space. As an example, Edith Wharton describes, in a broad-based manner, the Moroccan
Islamic architecture as being defeated by time (Wharton 2005, 51).Her
description seems to exceed her approaching of architectural designs
to cover metaphorical and metaphysical implications as she relates the
"half-ruined" architecture with the faith of Islam as vanishing before the
ongoing hegemony of Christianity. The same descriptive conviction is
manifest in a number of French colonial postcards of religious sites.

The selected visual configuration of shrines and mosques covers a num-

---

11 This explains why the French decided to build a new city in the southern suburb of Old
    Fez.

12 Bekkaoui describes how *"Medieval Spain was a battleground of fierce and long wars"* between
    Christianity and Islam. The Muslims won these wars, which destabilized the Christian re-
    ligious conceptions of non-Westerners.

ber of postcards that are over-loaded with limitless images framing the French conception of Fez's religious and spiritual spaces. There is a whole set of postcards that are captioned under the phrase, *Le Maroc Pittoresque* (Picturesque Morocco). The mosque recurrently appears to be associated with the 'half-ruined' ramparts as a preparation for subsequent denunciation of its profound influence among the Muslims.

Most of these postcards are edited by P. Grébert, in Casablanca and Levy and Neurdien Reunis, in Paris. These two editors differ slightly in terms of the general view that they both target. However, taking into account the invested textual conventions within the core of their imagery, we come to locate certain instances of interlocution between the different visual segments composing the overall view. What may please the Western viewer in these postcards is the emphasis made on the mosque that functions as an anchorage point where Western tropes of the Islamic faith can be loosely fastened. The colossal presence of the mosque that is intimidated by the decaying texture of the ramparts is reinforced as a symbol of a repeated fate of recession through the inclusion of remote, but made visually near-by, mosques. Such a representation reflects the French colonial propensity for ranking and categorizing spatial and cultural components of the city of Fez. It is true that the mosque is made prominent within the visual ensemble, but its prominence, from a colonialist perspective, is made equivalent to the size of destruction being suffered by the Islamic civilization.

In the case of painted colourful postcards, covering 'prototypal' spatial ingredients, in addition to the inclusion of a wider scope of vision, there is a clear visual testimony to Orientalist paintings, especially with some postcards hosting a dim view of camels, in the manner of Arabian Nights' caravans, passing towards the gate. The picture image, in this context, is meant to recount a visionary experience which, not less interesting than Orientalist heroic sagas, the painter has kitted out with the basic visual data to render the sights more adaptable to what already haunts the Western imagination. The same dim procession of camels may be seen as expressive of a burning colonial desire to trespass on the city's core, whose 'exotic' secrets were shielded except from certain travelogues and paintings' excerpts.

Yet, the mosque remains noticeably the religious umbrella, under which this backward mode of living persists. Most photographers' 'zooming out' seems to foreground, with imperial standards in mind, colonial mastery of space. This metaphorical imprisonment of human environment is enticed by the broad view that the postcard provides. In other words, the operation is quite similar to the strategies followed in imperial travelogues, particularly when writers tend to pack their narrative with descriptive snippets that share common consent with the Rhetoric of Empire. Furthermore, the fact that these cards are coloured with a 'desert-like-colour' transports the viewer back to the imagery of the Arabian landscapes.

Other mosques were built in shrines, like the mosque of Moulay-Idriss shrine. Their depiction seems to conjure the exotic images of the Orient. The desire to shed light on traces of grandeur and glory that the city enjoyed in the past aims at fascinating the viewer with a 'vanishing' powerful 'Other' whose visual containment becomes symbolically tantamount to its subjugation.

The intense exposure of human environment to the logic of otherness stems from a whole tradition of western ideological apparatuses that aim at reconstructing other cultures, following the model of western civilization. Figure 1.3 illustrates the presence of the French in Fez, counting as a visual message depicting the changes implicated in the social environment of the city. The accessibility to alien space is detected and celebrated. The observing position (or rather the zooming viewpoint) from which the photographer was 'licensed' (by his colonial preoccupations) to shoot took into account the frozen instance of natives getting in and out the gate along with the presence of the two mosques as a salient background of the 'unspoken' confrontation that is taking place between Franciscans, with their European clothes, and the natives, with their 'uniform dimness'. The Franciscans, with their religious roles as missionaries, are not only rivalling the cultural and religious role of the city, but also insinuating other forms of reconstruction and appropriation which seek the destabilizing of the city's local brand of cultural specificities.

As for shrines, the selected postcards do not illustrate them from within except for few instances where the inside of the shrine appears framed in a very limited field of vision. The reason why such depiction remains inadequate as a source of visual documentation is that religious settings like the inside of mosques and shrines are not accessible to the Christians (except for a few postcards illustrating the presence of the French soldiers, during the events of Fez, inside the mosque of Bab Gissa, edited by Niddam and Assouline1912). What lasts for photographers is what the gate of these places makes narrowly available for the lens of their cameras. Most Fez's religious sites, therefore, survive intact even after colonial intrusion.

FEZ. - Nouvelle Porte de Boujeloud

Édition Haïm-David Barera

Figure 1.3: Fez- Nouvelle Porte de Boujeloud

Figure 1.4: Fez- Entrance of Moulay-Idriss Mosque

The photographic documentation of shrines presented in the French colonial postcard functions as a sort of mapping to the spatial identity. Its
prime task is to document spatial structural ingredients to build a system
of visual mapping to the city[13] (Berg 2008, 8). The sense of orientation
that the picture image provides seems more intelligible than scripted di-

---

13   Berg refers to Du Camp and Salzmann whose collected images served to "localize the
      structure functioning as photographic maps," thereby replacing topographies of Egypt.

rectives. However, in certain settings there are some spatial constraints which hinder this process. The interiors of shrines and Mosques are significant examples. Figure 1.4 pictures the entrance leading to the Tomb of Moulay Idriss II. The photographer was allowed much freedom to manipulate specific angles and appropriate frames conforming to conventional standards of Western composition of visual facts. In other words, the ethnographic interest is apparently not directed towards 'documenting' random knowledge about the shrine though the zooming technique is restricted in a rigid manner.

The official ban that is exerted by the religious institution of the space in question is seen as fragmental moments of humiliation that the Western gaze has to experience due to its incessant and untiring quest for gathering (or constructing) information. To shift from the observing Self's position onto the Other's interlocution, one may pause to admire these highly decorated architecture, which stands as a significant emblematic 'trace' of the Islamic civilisation. The two women at the entrance remain as anonymous as the targeted religious environment. However, their 'intended' inclusion along with their association with the setting entails reconsideration of the standards imposed by the Orientalist tradition.

Other postcards display most of the shrine site not as a spiritual resort for some worshipers, but rather as necessarily a place accommodating shelter for beggars. The existence of beggars in a place whose structure is rich with blazing shapes of the Islamic architectural designs invokes in the viewer's psyche dialectical images that may destabilize the previously internalized standards of reception.

The shrines and mosques are religious settings and are possibly the most desired by colonial photographers seeking to cover a 'foil' for their faith. However, their institutionally maintained closure impedes the photographer's attempt to bring their sacred interior into extreme visibility. Many postcards illustrate how picturing religious settings raises objection in the part of the natives. Before shooting the photograph, some photographers must have apparently been blitzed by the natives' audacious and repudiating looks.

To sum up, despite endless images of poverty and misery which are documented in association with Fez's shrines and mosques, their inner sides remain mostly intact and inaccessible. The general visual message that most postcards tend to communicate is about the dissemination of a constructed spatial identity which lag behind the standards of Western urban development.

b. Old Medina and Colonial Appropriation

The complex and heterogeneous nature of the postcards configuring Fez necessitates a thorough investigation of the major transformations being effected on the city's cultural identity due to different forms of visual representation. In addition, we should consider the new architectural polity that French Morocco, under the administration of General Lyautey, upheld as a manifest indication of the French 'civilizing mission' in Fez. Innovations in the city's architectural morphology were salient features stretching from the northwest of the old Fez to form what has been known as Ville Nouvelle (The New City) or Dar Dibbagh. Lyautey's official invitations to well-known architects of the time, like Maurice Tranchant de Lunel and Henri Prost, aimed at designing urban areas for foreigners, with strong emphasis on making this pattern different from the old city[14] (Mezzine 2010, 261- 263).

To visually cover and document this enterprise, a number of artists and photographers were mobilized on a grand scale. Some of them were part of the colonized subjectivities, like the oil painter Azouaou Mammeri who painted the Moroccan cities of Rabat and Fez (Benjamin2002). Benjamin claims that "Mammeri developed a way of summarizing detail in a racy geometric manner that he shared with certain colonial painters of the 1920's" (44). His 'artistic' work was not dissimilar from that of Edith Wharton's in that they both sided with the French 'civilizing mission' and preached the French 'rightfulness' to take charge of 'modernizing' Morocco and pulling it through out of its 'backward' state of 'immobility'.

As for photography, colonized subjects in Fez were also engaged in the visual documentation of the native landscape and people in numerous postcards. Patricia Goldsworthy refers to the Jewish photographer, Joseph Bouhsira who was "the first Moroccan to own a studio" (Goldsworthy 2009, 148). His photographs range widely on different themes, including a strong emphasis on the Moroccan Jewish community. Other photog-

---

14   Mezzine affirms that the Makhzan took care of the conservation of the old city through passing the acts of 26th November 1912 and 13th February 1914 which prohibit any intervention of modern architecture.

raphers were mainly Europeans and their mission was part and parcel of the major French colonial enterprise in Morocco. A major proportion of their work was dedicated to featuring the old and the new parts of Fez. Their modes of representation show an astonishing fidelity to preserving the recommended distinction between the native space and the colonialist one. The recurrent presence of gigantic ramparts and tall outstanding minarets in photographs picturing the old Fez is highly expressive of the prevailed tendency among photographers. Such a way of seeing entails the photographer's unconditioned allegiance to the Orientalists instructions, which tend to view the photographed Oriental landscape as if it has sprang up from an oil painting.[15]

Most of the photographs selected to inform this analysis are shot from a distance that creates a wider telescopic vision incorporating the smallest details meanwhile intimidating the general ensemble to prevent the emergence of any natural 'artefact' that would intimidate, in its turn, the French mode of expression. This 'rhetorical totalizing view'[16] is only made available from an outside viewpoint with the purpose to create a fictional presence of the city. This visual construction can be underpinned by the idea that "photography…is hardly immune to the bandishments of Orientalism, and even a presumably innocent or neutral view of architecture can be ideologized" (Nochlin 1991, 39).

Some photographs tend to share a propensity to document decorated arched entrances, fountains of different shapes, marbled pillars and certain daily activities which conjure up the museum-like landscape of old Fez. All these ingredients are significant for the ultimate Orientalist 'recipe' that is meant to invoke a kind of familiarization (and also sense of security against the 'other') with the depicted space within the French shared imagination in the metropolis. This is done through the demarcation of a homogenous 'other' that would appear analogous to the previously constructed image carved in the West's collective memory.

---

15   Here I have in mind Roger Benjamin (2002) who explains how oil painters, like the Algerian artist Mammri, gained access to European modes of knowledge that influenced their paintings (46).

16   In the context of photographs being shot from a distance, the city 'swallows' minor spaces and deprive the viewer from experiencing visual containment of the swallowed details. Here I adapt Dickens' description of the city as a destructive animal swallowing every tiny segment that are part and parcel of its overall composition, (cited in Williams1973, 196).

The distance from which the photographs were shot reveals a metaphorical murder of the place in question. It has enabled the camera, in some instances, to visually stuff unparalleled ramparts into a narrow field of vision to create a 'paranoid' space, whose sense of fortification appertains to the Middle Ages. The pictured landscape is appropriated to reveal varied degrees of 'hostility' or 'fear' towards outside threat; the created impregnability of the space signals the heroic adventure and challenge awaiting the French colonizing mission.

Depictions of the old city are mostly packed with symptoms of a closed mode of life. They produce a spectacle of a space with a human essence that functions as the polar opposite of 'white humanity'. The need for a reproduction of this latter's mode of life within the colonized land comes as a colonial tendency to foster a spatial dialectic where colonial occupation is legitimized. This was only possible through the French imposition of European architectural models to counterbalance the monumental designs of old Fez. The urban changes that took place developed "at a due distance from the old town centres" (Khallouki 2002, 3).

The new cityscapes came as an emergent architectural décor contrasting with the old architectural patterns of old Fez. They may also count as a form of spatial intrusion that was brought forth to further materialize the ideological battle in Morocco. However, this intrusion seems to have been subjected to some restrictions as Fez managed to preserve its cultural heritage unspoilt, allowing urban innovation to happen outside its architectural realm. As an example, Roger Le Tourneau describes the arched Bab Boujloud as a polychromic and spatial landmark which ended the impregnability of Fez and allowed its visitors to access further spatial details which defines the inside of Old Medina (Le Tourneau 1987, 109). His remark aimed probably to show that the door was an inaugural spatial change in colonial Morocco, a change which played an important part in extending the use of polychromic mosaic from the inside of palaces and mansions to a gate allowing smooth penetration to the heart of the city.

Yet, the construction of the new Bab Boujloud was preceded by another French attempt to build a gate that conforms to European architectural style. Figure 1.5 represents this doomed attempt. It is a European spatial identity that was introduced in 1913 to function as the city's sole entrance giving access to the covered market that plunges to the right in the old city

(109). Its construction was adjacent to a small gate, built during the reign of Mohamed al-Nassir Bnu al-Mansour. The French gate fostered public resentment and the Qarwiyyine Ulama started to preach against it in their Friday's sermons.Khalid Bekkaoui explains that the Ulama (religious scholars) believed that "walking under it (the French gate)…would turn the pious Muslim believer into a Christian renegade" (Bekkaoui 2007, 1). As a consequence, the resident general, Marshal Lyautey ordered the destruction of the gate which was soon replaced by a gate pattern that conforms to the Islamic arched entrances, as demonstrated in 1.3.

The caption says, *Bab Boujloud,* with a parenthetic remark, *The Gate of the French,* added as an allusion to the public protest rallied against the gate. However, the postcard in 1.3 acts as a legitimate resistance to such appropriation insinuating meanwhile that the colonized space has very limited tolerance to the French colonial interference.

Figure 1.5: Fez- Bab-Boujloud, dite «Porte des Francais»

The new blocks of buildings and streets were constructed for hosting foreign settlers from all walks of life. Their creation must have come as an attempt to build up a spatial organism of a counter-discourse challenging the city's 'prolonged past' (Wharton 2005, 50). They emerged to 'shape the city's future' under the French supervision and end up its exclusion from the Eurocentric linearity. Also, the heterogeneous nature of colonial vision may necessitate another reading of the occurrence of such European spatial layout. From a social and economic perspective, the new city can be understood as a Euro-colonial form of spatial marginalization to the Oriental local center, known as Old Medina. This overmastering of the old city seeks concrete forms of legitimizing the French colonial presence in Fez. The latter may still preserve its historical value but this time through the 'exoticizing' lens of the colonial eye. Its existence may serve to function, from a Western point of view, as a museum-like mode of living available to fulfill the colonial expectation of the timeless Orient.

In this respect, we ought not to forget that the dimensions of the city's immobility and timelessness is a Western self-inflicted problem and its conception as a geographical entity was just another 'commodity' replete with colonial tropes instructing additional ways of seeing the 'Orient'. In addition, the new architecture may insinuate the French desire to lessen the traumatic amnesia of the settlers who had been in a prolonged contact with the alien space in question.

If we happen to open "a real textual terrain for native self representation and self-assertion" (Bekkaoui 2007, 47)[17], we may end up designing a dialectical map of the different experiences that the colonial administration had in its various forms of contact with the native. There are numerous cards illustrating 'prestigious' colonial interventions within the general surrounding of the city of Fez. Their visual content acts as an attempt to prevail (or rather veil) the fallacy that the French colonial administration had a 'noble' presence in Fez with another 'noble' aim of accomplishing a civilizing mission. It is a form of discourse that conspicuously enchants the skeptics and opens the door wide for unequal confrontations between two spatial identities.

The modern quarters being visually depicted were designed to provide the French colonial officials with a 'well-earned' rest. This must have also served to facilitate their official missions, fostering sense of home among the French expatriates. However, within the same visual narrative, the native element seems to level degrees of inconsistency against the discursive standards informing the colonial discourse in question. The presence of some veiled women in certain cards renders the newly built 'Europe-

---

17   Khalid Bekkaoui foregrounds the need for voicing the native's counter-hegemonic opposition through opening a textual terrain for the native's self-assertion and self-representation.

an' quarter diasporic. The fact that they were captured in motion signals a native social dynamism taking place at the very heart of an intruding spatial identity. At this juncture, the colonial text is bound to suffer symptoms of discursive impotence while communicating a form of a spatial change that is meant to propagate the success of colonial assimilation. Veiled women, and probably other native ingredients, though they form a spectacle of distant nature, subject the overall space to a state of solitude which makes it estranged from its cultural background.

In cataloguing these spatial identities, I have sought to present the French 'experienced reality' of Fez gained through individual ethnographic encounters with the city[18] (Pink 2001,19). Most of them are rarely innocent or freed of fictional construction of reality. The 'embellishment' of space with modern architectural designs may count as ethnographic indications of social mobility stimulated by France in Fez. Though this act can be highly critical of the old city's backwardness, the distance being maintained between the two spaces implies that the "perpetually prolonged past" of Fez is an everlasting reality, a claim that has proved its felicity since then and continued up till the present time. In other words, Fez still provides its foreign visitors, as it used to do with its colonizers, with the opportunity to witness medieval Eastern life. Its tawny ramparts still bear testimony to an ancient architectural morphology which still gives the Western tourists an unprecedented thrill to encounter the fictional Orient being depicted recurrently by ancient travel writers.

French colonial postcards have managed to accumulate a great deal of visual 'documentation' of non-Western cultures and territories. Their mapping strategy of Eastern identity and geography is tantamount to the role played by nineteenth century European maps and travel narrative. In addition, the creation of fictional maps of unknown geographies has inspired their readers with metaphorical constructions of the Orient replete with tales of exoticism, adventure and mystery. Such an inspiration counted as an open invitation to adventure accompanied with 'useful' guidance to assure the survival of the white man in an alien land.

The role of colonial photography seems to be analogous in various re-

---

18   Sarah Pink argues that ethnographic knowledge can only be subjective construction, "a 'fiction' that represents only the ethnographer's version of a reality, rather than an empirical truth."

spects, if not basically complementary, to the 'linguistic' maps devised by European fictions and travelogues. Photographs, notably postcards, were effective enough to translate the Oriental fact into forms of information much more appreciable than the art of writing. In other words, the experience of the Oriental 'world' through descriptive and fictional accounts might have pleased the Western imagination but not its retinal reception. In this respect, the visual mapping of Fez's old cityscapes served, in certain instances, the construction of the Orient's spatial primitiveness, a visual stereotypical depiction which substitutes pictorial reproduction for the representational value of words, to reaffirm the Western matrices of polar opposition.

Geographical fantasies are repeatedly encountered in a number of postcards featuring the city of Fez in a disordered shape where the presence of the natural landscape is prominent and almost swallowing the disproportionate urbanized area. Such a manipulated way of seeing echoes a whole tradition of hegemonic discourse that seeks containment of non-Western peoples and places, through linguistic and visual forms of representation.

Conclusion

In conclusion, the examination of colonial postcards depicting various spatial aspects of Fezreveals a pervasive pattern of Orientalist discourse perpetuating stereotypes and narratives of Western superiority while exoticizing the cultural identity and agency of the depicted Orient. Through selective framing and portrayal, these images construct a distorted view of Fez as stagnant and exotic, reinforcing colonial power dynamics and celebrating Western triumph over Islamic civilization. Despite attempts to capture and control indigenous spaces, the postcards also reveal moments of resistance within the visual landscape, underscoring the complexities of power, representation, and identity in the colonial encounter. By critically engaging with these images, we can uncover deeper layers of meaning, reclaiming the historical narrative to reflect marginalized voices and offering a more nuanced understanding of colonialism's enduring impact on perceptions of the Orient.

Acknowledgements

The selected sets of French colonial postcards that capture the essence of the city of Fez are drawn from the private collection of Dr. Majid Tazi Saaoud, a physician and postcard collector from Fez.These invaluable historical artifacts not only provide a vivid contextual analysis but also offer a rare glimpse into the past. We are deeply grateful for Dr. Saaoud's generosity in sharing these treasures, which enrich our understanding and appreciation of Fez's rich heritage. Also, special thanks are given to Professors Khalid Bekkaoui, whose expertise has acted foundationally in shaping the direction and the quality of this work, and to the staff of *Bibliothèque Nationale du Royaume du Maroc*, in Rabat and the staff of *Bibliothèque de la Fondation du Roi Abdul Aziz Al Saoud*, in Casablanca for their generous help and guidance.

References

Al-Jazaani, Ali.1991. *Jana Zahrat al-Ass fi Bina'a Madinat Fass.* [*The History of the City of Fez*], edited by Abdelwahhab Ibnu Mansour. Translated by Mine. Al-Matba'a al-Malakiya.

Barthelemy, Anthony Gerard. 1987. *Black Face, Maligned Race: The Representation of Blacks in English Drama from Shakespeare to Southerne.* Louisiana State University Press.

Bekkaoui, Khalid. 1998. *Signs of Spectacular Resistance: The Spanish Moor and British Orientalism.* Najah El Jadida Press.

———. n.d. "Fez Medina: Creation, Conquest and Contraband." In *The Contraband Modern in The Fez Medina.*http://www.open.ac.uk/Arts/ferguson-centre/fes-medina/papers/khalid-bekkaoui-paper.htm.

Benjamin, Roger. 2002. "Colonial Tutelage to Nationalist Affirmation: Mammeri and Racim, Painters of the Maghreb." In *Orientalism's Interlocutors: Painting, Architecture, Photography*, edited by Jill Beaulieu and Mary Roberts, 43–78. Duke University Press.

Berg, Keri A. 2008. "The Imperialist Lens: Du Camp, Salsmann, and Early French Photography." *The Journal of Early Popular Visual Culture* 6 (1): 1–18.

De Certeau, Michel. 1984. *The Practice of Everyday Life.* Translated by Steven Rendall. University of California Press.

Hodge, Carl C., ed. 2007. *Encyclopedia of the Age of Imperialism, 1800–1914.* Vol. 1. Greenwood Press.

Jacobs, Jane M. 1996. *Edge of Empire: Postcolonialism and the City.* Routledge.

Khallouki, Mohamed Tamsamani. 2002. *The Golden Book.* Translated by Julia Weiss. Casa Editrice Bonechi.

Le Tourneau, Roger. 1987. *Fès avant le Protectorat.* Éditions la Porte.

Lidchi, Henrietta. 1997. "The Poetics and the Politics of Exhibiting Other Cultures." In *Representation: Cultural Representations and Signifying Practices,* edited by Stuart Hall, 151–208. SAGE Publications.

Goldsworthy, Patricia Marie. 2009. *A Dissertation on Colonial Negatives: The Prohibition and Commodification of Photography in Sharifian and French Morocco.* Self-published.

Mezzine, Mohamed, ed. 2010. *Tarikh Madinat Fas [The History of the City of Fez].* Translated by Mine. Sipama Imprimerie.

Pink, Sara. 2001. *Doing Visual Ethnography: Images, Media and Representation in Research.* SAGE Publications.

Price, Derrick, and Liz Wells. 1996. "Thinking about Photography: Debates, Historically and Now." In *Photography: A Critical Introduction,* edited by Liz Wells, 9–64. Routledge.

Said, Edward. 1993. *Culture and Imperialism.* Chatto & Windus.

Slavin, David Henry. 2001. *Colonial Cinema and Imperial France, 1919–1939: White Blind Spots, Male Fantasies, Settler Myths.* The Johns Hopkins University Press.

Spurr, David. 1993. *The Rhetoric of Empire: Colonial Discourse in Journalism, Travel Writing, and Imperial Administration.* Duke University Press.

Staszak, Jean-François. 2004. "Primitivism and the Other: History of Art and Cultural Geography." *GeoJournal* 60: 353–64. Kluwer Academic Publishers.

Wharton, Edith. 2005. *In Morocco.* Edited by Khalid Bekkaoui. The Moroccan Cultural Studies Centre.

Williams, Raymond. 1973. *The Country and the City.* Cox & Wyman Ltd.

Nomadism, Border(s) and Geoerotics: Postcolonial Rhizomatic Reading of Kamila Shamsie's *Kartography*

Abhisek Ghosal, PhD.

Abstract

Inoperativity of stratified and territorialized postcolonial thinking falls short of explaining (non)-hierarchical interactions among colonizers, colonized and the Earth—an important planetary phenomenon that stands fraught with the multiplicity of border(s) which are contingent upon a series of elusive and deterritorial assemblages, thereby putting the notion of 'belongingness' under the scanner. This article engages postcolonial rhizomatic thinking to work out an ethico-politics of 'nomadic thinking' in the context of Kamila Shamsie's *Kartography* to put forward a two-fold argument: it is by working out an ethico-politics of 'nomadic thinking', processual and differential aspects of geo-territorial border(s) could be figured out, and in doing so, the question of 'belongingness' could be re-cartographed, aiming at wedding it to the strands of chaosophical immanentism.

Keywords: Rhizome, Geokinesis, Ethico-Politics of Nomadism, Chaosophical Immanentism, (Trans)position

Introduction

The starting point for political theory and action should no longer be the state and its policies but rather the socially constitutive figure of the migrant and human [...] three interrelated tactics that will likely be necessary, but not sufficient, conditions for winning and sustaining a borderless world: sanctuary, solidarity, and status. (Nail 2019, 23-24)

> RHIZOMATICS = SCHIZOANALYSIS = STRA-
> TOANALYSIS = PRAGMATICS = MICROPOLI-
> TICS. (Deleuze and Guattari 1987, 22)
>
> We live in a world of borders. [...] The border is "a process
> of social division." What all borders share in common
> [...] is that they introduce a division or bifurcation of
> some sort into the world. (Nail 2016, 1-2)

Thomas Nail has pertinently argued that human beings nowadays dwell in an age of movement actualised by several socio-cultural, political and economic phenomena, including rapid technological advancement, easy and accessible transportation system, geopolitical displacement of migrants across borders, worldwide dissemination of neoliberal economic framework, information flow, to name only a few. What it points at is that under the glaring stare of postcolonial conditions, human beings ride the vector of migrancy to move across different kinds of border(s), among which are territorial, political, cultural, social, economic, and technological, either to come to terms with the onslaughts of postcolonial memory and trauma, or to deal with the politics of *bio-geo-eco-territorialization*.

Polysensorial and multifaceted movements across borders, caused by the geopolitical conflicts embodied in the form of War, entail cross-border inflows and outflows of migrants who are forced to take on the politics of *inside/outside* to settle down on the margins of a sovereign territory. On the one hand, so-called "stateless" migrants have to tackle the exploitative territorial governmentality of the State and on the other hand, they are forced to negotiate *geological pedesis* of the Earth to reorganize and reterritorialize themselves in the *zones of indiscernibility* embodied through geo-territorial tensions and *deterritorial assemblages* of colonized, colonizers and the Earth.

Pitted against the problematic of movement and belongingness, this article seeks to put the spotlight on the inoperativity of postcolonial strands in elucidating *non-hierarchical* and *non-arborescent* interactions among refugees, State and the Earth while aiming at providing a postcolonial rhizomatic model of thinking to contextualize an ethico-politics of nomadism to back up onto-epistemic fluidity of migrancy that stands capable of taking up, what Deleuze and Guattari call, "lines of becoming" to evade the magnetic pulls of stratification, codification and territorialization. In a nutshell, this article seeks to foreground processual and differential dimensions of border(s) with the help of *nomadic thinking* aided by postcolonial rhizomatics to re-cartograph the question of *belongingness* in the context of Kamila Shamsie's *Kartography*.

Limits of the Postcolonial: From Stratified Thinking to Multiplicity of Border(s)

> Postcolonial writing characteristically sees space as heterogeneous and malleable. [...] It suggests that the identity politics, implicit or explicit, in postcolonial writing offers a particular challenge to discourses that see place as a stable entity. (Thieme 2016, 2)

> Where the migrant moves along the paths formed by striated space, the nomad is "distributed by turbulence across a smooth space." (Bull 2004, 223)

> Multiplicities are rhizomatic. [...] A multiplicity has neither subject nor object, only determinations, magnitudes, and dimensions that cannot increase in number without the multiplicity changing in nature. (Deleuze and Guattari 1987, 8)

In "Deleuze and the Postcolonial: Conversations, Negotiations, Mediations," Simone Bignall and Paul Patton reflectively contend that exiting strands of postcolonial stand fraught with the "forces" of territorialization and thus cannot come to the help in understanding the plane of "exteriority" embodied through self and other. It means that the inoperativity of stratified postcolonial interventions cannot help one explain constant "negotiations" and "mediations" between self and other. It calls for taking into account the philosophical insights of Deleuze and Guattari. They are of the viewpoint that if the colonised man fails to break away from conformist ways of thinking, he "won't get away from a master's or colonist's discourse," an established discourse" (Deleuze 1990a, 125).

Thus, Bignall and Patton emphasise forging an epistemic linkage between Deleuzian thoughts and the postcolonial, hoping that:

> Communication with Deleuzian concepts may prompt a critical *becoming* of postcolonial theory, providing a useful philosophical perspective for evaluating and improv-

> ing the adequacy of the existing solutions proposed to
> resist and transform the conditions defining the problem
> of colonialism. (2010, 12)

It suggests that an epistemic wedding between Deleuze and the Postcolonial entails reparative refashioning of the subversive and transformative discourses of the postcolonial, intending to alter the grammatology of postcolonial interventions so that the affective assemblages of "exteriority" could be figured out to elucidate colonized people's ceaseless mediations with what Deleuze and Guattari call "striated" and "smooth" spaces of knowledge. Deleuzian tweak with postcolonial discourses leads one to mark the onto-epistemic "diagrammatism" of geo-territorial spaces which are often subjected to colonialist discourses, supposing that colonisers have established territorial sovereignty through the practices of European socio-cultural traditions of dominance.

Whereas colonialist discourses force colonized people to subscribe to "striated" spaces of knowledge, colonized people need to look forward to exploring "smooth" spaces of intellectual becoming so that "diagrammatic" transformations of spaces along the "lines of departure" could be set forth to question tenability and viability of colonialist discourses in the age of Movement.

Following Deleuze's Externality thesis, it could be argued that the "outside" of the territorial border(s) is seemingly governed by the state which at times cannot regulate the outside's nuanced "negotiations" and "mediations" with the *geological pedesis* of the Earth. In other words, territorial border(s) cannot be taken into cognisance as an inflexible and unchangeable referent since these are both often drawn and redrawn in alignment with the political governmentality of the State and are subjected to self-decay and processual ungrounding of the Earth. To elaborate on differential intensities of the border(s), one may tenably argue that territorial border(s) stand charged up with quanta of deterritorialization which enables them to take up "lines of becoming" in the "zones of irreducibility," thereby suggesting that there exists a *micropolitics* of border-thinking—epistemological strands of which are *intensively* connected with what Thomas Nail terms "kinopolitics" in *Theory of the Border*. Nail reflects:

> Kinopolitics is the theory and analysis of social mo-
> tion: the politics of movement [...]The conceptual
> basis of kinopolitics is the analysis of social flows [...]
> The second basic conceptual term of kinopolitics is the
> junction. If all of social reality comprises continuous
> flows, junction explains the phenomenon of relative or
> perceived stasis [...] A junction is not something other
> than a flow; it is the redirection of a flow back onto itself
> in a loop or fold [...] The third basic conceptual term
> of kinopolitics is circulation, which connects a series of
> junctions into a larger curved path [...] Circulation, just
> like flows [...] is a continuum. In this sense, circulation
> is both inside and outside at once. It is a multi-folded
> structure creating a complex system of relative insides
> and outsides without absolute inclusions and exclu-
> sions, but the insides and outsides are all folds of the
> same continuous process or flow. (2016, 24-29)

Nail clearly articulates that "kinopolitics" is primarily grounded in the
dialectical interplay among "flow", "junction" and "circulation," which accounts for how border(s) get governed by the tension between "flow" and
"fold." In other words, territorial border(s), instead of being a codified
geopolitical instrument, are constitutive of "flows" of social motion that
get folded into itself, forming the relatively stable plane of "junction"—a
series of which make up "circulation" that has neither permanent inside
nor permanent outside. In short, territorial border(s) are made up of
"multi-folded" structures of both "inside" and "outside" and thus stand in
a state of "continuous process or flow" interspersed with the movements
of both human and nonhuman agents.

Then, one may be reminded of the productive potentials of "folding," as
understood by Deleuze in *The Fold*:

> A fold is always folded within a fold, like a cavern in a
> cavern [...] Unfolding is thus not the contrary of fold-
> ing, but follows the fold up to the following fold [...]
> Folding-unfolding no longer simply means tension-re-
> lease, contraction-dilation, but enveloping-developing,
> involution-evolution. (1993, 6-8)

247

Taking recourse to Deleuzian intervention into the phenomenon of "folding," it can be argued that territorial border(s) consist of "folding-unfolding" dynamics and therefore, are capable of triggering "co-intensive" and "co-extensive" spaces of differential becoming into being represented by "borderspace" that stages heterogeneous and non-arborescent movements of human and nonhuman beings along the "lines of rupture." Following this critical contention, it has become clear that as "borderspace" stands checkered by cross-movements of different human and nonhuman agents, it perfectly accounts for the "differentiation" of border-thinking embodied through the constant "negotiations" and "mediations" of migrants with the *geological pedesis* of the Earth.

In continuation with this vein, it needs to be added to the earlier contention that the kinopolitical movements of territorial border(s) are largely governed by a sort of *intensive micropolitics* that leads border(s) to go along the "minor" lines of escape so that the onto-epistemological fluidity of border(s) cannot be territorialized in terms of stratification and codification. This "supple segmentarity" of territorial border(s) finds home in the production of new "collective assemblages of enunciation"—physical manifestations of which are found in the constantly altering nature of "borderspace." It can be contended that following the notion of "absolute positive deterritoralization" (2017, 36) found in Nail's *"What is an Assemblage?"* new "collective assemblages of enunciation" get reflected through an emergent multiplicity which can be figured out only in terms of "determinations, magnitudes, and dimensions" (Deleuze and Guattari 1987, 8). It means that territorial border(s) cannot be reduced to mere spaces of "liminality;" rather, these need to be opened out to the politics of "trans(in)fusion" so that State machineries cannot contain the aberrant dispersals of migrants who are not only wedded to an ethico-politics of nomadism but also whose "aleatory" movements can potentially unsettle structured territorial governmentality exercised in favour of the State.

Samuel Weber has thus contended in *Singularity: Politics and Poetics*:

> What is "singular" can only be conceived or experienced
> as an event that quite literally comes out (ex-venire) of
> that which it follows and exceeds [...] It can only be
> acceded to through a process that seems to be its direct
> contradiction: a process of repetition. But it is a repeti-

tion that is composed not just of similarity, but of irreducible difference. (2021, 2)

Weber means to argue that the seemingly repetitive process of singularity
stands characterised by "irreducible difference" and therefore is experienced as "a movement of transfer or of transformation" (2021, 2). Following Weber's critical intervention, it can be claimed that in the "zones
of irreducibility", the experience of singularity can best be figured out in
terms of "dimensions" and "directions," which hints at its epistemological
linkages with principles of multiplicity laid out by Deleuze and Guattari in
A Thousand Plateaus. In fact, in *The Logic of Sense*, Deleuze provocatively
claims: "Singularities are turning points or points of inflection [...] "sensitive" points [...] Singularity is *neutral*," (1990 b, 52) thereby suggesting
that singularityes can be neither compared with "denotation," nor with
"manifestation," nor with "significance," as these constitute the essence of
the meaning of an Event. It is quite true in the context of territorial bor-
der(s) in the sense that "borderspace" stands replete with "singularities"
which explains why it turns out to be a veritable "Body without Organs"
(BwO) for the physical enactment of "movement of transfer or of transformation."

Geoerotics, (Trans)positions and Nomadism: Working out Postcolonial Rhizomatic Thinking

One way to do this is to distinguish between two kinds of
movement that define the migrant. The first kind, made
up of units of space-time, is extensive and quantitative:
movement as a change of place, or translation. The second kind of movement is intensive and qualitative: a
change in the whole, a transformation. (Nail 2015, 13)

Being single and multiple, independent and interconnected, Nomadic Subjects and Nomadic Theory form a
complex singularity or a nondualistic assemblage. They
frame and actualise a nomadology that instils movement
and mobility at the heart of thinking (Braidotti 2011, 2)

Sensation is the zone of indeterminacy between subject
and object, the bloc that erupts from the encounter of
the one with the other. [...] Sensation has two dimensions, two types of energy: it is composed of affects and

percepts. (Grosz 2009, 84-86)

Whereas Deleuze and Guattari lay down geophilosophical insights in terms of a tension between "deterritorialization (from territory to the earth) and reterritorialization (from earth to territory)" (1994, 86) in *What Is Philosophy?*, thereby underscoring the workings of desire in governing the geological becomings of the Earth in alignment with the "lines of departure," Thomas Nail calls for taking the figure of the migrant into account as a "social vector" that stands capable of exceeding the limits of "stasis" and can well step into the state of perpetual "movement." Following these critical contentions, one may here tenably deduce that just as the nuanced movements of the Earth stand grounded in the dialectical interplay between "territory" and "the earth," movements of a migrant across the territorial border(s) do not seem to stand in between fixed points but find home in "kinopolitics."

In short, multifaceted movements of a migrant across the "borderspace" remain suspended in a state of "trans:" (trans)formation, (trans)duction, (trans)figuration, (trans)migration, (trans)mutation, (trans)ference; in a nutshell, (trans)position(s). Interestingly, whereas geoerotical becomings of the Earth are premised on the politics of "trans(in)fusion," thereby referring to the "geokinetic" dispersals of the differential intensities of the Earth, movements of a migrant across the "borderspace" are regulated by the 'forces' of kinopolitics. At this critical juncture, one may stop and think: what do both "geokinetic" movements of the Earth and "kinetic" displacements of a migrant across the "borderspace" entail? How can these nonhuman and human movements be "sensed?"

To respond to these problematic questions, one may be reminded of Rosi Braidotti's *Transpositions: On Nomadic Ethics*, in which she has categorically mapped the concept of transposition in the following terms:

> [Transposition is] a creative leap that produces a prolific in-between space [...] The term 'transposition' refers to mobility and cross-referencing between disciplines and discursive level [...] The notion of transposition describes the connection between the text and its social and historical context, in the material and discursive sense of the term. (2006, 6-7)

Braidotti means to argue that "transposition" could be taken into account as a conceptual framework that can help one spell out nuanced intersections between "cartographic" and "normative" trajectories. It means that taking "transposition" as a form of "conceptual creativity," (2006, 9) "a fluid flowing of becoming" (2006, 9) found in the "borderspace" can be cartographed. In other words, across the "borderspace," migrants resort to singular points of becoming that stand in connection with geokinetic movements of the Earth and kinetic ungrounding of the territorial border(s). It is by riding the vectors of "transposition," that migrants can potentially assume "a fluid flowing of becoming" and thus are often considered as potential 'threats' to the territorial sovereignty of a State.

In addition, migrants often take up the "creative" and "productive" loop of folding into itself, thereby constituting a series of complex "junctions"—a deterritorial assemblage of which forms the dynamics of "circulation." Interestingly, State machinery cannot figure out fluid "transpositions" of migrants through rigid and stratified codes and blocs, and therefore, end up being inflexibly and unalterably categorised as refugee, immigrant, asylum seeker, and stateless person, to name a few. Contrary to this sort of territorial governmentality performed by the State, migrants rely on "transpositional" movements to evade the snares of territorialization and physical detention. In a nutshell, migrants prefer to take up nomadic paths of singular becoming conditioned by the trajectories of both "kinopolitics" and "transposition" so that they can make much of the "smooth space" triggered into being by the intersectional overlapping among "flow," "junction" and "circulation" and State machinery cannot track them down across the "borderspace."

At this point, one may stop and think: how do nomadic pathways facilitate migrants to slip into fluid transpositional vectors of kinesis? In *A Thousand Plateaus*, Deleuze and Guattari hold that nomadic path is replete with "smooth" space which "is a field without conduits or channels. [...] is wedded to a very particular type of multiplicity: nonmetric, acentered, rhizomatic multiplicities" (1987, 371). It means that nomadic "transpositions" seem to result in leading migrants to take up "the line of escape" in the "zones of irreducibility" and thus migrants make use of nomadism as a "war machine" against the oppressive and restrictive, exploitative and regressive forces of the State.

What is interesting here to note is that as migrants follow nomadic singularities to traverse heterogeneous spaces of difference across the "borderspace," they do not get caught up in the pull of sedentary points of territorialization and thus State has to keep on devising political strategies to take stock of migrant movements having the power to unsettle politico-cultural-social *status quo* of the State. In addition, migrants devise "nomadic thinking" to take on State politics across the "borderspace" to put the "politics of affect" at play. In *Nomadic Theory*, Braidotti reflects:

> [Nomadic thought] borrows instead from Spinoza a positive notion of desire as an ontological force of becoming. This achieves an important goal: it makes all thinking into an affirmative activity that aims at the production of concepts, precepts, and affects in the relational motion of approaching multiple others. (2)

> The central tenet of nomadic thought is to reassert the dynamic nature of thinking and the need to reinstate movement at the heart of thought by actualising a non-unitary vision of the thinking subject. (2011, 7)

She clearly spells out that nomadic thought stands charged up with quanta of deterritorialization which explains how nomadic thoughts evade territorial settlement and look forward to the "forces" of reterritorialization. In other words, dialectical interplay between deterritorialization and reterritorialization conditioned by the "smooth" flows of desire play instrumental role in steering nomadic thoughts forward.

Taking the migrants' inclination to nomadic thoughts to counter State-sponsored violence across the "borderspace" into account, "connective" and "disjunctive" potentials of "desire" expressed through "rhizomatics" could be twisted into epistemic discourses of postcolonial to make it work effectively and productively in the context of transpositional and nomadic kinesis of migrants. Epistemic grafting of "rhizomatics" onto the postcolonial is intended to refashion hackneyed and stratified interventions of the postcolonial, which works by the logic of arborescent inroads.

In *A Thousand Plateaus*, Deleuze and Guattari reflectively contend that the characteristics of rhizome incorporate "Principles of connection and heterogeneity, [...] Principle of multiplicity, [...] Principle of asignify-ing rupture, [...] and Principle of cartography and decalcomania." (1987, 7-12) It means that a rhizome takes nomadic paths of becoming to end up in the production of "collective assemblages of enunciation." Taking the operative logic of rhizome into account, postcolonial rhizomatic thinking could be mapped as a fluid and deterritorial assemblage that can unfold nomadic transpositions of migrants that happened in the "borderspace."

Postcolonial rhizomatic thinking can cut across strata and territories, blocs and codes to look into the correspondences between kinopolitical transpositions of migrants and the geokinetic ungrounding of the Earth. Importantly, postcolonial rhizomatic thinking does not settle down in any enunciative field simply because it operates by the free flows of "de-sire" and nomadism. Therefore, it seems to be pretty useful in explaining non-conformist and non-arborescent transpositions of migrants who are often subjected to different kinds of rules and regulations ratified by the State, so that their movements across the "borderspace" can be catego-rised and regulated.

Thus, postcolonial rhizomatic thinking is designed to be a subversive and transformative critical framework that can bring out the might of nomad-ic becomings against the State-led restrictive and regulatory practices of communication. Postcolonial rhizomatic thinking entails the celebration of the ethico-politics of nomadism that pulls migrants back from getting caught up by State-led restrictions, and upholds the workings of transpo-sitional kinesis embodied by migrants.

Shamsie's *Kartography*: Postcolonial Rhizomatic Interventions into the Question of Belongingness

> Belonging is more problematic than is suggested by a rapid etymological overview. Belonging is associat-ed [...] with identity. [... Belonging] is at the root of conflicts between individuals, groups and entire nations [...] In theory, this belonging is meant to be a non-ma-terial phenomenon but it is extremely material: in fact, it becomes material by dint of its very immateriality. (Westphal 2019, 18)

> One travels by intensity; displacements and spatial fig-ures depend on intensive thresholds of nomadic deter-

> ritorialization (and thus on differential relations) that simultaneously define complementary, sedentary reter-ritorialization. (Deleuze and Guattari 1987, 54)

> Nomadism is a movement, a becoming that affects sed-entaries, just as sedentarization is a stoppage that settles the nomads. (Deleuze and Guattari 1987, 430)

On the one hand, Shamsie's *Kartography* relates a poignant tale of Kara-chi city that stands affected by the inflow of refugees in the post-partition scenario, and on the other hand, it stands as a differentiative actualization of what Braidotti calls "a fluid flowing of becoming." Experienced through the critical gazes of Karim and Raheen, two protagonists of the novel, Shamsie attempts to bring out the politics of identity that is at once deep-ly embedded in geokinetic transformations of Karachi city and at times becomes the primary cause for ethnic violence and socio-political up-heaval across the "borderspace." Karim who wishes to be "a map-maker," (2003, 23) looks forward to exploring how identity plays a crucial role in the process of self-identification with a territory and how it is used as a political weapon to cause discrimination and to underline differences between so-called "natives" of a land and "Muhajirs:"

> Coming across the border thinking we should be grateful for their presence [...] Who the hell are these Muhajirs to pretend it's their city! [...What] kind of immigrant is born in a city and spends his whole life there, and gets married there, and raises his daughter there? [...I] agreed with my father about land reforms, if I told them Karachi was my home just as much as it was anyone else's, would they look at me and think: another Muhajir. (2003, 41)

Following this textual instance, one may argue that just as identity hap-pens to be a fluid marker of one's territorial positionality, Karachi city has been altering in association with the geokinetic becomings of the Earth and as a result of which, it embodies ethnic clashes between "natives" and "Muhajirs" so far as problematic inroads of identity politics into the (trans) positional kinesis of the city and its "migrant" dwellers are concerned.

Along with the geokinetic alterations of Karachi city, dwellers of the city, like potent "social vectors," resort to riding migrancy to explore its nooks and corners, which results in direct confrontations between diverse ethnic communities. In the post-Partition scenario, due to huge inflows and outflows of people across the "borderspace," Karachi city undergoes geoerotic tension between deterritorialization and reterritorialization embodied by nomadic movements of Muhajirs and sedentary dislocations of "natives" respectively.

Whereas "natives" of Karachi city prefer to be governed by the official norms and regulations laid down by the State authority, Karim, a budding map-maker, chooses to indulge in nomadic singularities to "map" Karachi city in a non-arborescent fashion. The problematic dwelling of Karim in Karachi conditioned by his own border-crossing and political turmoil keeps him engaged in deciphering how "flow," "junction" and "circulation" characterize "kinopolitics" of the city that is at once charged up quanta of deterritoralization and at times speaks of the problematic aspects of one's belongingness to it.

As the city rapidly undergoes a series of geoerotic transformations both in terms of transcorporeal fusion and diffusion of bodies, one's belongingness can hardly be mapped in terms of inflexible and rigid segmentarities, knowing that belongingness is onto-epistemologically fluid and "diagrammatic" in nature. In other words, belongingness happens to be a putative "zone of irreducibility" which makes room for nomadic singularities to pull one back from being caught up in rigid territorialization and to lead him/her to take up "lines of flight" only to be landed on the terrain of reterritorialization.

In short, the sense of belongingness calls for the consideration of (trans) positional kinesis of migrants across spaces—differential becomings of which make up geoerotic flux in which Karachi slips into. Therefore, making sense of belongingness has to be tied up to both nomadic displacements of migrants and geoerotic transformation of Karachi.

Karim intends to "map" how the aspects of belongingness stand in flux, and thus it makes it quite difficult for a Muhajir to connect his sense of belongingness with rigid topographical makers of a city like Karachi which is constantly being written and rewritten by rhizomatic movements of migrants. Karim reflects: "Have you ever seen a proper map of this city? Not just one of those two-page things that you see in tourist books but a real, proper map of the whole city'?" (2003, 66)

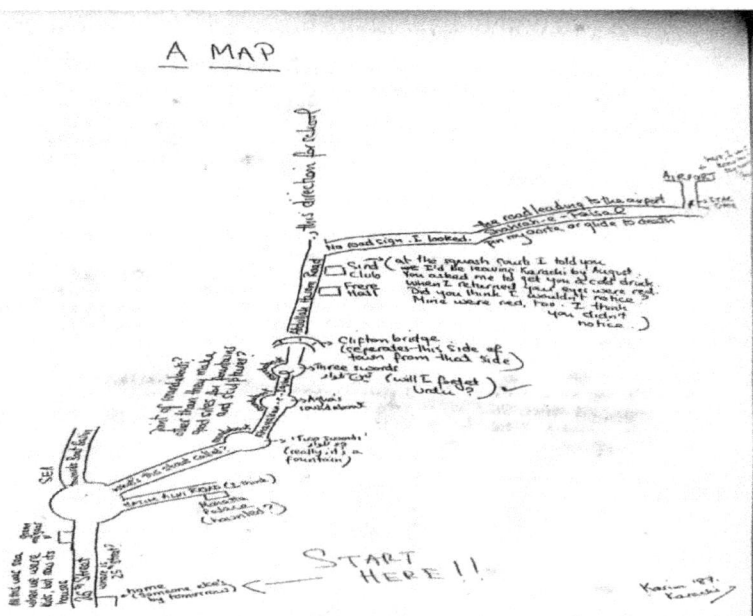

Fig 1. Karim's hand-drawn map found in Shamsie's *Kartography*

Being driven by a desire to be a mapmaker, Karim draws up a subjective map of Karachi, which stands in contrast to the official and government-certified one. This hand-drawn map of Karachi questions the normative representation of Karachi found in official narratives and calls one's sense of belongingness into question. As the hand-drawn map is replete with subjective referents, Raheen at once finds it quite amusing and astonishing:

> On one side was a map of Karachi. A useless, partial map of Karachi, which I had brought with me to America to see if they would bring me any kind of comfort, any kind of pain, on the days when I was most homesick [...] Streets leading to other streets, streets named, areas defined, places of interest clearly marked out. This map was Karachi's opposite [...] These fragments, which he pasted together, were only extracts, contextless; they did not—oh God, surely they did not—reflect anything but a partial truth of who I was, of who I had become in those defining years when he was in so many ways absent to me. (2003, 130-131)

This excerpt lays out Karim's subjective exploration of Karachi and thus the hand-drawn map consists of Karim's experiences of being in Karachi. Interestingly, when Raheen takes a look at the map, she finds a reflection of Karachi through the eyes of a Muhajir whose sense of belongingness is contingent upon geoerotic "trans(in)fusion" of Karachi through nomadic movements of migrants.

Whereas traditional postcolonial insights end up explaining how Karachi gets altered by the inflows of Muhajirs, a rhizomatic twist to postcolonial thinking can enable one to mull over how the act of mapping Karachi by Karim is linked up with mnemonic exercises of Raheen who tries to recall her sense of (be)longingness to Karachi in a non-normative and non-arborescent fashion. In other words, just as Karim draws up the map, defying its rigid and official landmarks, Raheen, too, indulges in the rhizomatic recalling of Karachi to make sense of deterritorial assemblages that constitute the epistemic configuration of belonging. In a nutshell, both Karim and Raheen resort to the operative logic of nomadism both to draw up and to figure out the geoerotic diffusion of Karachi through one's belongingness.

Postcolonial rhizomatic interventions into the question of belongingness entail a Deleuzo-Guattarian ungrounding of Karachi and its "migrant" inhabitants in the context of post-Partition. Deterritorial movements of Muhajirs across the "borderspace" make it very difficult for one to "map" the roots and routes of belongingness as ethnic violence continues to erupt abruptly thereby shaping up the exteriority of Karachi—a phenomenological event that gets precipitated into its differential intensities.

As a result, Karachi slips into intensive becomings which find reflections in Karim's map and leave an impact on Raheen's indulgence into the act of being (longing). Karim intuitively says: "'We learned to forget,' he said. Do you have a family to support?'" (2003, 176) This comment reminds one of how Karim underlines the necessity of the retrieval of the past to explore one's belongingness to a place that stands lashed by ethnic violence and bloodshed. It means the strands of belongingness transversally cut across temporal, spatial, topographical, geoerotical, and nomadic dimensions, which accounts for the need for postcolonial rhizomatic interventions that stand capable of exposing seamless interactions between nomadic movements of migrants and geoerotical transformations of Karachi.

While Karim's map is a never-ending exploration of Karachi's geoerotical becomings, Raheen's use of Karim's map as a tool to step into the realm of belongingness stands backed up by her rhizomatic thinking. But, Raheen finds the map problematic as it questions her understanding of the city where she grew up:

> Why did I keep on harping on about maps? How had they become the symbol of everything that had gone so wrong, so inextricably, in my relationship with Karim? [...] Or was it because every time Karim wrote to me from London and mentioned something about maps of Karachi I heard in his tone both a rebuke and a challenge? As if he knew the city better than I did. (2003, 179)

> I loved the idea of those early cartographers who thought Odysseus's voyage was as valid a source for map-making as the charts of travellers who had actually set sail themselves. (2003, 180)

> All around us, Karachi kept moving. (2003, 181)

These textual instances attest to the claim that Karim's map calls into question Raheen's memories of Karachi and pushes to rethink her belongingness to Karachi, which is insularly mapped in terms of certain rigid landmarks. Karim's individualistic mapping of Karachi lays bare the need for making unconventional and unauthorised inroads into Karachi's intensive becomings reflected through its geoerotical becomings.

What it suggests is that the question of belongingness cannot be pinned down to some rigid signifiers since both Karachi has been undergoing transpositional kinesis and its "migrant" inhabitants to take up "lines of departure" to explore the city along the trajectories of rhizomatics. In short, postcolonial rhizomatic insights help one reveal that belongingness is not only linked up with one's accessibility to Karachi in spatiotemporal terms but also is strongly embedded in one's negotiation with ethical, political, social and economic factors.

Conclusion

Before wrapping up the discussion, one may choose to ask: how does belongingness matter in understanding one's existence? Is belongingness just a matter of identity backed up by memory and nostalgia? Postcolonial rhizomatic readings of Shamsie's fictional forte, that is, *Kartography* answer these questions aptly. On the one hand, the ethico-politics of nomadic thinking leads one to figure out 'belongingness' a series of fluid singular particles since a nomad has to negotiate geo-territorial border(s) that ceaselessly undergo differential movements.

On the other hand, a rhizomatic twist to the postcolonial reading of Shamsie's *Kartography* drives one to link 'belongingness' to the operative matrix of chaosophic immanentism in the sense that deterritorial intensities of 'belongingness' take up aberrant "lines of flight" in the "zones of irreducibility" and therefore stand pervasive of one's dwelling places. In a nutshell, 'belongingness' transversally cuts across socio-political factors including places of dwelling as the epistemic configuration of 'belongingness' seems to be aleatory in nature and subsequently undergoes a process of differentiation to comply with the strands of chaosophical immanentism.

It is by now quite evident that *belongingness* cannot be restricted within memory and nostalgia—which happen to be two cognitive instruments, among others. "Smooth" spaces of *belongingness* stand capable of moving across the geo-territorial border(s), for these are charged up with quanta of deterritorialization. Therefore, the postcolonial rhizomatic reading of Shamsie's *Kartography* ends up in the re-epistemization of *belongingness* by subjecting it to the ethico-politics of nomadism and chaosophical immanentism.

References

Bignall, Simone, and Paul Patton. 2010. Deleuze and the Postcolonial: Conversations, Negotiations, Mediations. In *Deleuze and the Postcolonial*, edited by Bignall and Patton, 119. Edinburgh University Press.

Braidotti, Rosi. 2011. *Nomadic Theory: The Portable Rosi Braidotti*. Columbia University Press.

———. 2006. *Transpositions: On Nomadic Ethics*. Polity.

Bull, Malcolm. 2004. Smooth Politics. In *Empire's New Clothes Reading Hardt and Negri*, edited by Paul A. Passavant and Jodi Dean, 220-233. Routledge.

Deleuze, Gilles. 1990 a. *Negotiations.* Columbia University Press.

———. 1990 b. *The Logic of Sense.* Translated by Mark Lester. The Athlone Press.

———.1993. *The Fold.* Translated by Tom Colney. The Athlone Press.

Deleuze, Gilles, and Félix Guattari. 1987. *A Thousand Plateaus: Capitalism and Schizophrenia.* Translated by Brian Massumi. University of Minnesota Press.

———. 1994. *What Is Philosophy?* Translated by Hugh Tomlinson and Graham Burchell. Columbia University Press.

Grosz, Elizabeth. 2009. Sensation: The Earth, a People, Art. In *Gilles Deleuze: Image and Text,* edited by Eugene W. Holland, Daniel W. Smith and Charles J. Stivale, 81-103. Continuum.

Nail, Thomas. 2016. *Theory of the Border.* Oxford University Press.

———. 2015. *The Figure of the Migrant.* Stanford University Press.

———. 2019. Sanctuary, Solidarity and Status! In *Open Borders: In Defense of Free Movement,* edited by Reece Jones, 23-33. Athens: The University of Georgia Press.

Nail, Thomas. 2017. "What is an Assemblage?" *SubStance* 46, no. 1: 21-37. https://muse.jhu.edu/article/650026.

Shamsie, Kamila. 2003. *Kartography.* Bloomsbury Publishing India.

Thieme, John. 2016. *Postcolonial Literary Geographies: Out of Place.* Palgrave Macmillan.

Weber, Samuel. 2021. *Singularity: Politics and Poetics.* University of Minnesota Press.

Westphal, Bertrand. 2019. Belonging to the Periphery of the Planet. In *Spaces of Longing and Belonging: Territoriality, Ideology and Creative Identity in Literature and Film,* edited by Brigitte Le Juez and Bill Richardson, 17-32. Brill Rodopi.

Confessions of an Anonymous Barbie: an Identity Literacy Journey for Increasing Digital Citizenship Capacity

Jennifer Roth Miller, PhD.

Abstract

This work outlines a digital humanities- and writing and rhetoric-informed framework and pedagogy, presented as an approachable identity literacy journey, for building digital citizenship capacity through the visualization, investigation, and defamiliarization of personal identity. Nuances of critical and digital multiliteracies are explicated along with new language for the implicit mechanics of how identities and collective meaning-making are constructed, expressed, and maintained. Embodied creativity, serious play, and incremental counter performances leveraging art and anonymity in social media engagement and multimodal digital composition are highlighted as tactics for authentic contribution to collective meaning-making in social justice, political, and philanthropic movements and causes, entertainment, popular culture, identity, belonging, and other mundane issues facing global digital citizenship. Academics, students, and everyday citizens alike have the potential to become leaders as they apply and model these multiliteracies that directly relate to increasing encoding, decoding, and reception of diverse authentic original perspectives contributing to solutions to complex matters around the globe.

Keywords: Digital Citizenship, Digital Literacy, Critical Literacy, Multiliteracies, Pedagogy, Social Media, Identity, Slacktivism, Participatory Culture

Identity and belonging, particularly expressed and maintained on social media, have become a paramount channel for the amplification and replication of directed ideas. Therefore, everyday composition in the 21st century increasingly correlates directly with digital citizenship capacity—the ability to authentically participate with original thinking in decoding and encoding multimodal messages affecting collective meaning-making and understanding. Indeed, everyday people participate in the definition of a variety of topics from serious issues such as social justice, philanthropic, and political movements and causes, to fun activities such as entertainment and popular culture, personal identity creation and maintenance, and a variety of mundane matters regularly via social media engagement.

> Every time a person likes, shares, or posts a comment, photo, video, or meme, for example, momentum is given or taken away from collective understanding on any given topic. Increasingly, digital citizens are operating in these new contexts and genres that are participatory, digital, visual, and entertaining, yet they continue to be loaded with rhetorical cultural narratives, power structures, and dualistic thinking. This chapter will juxtapose relevant academic theory with the more fun, creative, visual, and self-expressive activities of social media to guide readers through a personal identity literacy journey to build digital citizenship capacity. Contents of this composition include: new theory, concepts, and language regarding digital citizenship; identity-based pedagogy for defamiliarizing implicit conditioning and rebuilding authenticity; and modeling of concepts.

Readers are invited to engage with the text by participating in an identity literacy journey—a journey that guides ordinary global citizens in unpacking and examining their own identity to build digital citizenship capacities. This journey is a personal activity, but it also includes a step-by-step pedagogy with exercises, materials, and theory that can be utilized with college-level students in the classroom. The fundamental goal of this work is to poise readers, whether they are faculty, students, or citizens, to become leaders in employing and modeling multiliteracies that directly correlate to increased encoding, decoding, and reception of varied authentic original perspectives contributing to solutions to the world's multifaceted issues.

Theory: A Digital Humanities and Writing and Rhetoric Perspective on Identity

This chapter analyzes identity and digital citizenship from an American digital humanities and writing and rhetoric perspective. Romanticism, modernism, and postmodernism are Western-based humanities terms that are used to describe and categorize dominant historical trends during the past few centuries in individual and collective thought and expression evident in literary, visual, and performing arts. Identity-focused scholars in the field of digital humanities (Gergen 1991, 6-17; Hayles 1999, 6-24; Turkle 1995, 36-49), employed historical categorizations to delineate and label tendencies in cultural mindsets and attitudes inherited from distinct periods. This terminology offers a common language and an anchor for the forthcoming discussion of identity and digital citizenship.

Nineteenth-century romanticist thought privileged the private emotional individual, morality, and expression of a unique inner depth or soul, passionate feelings, and inspired personal significance beyond the surface. Twentieth-century modernist thought leveraged pre-existing Enlightenment beliefs of reason and observation and romanticist beliefs of the virtuous autonomous individual, but further developed science, machine, business, and progress metaphors that privileged rigid absolute objective truths, logic, ways of being, and knowing. Twenty-first-century postmodern tendencies, which are currently unfolding, embody a technologically represented public comprised of a highly influenced and contradictory multiplicity of identities and personalities muddled by the additive ideas of romanticism and modernism.

Historically, the private singular moral individual inner self prioritized by romanticism evolved into a postmodern highly-exposed public comprised of exponential visual-based representations of individuals' identities that continue to be predisposed to absolute modernist truths and romanticist ideals, yet they are now conveyed through ever-evolving high-tech modalities and media. In sum, the postmodern condition is cumulative by retaining key attributes and ideas from earlier periods such as individuality, morality, and absolute truths, but an expression of individual identities is multiple and contradictory due to exposure to vast technological representations, reach, and remnants of conflicted romantic and modernist beliefs.

The reach of historical categorizations, particularly "postmodern," has been extended beyond the arts by multidisciplinary scholars (Barthes 1977, 15-20; Baudrillard 1994, 160-161; Gergen 1991, 6-17; Hayles 1999, 6-24; Turkle 1995, 36-49; Ulmer 2003, 5-7) as they have sought to forecast and understand the ways technologies continually influence culture, identity, self, experience, and perspective in the period unfolding following modernism. Much postmodern analysis has focused on criticism and forecasting utopian and dystopian disembodied, simulated, image-based representations of multiplicities of identity and experience. Indeed, a multiplicity of identities and imitative personalities are evident online as individual physical bodies have become visually-enhanced exponential representations leveraging technologies such as photos, video, filters, etc. Furthermore, extending a "postmodern" categorization and label to digital culture is relevant and useful to discussions of identity and digital citizenship because the arts have historically served as an effective medium for creative expression and reception of connotated meanings.

More recent digital humanities scholarship (Gries 2015, 3; Jenkins 2006, 19-21; Knoebel and Lankshear 2007, 205; Milner 2013, 2357; Ntouvlis and Geenen 2023, 1193-1211; Potts 2014, 11-13; Shifman 2014, 131-139; Vie 2014, 4; Wiggins 2019, 144) has shifted from forecasting what the "postmodern" will be to analysis of social media content creation and consumption such as that of memes, popular culture, political and philanthropic movements, disaster response, etc. In this sense, digital content can be considered postmodern creative expression(s) of identity, thought, ideas, experiences, and perspectives. Pieces of digital content serve as disembodied public representations of identities. Further, any individual consumes and creates numerous, often exponential, visual-based representations of personal selves.

Purpose and Organization

This chapter will juxtapose the concepts of romanticism, modernism, and postmodernism, as well as content consumption and creation, as a framework to elucidate digital citizenship multiliteracies for an undergraduate-level audience. A digital humanities and writing and rhetoric academic approach views college composition courses as a significant site for fostering multiliteracies to prepare students for citizenship and professions in a digital age (Cambre and Arshad-Ayaz 2017, 64-80; Knoebel and Lankshear 2007, 219-225; Miller 2022, 199-230; Selber 2004, 24-26;

Selfe 1999, 9-10). Therefore, impactful composition classroom pedagogy must bridge literacies for decoding and encoding ideas, thoughts, experiences, perspectives, and ultimately identities, creatively and artistically via a multitude of technological modalities and media.

The forthcoming pedagogy explicates "identity literacy" as an original concept and concurrently asserts that identity literacy is an overlooked, yet critical, facet of the multiliteracies necessary for global citizenship in the postmodern digital age. Readers are invited to complete the following exercises to experience identity literacy personally and gain the experience necessary to foster identity literacy in citizens and students in their network. Teachers and everyday citizens alike may cultivate identity literacy in others by modeling the product of identity literacy—a sincere relational expression of authentic original perspective.

Pedagogical materials are marked by the "Choose Your Own Adventure" headline borrowed from the "Choose Your Own Adventure" book series of the 1980s (Packard 1979, 1) to similarly extend a participatory invitation to readers. These sections are organized with prompts, exercises, and literacy descriptions. Supporting theory and accessible explanations for an audience of college-level students and/or adult citizens are also woven throughout the chapter and are marked by "Theory" headlines.

Choose Your Adventure: Start Here/Baseline

Imagine you are playing a game as you begin your journey with this reading, and you need to choose an avatar. Consider a character, celebrity, historical figure, or childhood toy that you would say you are most drawn to or identify with. For me, this avatar was the Barbie doll (Wikimedia 2025)—hence, this is why Barbie is referenced in the title of this writing. Search for and save a visual digital representation, photo, of your avatar in a word processing document titled "My Adventure." This document should be considered your personal space for identity literacy journaling.

Next, think about how you would introduce yourself in a variety of situations: at school; at work; among new friends; etc. Most people, start by describing where they are from, their profession, their role in the family, hobbies, likes and dislikes, etc. This is how you would introduce yourself if you were to sum up "Who am I?" Take a look at your social media profiles and post content to help pinpoint your identity. This activity, as the first of a series, is presented as casual journaling, however, pedagogical background, instructions for use as assignments, and more examples are accessible in a prior publication (Miller 2022, 199-230).

Baseline Journal Prompts:

1) First, choose an avatar (see above for clarification).
2) Think about your identity. Look at your social media profiles as guides.
3) Write "I am" statements for how you could introduce yourself to strangers. "I am a teacher, I am a mother," etc.
4) Identify 4-6 photos that represent your favorite "I am" statements.
5) Baseline Products:
6) First, find and save a photo or digital representation of your avatar.
7) Compile a list of "I am" statements.
8) Create a collage with 4-6 photos to introduce yourself visually (tech advice below).
9) Start a journal by saving these items in a document titled "My Adventure."

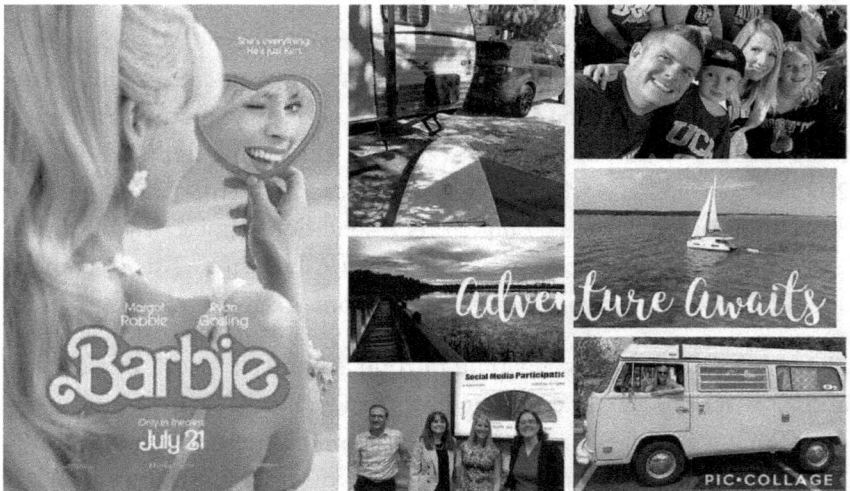

Figure 1: Examples of baseline products.

Baseline Multiliteracies:

Functional Literacy

Certain computer skills are required for the task of creating aesthetic multimodal content such as a collage, meme, or photo/video-based social media post. Functional literacy is the academic term ascribed to these technological abilities (Selber 2004, 24-25; Selfe 1999, 3). Smartphones and social media applications, such as Photos, Instagram, Snapchat, Facebook, etc. provide functional tools for creating multimodal content. If you are not familiar with the native smartphone photo applications and tools of social media, take some time to explore and experiment with them to build your functional literacy. Additionally, smartphone app stores and Internet search bars are also good places to search for "free collage maker," "free meme maker," "free content creator," etc. The example collages, memes, and content shared throughout this chapter were created with free applications available in the app store, on a smartphone, or social media platforms.

Theory: I am a Writer and Creator

For our discussion about digital citizenship, social media will be a main focus. Social media have become mundane composition genres for most people since their inception early in the 21st century due to their participatory nature; everyone can be a writer and content creator. Particularly college students are familiar with many social media applications and use them daily since these platforms have existed most, if not all, of their lives. Arguably, the activity that garners the most attention in social media composition, engagement, and participation is identity-based. Everyday posts often showcase photos, videos, text, ideas, activities, people, places, memes, etc. that a person identifies with.

Young people, in particular, have embraced social media and participate personally and professionally with many striving to become social media content creators and influencers. Posting on social media resonates personally for many users and is generally held in high regard due to a felt sense of potential. Yet, social media are still relatively new composition genres increasingly worthy of new research, analysis, and theory to more fully develop their potential.

Digital Citizenship

Digital citizenship involves active participation, decoding, and encoding, in collective meaning making and understanding regarding any given topic, but how can meaning-making be defined? Meaning making ideally entails the expression, reception, and amalgamation of many individuals' authentic non-influenced perspectives to contribute to and shape collective understanding of an idea. The term meme describes how ideas have the potential to constantly be in flux.

You are likely familiar with the Internet meme and how, as a genre, Internet memes humorously can negate or change the meaning of an original idea. The root term meme (Dawkins 1976, 245-260) updated to online materializations (Jenkins 2006, 2-4; Knobel and Lankshear 2007, 199-225; Lessig 2008, 69-71; Milner 2013, 2357-2390; Shifman 2014, 17-35; Varis and Blommaert 2014, 1-21; Wiggins 2019, 1-20), refers to how all ideas are versions of earlier ideas that continuously morph with additive meaning as they are replicated, supplemented, recontextualized, remixed, etc. In this discussion, we can view any topic, concern, cause, etc. that digital citizens weigh in on as a participatory idea in flux with potentiality - a meme.

Generally, digital citizens express their support or opposition to ideas by composing and posting multimodal messages on social media platforms ranging from likes, emoji reactions, and comments, to original textual, photo, or video posts. Every post, whether it is textual, visual, or increasingly multimodal either contributes to or takes away momentum from a collective understanding of any idea. You, as a digital citizen, are likely familiar with the mechanics of how ideas are presented to you in a range of daily feeds on the social media platforms you choose to engage with. Regardless of whether the posts originate from friends or family, various groups, news entities, advertisements, etc., we are all conditioned to respond in certain mundane ways that convey support or opposition: like, emoji reaction, comment, post a photo or video, etc.

Interestingly, digital citizens often successfully affect meaning-making by leveraging photo, video, and textual representations of bodies, faces, names, and voices. In this way, the digital offers a disembodied multiplicity of identity expression and reaches beyond a single physical body. As a form of passive indifference or polite resistance, we may also choose to not respond or engage at all.

The amalgamation of all responses to any given idea shapes its collective meaning and understanding. Imagine how artificial intelligence (AI) might draw meaning or how contributors on Wikipedia continually revise meaning. In this sense, meaning-making is participatory and influenced by a push and pull or ebb and flow of digital responses from digital citizens to ideas presented on social media. The mundane activity of responding on social media to various ideas is the work of digital citizens, so as a social media user, you hold great potential to shape the collective meaning, response, and action regarding any idea, big or small. With this potential, also comes a responsibility for developing literacies and capacities for decoding rhetorical ideas and encoding original thinking.

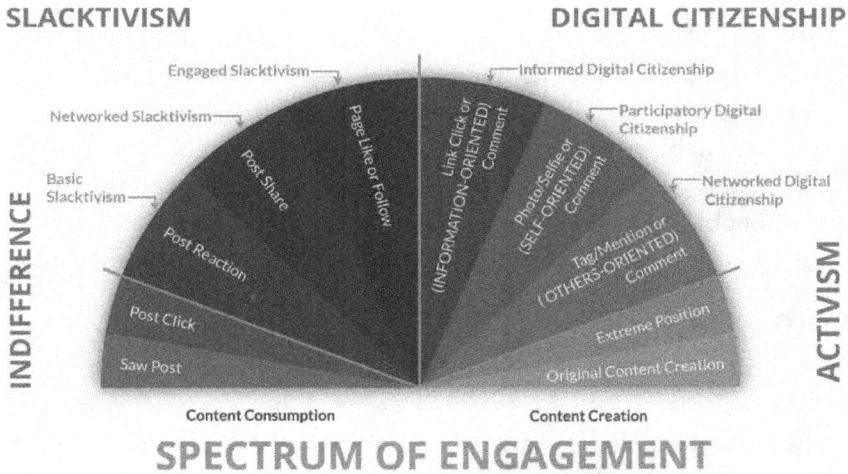

SLACKTIVISM   DIGITAL CITIZENSHIP

INDIFFERENCE   ACTIVISM

Engaged Slacktivism

Networked Slacktivism

Basic Slacktivism

Post Share

Page Like or Follow

Post Reaction

Link Click or (INFORMATION-ORIENTED) Comment

Photo/Selfie or (SELF-ORIENTED) Comment

Informed Digital Citizenship

Participatory Digital Citizenship

Networked Digital Citizenship

Tag/Mention or (OTHERS-ORIENTED) Comment

Post Click

Saw Post

Extreme Position

Original Content Creation

Content Consumption   Content Creation

SPECTRUM OF ENGAGEMENT

Figure 2: Spectrum of Engagement Model (Miller 2018, 81).

This visual model illustrates a spectrum of digital citizenship engagement actions and any potential action's influence on collective meaning-making and understanding. A line, representing a continuum, from the consumption of ideas to the creation of ideas, runs along the bottom of the diagram. Each action represented as a pie-shape piece of the semicircle situates the range of its function from consumption to alteration to opposition to the creation of a new idea. This spectrum only includes actions that were witnessed from a prior research study, and certainly, more actions could be added to the spectrum respective to how they embody content consumption, supplementation, alteration, opposition, or creation.

Considering the actions represented on the diagram, if a digital citizen saw a post, for example, but did not respond, the action represents the sole consumption of an idea. However, if a digital citizen responds by posting a like, emoji reaction, photo, symbol, meme, or comment, new content has been added to supplement or alter an idea; that new content pushes and pulls on the collective meaning or understanding of the idea. New content as slight as an emoji reaction, adopting a symbol, or even a share has generally been criticized in the past as slacktivism, trivial identity-enhancing behavior, yet evolving scholarship (Miller 2018, 82; Varis and Blommaert 2014, 7-8; Vie 2014, 4) argues that slacktivism actions offer incremental meaning making value because they recontextualize an idea in new networks adding additional meaning.

Creativity and art in the visual remix of ideas, perhaps as an Internet meme or a relevant personal photo, for example, become increasingly additive to meaning. Also of significant interest is that extreme positions in activism tend to be primarily dualistic and oppositional, inciting stalemate, so the mild actions that incrementally push and pull on meaning-making offer thought-provoking value in digital citizenship. This chapter further probes this "sweet spot" of digital citizenship potential and responsibility.

Responsibility

Along with the significant potential digital citizens possess to participate in meaning-making comes substantial responsibility for uncovering, safeguarding, and expressing a distinct individual authentic perspective; but authentic perspectives are mysterious because they exist outside cultural conditioning. Critical literacy is a concept you have likely encountered throughout your education that strives to foster authentic perspectives through a critique of invisible influences on mainstream approaches to life, solving problems, and "truths" (Lanius and Hassel 2018, 195-196; Palczewski, DeFransisco, and McGeough 2019, 129-138; Selfe 1999, 24). Further, critical theories urge people to consider the power structures behind socially constructed mainstream cultural beliefs, practices, and narratives. Though useful, critical literacy and theories don't immediately transfer because they tend to remain highly theoretical and also dualistic in their critique of what becomes more approachable when illustrated as cultural lenses.

Figuratively, cultural lenses are the "eyeglasses" citizens are conditioned to see the world through, and developing the multiliteracies to not only "see" without the cultural "eyeglasses," but also to "see" the "eyeglasses" themselves is an important missing link in digital citizenship capacity. These metaphors illustrate a critical literacy gap I termed "identity literacy." Identity literacy takes a step back from critical literacy to first illuminate cultural lenses personally and separate them from identity. Separating, naming, and visualizing lenses outside the body or mind allows examining them less defensively.

Additionally, identity literacy draws from the philosophical approaches of "cultural memetics" (Dawkins 1976, 245-260) and "ecological thinking" (Code 2006, 4-9) to reconceptualize static "truth" or knowledge as fluid meaning-making shaped by overlaps in the pursuit of diverse authentic perspectives and objectives. Therefore, self-understanding including and excluding cultural lenses is critical for nurturing digital citizenship capacity. The forthcoming section unpacks an amalgamation of cultural lenses inherited from romanticism and modernism to further develop multiliteracies to "see" beyond cultural "eyeglasses."

Binaries

Let's begin exploring one of the most significant romanticism- and modernism-based lenses that affect social media engagement and digital citizenship. The romanticist idea of the righteous self and modernist idea of objective truth has been reconciled in early postmodernism as binary thought. United States (and increasingly global) digital culture tends to favor dualistic thinking as a lens. Every day, we are presented with binary (two oppositional) choices such as: true/false, right/wrong, good/bad, like/don't like, support/oppose....

A list of familiar binaries could go on indefinitely. You are likely familiar with binary choices, but what you likely haven't directly considered is the role duality plays in the illusion of choice. Binary choices make it seem like you have choices, but at the same time, they only give you two choices – two controlled predetermined choices. Rarely is any topic or idea as simple as right or wrong or true or false, yet cultural pressure to identify with one side of a polarized binary is intense. Dualistic thinking is a programmed belief system that poises citizens to take sides in support or opposition on issues rather than engage in and express original thinking and diverse authentic perspectives that could broaden collective understanding and generate more potential solutions to the world's big problems.

A useful allegory for understanding this conundrum involves a train. Think about a high-speed train that will travel across tracks from point A to point B. You board the train and you have a choice to sit on the right side (choice 1) or left side (choice 2) of the center aisle. You think you have a personal choice to sit on either side of the train and, yes, you do have a controlled choice limited to choosing a seat on the right or left. However, ultimately that train is rushing along the tracks to the same predetermined destination regardless of what side of the train you sit on.

Just like this train, many of our choices as digital citizens are controlled and limited by dualistic thinking and binary choices. The primary choice on social media is to click like/love/share (like) or ignore/be silent/criticize (dislike) something. Support or oppose a (good/bad) idea. Adopt the idea or reject it. Dualistic programming obfuscates other actions that could better supplement participatory collective meaning-making. By explicitly defamiliarizing the ideas of the virtuous singular inner self prioritized in romanticism and absolute objective truth stressed by modernism, the affordances of postmodernism can be more effectively leveraged for digital citizenship.

The spectrum of engagement model is an original thinking tool that helps digital citizens envision additional creative actions beyond sole binary consumption or rejection of ideas. The actions in between complete consumption or outright rejection of ideas are where collective and participatory meaning-making, understanding, equality, and solutions reside. When citizens express a perspective (choice) outside of choice 1 or 2, they disrupt the volume of both choice 1 and choice 2 and ultimately steer the issue (train) in a slightly different direction.

Social Institutions

A looming curiosity builds in this discussion concerning what the implicit power structures referenced in critical literacy are. An entire body of scholarship (Lanius and Hassel 2018, 101-102; Palczewski, DeFransisco, and McGeough 2019, 129-138) is dedicated to unpacking dominant cultural belief systems and power structures controlling cultural "truths." Hegemony is a scholarly term ascribed to general mainstream cultural beliefs, approaches to life, and social institutions. Social institutions represent ways to group and name hegemonic beliefs, structures, and mechanics. The main agreed-upon social institutions, representing the postmodern global human condition, include: family, education, work, religion, and media.

Below are very brief, and purposely loose, descriptions of social institutions based on conversations that have arisen in scholarship and the classroom that will likely help you begin to contemplate how these social institutions function personally in your life. These descriptions are American or Western culture-oriented, so readers from other cultures may want to adapt them to better fit their own culture. The intent is to give you a starting point from which you can begin to separate cultural conditioning from your own authentic self-understanding. Self-understanding is the prerequisite or starting point from which original thinking and expression of your own authentic perspective can arise.

Family

> Traditional nuclear family values
> Hierarchical gendered roles, child rearing, codependence
> Shared identity, future, love
> Dating, romance, heteronormativity

Education

> Truth, knowledge, history, hidden curricula
> Quantitative, logical, STEM (science, technology, engineering, math), and achievement-oriented
> Gendered and hegemonic socialization rewarded with privilege
> Corrective enforcement and patrolling via judgment, bullying, shaming, harassment

Work

> Progress, capitalism, the American dream, purpose
> Truth, knowledge, hegemonic masculinity
> Quantitative, logical, STEM, and achievement-oriented
> Gendered, raced, and classed jobs, wage gaps, subordination

Religion

> Belief in a higher divinity, infallible power
> Hierarchical gendered roles, child rearing, codependence

Heteronormativity, love, service, morality
Link to nationalism, ethnicity, colonialism

Media

Consumption, consumerism, entertainment, popular culture, and multimodally-focused
Replication of identity and beauty norms and gazes
Hegemonic socialization rewarded with privilege
Corrective enforcement and patrolling via judgment, bullying, shaming, harassment
Replicates and amplifies all social institutions

Choose Your Adventure: Externalizing Identity

Ulmer (2003, 5-7) explicated a blueprint for a "mystery" exercise to externalize and visualize the mystery of an individual's natural home standpoint, arguably identity, which he asserted is shaped by four discourses: career; family; entertainment; and community.

Mystory Discourses

1) Career Discourse: Think about your university major or a field of disciplinary knowledge in which you have some interest or have worked. What are the distinct values and beliefs of that discipline? What drew you to the field? What do you admire about professionals working in that field?

2) Family Discourse: Think of a few memories that stand out from your childhood. Prominent memories often represent significant learning moments, paradoxes, problems, or traumatic events. What do you think is significant about your family memory? How did you feel? Was there conflict? What did you learn from it?

3) Entertainment Discourse: Think of favorite movies, gaming storylines, advertisements, TV shows, or books you have watched or read. Think about any favorite characters. Think about common problems/resolutions. How do these narratives make you feel? Then relate these findings to what you discovered from the other discourses. Is there any overlap or any theme?

4) Community Discourse: Think about community events, leaders, heroes, and activities that embody the communities you are a part of. Re-

ligion, race, nationality, and ethnicity represent communities we may belong to. What are the values and beliefs of the community? What are the problems, conflicts, and ideal resolutions for the community? What did you learn in school about the beliefs, values, and history of your local community, nation, and the world? Do any historical events stand out?

You should now revise your introduction collage to include four new personal photos that illustrate your relationship with each of the four mystery discourses. You may use past photos or take new photos to illustrate your natural home standpoint. Please avoid using generic Internet photos, because this exercise is about self-understanding.

Mystery Journal Prompts:

1) Learn about binaries, social institutions, and Ulmer's four discourses in this reading.

2) Revise your collage into a mystery with one personal photo representing each of the four discourses: career, family, entertainment, and community.

3) Look for and journal about themes, patterns, conflict, contradiction, paradox, or discomfort in your mystery. The questions in the four discourses section are a guide.

Mystery Products:

1) Revise your collage into a mystery with one personal photo representing each of the four discourses: career, family, entertainment, and community.

2) Add a tagline highlighting any identity theme, pattern, conflict, contradiction, discomfort, or paradox you discover.

Mystory Multiliteracies:

Functional literacy
Semiotic literacy
Identity literacy
Critical literacy

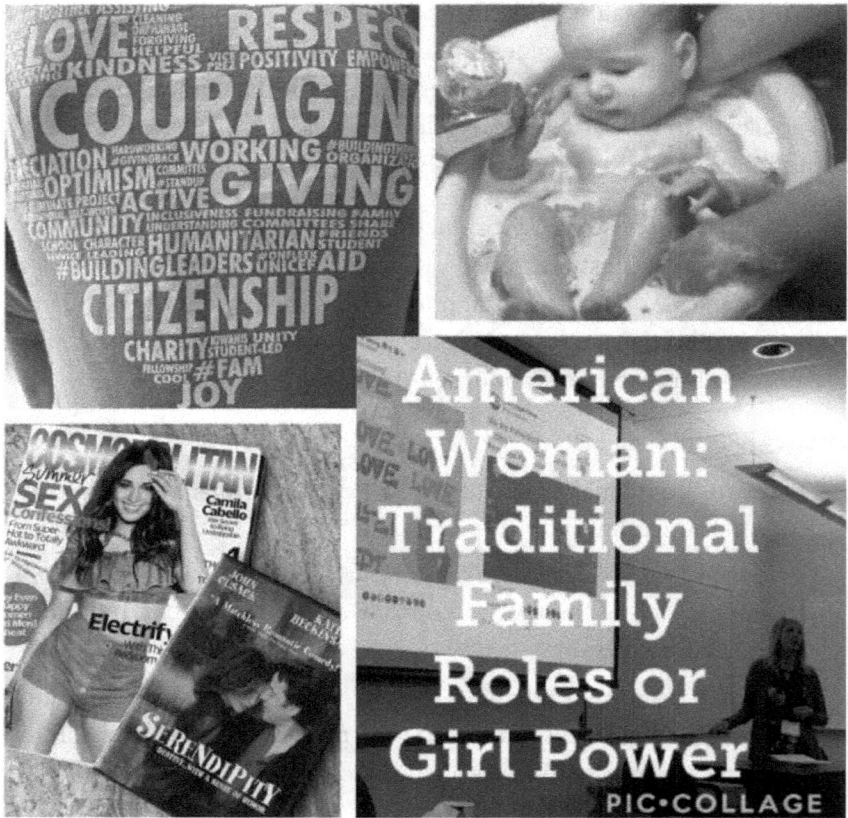

Figure 3: Example mystory.

The mystery is a tool to extract subconscious personal conditioning by supplying a genre to externalize and visualize it in a collage. Scaffolding from the functional literacy skills employed to create a collage, now the focus shifts to experiencing semiotics, identity, and critical literacies. Discovery of how cultural narratives and binaries are illustrated visually in personal photos provides a dramatic opportunity to experience the nuances of these multiliteracies.

Semiotic literacy involves the capacity to recognize, interpret, and leverage patterns of repeating visual signs in decoding or encoding multimodal messages (Miller 2022, 199). Identity literacy works in tandem with semiotic and critical literacies to personally recognize the presentation, consumption, and replication of cultural narratives and binaries in a person's life and small circles. Finally, critical literacy is the critique of hegemonic cultural narratives and structures (Lanius and Hassel 2018, 195; Palczewski, DeFransisco, and McGeough 2019, 129-138; Selfe 1999, 24).

Theory: Conditioning to Authentic Original Perspective

The necessary hallmark of the mystery activity is to experience a degree of discomfort when a theme, pattern, contradiction, conflict, or paradox among the visual signs contained in your collage is discovered. Discomfort marks the "aha moment" when deviation becomes accessible because it represents a crack, fissure, gap, or hole in the promise or authenticity of the hegemonic narratives (Palczewski, DeFransisco, and McGeough 2019, 116 -124). Discomfort and access often originate from exploring otherness, defensiveness, shallowness, inequality, or traumas such as bullying or harassment.

How might the hegemonic narratives have let you down, not served you well, privileged, or limited you? How might they appear fake or shallow in relation to real life? Do not move on from the mystery until you have uncovered and articulated a theme, pattern, contradiction, conflict, or paradox. Take a look at Figure 3 for a mystery example. A more detailed textual explanation of this example is explained in the conclusion of this chapter to provide additional direction if you are having trouble identifying your "aha moment."

The mystery exercise is often uncomfortable. Some people feel very defensive of what they see in their mystery at first glance. Conversely, comfort is offered when hegemonic ideas are consumed and replicated. Indeed, the rewards of privilege and praise feel good. Performing your natural home standpoint will always feel comfortable, like coming home.

As a simple example, I love to shop, especially for beauty products. I often describe the purchasing and use of beauty products as retail therapy, because it feels good to look the way my culture deems a "pretty" woman should look. I also enjoy the privilege of being seen as attractive. However, more purposeful active choices become comprehensible with an awareness of when privilege, praise, and comfort are offered in exchange for the consumption and replication of hegemonic ideas.

To ease any defensiveness you may feel, know that being aware doesn't mean your conditioning has to be disregarded altogether. Yet, a weighing of the consequences and consideration of slightly alternative choices become possible through this often uncomfortable work. Some uncomfortable "aha moments" in the mystery, for example, center around hierarchical relationships in religion and family, unrealistic or conflicting ideals, or staged cliché social media posts. Growing from this discomfort involves reconciling, rather than fully rejecting, conditioning.

Change is surprisingly "typically the result of sly, subtle adjustments that somehow meet the needs of both the operations of power and the needs of the vulnerable" (Cintron quoted in Grabill 2007, 4). The spectrum of engagement is a tool that aids digital citizens in envisioning minor adjustments in the messages they encode moving from sole consumption or opposition of hegemonic ideas to slightly and incrementally enriching those ideas. In other words, authentic original perspectives resonate most effectively when slight incremental and purposeful adjustments to dominant narratives are illustrated such as portraying equality in spiritual and family activities or authentic posts featuring raw natural beauty and presence.

New Language Resignifying Identity and Belonging

Romanticism prioritized an individual noble interiority and modernism retained the idea of sovereign identity, but added the notion of rigid, absolute, and objective truth in what is deemed true and false, good and bad, right or wrong, etc. These hegemonic elements prevail in postmodernism. However, continuously advancing technologies catapult exponential visual representations of identities into an increasingly public social sphere.

While these historically dominant approaches to identity stressed individualism, a collective element has always existed in varying degrees across cultures. Relationships and interaction among others have continuously contributed to constructing and solidifying identity by offering the privilege of belonging, yet social circles of influence and acceptance have grown significantly larger in reach, magnitude, and power increasingly from romanticism to postmodernism. The forthcoming section employs new language to explicate implicit social dynamics of identity and belonging.

Every one of us innately possesses potential power if we can understand and express, through composition, our own unique authentic perspective and original thinking on any given idea. Cultural belief systems that prioritize dualistic thinking and certain narratives work to coopt citizens' power and direct perspectives. Replication, amplification, the illusion of choice, privilege exchange, nodes of enforcement, small circles of codependence, codependence, and codependent activism are new languages that help explicate the sophisticated and obfuscated mechanics of how citizens' power is regularly collected and coopted. New language regarding safeguarding personal power includes: identity literacy; content consumption continuum/spectrum of engagement; authentic original perspective; sincere relational expression; interdependence; overlapping objectives; and allies for interdependent flow.

The Problem

Replication

Power structures collect and stockpile citizens' power when individuals are successfully influenced to consume and spread ideas in the form controlled by the structure.

Amplification

Controlled ideas become louder, omnipresent, and dominant when a critical mass of individuals consume and spread ideas in the form controlled by power structures.

Illusion of Choice

Dualistic thinking and binary choices direct individuals' energy at safeguarding controlled ideas. The illusion of choice pigeonholes individuals in support or opposition of controlled ideas and limits the expression of an array of authentic original perspectives. Dualistic ideas can be easily controlled by two powerful opposing entities.

Privilege Exchange

Privilege, usually in the form of opportunity, praise, or belonging, is the social reward for adopting, replicating, and enforcing ideas in the form controlled by power structures. Sometimes people receive privilege based on the ways they look or behave. For some people, privilege can be acquired by modifying looks or behavior to adhere to mainstream preferences. For others, modification is more difficult or not possible. Identity is a performative opportunity for privilege.

Nodes of Enforcement

The illusion of choice and polarity of binary choices directs individuals who have bought in at enforcing controlled ideas. Privilege, praise, shame, and judgement (through relationship) become the limited work of individuals after individual power has been coopted. Bought-in individuals become nodes of influence replicating, amplifying, and enforcing controlled ideas in their own smaller networks of reach.

Small Circles of Codependence

The small social circles to which we belong (communities, families, schools, work teams, churches, social media networks) are made up of members who believe and uphold the values of the social institution it respectively represents. The values are enforced and behavior is socially patrolled in the form of awarding or removing privilege – opportunity, praise, belonging, judgment, shame, bullying, etc. Enforcement and patrolling are usually subtle and camouflaged as blind truths of the circle, yet these actions are very effective in limiting the expression of authentic original perspectives outside of controlled ideas.

Codependence

A culture of codependence involves social pressure to be overly concerned with enforcing and patrolling the uptake of hegemonic ideas, actions, and performative identity by others. Codependent behavior relies on an extreme belief in modernist objective truths. Codependent conduct also involves an element of romanticist-based morality in that the singular, good, right, objective, and absolute truth should be advanced and enforced. Codependence fuels the networked behavior of nodes of enforcement and small circles of codependence in awarding or revoking privilege.

Codependent Activism

Activism tends to remain stuck in dualistic thinking influencing others to join in solely supporting or opposing an issue. The problem is a range of other less privileged authentic original perspectives is drowned out by the amplification of only binary (supporting/opposing) voices. Codependent and hierarchical activists, additionally, leverage privilege to speak for others.

Solution

Identity Literacy

Identity literacy works in tandem with functional, semiotic, critical and rhetorical literacies, to personally recognize the presentation, consumption, and replication of hegemonic cultural narratives and binaries in a person's life and small circles.

Content Consumption Continuum – Spectrum of Engagement

The introduction of the spectrum of engagement, particularly the content consumption continuum, as a model, provides a tangible multiliteracies tool to enable engagement beyond sole consumption or rejection of the ideas we are bombarded with every day.

Authentic Original Perspective

Authenticity, or self-understanding, beyond cultural conditioning, informs original thinking, and original thinking informs the expression of an authentic original perspective. Original thinking is independent of identity but does involve an approach to life or an authentic perspective informed by lived experiences outside of conditioning. The responsibility is delineating outside influence, safeguarding coopt, and maintaining sincere relational expression.

Sincere Relational Expression

Sincere relational expression of authentic original perspective is each citizen's equal raw unit of expressive power that exists outside cultural conditioning. As a utopian ideal, each citizen is worthy of an equally valued authentic original perspective contributing to collective meaning making regarding any given matter. However, a multiplicity of digital representations can exist for any perspective amplifying some over others, contributing to a disparity in perspectives being equally relational. Sincere relational expression is interdependent rather than codependent in that it resists influencing and coopting others' expressive power.

Interdependence

Collective versus individual, or "we/I," is a powerful limiting binary, because "we" cultivates codependence, and "I" promotes opposition and stalemate. Broadening this binary to valuing a sincerely relational amalgamation of an array of authentic original perspectives fosters equality in collective meaning-making, understanding, and digital citizenship. Further, a safe, peaceful, and productive, rather than controlled oppositional collective could materialize as interdependent allies express authentic original perspectives to pursue authentic overlapping objectives and interdependent meaning-making.

Overlapping Objectives

Overlapping objectives is a concept drawn from activity theory representing intersections of shared interests among individual actors (Kapelinin and Nardi 2006, 31-32). Interdependent allies identify common interests while valuing the authentic expression of varying approaches and perspectives because they have confidence in a higher outcome resulting from increased manpower toward overlapping objectives and meaning-making. Interdependence is the work of genuine allies who speak for themselves to express their own authentic original perspectives, goals, and thinking safely and peacefully to equally contribute to collective meaning-making, understanding, productivity, and solutions.

Allies for Interdependent Flow

"Love," a good and moral ideal originating out of romanticism, has become a dominant narrative of codependence coopted by social institutions, particularly family, religion, and media. The word "love" increasingly enables small circles of codependence, nodes of enforcement, and the "we/I" binary. Rather, the new language of "allies for interdependent flow" better describes a free, safe, and equal flow of sincere relational expression of authentic original perspectives between allies aimed at overlapping objectives. In other words, fostering an unobstructed "interdependent flow" of authentic original perspectives rather than awarding privilege such as belonging and attention for shared identity is a better description of sincerely relating with others.

A funk band is a useful metaphor (Banks 2005, 5-6) for understanding the concepts of sincere relational expression, interdependence, and overlapping objectives. The sincere relational and authentic overlapping objective of the members of the band is to make pleasing music, yet each member plays a different instrument making a different sound each in their unique way. Each member of the band is concerned with their instrument and sound—authentic original perspective. However, when valued and heard in unison, the sounds combine to make richer meaning— music. A patchwork quilt is similarly comprised of disparate fabrics that join in collective purpose and meaning (Banks 2005, 5-6). The analogies woven throughout this chapter aim to demonstrate the potential of creativity and art, play, in communicating connotated authentic original perspectives to shape meaning-making.

Postmodernism and a New Language of Play

Play, in particular, has become a central tenet of the postmodern condition. A significant portion of the mundane activities people engage in online are entertaining and fun. From gaming to social media engagement, an invitation to play with the self construction of identity is extended from the start by selecting a profile photo – creating an avatar.

Avatars, disembodied semiotic representations of selves, can range from real photos and symbols on social media to animations in gaming. In any case, the accessibility of postmodern high-tech tools inspires a significant element of imagination, fantasy, creativity, and artistry for everyday citizens that before was reserved only for the media. Postmodernism, more than ever, heightens our capacity to serve as actors playing parts in the privilege-centered theatre, cinema, dramas, and games of life.

Multiple and simultaneous roles and representations, often conflicting, can be tried out and played with in the digital much like a child playing with a Barbie doll. The early stages of postmodernism have wrestled with simple identity play fixed in entertainment, content consumption, and replication. Some noteworthy manifestations of postmodern play have been named by scholars interrogating serious play: "pastiche personality," "strategic manipulator" (Gergen 1991, 149-150), "identity play" (Turkle 1995, 11-14), and "participatory culture" (Jenkins 2006, 2-4).

The early postmodern tendency, performing as a pastiche personality and strategic manipulator in identity play, has been to strategically observe, draw from, manipulate, construct, and present multiple contradictory representations of varying identities for personal advantage and privilege. Another early postmodern inclination has involved a shift to a participatory culture of citizens that consume content and experiment creating content in a primarily entertainment and popular culture context such as fandom – fans participating in the continual development of plot-related content such as for Star Wars (Jenkins 2006, 135).

Postmodernism has undeniably extended a meaningful invitation to play, which digital citizens have embraced to date for identity and entertainment purposes, yet a call for serious play beckons. Serious play, intentional play employed as a digital citizenship skill, offers the potential to unlock a range of authentic original perspectives broadened beyond the inheritances from romanticism and modernism to enrich collective meaning-making. The final section of the identity literacy pedagogy shared in this chapter engages serious play to aid citizens in discovering their authentic original perspective for digital citizenship.

Choose Your Own Adventure: Serious Play for Discovering Authentic Original Perspective

Your mystory visualized and externalized the cultural lenses or conditioning that influence identity. Now, the final journal activity will help you comprehend yourself beyond conditioning to identify and sincerely express your authentic original perspective on any given idea or relational situation. Authenticity, the quality that informs original thinking and authentic original perspective, refers to a raw outlook outside of cultural conditioning and is a prerequisite for original thinking.

A parallel can be drawn between the deep inner self prioritized in romanticism, yet postmodern authenticity and original thinking strive to strip away the problematic remnants of romanticism and modernism, particularly codependent individual morality and absolute truths. Your "aha moment" in the mystery is the access point to your authenticity. What have your life experiences about your mystory allowed you to understand personally? How could you express that unique perspective sincerely to push and pull on meaning-making regarding the issues you care about? The following playful exercises may further open that access point to your authenticity.

Take some time to revisit and play with your list of "I am" statements. Add as many more "I am" statements as you can. Then make a list of statements describing your "best life" (Oprah Magazine Editors of O 2005, 8) —what would your fantasy life be like if you had no limitations. Then list your "joys"—what makes you happy? You can continue to make lists of anything you want here, but these prompts are a good start. The purpose is to explore yourself deeply beyond your conditioning. Exchange truth and purpose for perspective, play, and imagination. These lists should be casual, relaxed, and fun creative brainstorming activities.

Now analyze each statement and cross out any that are influenced by social institutions, binaries, or Ulmer's four discourses. The goal here is to see what is left. Circle or highlight the statements that are left. This often is an iterative process where you cross statements out, but then add more statements and check them for influence.

Writing from directed prompts in a journal is one way to explore your authenticity, but creative writing, poetry, art, and anonymity are other tools for self-exploration. Play with these tools to creatively and multimodally express "What am I really?" In other words, what's left on your list of "I am" statements that aren't influenced by social institutions?

Multimodal arts offer significant potential as a medium for the indirect expression of original ideas (Barthes 1977, 15-20; Ulmer 2006 43-44). Further, other scholars such as Turkle (1995, 11-14) found anonymity, removing your body, face, or name from expression, to be a significant tool for exploring or expressing non-mainstream facets of authenticity or potential identity. Anonymity fosters authenticity by offering a buffer, a degree of freedom, and more safety from revoked privilege – judgment, harassment, bullying, etc.

Serious Play for Discovering Authentic Original Perspective Journal Prompts:

1) List more statements of "I am," "Best Life," and "Joys."

2) Iteratively analyze and cross out any that are influenced by social institutions, binaries, or Ulmer's four discourses.

3) Circle or highlight "What's left?" Consider "What am I really?"

4) Play with authenticity by experimenting with creative writing, poetry, art, and anonymity.

Serious Play for Discovering Authentic Original Perspective Product:

5) Create an original piece of multimodal content - a social media post, meme, art, or poetry, for example, exploring the relationship between your authenticity and conditioning. Consider circling back to your avatar to make a meme or write an "I am" poem about "what's left." Highlighting a conflict you uncovered in your mystery or inventing a new language may inspire you, and remember anonymity may provide safety as you explore and express your authenticity.

Figure 4: Serious play for discovering authentic
original perspective product examples.

Serious Play for Discovering Authentic Original Perspective Multiliteracies:

Functional literacy
Semiotic literacy
Identity literacy
Critical literacy
Rhetorical Literacy

Scholars have jointly continued to interrogate and deepen the understanding of the concept of multiliteracies in postmodern years (Cambre and Arshad-Ayaz 2017, 64-80; Knoebel and Lankshear 2007, 219-225; Miller 2022, 199-230; Ntouvlis and Geenen 2023, 1193-1211; Selber 2004, 24-26; Selfe 1999, 9-10). This chapter has explicitly sought to explicate additional facets of multiliteracies in the age of social media. Functional, semiotic, identity and critical literacies are facets comprising the ultimate goal of rhetorical literacy - the ability to multimodally encode authentic original perspective creatively, artistically, and semiotically. To aid in further developing functional and rhetorical literacy skills, try searching for and experimenting with a "free content creator" or "free AI art generator" to bring creative ideas to life.

Closing Remarks from an Anonymous Postmodern Barbie

I am an anonymous Barbie. I am a postmodern pastiche personality and strategic manipulator. I receive and enjoy attention, comfort, and privilege for making myself look what is considered attractive for an American female and performing the role of a "good" traditional mother, wife, and family member. I simultaneously pursued the highest levels of education, scholarship, and career as a teacher. My mystory "aha moment" revealed contradictory and unrealistic narratives of traditional (patriarchal) family roles and girl power (female achievement through masculinity). I am married to an anonymous Ken. His mystory "aha moment" revealed a repetitive idealistic theme of "the heroic man," yet one person carrying the weight of every family members' personal responsibilities and all decisions is burdensome and creates an unequal hierarchical family structure.

Our mystories conveniently portrayed what it meant in our circles to be a "good" woman and a "good" man. Like many postmodern parents, we posted many perfectionistic photos and videos of our "good" family and life on social media. Those multiple public visual digital representations of our constructed and relational identities were consumed, liked, reified, and amplified hegemonically by those in our networks.

However, our mystery realizations supplied us with a small glimpse into how unrealistic, inconsistent, and limiting those dominant narratives often are in comparison to how "real life" unfolds with messiness, chaos, and disparity. From that small peek into our fuller authenticities, a crack evolved to a fissure, from which we could begin to "unlearn" our conditioning to be only a "good" girl and boy (in a normative sense). Unlearning together with our children, ultimately helped our immediate family relate more positively as interdependent allies. Together, we rebuilt a family culture of interdependent overlapping objectives, equality, personal responsibility, authenticity, and joy, which we model for our children and actively engage them in.

Romanticist and modernist lenses of idealist objective singular truth in what is perceived as "good" and "true" slowly gave way to embracing previously obfuscated facets of our authenticities in the messiness, chaos, and disparities of postmodern life. While postmodernism is well underway, the remnants of romanticist and modernist offerings remain quite comforting to us. This anonymous Barbie confesses to subconsciously reverting to performing as a pastiche personality and strategic manipulator from time to time during these transitory times, but the goal is to consistently model sincere relational expression of authentic original perspective.

Your confessions won't be the same as mine, but your mystery revelation likely will center around objective or binary conceptions of "good" "truths" in your network. So I ask you this: do you consider yourself a "good" person like Barbie and Ken? What if I suggested performing "good" resulted in more harm than worth? More specifically, codependently upholding "good" "truths" can and often does subordinate, marginalize, oppress, limit, and stalemate solutions to the world's complex problems.

This chapter explored how privilege is awarded for performing what is deemed "good" and "true" by social institutions. In turn, the people most capable of performing cultural narratives of "good" behavior and "truth" hold great potential to either reify or disrupt power structures. This chapter served as an identity literacy guide; this process of defamiliarizing conditioning poises digital citizens to better model sincere relational expression of authentic original perspective, a purposeful interdependent (rather than codependent) act that disrupts power structures and more appropriately positions us all as interdependent allies for the overlapping objectives of collective meaning-making, liberation, equality, and peace.

Three specific tactics for sincere relational expression of authentic original perspective for digital citizenship were modeled throughout this chapter:

- multiliteracies for uncovering and highlighting contradictions ("aha moments");
- resignifying, creating, and using new language; and
- embodied creativity, serious play, and incremental counter performances leveraging art and anonymity.

While our discussion has been social media oriented, these citizenship strategies have an effect in both physical and digital spaces, which is why our bodies, physical and digital representations, are such effective canvases.

What I am hoping to inspire in you may seem daunting, but know this; the importance lies not so much in exactly what you communicate (no right/wrong binary), but rather in creatively relaying something, however slightly, different than the dominant narratives and binary choices (true/false, good/bad, etc). The central goal is to jam the hegemonic signal by lessening the amplification. In other words, impactful digital citizens move away from sole consumption and repetition of dominant messages in the form controlled by power structures. These playful, creative, and often artistic, incrementally different strategic expressions create space for more non-dualistic authentic original perspectives to be seen and heard to contribute to more equitable meaning-making and solutions by lowering the volume of dominant messages.

My Passion and Why

What a journey it is to peel back the layers of cultural conditioning, study yourself, and hone sincere relational expression of authentic original perspective with serious play for digital citizenship! The why and passion for sharing this process, new language, and tools are to help alleviate the unnecessary pain of hegemony – control, codependence, judgment, and isolation. I've felt this pain myself and have witnessed and empathized with it in countless others. I've observed how the backlash manifests in different ways and outcomes, but ultimately it hurts us all - all genders, races, ethnicities, cultures, families, family members, ages, and communities. I hope you will come back to this process at different points in your life. Social construction and identity are parts of you that will often offer privilege and comfort, yet bring discomfort at various stages of life too. This process is not only for digital citizenship; it is therapy. Each person who reclaims their innate power by fully discovering and embracing their authenticity and modeling sincere relational expression of their authentic original perspective helps heal families and communities and increase freedom, equality, interdependence, flow, and peace.

Acknowledgment

I, Jennifer Roth Miller, created and own all the images in this chapter. I acknowledge these images will be published by Westphalia along with my chapter in a scholarly edited collection on identity and belonging. The publicly posted Barbie movie ad remixed into new content in figure 1 is included solely for educational purposes.

References

Banks, Adam. 2005. *Race, Rhetoric, and Technology: Searching for Higher Ground*. Routledge.

Barthes, Roland. 1977. *Image, Music, Text*. Hill and Wang.

Baudrillard, Jean. 1994. *Simulation and Simulacra*. The University of Michigan Press.

Cambre, Carolina and Adeela Arshad-Ayaz. 2017. "Literacies Future Past: Inwardness as Ethical Information." In *Information Ethics and Global Citizenship*, edited by Toni Samek and Lynette Shultz. McFarland Publishers.

Code, Lorraine. 2006. *Ecological Thinking: The Politics of Epistemic Location*. Oxford University Press.

Dawkins, Richard. 1976. "Memes: The New Replicators." In *The Selfish Gene*, by Richard Dawkins. Oxford University Press.

Gergen, Kenneth J. 1991. *The Saturated Self: Dilemmas of Identity in Contemporary Life*. Basic Books, A Division of Harper Collins Publishers.

Grabill, Jeffrey. 2007. *Writing Community Change: Designing Technologies for Citizen Action*. Hampton Press.

Gries, Laurie E. 2015. *Still Life with Rhetoric: A New Materialist Approach for Visual Rhetorics*. Utah State University Press.

Hayles, N. Katherine. 1999. *How We Became Posthuman: Virtual Bodies in Cybernetics, Literature, and Informatics*. University of Chicago Press.

Jenkins, Henry. 2006. *Convergence Culture: Where Old and New Media Collide*. New York University Press.

Knobel, Michele, and Colin Lankshear. 2007. "Online Memes, Affinities, and Cultural Production." In *A New Literacies Sampler*, edited by Michele Knobel and Colin Lankshear. Peter Lang.

Kaptelinin, Victor and Bonnie A. Nardi. 2006. *Acting with Technology: Activity Theory and Interaction Design*. MIT Press.

Lanius, Christie and Holly Hassel. 2018. *Threshold Concepts in Women's and Gender Studies: Ways of Seeing, Thinking, and Knowing*. Routledge, Taylor and Francis Group.

Lessig, Lawrence. 2008. *Remix: Making Art and Commerce Thrive in the Hybrid Economy*. Penguin Books.

Miller, Jennifer Roth. 2018. "Digital Citizenship Tools for Cause-Based Campaigns: A Broadened Spectrum of Engagement and Participation-Scale Methodology." PhD diss., University of Central Florida. https://stars.library.ucf.edu/cgi/viewcontent.cgi?article=7022&context=etd

———. 2022. "Unlocking Digital Citizenship with Visual Pedagogy: Teachings from an American Gender Issues in Communication Course." In *Visual Pedagogies: Concepts, Cases, and Practices*, edited by Carolina Cambre, Edna Baromi-Perlman, and David Herman, Jr. Brill.

Milner, Ryan M. 2013. "Pop Polyvocality: Internet Memes, Public Participation, and the Occupy Wall Street Movement." *International Journal of Communication* 7 (2013): 2357-2390. https://ijoc.org/index.php/ijoc/article/view/1949/1015

Ntouvlis, Vinicio and Jarret Geenen. 2023. " 'Ironic Memes' and Digital Literacies: Exploring Identity through Multimodal Texts." *New Media & Society*, 27 (2): 1193-1211. https://doi.org/10.1177/146144482 31189801

Oprah Magazine Editors of O. 2005. *Live Your Best Life: A Treasury of Wisdom, Wit, Advice, Interviews, and Inspiration from O, The Oprah Magazine*. Oxmoor House; The Best of O, The Oprah Magazine.

Packard, Edward. 1979. *Choose Your Own Adventure: The Cave of Time*. Bantam Books.

Palczewski, Catherine H., Victoria P. DeFransisco, and Danielle D. McGeough. 2019. *Gender in Communication: A Critical Introduction*. Third edition. Sage.

Potts, Liza. 2014. *Social Media in Disaster Response: How Experience Architects Can Build for Participation*. Routledge.

Selber, Stuart. 2004. *Multiliteracies for a Digital Age*. Southern Illinois University Press.

Selfe, Cynthia L. 1999. *Technology and Literacy in the Twenty-First Century*. Southern Illinois University Press.

Shifman, Limor. 2014. *Memes in Digital Culture*. MIT Press.

Turkle, Sherry. 1995. *Life on the Screen: Identity in the Age of the Internet*. Simon & Shuster Paperbacks.

Ulmer, Gregory L. 2003. *Internet Invention: From Literacy to Electracy*. Pearson Education, Longman.

Varis, Piia and Jan Blommaert. 2014. "Conviviality and Collectives on Social Media: Virality, Memes and New Social Structures." *Tilburg Papers in Culture Studies,* paper 108: 1-21. https://pure.uvt.nl/ws/files/4933758/paper108_Varis_Blommaert_memes.pdf

Vie, Stephanie. 2014. "In Defense of 'Slacktivism:' The Human Rights Campaign Facebook Logo as Digital Activism." *First Monday,* 19: 4-7. http://firstmonday.org/ojs/index.php/fm/article/view/4961

Wiggins, Bradley E. 2019. *The Discursive Power of Memes in Digital Culture: Ideology, Semiotics, and Intertextuality.* Routledge.

Wikimedia Foundation. 2025. "Wikipedia: Barbie." Last modified February 7, at 4:30 (UTC). https://en.wikipedia.org/wiki/Barbie

Autoscopic Selves: Ego as Resistance in Postindependence Narratives

Rania Elshabassy, PhD

Abstract

Though issues of subjectivity, ipseity and alterity unfold in the writings of philosophy more than a century ago, contemporary theorists still bring to the fore problems such as xenophobia,xenophilia, philosophical autism and the lack of genuine equality in an era of utter post-modernism; which develops in unequal transnational regions. Within the framework of postcolonial literary theory, this article explores Tayeb Salih's Season of Migration to the North and Alaa Al-Aswany's The Isam Abd al-Ati Papers as undoings of a Manichean self/other relationship. The novels are investigated as imagined symbolic resolutions of the real contradiction of a postmodern and post-independence Sudanese and Egyptian vague sense of self and unbalanced relationship with a Western other. Through an interplay of doubling and witnessing, the narratives present autoscopic protagonists, who act as allegorical dramatizations of the existence of ipseity and alterity within the contours of a single subjectivity, challenging essentialist notions of identity and proposing a hybrid subjectivity that resists colonial ideologies. Autoscopy (a mode of cognitive decolonization—an act of epistemic resistance through which the self confronts its internalized otherness) renders certainty, constancy, stability and fixation impossible; hence loosening the self's grip that has long been fixed on a subjectivity formed by oppression and subordination. Once this is achieved, suggesting other forms of subjectivity and relating to others becomes a genuine possibility.

Keywords: Autoscopy, Agential Subjectivities, Cognitive Decolonization, Hybrid Identity, Xenophobia, Xenophilia

Introduction

The right to "self-fashioning," the possibility of reconstructing a subjectivity and recognizing the other (the different and unsettling) are at the heart of contemporary theoretical and interpretive discussions (Huttunen, et al. 2008, xiv). Though issues of subjectivity, ipseity and alterity unfold in the writings of philosophy more than a century ago, contemporary theorists still bring to the fore problems such as *xenophobia, xenophilia, philosophical autism* and the lack of genuine equality and recognition (as difference) in an era of utter postmodernism; which develops in unequal transnational regions.

Within the framework of postcolonial literary theory, this article explores Tayeb Salih's *Season of Migration to the North* (1966) and Alaa Al-Aswany's *The Isam Abd al-Ati Papers* (2004) as (re)creation of a *Manichean* self/other relationship founded on pre-established codes of *identity*. Both authors, as this article attempts to prove, deconstruct established codes of subjectivity—disturbing and calling into question a self-other relationship conceived in binary terms—in an attempt to create new ways of being and of relating to otherness and difference.

The analysis examines Salih's and Al-Aswany's novels as imagined symbolic resolutions of the real contradiction of a postmodern and post-independence Sudanese and Egyptian vague sense of self and unbalanced relationship with a Western other. Both writers, in this reading, endeavor to reconfigure a postmodern subjectivity: one that is self-liberated via an awareness of and a confrontation with a constructed otherness within the self. Negotiating difference and the relationship with each *other* in their novels, the novelists, as the argument will run, present a notion of the self as multiple and contradictory in an attempt to transcend a self/other opposition that hinders subjective freedom and leads to either *xenophobia* or *xenophilia*.

Subjectivity: a *Playful* Sign

Divided as they are in their treatment of a conception of subjectivity (identity), postmodern, poststructuralist and postcolonial critics agree on a link that ties a notion of human freedom to a definition of subjectivity and a relation (or the lack of it) with the *other*. The opposition of ipseity, identity, sameness, being, unchangeability, on the one hand, and alterity, nonidentity, development, becoming, and changeability, on the other, unfolds in the debates over subjectivity and the relationship with the other since Descartes and down to phenomenologists and existentialists. Suppressing all notions of diversity or multiplicity, Enlightenment philosophies have not called the nature of the self as a whole, constant entity to question.

Thinking, for Descartes, is being; and his doubting, unified, and stable "self" is the starting point of philosophy. The Hegelian subject is, similarly, a continuous, stable whole; and subjective freedom is attainable, solely, through unity that is achieved via a realization of identity- in-difference: the self is the self because it is not the other. This bequest of the Enlightenment has not stopped short of influencing critiques of subjectivity set up by postmodernist, poststructuralist and postcolonial critics who bring forth different perspectives on the 'ideals' of the Enlightenment.

With the advent of modernism and postmodernism with their conceptions of uncertainty, relativism, and indeterminacy, older notions of absolutism and utter Truth were totally disrupted. As a consequence, among other conceptions, the notion of an unchangeable, stable self appeared as an illusion and has been replaced by multiple and diverse subjectivities. Suspecting any notion of absolute truth or fixed essences, postmodern and postcolonial critics have rejected the Enlightenment's totalizing philosophical tradition and its conceptions of duty and universal laws as means to suppress *alterity* and subjective freedom. Deconstructing a notion of an autonomous and internally coherent subject, they proposed the notion of a *constantly* shifting subject position.

The predicament of the "apophantic structures of knowing," for Husserl, for instance, is their tendency to reduce otherness to the same; "each entity populating the plenum of the world is reduced to the same, each time, and any identifying difference falls through the sieve of the established methods." (Liberman 2007, 7) For him, *apophansis* is a "delimiting force;" and by applying dogmatic positivism, philosophers substitute a narrow theoretically determined "Truth" for an "actually experienced and experienceable world." (Liberman 2007, 3) Moreover, Jorge Luis Borges proposes that "personality is a mirage maintained by conceit and *custom*, without metaphysical foundation or visceral reality." (Borges 1999, 3)

These ideas are in line with Lacan's psychoanalytic model, which holds that the subject is essentially decentered and formed by a symbolic order that comes before it. According to Lacan, the child identifies with an image of coherence that conceals an underlying fragmentation during the mirror stage, which is when subjectivity manifests through a misrecognition (*méconnaissance*). Thus, the self is a product of language and the unconscious, enmeshed in a never-ending conflict between the Real, the Symbolic, and the Imaginary. The Enlightenment ideal of a transparent, self-knowing subject is further undermined by Lacan's claim that the unconscious is structured like a language, which positions identity as contingent, postponed, and mediated by the Other's speech and gaze.

The predicament of the Western philosophical tradition from Plato over Descartes to Kant and Hegel, they argue, lies in how it focuses on the experiences and consciousness of the self of the Western male subject—the "one self-identical" subject—"delegitimizing the presence of otherness and difference which do not fit into its categories." (Benhabib 1992, 212) Accordingly, Spivak proposes a "deconstructive" politics of reading that while acknowledging the "determination as well as the imperialism" of these "magisterial texts," raises the question of how to use these texts as "our servant." (Spivak 1999, 7)

Moreover, it is against this conception of universalism (even the "enlightened form" that permits diversity) that Homi Bhabha proposes his notion of a "radical particularism." He reiterates: "the universalism that…permits diversity masks ethnocentric norms, values and interests." (Brinker-Gabler 1995, 56) As a substitute for diversity, Bhabha proposes a "politics of difference," namely the "notion of a politics which is based on unequal, multiple, and potentially antagonistic, political identities." (Brinker-Gabler 1995, 57) Conflict is an inevitable condition among a group of different and ever-changing selves due to their different sorts of interests, different kinds of cultural histories, different postcolonial lineages, and different sexual orientations. The place of "difference and otherness", for Bhabha, "is the space of the adversarial." (Brinker-Gabler 1995, 58) Similarly, Spivak denies a position of identity whereby knowledge might be predicated on identity: "Whatever the political necessity for holding the position, and whatever the advisability of attempting to identify (with) the other as subject to know her, knowledge is made possible and is sustained by irreducible difference, not identity." (Spivak 1988, 253-254)

In addition, Catherine Belsey marks subjectivity as "a matrix of subject-positions, which may be inconsistent or even in contradiction with one another." (Belsey 1985, 48) Endorsing Belsey's argument, Judith Butler, in her *Gender Trouble: Feminism and the Subversion of Identity*, also argues for identity as a variable or ever-changing construction. She argues against the originality and inevitability of identity by proposing a view of identity as "a kind of persistent impersonation" that only "passes as the real." (Butler 1990, viii) Holding a view of the whole, unified identity as an illusion, Butler argues that: "Since "identity" is assured through the stabilizing concepts of sex, gender, and sexuality, the very notion of "the person" is called into question by the cultural emergence of those "incoherent" or "discontinuous" gendered beings who appear to be persons but who fail to conform to the gendered norms of cultural intelligibility by which persons are defined." (Butler 1990, 17)

Moreover, critics trace contemporary "philosophical autism" back to the Hegelian master-slave dialectic. The Hegelian self/other relationship is a struggle for recognition; the self attains self-consciousness through recognising the other. Hegel's "other", as Shaun Gallagher argues, is a slave who is made to work for the master; an "object" that is denied "subjectivity." (Gallagher, et al. 2004, 7) According to a notion of "reciprocal recognition", being-for-the self is attained solely by being recognized and acknowledged by the "other." Gallagher identifies the problem as such: at a time when self-consciousness is only attainable by the fact of its existence for another self-consciousness, both slave and master alike are denied this recognition. Regarded as an object incapable of conveying any sense of recognition, the slave leaves the master with "an unfulfilled self-recognition;" (Gallagher, et al. 2004, 8); and simultaneously, finds fulfillment in his work rather than in any social relation.

This, according to Gallagher, results in "purely external and a-pathetic" relations between "subjects who from within their first-person lives are unable to communicate as subjects with others whom they can approach only in third-person perspectives." (Gallagher, et al. 2004, 8) Along the same lines, rewriting Hegel's dialectic of recognition and Lacan's mirror stage in the colonial context, Fanon renders mutual recognition for the colonized *black* subject under the *white* gaze impossible. Objectifying the black subject under the colonizer's *look* as a racialized body, a fixed image, rather than as a subject deserving of acknowledgement, the colonial structure rejects the reciprocal model provided by Hegel's dialectic. Furthermore, drawing on and challenging Lacan, Fanon reveals how racial trauma overdetermines the mirror stage for the *black* subject. This creates a political, ontological, and psychological alienation for the racialized subject, trapping them in a vicious cycle of recognition being both desired and structurally denied (Fanon 1952).

Subjectivity: a *Kaleidoscopic Ground*

Engaging with Hegel, Adorno, Deleuze, and Guattari in a dialectical manner, Fredric Jameson highlights both, aforementioned, 'images' of 'identity' as "absolutizing and frightening" extremes (Jameson 1990, 16). In its first image (what Jameson marks as "neurosis"), identity is perceived as sameness: namely, "repetition as such." (Jameson 1990, 16) It is that of the 'closed' self that is basically a return of the (self)same again and again. It is a closed self that does not 'open up' new strata of analysis. The second, which is a counter-image of identity as sameness, develops due to the first's inability to "stand the new; to be 'open' to it;" to imagine and conceptualize what one cannot, *ipso facto*, "imagine or foresee; what has no equivalent in…[one's] current experience." (Jameson 1990, 16) It is that "terrifying rush of the non-identical"- that of the postmodern "schizophrenic hero." (Jameson 1990, 16) It promotes a primordial flux of schizophrenic difference. It is the "unrepresentable vision of the ceaseless flow of the new, the unrepetitive, the great stream which never comes twice." (Jameson 1990, 16) It is the Deleuzean "flux" of continuous and everlasting change, "in which neither subject nor object can yet be imagined, but only the terror and exhaustion of radical difference without markers or signposts." (Jameson 1990, 16)

Identifying both views as two horns of a dilemma, Jameson proposes what he defines as a "garden-variety 'psychic identity'" as a "compromise" formation (Jameson 1990, 18). For him, both models of identity hamper the possibility of 'agency', individuality and subjective freedom. Contrary to those critics who endorse an abandonment of conceptuality (seen as the weapon for idealism, domination, imperialism and the repression of *alterity*), Jameson marks conceptuality as indispensable. For him, disposing of "philosophical concepts" altogether does not effect real change as they "continue to inform daily life in the guise of common-sense realism." (Jameson 1990, 18) However, the concept, as revealed in Jameson's explication, is not to be conceived as the "Universal… encompassing container of the particular content." (Jameson 1990, 18) The concept itself is the "site of antagonism [and] self-contradiction." (Jameson 1990, 18) Opening up the concept itself to include other, even conflicting, forms of conceptuality is the means to get out of the "iron cage" of a concept (Jameson 1990, 18). Opening up the concept of identity itself is what makes 'generating the new moment, temporal change, out of mythic repetition and sameness' a possibility (Jameson 1990, 18). He proposes dialectical thinking, namely using the concept against itself, as the answer to the question he poses: "Is it possible to do something to the concept, which otherwise tendentially locks us into sameness, to use it as a mode of access to difference and the new? " (Jameson 1990, 17)

Identity, according to him, is the site of numerous and even contradictory discourses. The significance of the dialectical process Adorno introduces in his *Negative Dialectics*, for Jameson, lies not only in the way it urges us "to think another side, an outside, an external face of the concept ", but also in its assertion that "we must vigilantly remember and reckon that other face into our sense of the concept while remaining within it in the old way and continuing to use and think it." (Jameson 1990, 25) Accordingly, thinking *subjectivity* would denote thinking *ipseity, alterity* and the system that produces both faces, simultaneously, as "the thought...is itself inevitably the result of a system that escapes it and which it perpetuates." (Jameson 1990, 30) Beyond both the old *bourgeois ego* and the *schizophrenic subject*, Jameson proposes a third possibility which is a *collective subjectivity*. It is a subject that tells a story which does not belong to it.

Jameson expands on this dialectical framework by criticizing other well-known theories of alterity, including Heidegger's *Mitsein* and Fanon's *Look,* for ignoring the structural and conflictual aspects of subjectivity. For him, Heidegger's theory of the *Other* is a "feeble theory" because *Mitsein* results in that "everything conflictual in my relations with the other people is [...] smothered under the indistinction of what is elsewhere blandly called 'intersubjectivity.'" (Jameson 1998, 104) In addition, returning the dominating and subjugating 'Look'—as suggested by Fanon—does not effect real change because it does not "alter the terms of the problem and the situation from which it springs. Europe remains the place of the universal, while Caliban's art affirms a host of merely local specificities." (Jameson 1998, 105) Returning the gaze of the *other* proves an ineffective tool for overcoming the Sartrean Look (that dominates people by turning them into things) as it "cannot overcome the contradiction betrayed by the fact that the identity thereby chosen in Sartrean 'shame and pride' is still conferred on Caliban by Prospero and by the First World colonizer". " (Jameson, CT 1998, 107)

Jameson suggests that "a different reign of visibility can thereby be imagined": a medium that transcends the "colonial gaze." (Jameson, CT 1998, 107) The merit of focusing on the utopia for the subject's "own collectivity"—which is "appropriated by [the subject's] act of resistance"—is the generation of a space beyond. This space in its specificity and particularity surpasses the "colonial gaze." (Jameson 1998, 108) Though Jameson does not deny the risk of having "a utopia of separatism, a cultural nationalist space swept free of the colonial gaze" as a consequence; and though he admits the difficulty in sustaining such visions in a transnational global world, the importance of such visions, for him, lies in their assertion of a genuine "possibility of Otherness" and a "transfiguration of the visible space of domination." (Jameson 1998, 108)

Adopting Jameson's concept of identity, this article explores both Salih and Al Aswany's endeavors to decenter an essentialist notion of identity that, together with warranting that the self is indisputably the self and the other is unequivocally its other, hinders genuine self-knowledge; and thwarts a balanced relationship with the other. It will, first, examine their attempts to dismantle a *fixed* notion of subjectivity and to question the dynamics that structure a self-other relationship via bringing together *self* and *other* within the contours of a single identity-that of an autoscopic protagonist. Both authors use autoscopy (duplication as a motif) as a *Heilsweg*.

In an attempt to create new complex subject-positions, the narratives, as the argument will run, introduce autoscopic protagonists as allegorical dramatizations of a diverse post-independence identity within which ipseity and alterity coexist. The autoscopic protagonists encounter doubles of their creation to overcome a psychological fracture. Secondly, it will examine both novelists' use of 'witnessing' as a process through which they rewrite a "concrete," "self-constitut[ed]" post-independence Sudanese and Egyptian subjectivities—proposing 'Ego' as a terrain of resistance and transformation: "a defense mechanism…a weapon [and] an instrument of praxis and survival" in a post-independence Sudan and Egypt (Jameson 1990, 17).

Autoscopy: a Strategy of Resistance and Survival

According to *A Dictionary of Psychology*, *autoscopy* (from Greek *autos* self +*skopeein* to watch) is the experience of perceiving one's face, body, or part of the unconscious as an external entity. Peter Brugger defines "autoscopic phenomena" as a "heterogeneous class of reduplications of one's own body and perceived self." (Brugger 2002, 180) In their various types, autoscopic experiences stand on the axis of an "increasing detachment from one's own body as a point in space on which the observer's perspective is normally centered and from which the world is observed." (Brugger 2002, 180) An encounter with a doppelganger, *heautoscopy*, one of the types of autoscopic reduplications, is, according to Brugger, "a reduplication not only of bodily experience, but also of aspects of one's psychological self." (Brugger 2002, 179)

The observer projects bodily feelings onto the doppelganger which implies "a mental rotation of one's own body along the vertical axis." (Brugger 2002, 179) The original and the duplicated bodies "are not mirror images of one another." (Brugger 2002, 179) In heautoscopy, the doppelganger can be experienced "as highly supportive, but also as offensive and sometimes overtly aggressive." (Brugger 2002, 187) He can either play the role of the saviour or that of the pursuer. Moreover, the double, in heautoscopy, "may speak with, or touch the subject…The double may be motionless, expressionless, imitate the subject's own facial expressions and movements…or act independently." (Mishara 2010, 596-597) Often does the double become the leader who "takes over the I "—who "usurps the 'real self'." (Mishara 2010, 626) What distinguishes *autoscopy* from other phenomena of illusory reduplications of the self, according to Brugger, is the core position the psychological affinity to one's own double or doppelganger occupies in the autoscopic experience.

The experience of encountering a double or a doppelganger has been grappled with, from different perspectives, in many literary and cultural works since the late eighteenth century and down to Modernism and Postmodernism. Though the Classical, Romantic and early Modern periods have classified the phenomenon of self-duplication as a psychological crisis, underlying the horror raised by such experiences, the permeation of late modern psychological theories has robbed it gradually of this nomenclature by highlighting the normal diversity of the self.

Written in the late 1980s (almost thirty years after Egypt attained its in-dependence) *The Isam Abd el-Ati Papers* share with *Season of Migration to the North* (published in 1966—almost ten years after Sudan achieved independence) its concern with the blurred position of the subject. The protagonists' struggle against the legacies of colonization, in my reading, provides the foundational base of both novels. Both protagonists are pre-sented as bifurcated psyches: subjectivities made up of a postcolonial *self* and its *other[s]*. It is not a self-other peaceful coexistence that both writ-ers present, though. The subject itself is a site of conflict, antagonism and contradiction. Embodied as the colonial subject who carries the 'germ' imported by the colonizing *other* in Salih's novel, the *other* in Al Aswany's text is a Western woman (Salih 1969, 75).

In this argument, both writers engage in a bifocal endeavor. Firstly, pre-senting *autoscopic* narrators as the main characters of their novels, both authors aim at shaking the self's convictions; that is, they aim at an "un-fixation" of the self's "belief." (Sweet 2002, 7) Blurring the clear distinc-tion between reality and illusion, autoscopy renders certainty, constancy, stability and fixation impossible. Both authors, in my reading, attempt to loosen the self's grip that has long been fixed on a *subjectivity* formed by oppression and subordination (as one of the *habits* of subalternity). Once this is achieved, the second endeavor: suggesting other forms of subjec-tivity and relating to others becomes a genuine possibility. Via their auto-scopic narrators—who act as allegorical dramatizations of the existence of ipseity and alterity within the contours of a single subjectivity—both narratives, in this reading, *react* symbolically to an unstable relationship with the other. Autoscopy is the authors' means to draw the self's atten-tion to the falsehood of essentialism, certainty and fixation; hence, the self is encouraged to reconfigure its own subjectivity.

However, the mere proposition of multiple, diverse, interchangeable and ever-changing subjectivities is not sufficient to eschew a xenophobic or a xenophelic relationship between self and other—in favor of a balanced relationship. It is to resolve this contradiction that both writers, meta-phorically, propose *witnessing*, in their narratives, as a process to establish a productive rapport with the other; a notion that the following analysis of both texts will attempt to prove.

Trailing Subjectivities in *Season of Migration to the North* and *The Isam Abd el-Aty Papers*

In *Season of Migration to the North*, Salih challenges the notion of a unified stable subject. The subject itself is a site of conflict. The reader gets the picture of a *self* that veils an unconscious *other* from the very beginning. The narrative presents an instance of a xenophobic relationship between a Sudanese *self* and its *other*—another Sudanese self-tainted by the germ of colonization. The narrator says: "I feel hatred and seek revenge; my adversary is *within* and I must *confront* him [...] my adversary [is] Mustafa Sa'eed." (Salih 1969, 106-7 emphasis added)

Salih opens up a channel of communication between *self* and *other*, through which the *self* confronts the *other* as a construction within its own subjectivity. Such a confrontation of otherness is presented in the novel as a need. Talking about Mustafa Sa'eed, the narrator says: "He wants to be discovered, like some historical object of value [...]. It was no coincidence that [...] he had then told me his life story incompletely so that I myself might unearth the rest of it." (Salih 1969, 122) Furthermore, via an allegorical destabilization of a conception of identity as a unified, stable entity—dismantling the apparently definite boundaries between *self* and *other*—Salih seeks to challenge a self/other binary besides contesting a fabricated status of the self. He urges the self to interrogate the boundaries constructed between itself and its *other*.

The relationship between the narrator (the postcolonial subject) and Mustafa Sa'eed (the colonial subject) is the pivot around which the narrative revolves. Set in a post-independence Sudan, the story is narrated by a nameless narrator. After seven years of studying in England (achieving a Ph.D. in English literature), the narrator goes back to his small village in the Sudan not long after the Sudanese independence in 1956. There, he meets Mustafa Sa'eed, a "stranger" about fifty years old, who "had come... five years ago," bought a farm and a house, married Mahmoud's daughter and had two kids (Salih 1969, 2). During a community drinking session, Sa'eed raises the narrator's doubts by reciting an English poem in an "impeccable accent." (Salih 1969, 11) When the narrator (almost sure that Sa'eed isn't that simple farmer he claims to be) confronts him, Sa'eed feels obliged to relate his story to the narrator lest "his imagination run[s] away with him." (Salih 1969, 14)

The narrator's tendency towards *denial, repression,* and *negation* calls the reader's attention the moment he begins narrating his story. The narrator goes back to his small village in the Sudan, his home country, after spending seven years studying in Europe. Yet, he describes it as "an(other)" story that is not of much importance because the "important thing" is—ironically—that he has returned home to his people (Salih 1969, 1 emphasis added). The harder the narrator tries to prove the insignificance of his experience, the more obvious his mental anguish becomes to the reader. It is not merely that there is little to recount about his seven years in Europe; the narrator repeatedly emphasizes that this period brought no change in him or his relationship with his people. The "fog" that "rose up between them…the first instant" (paradoxically because of having thought a lot about them during his absence) "clear[s]" the second day of his arrival (Salih 1969, 1).

Although he claims that nothing has gone wrong, he needs the old "palm tree standing in the courtyard" of his old house to be assured that "all was still well with life." (Salih 1969, 1) He needs his parents, sisters and brother to be sure that "life is good and the world as unchanged as ever." (Salih 1969, 2) He needs his grandfather to feel "a sense of stability" of continuity and wholeness: to feel that he is not "a stone thrown into the water but seed sown in a field." (Salih 1969, 4) To the narrator's astonishment, it is particularly at that time of denial and negation that he encounters Mustafa Sa'eed for the first time; and is struck by his strangeness. The narrator encounters Mustafa at the time when he like a "child," sees "its face in the mirror for the first time;" and when he starts "renew[ing]" his relationship with his own people (Salih 1969, 3).

The synchronization of the narrator's return to his village and his encounter with Sa'eed, together with that aura of strangeness, mystery and vagueness that the narrator surrounds Sa'eed with from the beginning urge the reader to delve deeper into this character that has much more about it than what is revealed. Throughout the novel, the narrator consistently describes Sa'eed as enigmatic. Gradually, both the narrator's story and Mustafa's intertwine and the picture of Mustafa as an externalized part of the narrator's consciousness unveiled to the reader. The sense the reader gets of Mustafa as the narrator's doppelganger is enforced by the narrator's remarks throughout the novel. Even when Mustafa dies, the narrator does not stop meeting him. He goes thusly: "I still continue to meet up with him from time to time…Mustafa Sa'eed has, against my will, become a part of my world, a thought in my brain, a phantom that does not want to take itself off." (Salih 1969, 40) When the narrator moves to Khartoum, Mustafa's phantom does not leave him—"like a genie who has been released from his prison and will continue thereafter to whisper" in his ears (Salih 1969, 43). The blurring of identities reaches a poignant moment when the narrator enters Mustafa's secret room—supposedly for the first time—and finds its odour strangely familiar. Confronted with a photograph, he is startled to recognize not Sa'eed, but himself: "This is not Mustafa Sa'eed—it's a picture of me frowning at my face from a mirror." (Salih 1969, 107)

The author builds the relationship between the narrator and Mustafa Sa'eed on axes of sameness and difference. Being the narrator's doppelganger, Sa'eed is not a mirror image of him. While the narrator reaches for the past, Sa'eed carries with him the legacy of a past which he exerts every effort to erase or forget. When the narrator is frightened to lose his roots, Sa'eed cannot disengage from a culture that has captivated him. Born to two Sudanese families; the narrator and Mustafa connect differently to their kin and roots. "I returned:" this is how the narrator begins his story—disclosing a great relief, strong love and affinity with his family, his people, and his tribe and the important role they play in his life (Salih 1969, 1).

The narrator goes back to "yearning" for his people and the "warmth" of the tribe in that 'small village at the bend of the Nile' after seven years of "long[ing]" for them and "dream[ing]" of them in a "land whose fishes die of the cold." (Salih 1969, 1) It is not only love that the narrator receives from his people; more significantly, they provide him with a profound sense of continuity, assurance, stability, and security. He reflects: "I felt not like a storm-swept feather but like that palm tree, a being with a background, with roots, with a purpose"; and further affirms, "I feel that I am important, that I am continuous and integral." (Salih 1969, 1) Contrary to the narrator's, Mustafa Sa'eed 's roots cannot be confirmed. His father, who dies before he is born, is from the "Ababda, the tribe living between Egypt and the Sudan" and his mother, his only kin and towards whom he hardly has any feelings, is a slave from the south, from the tribes of Zandi or Baria (Salih 1969, 42). Unlike the passionate narrator, Mustafa has not been attached to his mother nor has he had any feelings of gratitude for anyone who has helped him. Mustafa is simply "different." (Salih 1969, 16) He tells the narrator: "I was like something rounded, made of rubber: you throw it in the water and it doesn't get wet, you throw it on the ground and it bounces back." (Salih 1969, 16)

Moreover, the challenges of knowing and relating to the *other* are at the core of the novel. Yet, the same difference between Mustafa and the narrator shows in the way both react upon encountering *otherness*. The narrator describes himself as "one of those birds that exist only in one region of the world." (Salih 1969, 39) His tendency towards neutralizing difference and otherness is unveiled in the way he makes Africans of those Europeans he meets in London: "I would imagine the faces over there as being brown or black so that they would look like the faces of people I knew." (Salih 1969, 39) For him: "Over there is like here, neither better nor worse." (Salih 1969, 39) Thus, being asked by his people about how Europeans are like, he tells them: "Europeans [are], with minor differences, exactly like them...that they [have] good morals and [are] in general good people." (Salih 1969, 2) Contra the narrator, Mustafa enforces his alterity and confirms a stereotype to manipulate the *other*. He "fabricate[s]" stories about "deserts of golden sands and jungles where non-existent animals called out to another." (Salih 1969, 30) He reads poetry, talks of religion and philosophy, says things about "the spirituality "of the East (Salih 1969, 24). He "transform[s]" himself in the eye of the other into "a naked, primitive creature, a spear in one hand and arrows in the other, hunting elephants and lions in the jungles"; and it is "fine" with him as long as it helps him to seduce his "prey." (Salih 1969, 30) Deliberately building up "lie upon lie," Sa'eed enforces a "myth" created by the "other." (Salih 1969, 115)

It is via such a symbolic blurring of the boundaries between sameness and difference—highlighting an existence of otherness as a construction within the self, in this reading—that Salih calls upon the self to question the truth of a constructed identity, which has long been imposed on it. A self-liberated subjectivity can be attained, for Salih, when the marks the *other* has engraved in the psyche are "consciousnessize[d] and the mechanisms of projection used by the "other" to "impose" a "collective unconscious" are exposed (Fanon 1952, 80). What Salih seeks is to get post-independence subjectivities to figure out "the truth about themselves" to get them to figure out that part of their own subjectivity that has been invented for them, and in which they have been made to believe (Salih 1969, 53). It is only, then, that they can work through it and move forward. It is only when the self confronts the other within—when it comes to seeing how the other has long worked to reshape its identity—that it can begin to move beyond it. Mustafa—the colonial subjectivity—asks the narrator to tell his children his own story lest his life "emerge[s] from behind the unknown like an evil spirit and cause them harm." (Salih 1969, 53) Indeterminacy unfolds at the thematic core of the novel. Multiple perspectives and significations inhabit the novel—dismantling all notions of unification and essentialism. The novel does not inscribe a simplistic self/other dichotomy. Via a play of positions and an 'unfixing' of the significations of self and other, Salih, allegorically, presents subjectivities as identities in flux—in constant and permanent change.

Positing this notion of subjectivity as the ground of the intersection of self and other, Salih postulates new forms of testimony that question the truth claims of representation, besides those of selfhood, and call upon the different 'sel(ves)' and 'other(s)' to give up their "simplistic perception" of one another (Fanon 1961, 94). Though things may appear simple, still and stable, "simplicity is not everything." (Fanon 1952, 40) Hence, Mustafa's "life story" is dedicated: "[t]o those who see with one eye, speak with one tongue and see things as either black or white, either Eastern or Western." (Salih 1969, 119)

Similarly, in his *The Isam Abd el-Ati Papers*, Alaa Al-Aswany discloses the same concern with the issues of a postmodern, post-independence Egyptian subjectivity and a self-other relationship. He opens a space in his narrative to challenge his Egyptian readers to reconsider Egyptian subjectivity and its relationship with the other away from binary terms. The legacy of colonization provides the context of Al-Aswany's narrative as is the case with Tayeb Salih's. The novel posits an interaction between the residues of a colonial past and a capitalist present. In this reading of the novel, Al-Aswany destabilizes the notion of a monolithic, unified identity to reinvent a notion of subjectivity as multiple and diverse entities.

Written in the first person, the novel is narrated by Isam, a middle-aged highly educated Egyptian who suffers from the *mal* social conditions 'after nationalization.' (Al Aswany 2009, 27) In the novel, Isam's life story intertwines with his father's, highlighting frustration, corruption, hypocrisy, bureaucratic decay, and the suppression of talent and creativity as defining features of society across generations. Against the expectations of his father, Isam does not accomplish much in obtaining his baccalaureate in science. Being appointed as a researcher in the government's Chemistry Authority, Isam lays a hand on the excruciating reality. His disappointment and frustration increase (having to face a world of hypocrisy, corruption and lies embodied by his coworkers at the Authority) which results in his alienation and withdrawal from his society to live in a dream world of his own creation. At this point, he meets Jutta—his *doppelganger* and his soul-image.

In the novel, Al-Aswany shares with Salih both his concern with the marks left by an encounter with otherness on subjectivity and his attempt to emancipate the mind almost thirty years after Egypt attained its independence. The novel's narrator claims: "The history of Egypt is in reality nothing but a continuous series of defeats inflicted upon us by all the nations of the world, starting with the Romans and going all the way to the Jews." (Al Aswany 2009, 3) Subjectivity is displayed as a text within the novel: an inscription of a Postmodern Egyptian social, economic, and political scene. While Al-Aswany's narrative may initially appear solely concerned with portraying alienation, displacement, disorientation, and psychic fragmentation as consequences of living under postmodern coercive social, economic, and political conditions, the reader is gradually prompted to probe deeper into the underlying causes of these dire individual and collective states.

As the narrator observes: "To look at, a drop of water is as pure and transparent as crystal, but if you magnify it under a lens, a thousand impurities appear." (Al Aswany 2009, 47) The narrator emerges as a fragmented subjectivity, frayed by coerced encounters and persistent clashes—an idea underscored early in the novel when he says: "We are the corrupt, indeterminate outcome of the miscegenation of the conquerors' troops with their captives from the defeated population." (Al Aswany 2009, 3) Wrestling with notions of a past grandeur, a present decay and internalized Western values, the narrator ends up with a split self and a vague sense of his subjectivity.

Showing close affinity with Salih's narrator, Isam Abd el-Atty internalizes a Western other within the self. The self-other relationship in Al-Aswany's novel is one of xenophelia, though. It is a relationship marked by strong admiration that reaches the degree of infatuation representative of an unresolved identity crisis. Contrary to Salih who presents an instance of a xenophobic subjectivity that regards the other as an "adversary within," (Salih 1969, 106) Al-Aswany's narrator is deeply fascinated with the other whom he "devour[s]" (Al Aswany 2009, 68). A notion of the supremacy of the *other*—the West or Europeans and Americans—is deeply rooted in the narrator's mind that it becomes an essential part of his life and worldview.

According to Todorov, xenophelia constitutes an "act of imaginative projection into the culture of an*other* rather than the mutually challenging process of intra- and intercultural engagement." (Bammer 1995, 50) It is an "attempt to disown the culture-in-process of which we are a part; it is a call not for change, but for substitution…an act of self-displacement," he reiterates (Bammer 1995, 50). In *The Isam Abd el-Aty Papers*, the narrator immersed in despair, frustration and disappointment slips into self-loathing and a blind infatuation and obsession with the other. Consequently, he starts seeing Egyptians as: "Base, stupid, parasitical, and spiteful," in comparison to Americans and Europeans– God's "most exquisite creatures." (Al Aswany 2009, 68- 79)

The author aims to draw the self's attention to the dangers of blind infatuation with the West—exposing the illusion that underpins such fascination. Falling in love with the "spirit of the West", as he explains, the narrator—"totally bewitched"—walls himself off the people around him, starts buying European and American magazines and spends the night smoking hashish, watching the pictures in the magazine and dreaming (Al Aswany 2009, 65). He narrates:" I tried to read a political article in the American magazine but got bored and stopped. It was the pictures alone that attracted me. Everything in the pictures seemed marvellous; even the smallest things had a quiet glamour. A life of exuberance, variety, and resplendence." (Al Aswany 2009, 65) Looking at this passage through the lens of Bakhtin's dialogical novelistic utterances, the reader can easily recognize the author's endeavor to convey an image of a supreme, flawless European and American other—internalized by a Postmodern Egyptian self—as a chimera of the self's own creation. It is only "pictures" that he is interested in, a mere image or an appearance that he uses to create his own impressions and illusions. This view becomes more and more obvious throughout the novel until the reader gets to know that Jutta (a dramatization of an internalized otherness within the self) is, herself, an illusion; that she has never existed and is in fact a figment of the narrator's imagination.

Through an allegorical dramatization of internalized otherness, Al-Aswany prompts subjects to reconsider and reconfigure both their sense of self and their relationship with the other. Carrying the burden of a past of defeat and helplessness together with an internalized fascination with the West, Isam's "new cannot be born." (Gramsci 1971, 107) The narrator's father is a metaphorical representation of the firm grip of the narrator's past on his present. Their relationship unfolds, within the narrative, as a love-hate relationship. Reading Abd el-Atty, the narrator's father, as an emblem of the narrator's past that "clings onto" him, the reader can easily detect the authorial voice embedded within the narrator's words.

Both Salih's and Al Aswany's narrators exhibit divergent responses to the otherness embedded within the self. Contrary to Salih's narrator, Isam Abd el-Aty succumbs to self-loathing and idealizing the *other*. Isam is cognizant of the lingering effects of colonization. However, the reader cannot overlook that the narrator, too, suppresses the profound—albeit different—psychic impact of a forced encounter with otherness on him. If Salih's narrator pretends that nothing has gone wrong and that all is well as it has always been, Isam Abd el-Aty, too, denies and negates the pain inflicted on him. Rather than facing his loneliness, alienation and displacement as an affliction, he starts seeing this displacement as a 'blessing' or even a triumph. The reader realizes the narrator's 'unbalanced feelings' which he himself is "incapable of determining if [they] are attributable to [his] overly developed awareness or to the circumstances of [his] upbringing." (Al Aswany 2009, 6) The discrepancy between the narrator's words and his deeds highlights this confusion even more. He announces his hatred of Egyptians who cover their flaws with lies about their 'greatness' and superiority, at the time when he is immersed in a deep sense of his own superiority. The sense of his bafflement and perplexity is accentuated by his inability to decide the role of fate in his life. He cannot make up his mind if he is the controller of his own life, and is thus responsible for these choices, or if he is a "tragic hero accepting the blows of fate with a noble, courageous heart," or if he is merely a "small wooden doll whose movements are controlled by numerous strings... [which] are gathered in a single hand, outside the box." (Al Aswany 2009, 7-8)

Isam's downfall is presented as a gradual process throughout the novel. His awareness of the frustration of all the dreams of a revolutionary generation embodied by his father and his friends initiates this process. About his father and his friends, he says: "When they came to Cairo thirty years before, two young artists full of determination and ambition, had it ever occurred to them that things would turn like this?" (Al Aswany 2009, 16) Then being unable to figure out the raison d'être of the failure of the talented and creative people of his father's generation to effect real change, he surrenders to his disappointment and frustration. Disdaining such a society that annihilates talent and creativity, the narrator—totally wrapped up in himself—seeks refuge in his own isolation, which ends up with his neurosis. What should be noted is how Al-Aswany focuses on the difference between the narrator and his father who could still compare his present situation to the past before nationalization and lay a hand on the problem. The narrator, on the contrary, appears as a lost self; a dangling subjectivity lost among different histories—unable to identify with any of them or to reinvent its own. As a consequence, he chooses to live in his illusions.

Weighed down by feelings of melancholy and disappointment and being unable to cope with his society, Isam seeks an alternative. He reiterates: "[T]he more certain I become of how useless we are, the more their spirit appears to me to be running over with amazing potential." (Al Aswany 2009, 67) What the narrator's words disclose to the reader is that this otherness has long been engraved within his own self—as part of his psychological make-up—and he only needs to dig it up from within. It is at this point that he meets his "Beloved"—Juttav—a German lady at the German Cultural Centre in Egypt. Gradually, the reader gets to recognize Jutta as Isam's double, a projected part of his unconscious, a mere figment of his own imagination. The relationship between Isam and Jutta (the Western other) appears in the novel as an unbalanced self-other relationship—very similar to the relationship between the narrator and Mustafa Sa'eed. Not only is the self bewitched by the other, but the other is the source of the self's inspiration and power on which it depends for its existence and well-being. He tells Jutta: "In fact, I'm a weak person and usually incapable of confrontation...I behaved bravely tonight because

I was with you." (Al Aswany 2009, 83) Containing her with his "feelings as [he] contained her with [his] body", the narrator could escape from "the familiar ugly reality that was forever crushing [him] in its unforgiving grip." (Al Aswany 2009, 84)

Witnessing: Constructing a Concrete Subjectivity

In both their novels, Salih and Al-Aswany, in this reading, draw 'witnessing subjectivit[ies]': subjectivities that are self-constituted by undergoing a process of "witnessing as address-ability and response-ability" which is "the founding possibility of subjectivity and its most fundamental obligation," argues Kelly Oliver (Oliver 2004, 205). Carrying both meanings of being an eye-witness and the religious meaning of blind belief, 'witnessing' is a process Oliver proposes as a means to reconstruct both a subjectivity and a self-other relationship. Through 'witnessing', self and other, in both texts, encounter the unfamiliar with all its alterity. In a process of witnessing, the 'othered' (occupying the position of a speaking subject) is allowed not only to testify to his objectification and oppression but also to regain a lost subjectivity by speaking—by having a voice and uttering his own individuality and specificity. Having autoscopic characters as the novels' protagonists, Salih and Al Aswany present subjectivities that are, simultaneously, the writers, readers and interpreters of their own life.

In his novel, Salih exposes the heterogeneity of the Sudanese cultural identity. Through 'witnessing', he dismantles a 'reductionism' that reduces people to categories and a 'constructionism' that masks the other's individuality, particularity and specificity. Difference, as shown in the novel, is the "starting point of reflection and action." (Benhabib 1992, 153) It is only in the court in England where "the ritual was being held primarily because of [him]," as an individual, that Sa'eed feels "superior" to them (Salih 1969, 75). Voicing his own alterity, Mustafa Sa'eed says: "I'm no Othello. Othello was a lie." (Salih 1969, 75) In a similar vein, Hosna remains locked in absolute voicelessness throughout the novel, until she kills Wad Rayyes. When she kills him, refusing to succumb to their rules, she steps out of a shared sign system and announces her alterity—silencing them.

The novel highlights and disavows a tendency to deny cultural differences that may not confirm with one's norms and practices. The narrator says: "By the standards of the European industrial world we are poor peasants, but when I embrace my grandfather, I experience a sense of richness as though I am a note in the heartbeats of the very universe." (Salih 1969, 58) Moreover, whereas the colonizer has denied the 'self' individuality, it is no better in a post-independence age because the 'self' is still denied this right by being denied representation and participation as an agent in the public sphere. The narrator answers Mahjoub's question: "What are you doing in Khartoum? What's the use in our having one of us in the government when you're not doing anything?"—saying: "Civil servants like me can't do anything…If our masters say 'Do so-and-so', we do it." (Salih 1969, 96) It is a matter of a different master. Mahjoub, the head of the National Democratic Socialist Party in the village, tells the narrator: "The world hasn't changed as much as you think…The world will really have changed when the likes of me become ministers in the government. And naturally that…is an out-and-out impossibility." (Salih 1969, 79)

In a similar vein to Salih, Al-Aswany highlights the misconception of the alterity of the other as what controls a self-other relationship. Through "witnessing," the narrative positions the narrator's voice against Jutta's. Describing the photos presented in a photographic exhibition held at the German Cultural Center, the narrator underscores the same rift (that Salih's novel highlights) between the self's notion of its subjectivity and a represented image of selfhood. Isam tells Jutta: "You love Egypt in exactly the way you'd love an exotic show at the circus, or rare animals at the zoo." (Al Aswany 2009, 71) However, the reader gets to see how Isam, assuming that he "know[s]", falls into the same trap of appropriating the other (Al Aswany 2009, 69). The author emphasizes dialogue as a strategy for dealing with the other—for establishing a balanced self-other relationship. Isam is first introduced to Jutta as a "voice." (Al Aswany 2009, 70) Though they disagree about almost everything they talk about, Isam and Jutta get to know each other through their conversation. Reversing the paradigm of the European who proves his superiority to an inferior other, the novelist provides an opposite model. Isam is the one who criticizes Egypt and the Egyptians at the time when Jutta expresses her love and appreciation of Egypt and the Egyptians. To Jutta's surprise, Isam tells her that he is "unfortunately" an Egyptian, to which she answers: "How strange you should feel sorry because you're Egyptian. Since I was a child. I've longed to be Egyptian." (Al Aswany 2009, 71)

Both Salih and Al-Aswany propose 'witnessing' (as a mechanism of addressing and responding adopted by both self and other) as the means to restore the self's agency and to rise above a Manichean self-other relationship. Emphasizing multivocality and dialogism, both texts create a space that makes it possible, as Homi Bhabha says, "to emerge as others of our selves." (Bhabha 1995, 209) They create a space where it becomes possible to interrelate; that is, to "experience knowledge of the other." (Waldenfels 1995, 35) They make possible a dialogue that is the only means for creating a stable relationship between individualized selves and others—not coded versions of subjectivity. However, by creating this space where self and other can engage in a dialogue, both writers underscore the role of the *collectivity* whose absence throws a monkey wrench into the attainments of such a dialogue. The reader cannot fail to realize how both novels end on a melancholic note. Whereas Salih's protagonist (unable to cope with otherness within and without) ends up in the middle of the river almost on the verge of drowning, Al-Aswany (entangled by the same otherness) ends up in a mental hospital. Highlighting a self-other dialogue as a resolution for a problematic, unbalanced self-other relationship—whether xenophobic or xenopheliac—both writers emphasize the role of collectivity. The willingness of the collectivity to engage in such a self-other dialogue is conveyed by both novelists as a necessity for the success of such an endeavor. Finding that he was "in a state between life and death," Salih's narrator "screamed with all [his] remaining strength, 'Help! Help!'" (Salih 1969, 132-133) Denied this 'help,' Isam Abd el-Aty in Al Aswany's novel ends up in a mental hospital feeling that "he will never be able to... leave." (Al Aswany 2009, 92)

In conclusion, autoscopy, as deployed in the novels, creates hybrid subjectivities--which Bhabha might refer to as a "third space" of enunciation or a location of identity that is "neither the one nor the other"—undermining the essentialist ideas of the self that form the basis of colonial ideology—which aims to fix identity and difference in unbending hierarchies (Bhabha 1995, 37). Via their autoscopic protagonists, both authors dramatize radical, emancipatory and agential subjectivities that subvert colonial logic by observing and recounting their fragmentation-revealing the violence of identity as an imposed structure. As a literary and epistemological approach to cognitive decolonization, autoscopy dismantles the imperial fiction of a unitary subject by letting the self reflect on itself and bear witness to its fragmentation. Rather than a passive doubling or mimetic device, autoscopy is employed by both authors as an act of cognitive insurgency.

References

Al Aswany, Alaa. 2009. "The Isam Abd-el Aty Papers." In *Friendly Fire*, by Alaa Al Aswany, translated by Humphrey Davies, 1-92. Cairo: The American University in Cairo Press.

Bammer, Angelika. 1995. "Xenophobia, Xenophelia, and No Place to Rest." In *Encountering the Other(s)*, edited by Gisela Brinker-Gabler, 45-59. State University of New York Press.

Belsey, Catherine. 1985. *Constructing the Subject: Deconstructing the Text. Feminist Criticism and Social Change.* Edited by Judith Newton and Deborah Rosenfelt. Methuen.

Benhabib, Seyla. 1992. *Situating the Self.* Routledge.

Bhabha, Homi K. 1994. *The Location of Culture.* Routledge.

———. 1995. "Cultural Diversity and Cultural Differences." In *The Post-Colonial Studies Reader*, edited by Bill Ashcroft, Gareth Griffiths and Helen Tiffin. Routledge.

Borges, Jorge Luis. 1999. "The Nothingness of Personality." In *Selected Non-Fictions*, edited by Eliot Weinberger, translated by Eliot Weinberger, 3-9. Viking.

Brinker-Gabler, Gisela, ed. 1995. *Encountering the Others.* University of New York Press.

Brugger, Peter. 2002. "Reflective Mirrors: Prespective-taking in autoscopic phenomena." *Cognitive Neuropsychiatry* 7 (3): 179-194.

Buchanan, Ian, ed. 2007. *Jameson On Jameson.* Duke University Press.

Butler, Judith. 1990. *Gender Trouble: Feminism and the Subversion of Identity.* Routledge.

Fanon, Frantz. 1952. *Black Skin, White Masks.* Grove Press.

———. 1961. *The Wretched of the Earth.* Grove Press.

Gallagher, Shaun, Stephen Watson, Philippe Brun, and Philippe Romanski. 2004. *Ipseity and Alterity.Interdisciplinary Approaches to Intersub-*

jectivity. University of Rouen Press.

Gramsci, Antonio. 1971. *Selections from the Prison Notebooks.* Translated by Quintin Hoare and Geoffery Nowell-Smith. International Publishers.

Herdman, John. 1991. *The Double in Nineteenth-Century Fiction. The Shadow Life.* St. Martin's.

Huttunen, Tuomas, Kaisa Ilmonen, Janne Korkka, and Elina Valovirta. 2008. *Seeking The Self, Encountering The Other.* Cambridge Scholars Publishing.

Iser, Wolfgang. 1989. *Prospecting: From Reader Response to Literary Anthropology.* John Hopkins University Press.

Jameson, Fredric. 1981. *The Political Unconscious.* Cornell University Press.

———. 1990. Verso.

———. 1998. *The Cultural Turn.* Verso.

Lacan, Jacques. 1989. *Ecrits. A Selection.* Translated by Alan Sheridan. Routledge.

Liberman, Kennetth. 2007. *Husserl's Criticism of Reason.* Lexington Books.

McHale, Brian. 1987. *Postmodernist Fiction.* Methuen.

Mishara, Aaron L. 2010. "Autoscopy: Disrupted Self in Neuropsychiatric." In *Handbook of Phenomenology*, edited by Daniel Schmicking Shaun Gallagher, 591-634. Springer.

Oliver, Kelly. 2004. "Witnessing Subjectivity." In *Ipseity and Alterity.Interdisciplinary Approaches to Intersubjectivity*, edited by Stephen Watson, Philippe Brun, Philippe Romanski Shaun Gallagher. University of Rouen Press.

Said, Edward. Autumn 1985. "An Ideology of Difference." *Critical Inquiry* (Chicago University Press) 12 (1): 38-58.

Salih, Tayeb. 1969. *Season of Migration to the North.* Translated by Denys

Johnson-Davies. Heinemann.

Spivak, Gayatri. 1999. *A Critique of Postcolonial Reason.* Harvard UP.

———. 1988. *In Other Worlds. Essays in Cultural Politics.* Routledge.

Sweet, William, ed. 2002. *Philosophy, Culture and Pluralism.* Bibliotheque Nationale Du Canada.

Waldenfels, Bernhard. 1995. "Response to the Other." In *Encountering the Other(s): Studies in Literature, History and Culture*, edited by Gisela Brinker-Gabler. State University of New York.

Zizek, Slavoj. Winter 2006. "A Plea for a Return to Difference (with a Minor Pro Domo Sua." *Critical Inquiry* (Chicago UP) 32 (2): 226-249.

Home and Away: Diasporic Hindi Fiction of Women Writers

Prachi Priyanka, PhD.

ABSTRACT

Strong connection to home provides migrants with a unique expatriate sensibility to examine, understand and respond to challenges they face in their present surroundings. By constructing "home" in their stories – diasporic writers can travel in time and space and generate a sense of identity despite being divorced from their roots. In diaspora imagination, home becomes a metaphor and metonymy for the retrieval of an individual's past and search for solace in the romantic or nostalgic imagination. While nostalgia and home define the experience of first-generation immigrants, the second and third-generation diaspora population step into a far more complex jumble of existence and relationship with both nations. It is this constant struggle to accommodate different worlds and belong nowhere that eventually gives way to the formation of new cultural identities. My particular objective is to foreground concerns of diasporic Hindi literature through the works of acclaimed Indian women writers like Pushpa Saxena, Sudha Om Dhingra, Archana Painuly, Purnima Varman, Usha Raje Saxena and Divya Mathur. In these texts, home and nation are re-narrated, not in terms of a monolithic space, but as a historically constituted terrain that touches upon ideas related to family ties, a sense of alienation and yearning for ancestral roots. The characters in these literary texts often navigate through psychic dimensions of nostalgia for people and places they call home – where home tends to acquire a spiritual character. This paper aims to assess the shifting boundaries of belonging as represented through the narratives that mediate between cultural experiences and complications of sustenance. The paper will also explore the complexities of self-representation in diasporic women's writings in Hindi and highlight their active agency in preserving the memory of homelands.

Keywords: Hindi Diasporic Fiction, Indian Diaspora, Homelands, Women Writers, Nostalgia, Identity

Introduction

The study of diaspora has evolved significantly over the last few decades, becoming a crucial lens through which to examine transnational identities, cultural displacement, and the fluidity of belonging in a globalized world. Traditionally understood as the dispersion of people from their original homeland, the concept of diaspora has expanded to encompass a range of experiences shaped by voluntary migration, forced displacement, exile, or economic necessity. The diasporic condition is marked by a continual negotiation between memory and adaptation, between rootedness and rootlessness. Central to this discourse is the idea of "home"—both as a lost origin and a recreated space—and the emotional resonance it carries in the lives of migrants. Within the vast landscape of diaspora studies, the South Asian diaspora has garnered substantial scholarly attention, particularly due to its complex colonial and postcolonial migratory histories, its vast linguistic and cultural diversity, and its evolving relationship with both host and home countries. Among the multiple linguistic communities that constitute the South Asian diaspora, the Hindi-speaking diaspora presents a distinctive case, especially in the literary realm, where questions of identity, memory, and cultural continuity are intricately woven into narratives of displacement and longing.

The Hindi-speaking diaspora includes migrants from North India who primarily communicate in Hindi or its dialects, such as Awadhi, Bhojpuri, and Braj, and who have settled in diverse parts of the world including North America, the United Kingdom, the Caribbean, the Middle East, and Southeast Asia. Historically, waves of migration from the Hindi heartland have taken place under varying socio-political and economic conditions—from indentured labour under British colonialism to contemporary voluntary migration for education and employment.

These movements have resulted in the formation of transnational Hindi-speaking communities that continue to maintain emotional and cultural ties to India, while simultaneously negotiating their identities in multicultural societies. The diasporic experience of Hindi-speaking individuals is further complicated by the dual demands of assimilation into host cultures and the preservation of linguistic and cultural heritage. This tension becomes particularly salient in literary expressions, where writers not only recount personal and communal histories but also reflect on the mutable nature of "home" and the fragile constructs of belonging.

In diasporic Hindi literature, women often emerge as custodians of culture, memory, and familial bonds—roles that place them at the heart of the discourse on home and belonging. Their narratives reveal how the experience of migration is not merely a spatial or economic shift but a profound emotional journey marked by longing, loss, and the search for identity. Female protagonists in these stories often navigate between traditional expectations and modern realities, between inherited cultural roles and the liberating yet alienating freedoms of the diaspora. Through their literary voices, writers such as Pushpa Saxena, Sudha Om Dhingra, Archana Painuly, Purnima Varman, Usha Raje Saxena, and Divya Mathur offer nuanced representations of diasporic life that challenge monolithic ideas of home and nation. They reimagine belonging as a fluid, evolving process rather than a fixed state, and in doing so, they contribute significantly to both Hindi literature and the broader field of diaspora studies.

This paper explores the intertwined themes of longing and belonging in the works of diasporic Hindi women writers, examining how their narratives navigate the emotional and cultural complexities of displacement. Rooted in personal and collective experiences of migration, these writers articulate a deep sense of nostalgia for the homeland while simultaneously grappling with the challenges of integration and identity formation in foreign lands. Through their literary expressions, they construct nuanced portrayals of home—not merely as a geographical space but as an evolving emotional and psychological construct. By focusing on their unique perspectives, this study seeks to uncover how diasporic Hindi women writers negotiate the tensions between memory, identity, and cultural continuity in the diaspora.

In the works of these writers, the concept of "home" evolves beyond a mere physical location to encompass a more complex and multifaceted space. For these writers, home becomes a dynamic emotional, familial, and cultural construct that reflects their characters' experiences of migration, displacement, and longing. Through their narratives, home is portrayed not as a static or geographical site but as a deeply psychological and spiritual space, one that exists in memory, imagination, and emotional attachment.

Memory, Nostalgia and the Idea of Home

The concept of "home" occupies a central place in diasporic discourse, yet it is inherently unstable, fluid, and contested. In diaspora studies, *home* functions not only as a physical or geographical location but also as a metaphor and metonym that captures a range of emotional, cultural, and psychic attachments. As a metaphor, home symbolizes belonging, identity, and rootedness—an idealized space that provides emotional security and cultural coherence. As a metonym, it often stands in for broader notions of nation, tradition, language, and familial memory. Within diasporic literature, particularly among first-generation migrants, "home" is frequently romanticized as a place of origin and authenticity, even as it becomes inaccessible or imaginary over time. The act of reconstructing home in fiction becomes a way for writers to bridge the temporal and spatial gaps created by migration, allowing them to preserve memory and assert identity in the face of displacement and cultural fragmentation.

Theorists such as Stuart Hall, Avtar Brah, and Salman Rushdie have profoundly shaped contemporary understandings of home, nostalgia, and identity within the diaspora. Stuart Hall argues that cultural identity in the diaspora is not fixed or singular but is instead a process of becoming—constantly produced and reproduced through memory, representation, and difference. In this context, home becomes a shifting signifier, more rooted in the act of remembering than in geographical fixity. Avtar Brah, in *Cartographies of Diaspora* (1996), introduces the concept of "homing desire"—the emotional pull towards a place that may never have been experienced directly. For Brah, the diaspora is characterized by "multiple belongings" and "diasporic space," where home is simultaneously real and imagined, personal and collective.

Salman Rushdie, writing from the vantage of a postcolonial exile, famously described the diasporic writer as one who views the world through "broken mirrors," suggesting that the act of remembering home is inherently fragmented and fictionalized. His assertion that "the past is a country from which we have all emigrated" encapsulates the diasporic tension between memory and reality. These theoretical perspectives collectively underscore the diasporic condition as one marked by dislocation, but also by a creative reimagining of belonging and cultural continuity.

Incorporating feminist and postcolonial perspectives into the analysis of diasporic literature allows for a more nuanced understanding of how migration affects individuals differently based on gender. While postcolonial theory critically examines the legacy of colonialism, displacement, and identity formation, feminist theory brings into focus the specific ways in which women's experiences are shaped by patriarchal structures both in the homeland and in the diaspora. Women in diasporic communities often bear the dual burden of cultural preservation and adaptation, expected to uphold traditional values while simultaneously navigating the challenges of a new sociocultural context. Their positionality is thus distinct—straddling the roles of cultural transmitters, caregivers, and identity mediators. This duality offers a rich ground for literary exploration, as many diasporic women writers interrogate the ways in which gender influences experiences of loss, nostalgia, assimilation, and resistance. Their narratives bring to the fore the intimate, emotional dimensions of migration, such as the longing for familial ties, the emotional labour of sustaining "home" in exile, and the psychic toll of cultural dissonance.

In the study of diasporic women's narratives, nostalgia emerges as a powerful emotional and literary element that shapes identity and experience in exile. It reflects a deep yearning for the homeland, encompassing memories of traditions, family, language, and cultural practices that provide emotional anchorage amidst displacement. For many women, this longing is intricately tied to domestic and cultural symbols—such as food, clothing, and festivals—which are remembered with both affection and ambivalence. While these memories offer comfort and continuity, they also highlight the contradictions of nostalgia: the homeland becomes idealized, even as it represents traditional gender roles that may have once been restrictive.

Nostalgia often drives women to preserve and transmit cultural values to the next generation, positioning them as custodians of identity within the diaspora. At the same time, it can create tension between the idealized past and the realities of both the changed homeland and the host land, where integration may be difficult. In literature, this emotional landscape is vividly portrayed through fragmented narratives that shift between past and present, expressing a sense of hybrid identity and cultural negotiation. Ultimately, nostalgia serves both as a coping mechanism against rootlessness and as a lens through which diasporic women articulate their complex relationship with belonging, memory, and selfhood.

Women's migration experiences are qualitatively different from those of men, not only because of gender-based roles and expectations but also due to the specific emotional, cultural, and corporeal burdens they carry. In diasporic Hindi fiction, women writers often explore how these gendered realities influence the process of identity negotiation and cultural belonging. For instance, the theme of negotiating tradition versus autonomy recurs frequently in the narratives, especially in contexts where women are expected to preserve "Indianness" through language, dress, food, and religious practices. At the same time, the diasporic setting may offer women new avenues for self-expression, economic independence, and social mobility, though often at the cost of alienation and cultural conflict.

These contradictions become a fertile ground for literary expression, allowing writers to interrogate both the constraints and the opportunities that migration affords women. In their stories, the domestic space often becomes a symbolic battleground where cultural continuity and transformation collide. Through their unique perspectives, diasporic Hindi women writers foreground the interiority of the female experience, often challenging patriarchal norms while simultaneously grappling with the emotional weight of exile and longing.

In migration narratives, the concept of home is rarely stable or singular. For diasporic individuals, home is not merely a geographic location; it is a site of memory, imagination, and emotional investment. It can signify a lost homeland, an ancestral village, or even a symbolic space of cultural authenticity. Diasporic literature frequently dwells on this ambivalence—home is remembered and idealized, even as it becomes increasingly inaccessible or mythologized over time. The significance of home in these narratives lies in its capacity to anchor identity amidst the flux of migratory existence. Writers often invoke home as a metaphor for belonging, using it to express both a yearning for rootedness and a critique of cultural displacement. This is especially true for first-generation immigrants, for whom the memory of home is often tinged with nostalgia and longing. The homeland is romanticized as a space of familiarity, tradition, and emotional fulfilment, even as the migrant simultaneously engages with the alienation and dislocation of life abroad.

In "Food and Belonging: At 'Home' in 'Alien-Kitchens'," the Indian American cultural critic Ketu Katrak suggests that culinary narratives, suffused with nostalgia, often manage immigrant memories and imagined returns to the homeland. As an immigrant subject distanced geographically and temporally from her childhood home in Bombay, food becomes both an intellectual and emotional anchor. And yet, she also acknowledges how the experience of dislocation, modulated by a nostalgic longing for the familiar, is also deeply rooted in the creation of imaginary fictions which distort the lived realities of her prior life. She notes:

> Food was not pleasurable to me as a child. Thinking about this now adult, I can say that food was an overdetermined category for my childhood years; it tasted of the heady tropical environment, and it del who was in and out of favor with my father. I tasted anxiety in the fried a bit too brown and tension in the too many dark burned roasted papad. One never knew what would be considered faulty at a particular meal, and the uncertainty overwhelmed any pleasure in what was eaten. (266-67).

Katrak's honesty registers the affective value of food and smells, in the process reflecting the nostalgia structuring memories of home for the immigrant subject. In "Imaginary Homelands," Rushdie sets in motion a complex investigation into the condition of the diasporic exilic writer. As he so eloquently puts it, "It may be that when the Indian writer who writes from outside India tries to reflect the world, he is obliged to deal in broken mirrors, some of whose fragments have been irretrievably lost." (9) Seeing the past through the shards of a mirror inevitably distorts the idealized memory one has of a "homeland:" owing to the exigencies of displacement and dis- location certain memories are remembered, while others, literally, are re-membered.

In Purnima Varman's story "Flight," Sakshi's connection to her cultural roots is expressed through food, as well as her longing for the comfort and familiarity of home. When she says: "'Mum, I'm starving! Can you cook some rajma chawal? You know it's my favourite.'" - It reflects the emotional bond with her family and her yearning for the tastes and experiences of her heritage, even while living in a foreign land.

However, for second and third-generation diasporic individuals, the notion of home becomes even more complex. Born and raised in foreign cultural contexts, these individuals may have only tenuous or imagined connections to their ancestral lands. For them, home is not inherited but constructed—shaped by parental narratives, cultural practices, and mediated memories. Their sense of belonging is often fragmented, oscillating between the cultural codes of the host country and the inherited legacies of the homeland.

This dual consciousness frequently manifests in a crisis of identity, where neither space offers full acceptance or comfort. Such complexities are richly explored in the literature of the Hindi-speaking diaspora, particularly in the works of women writers who bring a gendered perspective to the exploration of home, memory, and displacement. Through their stories, these writers articulate how gender, migration, and language intersect to shape the contours of diasporic subjectivity.

Emotional Landscapes in Diasporic Hindi Women's Fiction

In the works of diasporic Hindi women writers such as Pushpa Saxena, Sudha Om Dhingra, Archana Painuly, Purnima Varman, Usha Raje Saxena, and Divya Mathur, the concept of "home" evolves beyond a mere physical location to encompass a more complex and multifaceted space. For these writers, home becomes a dynamic emotional, familial, and cultural construct that reflects their characters' experiences of migration, displacement, and longing. Through their narratives, home is portrayed not as a static or geographical site but as a deeply psychological and spiritual space, one that exists in memory, imagination, and emotional attachment.

In the works of these writers, home is often depicted as a space tied to deep emotional connections, particularly those formed through family ties and cultural roots. For instance, Pushpa Saxena's characters frequently experience a deep yearning for the emotional security and intimacy of their home country. Similarly, Sudha Om Dhingra explores how her diasporic characters find themselves haunted by the memories of their home, where familial bonds serve as a reminder of who they are, and where they feel their most authentic selves.

This emotional attachment to "home" persists, often overshadowing the physical distance between the characters and their homeland. For these writers, home is more than a place—it is a space within, an internalized sense of belonging that shapes identity in the face of migration. Archana Painuly, for instance, uses her characters' emotional journeys to show how they seek to recreate home through relationships and community in the diaspora. Here, the psychological weight of home is intertwined with loss, as the characters grapple with the inability to fully recreate the security of home in a foreign land.

The spiritual and cultural aspects of home are significant in these narratives, where characters grapple with the dual identity of living in a foreign land while holding on to their cultural heritage. Divya Mathur explores this tension in her works, showing how home is also a space of cultural preservation. Her characters often engage in practices such as celebrating festivals, maintaining rituals, and speaking in their native tongue to maintain their connection to home. In these narratives, the space of home is both a cultural and spiritual sanctuary, a means to resist the pressures of assimilation and to assert a diasporic identity.

In many cases, the search for home in the diaspora is a search for cultural authenticity. The characters in these stories often feel dislocated, struggling with the contradictions between the expectations of their host country and the memories of their homeland. However, their longing for home is not simply nostalgic; it is also a form of resistance. They assert their right to preserve their cultural identity in a world that often pressures them to conform. The idea of home, thus, becomes a space of spiritual resilience, where memories and cultural practices serve as anchors for the self.

Finally, the concept of home in diasporic Hindi women's writing is constantly re-narrated and reimagined. Home is not only a nostalgic yearning for the past, but also a space that evolves and transforms as the characters navigate their identities in the diaspora. Archana Painuly captures this transformation in her characters, who begin to redefine what home means to them—blurring the boundaries between their homeland and their new environment. Home becomes something that is constantly being reconstructed and redefined, based on the characters' evolving relationships with themselves, their families, and their cultures.

Cultural Alienation and the Dual Identity of the Diaspora

Cultural alienation is another prominent theme in diaspora literature, and it is intrinsically linked to the dual identity of the diaspora writer. The feeling of not fully belonging to either culture—neither the adopted country nor the home country—shapes the psychological and emotional landscape of many diasporic characters. This cultural dislocation is often portrayed as an existential struggle, as characters navigate the tension between retaining their cultural heritage and the pressure to assimilate into their new society.

Hindi diasporic women writers offer a rich and multifaceted portrayal of the emotional terrain inhabited by migrant women, bringing to light the personal and collective challenges they face in navigating life between cultures. Their stories capture a spectrum of experiences—ranging from identity loss and cultural displacement to marriage, aging, domestic violence, and the longing for emotional security. These narratives are not merely reflections of personal experiences but are deeply embedded in the larger socio-cultural and historical realities of migration, particularly as they affect women. By intertwining the personal with the political and the emotional with the social, these writers use fiction as a platform to explore the complexities of diasporic life and the inner worlds of their characters.

Themes of identity, loss and cultural adjustment form the emotional backbone of many diasporic stories. The act of migration is not just a physical movement but a profound emotional rupture that severs people from their cultural moorings and social familiarity. Ila Prasad's *"The Table"* metaphorically captures this sense of displacement through the image of an old wooden stool, uprooted from a rural Indian home and transported to Texas. Prasad writes how "the partly broken, discoloured wooden stool … had become a glorious dining table" for the birds (Māthura 2015, 117). This seemingly simple object becomes a powerful symbol of the immigrant's journey—initially disoriented and disconnected, but gradually adapting and finding a new place in a foreign environment. Similarly, many diasporic women writers draw from personal experiences to portray the emotional turmoil that accompanies cultural transitions.

In the story "Unmourned," when the protagonist sees a funeral van near her house, she wonders and wants to know more about her neighbour, However, the cultural differences make her pause as it might be taken as a form of intrusion in someone's private space. She thinks—"It was not like in India, where without knowing someone, you can walk into their house and ask anything and everything on humanitarian grounds." (179)

Adjusting to a foreign land's extreme climate is extremely difficult for Neha, who has come to pursue higher studies in Edinburgh. Toshi Amrita writes in her story "On a Cold Night:"

> Scotland was beautiful but bone-achingly cold! Inside the house, the floor felt as if it was made of a thin sheet of ice which declined to melt despite the central heating. Neha's loneliness was so intense it sent chills through her body, adding to the embrace of this fierce cold—and the desolation created by the darkness. The sound of the wind was eerie and made her shiver under the duvet. (202)

> The trouble was not just with the weather, but also the language which acted as a barrier to communication. Neha finds it difficult to understand the Scottish intonations of "Agnes, Bruce, Hamish—all foreign faces and foreign names with a foreign diction."

It is the nostalgia which hits her hard on certain days and she reflects on her past—

> Sometimes she felt that India was still the finest country in the world. Its food had body and taste, spices and aroma. There were no cold buffets, cold sandwiches or cold meats. India was warm—and Indians themselves were warm. She thought of her mum's hot chapatti with cauliflower or aubergine, or urad dal; mustard spinach and maize roti with a tall glass of buttermilk. She thought of Dad giving her a cup of tea in bed on Sundays, of Tannu's laughter and their whisperings till late in the night. Neha missed everything (205).

329

Ironically, towards the end of the story, Neha who feels betrayed by her sister, Tannu, slams the door in her face and does not yield to her pleas for help. At this point, she finds her behaviour reflecting not the country she belonged to, but the country she adopted as her home.

> She belonged to a country in which people believe that love is in the giving, not in the taking, where love has no conditions, no selfish motives. How cold she had become. As cold as the Scottish weather. She had become a small part of the snow-covered mountains. She was forgetting what she used to be. (213).

It is in a similar manner that Kamla—ill and ageing, identifies herself with the new surroundings of the foreign land:

> Beside this frozen, peaceful, unmoving lake, and the silently falling leaves, she lives and endures her life among a flock of other people, helpless and old like herself, waiting for the inevitable to come. Is this all that remains in the end? (201).

Marriage, often seen as a stabilizing institution, is explored by these writers as a site of both aspiration and disillusionment. Usha Raje's *"But Salina Had Only Wanted To Get Married"* poignantly depicts the shattered dreams of a poor woman who yearns for a fairy-tale wedding, only to face the crushing weight of economic and social realities. The story exposes the emotional toll of gendered expectations and unfulfilled desires. In contrast, Divya Mathur's *"My Better Half"* delves into the complexities of cross-cultural marriage, portraying the challenges faced by women who must reconcile their traditional upbringing with unfamiliar marital dynamics in a foreign culture. The story also tackles the persistent influence of extended family—especially the role of a dominating mother-in-law—and the emotional strain it places on women trying to assert their autonomy in a new cultural setting.

Virgin Meera by Dr. Pushpa Saxena and *The Better Half* by Divya Mathur are stories that explore themes of diaspora, identity, longing, belonging, and alienation, particularly through their female protagonists and their emotional landscapes shaped by betrayal, cultural displacement, and personal transformation. Set in a diasporic context, this story revolves around *Virginia*, an American woman who immerses herself in Indian culture under the influence of *Ravi*, an Indian PhD student in the U.S. Ravi teaches her Hindu philosophy and portrays an idealized version of Indian values, especially the spiritual and moral strength of Indian women. Virginia internalizes these ideals and becomes emotionally and spiritually invested in Ravi, only to be cruelly betrayed when Ravi returns to India and marries someone else due to family and societal pressures. Her devotion, compared to mythic figures like Meera and Ahalya, leaves her heartbroken and alienated.

The Better Half is a compact yet impactful story that explores the life of an Indian woman in London who lives in a strained marriage with a narcissistic husband. After years of subservience and silence, she finally finds her voice and asserts her independence. She is a part of the Indian diaspora but negotiates her space between the traditional expectations of womanhood and her lived reality as a modern woman in a foreign land. Her assertion of selfhood culminates in her refusal to continue a one-sided emotional relationship. *Virgin Meera* offers a more literal portrayal of diaspora, focusing on Ravi and Virginia's cross-cultural relationship.

Virginia, although American, tries to *enter* the Indian diasporic world by adopting its spiritual and moral codes. She is so full of awe about Indian culture—"The place where Rama, Krishna, Gautam, Aurobindo, Meera lived—how can you say that such a sacred land is a place of scarcity?' She sighed. 'I wish I had been born in India.'" The statement captures Virginia's romanticized view of India, her longing for a connection to its cultural and spiritual heritage, and her feeling of alienation from her current environment. Ravi finds himself incapable of persuading his father to accept Virginia in the family, but his father remained inflexible in his values and beliefs.

He threatened to go on a fast until death if a foreign girl from a foreign religion came to his house as a daughter-in-law." The conflict between cultural expectations and personal desires highlights Ravi's sense of alienation from his own family and the strong ties to his cultural and religious roots that complicate his relationship with Virginia. It reflects the emotional turmoil and the struggle to reconcile ancestral traditions with new experiences in a diasporic context. Her alienation stems from her idealization of a culture she does not fully belong to—making her both an outsider and a victim of its contradictions. In The Better Half, Liz *is* part of the Indian diaspora in the UK. Her displacement is less about cultural immersion and more about personal alienation within a diasporic domestic life. Her struggle is internal—living in a loveless marriage that reflects outdated gender roles carried over into a foreign land. Thus, while Virginia is emotionally dislocated by *entering* Indian cultural values, Liz is emotionally suffocated by being *trapped* within them.

Divya Mathur's "My Better Half" is a compelling narrative that deftly explores the intertwined themes of belonging and alienation through the lived experiences of its three central characters: Liz, Radha, and Goldie. At the heart of the story is Liz, a British woman navigating the complex dynamics of a cross-cultural marriage with Goldie, an Indian man whose loyalties and values appear to shift depending on context. Through Liz's journey, Mathur foregrounds the tension between emotional intimacy and cultural dislocation, laying bare the psychological landscape of a woman caught between two worlds.

Liz's experience of alienation is multilayered, stemming not only from her husband's infidelity but also from the cultural expectations imposed on her by her Indian in-laws. Her struggle to belong begins with her idealistic view of love and marriage, only to be gradually dismantled by Goldie's duplicity and the subtle but persistent undermining from his mother, Santosh. Santosh's insistence on traditional gender roles, such as Liz mastering Indian cooking and dressing in ethnic attire, reinforces a cultural script that excludes Liz's identity and preferences. Her alienation is further magnified in Baroda, where she is treated as an outsider by Goldie's family and the community, revealing how cultural codes of conduct demarcate the boundaries of inclusion.

Goldie, on the other hand, embodies a conflicting duality that blurs the lines between home and exile. While publicly presenting Liz as his "better half," he remains emotionally tethered to Radha, his former lover in India. His charm and performative Westernization mask a deeper allegiance to traditional values and personal entitlements that he is unwilling to relinquish. Goldie's failure to fully commit to either relationship—his marriage with Liz or his past with Radha—reflects his ambivalence about belonging. He remains caught between two identities: the Gopal of Baroda and the Goldie of London. This fractured selfhood becomes a source of emotional instability for both Liz and Radha.

Radha, as a figure of symbolic and literal alienation, challenges the reader's assumptions about female agency in diasporic narratives. Initially presented through the lens of nostalgia and loss, Radha is idealized by Goldie's family and community, yet her unmarried status and ambiguous sexuality complicate this image. Her reappearance in London as a pregnant, closeted lesbian seeking asylum from her oppressive environment in India places her at the intersection of cultural, sexual, and diasporic marginalization. Her eventual outburst and condemnation of Goldie expose the emotional exploitation she has endured and underline her exclusion not only from the Indian society she left behind but also from the diaspora that refuses to acknowledge her complexity.

Mathur uses the metaphor of displacement—both physical and emotional—to show how the idea of home is constantly negotiated. Liz's attempts to reclaim space within her marriage and household mirror her broader struggle to establish a sense of belonging within the Indian diaspora. Her eventual assertiveness, exemplified by her decision to walk away from Goldie, signifies a redefinition of home—not as a geographic or marital space, but as an emotional and psychological state of self-acceptance and solidarity.

The story ends with a symbolic moment of unity among the three women—Liz, Radha, and Rachel—who, despite their different backgrounds and experiences, find common ground in their rejection of Goldie's manipulation and their pursuit of autonomy. Ultimately, *My Better Half* examines how diasporic women negotiate belonging and alienation in the face of cultural expectations, patriarchal control, and personal betrayal. Through its richly drawn characters and emotionally resonant storytelling, the narrative underscores the resilience and agency of women who, despite displacement and marginalization, strive to carve out spaces of dignity, identity, and sisterhood.

In both stories, we witness how Indian men betray the trust of women under the guise of love, tradition, or morality—leaving the women to grapple with emotional devastation and reclaim their agency in vastly different ways. Together, these stories present a powerful dichotomy: the fragility of idealistic love vs. the strength of self-defined identity in the diasporic woman's experience.

In Susham Bedi's short story "Remains," the themes of nostalgia and longing are intricately woven into the emotional fabric of the protagonist's diasporic experience. A middle-aged Indian woman living in the United States, she is haunted by memories of her homeland—its familiar rhythms, cultural practices, and deeply rooted relationships. These memories evoke a deep yearning not just for a place, but for a former self that now feels distant and fragmented. The title itself, "Remains" symbolizes the emotional and cultural remnants that persist within her, even as she physically inhabits a new world. Her nostalgia is gendered and deeply personal, revolving around familial bonds, motherhood, and the loss of traditional roles that once gave her identity and purpose. She fondly remembers her time in India she spent living a grand way:

> The whole house used to be sparkling clean. The sitting room, kitchen, bedrooms—every part was suitably arranged and arrayed. A temple to good taste. ... The constant parties! Pulav, kebab, roast chicken, royal paneer ... she made everything with her own hands. Puffed-up phulbariyan, samosas, gulab jamun—there was no end to the different things she used to make. (197)

At the same time, Kamla's present life in the U.S. is marked by emotional isolation and disconnection from her husband and children, who have adapted more seamlessly to American culture. This contrast intensifies her longing for meaningful connection and belonging. Bedi paints a poignant portrait of a woman suspended between two worlds—one remembered with painful fondness and another that offers little emotional fulfilment. Kamla's sense of alienation and non-belonging to the host country is explicit in the lines:

> Because she knows only a few words in English they take her for either simple, foolish or stupid, sometimes even to the point where she is regarded as a strange creature from a different planet rather than another human being. Thinking about it, Kamla realises that sometimes they, too, seem like creatures from a different planet—creatures driven by somebody with a remote control.

Nostalgia in *"Remains"* is not mere sentimental reflection; it is a powerful expression of the psychological and cultural dislocation experienced by many diasporic women, highlighting the enduring pull of home and the silent endurance of identity in exile. When Kamla advises her son not to now tell anyone that she is living in a nursing home, they are unable to see her fear of being seen as abandoned and uncared for – even though all her needs were met in this new set-up. The daughter-in-law, therefore protests: 'Why, what's wrong with that? Isn't it a nice place? That kind of service, the level of care – you wouldn't find that anywhere else. And at home, well, we don't have a doctor present at all times, so [...]"

The aging process and intergenerational disconnect are also significant themes in diasporic fiction by women writers. Kamla, in *"Remains"* is an elderly Indian woman in a New York nursing home, grappling with the death of her husband and the indifference of her descendants toward the relics of her past. Each possession, while seemingly mundane to others, holds deep emotional significance for Kamla, encapsulating memories of love, tradition, and identity. The story serves as a powerful meditation on the loneliness of aging in exile and the slow erasure of personal history in the face of rapid cultural assimilation by younger generations. Torn between the geographical space where she lived all her life and the home where her children lived – she confesses to the readers:

> But this world is not hers. Her world resides somewhere among the acacia and neem trees . . . a glass of lassi and some radish parathas . . . bicycle bells, the shouting vegetable seller, cows basking in the streets, dogs barking in the alley – this long-familiar world, crisp and brittle like roasted grain.

These diasporic narratives also critically engage with the changing social landscape brought about by globalization, increased mobility, and shifting gender roles. As traditional norms rooted in patriarchy, religion, and economic dependency are challenged, diasporic women are often forced to renegotiate their sense of self. In the story "Remains," Kamla sees herself from a fresh perspective:

> An old inhabitant in a new country. The dreams of the past. Those old dreams, now seen through new eyes. She sees the new leaves fall. The more new things there are,

> the more she holds on to the old. New talks with old meanings. New meanings of old ideas. New ideas in an old language. New wrinkles in old skin! And in the wrinkles, old fears. Old and new all mixed up together! (199)

Migration offers both disorientation and opportunity—while it disrupts existing structures, it also creates new spaces for self-expression and empowerment. Women in these stories increasingly assert their independence, seeking personal fulfilment and professional achievement, even as they confront emotional and cultural conflicts. This dual engagement—with the past and the present, tradition and modernity—adds emotional complexity and thematic richness to their fiction.

Conclusion

Thus, the exploration of the South Asian—specifically Hindi-speaking—diaspora through literature offers a rich and layered understanding of the emotional landscapes of migration. The themes of home and belonging are not peripheral but central to these narratives, offering insights into how individuals and communities reconstruct identity in the aftermath of displacement. Literature becomes a space where memories are preserved, identities are negotiated, and new forms of belonging are imagined. In the case of diasporic Hindi women writers, this literary engagement is further deepened by their dual roles as cultural transmitters and active agents in redefining the contours of diasporic life. Their stories are not just about loss and longing but also about resilience, adaptation, and the enduring quest for a place to call home—whether real, remembered, or reinvented.

References

Bhatia, Nandi. 1998. "Women, Homelands, and the Indian Diaspora." *The Centennial Review* 42 (3): 511–26. http://www.jstor.org/stable/23740003.

Brah, Avtar. 1996. *Cartographies of Diaspora: Contesting Identities*. London: Routledge.

Jain, Shobhita. 2006. "Women's Agency in the Context of Family Networks in Indian Diaspora." *Economic and Political Weekly* 41 (23): 2312–16. http://www.jstor.org/stable/4418321..

Karmakar, Chandrima. 2015. "The Conundrum of 'Home' in the Literature of the Indian Diaspora: An Interpretive Analysis." *Sociological Bulletin* 64 (1): 77–90. http://www.jstor.org/stable/26290721..

Mannur, Anita. 2007. "Culinary Nostalgia: Authenticity, Nationalism, and Diaspora." *MELUS* 32 (4): 11–31. http://www.jstor.org/stable/30029829.

Māthura, Divyā. 2015. *Desi Girls: Stories by Indian Women Writers Abroad*. London: Hoperoad Publishing.

Across the Lines of Identity: The Sports Narrative of Indian Cinema

Manisha Poonia, PhD

ABSTRACT

This chapter delves into Indigenous identity and belonging as portrayed in Indian sports films, exploring how these narratives mirror and shape India's socio-cultural landscape. By critically analyzing the depiction of sports personalities, their challenges, victories, and the socio-cultural contexts they navigate, the chapter reveals how cinema constructs and disseminates narratives of identity and belonging. It examines how these stories intersect with broader discussions on nationhood, inclusivity, female empowerment, and cultural assimilation. Sports films illustrate how sports transcend geographical, cultural, and socio-economic barriers, uniting diverse individuals and fostering a sense of unity beyond societal divides. From grassroots initiatives to global tournaments, sports serve as a universal language, connecting people from various backgrounds. The chapter provides a comprehensive analysis of iconic sports films, highlighting universal themes of determination, resilience, and camaraderie that resonate globally. Furthermore, it emphasizes how Indian sports films portray underdog triumphs, team dynamics, and personal struggles, reflecting the shared challenges of humanity. The chapter also highlights how sports catalyze self-discovery and self-expression, especially for girls historically sidelined by society. Additionally, it considers the role of cinema chains like INOX and PVR in India's multiplex revolution, offering platforms for individuals to become societal icons. Ultimately, this chapter navigates the intricate terrain of identity and belonging within Indian sports films, demonstrating how these narratives reflect and actively shape the collective consciousness of a diverse and dynamic society.

Keywords: Identity, Dynamics, Resilience, Self-Discovery, Nationhood, Catalyst, Inclusivity

Introduction

> Sport has the power to change the world. It has the power to inspire. It can unite people in a way that little else does. It speaks to youth in a language they understand. Sport can create hope where once there was only despair.
>
> (Mandela 2000, 94)

Since the inception of human civilization along the banks of river valleys, sports have evolved into an essential facet of humanity's existence. More than just a physical activity, sports constitute a set of cultural practices imbued with profound historical and sociological significance. As an artistic form, sports illuminate various dimensions of society, including identity, education, health, the economy, politics, and families. As Garry Whannel encapsulates, "I am a firm believer that sports, both individually and collectively, have the power to transform lives, communities, and even entire nations." (Whannel 2005, 110) The shared experience of supporting a team or participating in sporting events can bridge divides and create a sense of identity among diverse groups. Sports transcend cultural, geographical, and historical boundaries, catalyzing and reflecting collective values, aspirations, and the competitive spirit.

Furthermore, sports have historically served as a platform for social change and activism. Figures like Muhammad Ali, Jesse Owens, and Pele have used their sporting achievements to advocate for civil rights, racial equality, and other social causes, inspiring millions and catalyzing progress toward greater inclusivity and equality. Sports have the unique ability to unite countries, speak a language, and embody ideals beyond the reach of politicians. Sports create a public image of inclusiveness, togetherness, and oneness, symbolically significant as sportspersons become key representatives of the nation. Sports stars actively represent difference and identity, involved in what Avtar Brah calls the political and personal struggle over the social regulation of 'belonging.' Celebrated as national heroes, these athletes are also embraced by specific groups, becoming symbols of pride and belonging, (Avtar Brah 2005, 45).

In India, sports are seen as a way of realizing the body's full potential, also known as '*Dehvad*' in ancient India. The initial thought foundation of the games in India lies in the history dating back to the Vedic Era, and it is mentioned in the Atharva Veda, Duty is in my right hand and the fruits of victory in my left. History shows that the Indian and Greek civilizations pioneered games like chess, chariot racing, and wrestling, and Indian epics like the *Ramayana* and the *Mahabharata* mention sports like hunting, archery, horseback riding, and archery, mace-warfare, fencing, and wrestling. Players like Sachin Tendulkar, MS Dhoni, Bajrang Punia, Neeraj Chopra, Virender Sehwag, Virat Kohli Yuvraj Singh Anju Bobby George. Sakshi Malik Mithali Raj, and Krishna Poonia have shown the path for glory to India on an international level and encourage the new generation to cheer for India.

Cinema, in India, represents a fascinating domain where storytelling converges with real-life achievements, societal issues, and cultural values. Over the years, Indian cinema has produced a diverse range of movies that have transcended the social and cultural barriers across the nation. As Dubey in his book *Cinema and Culture* pointed out:

Cinema is a captivating, if complex, root to the past. As a popular art set in the economic, cultural, and political spheres, the film inevitably bears the birthmark of its passage into light. As a technological art, crucially defined by its capacity for the automatic registration of sights and sounds, it comprises pieces of the culture it represents. Therefore, the film student must be at once a historian and an interpreter of art, able to shift constantly between the objective examination of the context of a film and subjective immersion in the experience it offers." (Dubey 2007, 66) Films of sports generally have achieved great success across the world.

In the context of films, 'across the line of identity' refers to portraying characters that transcend societal norms, stereotypes, or personal limitations related to their identity. It signifies going beyond the expected or defined boundaries that typically confine individuals based on gender, race, disability, or social status. Sports films often depict protagonists who defy these conventional boundaries. Therefore, across the line of identity, encapsulates the narrative arc where sports serve as a vehicle for characters to assert their capabilities, redefine their identities, and inspire others by surpassing their limitations. Thus, it vividly resonates with the existentialist ideas of Jean-Paul Sartre, where characters redefine their identities through their actions and choices.

Today sports movies have become a teaching and inspiration medium. Bora says; 'As because of shortage of time films become easier to understand and remember the communicated messages effectively' (Bora 2012, 56). Sports cinematic narratives forefront the bright side of Indian society like, the spirit of patriotism, unity in diversity, interest, and emotion, the transmission of love, and trust between sportsmen and Indian sports lovers, while also measuring the current issues of the society like, way of talent identification, gender discrimination, doping, injury, match-fixing, sports politics and corruption. So, today not only in India but also across the world films are working as a mirror in which the reflection of the society is clearly expressed. As Aggarwal Gupta depicts, 'mass media teaches values and behavioral patterns which in turn act as the agent of socialization' (Gupta 2001, 28-29).

In the early decades of Indian cinema, there were few films on sports, such as *Hip Hip Hurray (1984)*, *Boxer* (1984), *Awwal Number* (1990), and *Jo Jeeta Wohi Sikandar* (1992), often featuring utopian narratives where hard work, perseverance, and fair play triumphed. But the post-2000s era shifted towards youth-centric sports narratives, exemplified by films such as *Lagaan* (2001), *Iqbal* (2005), and *Chak De! India* (2007), *Paan Singh Tomar* (2012), *Saala Khadoos* (2016), *Sultan* (2016), *Mukkabaaz* (2017), *Gold* (2022), and *Ghoomer* (2023), which portrayed sports as a means to break societal barriers. Actual story-based films like *Bhaag Milkha Bhaag* (2013), *Mary Kom* (2014), *Budhia Singh: Born to Run* (2016), *MS Dhoni: The Untold Story* (2016), *Soorma* (2018), *Saina* (2021), and *Shabaash Mithu* (2022) highlighted the challenges and achievements of real-life athletes. Changing societal attitudes have also led to greater recognition of women's sports films such as *Mary Kom* (2014), *Dangal* (2016), *Saand Ki Aankh (2019)*, and *Panga* (2020).

Hindi films of the 1980s used the game as a thematic scaffolding for majorly family-based stories. Films of this type were generally attempts at embedding the post-Emergency (1975–77) inclusive, with sports being a minor addition to the canon of thematically variant films. The temporary extirpation of the Indira Gandhi regime in 1977, and the overwhelming sentiment for the '"people's struggle" on 'a par with the attainment of Independence' (Tarlo 2003, 22) was proclaimed through family rapprochement, collective furtherance, and spiritual homecoming. First, *Boxer* (1984), directed by Raj N. Sippy is based on boxing, knowing that Dharma works as a boxer with Kashmir silk mills. He is promised by the manager that if he wins the match then he will be sent to London, but Dharma loses the bout and is unable to box anymore because of injury. Later, his son became a boxer and he challenged the region's championship. *Hip Hip Hurray* (Prakash Jha 1984) depicts a school teacher's love and redemption by making the school football team tournament champions. Hindi cinemas 'almost total retreat into family life and its melodrama' (Radhakrishan 2023, 533) during the Post Emergency years thus support an overriding theme of 'unification' that was further encouraged by Congress' attempt to retrieve its Nehruvian everyman image.

Indian sports narratives after 2000 touched diverse subjects, *Hawaa Hawaai* (2014) showed the value of nutrients in sportsmen's lives. So, it circulates the message of diet and health in whole over the world which is the need for today's younger generation to remain healthy; *Meera Bai Not Out* (2008) showed that cricket become the medium of communication among nations and societies across the line of boundary. *Dhana Dhan Goal* (2007) and *Patiala House* (2011), showed Indian people's enthusiasm towards cricket for the nation. As Devan says, Cricket is a crucial vehicle for the formation of the Indian identity within India and Indian communities (Devan 2012, 1413-1425). *Chak De! India* (2007) directed by Kabir Khan Shows the efforts of the Indian Women's National Hockey Team by the team's new coach, disgraced men's star Kabir Khan (Shah Rukh Khan).

The film's prologue establishes the backstory of the team's coach, revealing how seven years earlier, Kabir Khan missed a critical penalty shot, thus securing India's loss to Pakistan at the World Men's Hockey Championship held in New Delhi. The particular rivalry in question is fraught with significance, invoking a continued resentment in India over the 1947 Partition. Later, Rajesh M. Basrur refers to the two countries. Further, Each player's arrival at the BharatPetroleum Groundin Chember (Negi

2012,18) reveals India's cultural and ethnic diversity. In the movie, all the girls have been recruited from India's various states and feel they represent that local identity, across the world khan insists "I am the captain of the Indian national women's team. I can't hear or see the names of states. I can hear the name of the country India" (Kabir Khan, 2007) and he asked the girl that reintroduce themselves with this single united identity that is Indian He reasserts his position that, ' this team needs only those players who first play for India, then for their teammates and then they have left for themselves' (Kabir Khan, 2007).

Thus this film spread the message of building national unity across the border. *Jo Jeeta Wohi Sikandar (1992)* imparts the lesson of belonging through its heartfelt narrative of rivalry, friendship, and personal growth. It showcases how true victory lies not just in winning but in camaraderie and self-belief. The dialogue *'Agar yeh do kadam tum aur badh gaye, toh tumse yeh race koi nahi cheen sakta'*, If you take these two more steps, no one can take this race away from you, (Aamir Khan,1992) emphasizes that a sense of belonging comes from mutual respect, unity, and the unwavering support of family and friends. *Paan Singh Tomar* (2012) imparts the theme of identity through sports by chronicling the life of an athlete who turns into a rebel. The film poignantly portrays Paan Singh's identity, shaped and reshaped by his experiences as a celebrated athlete and later as a disenfranchised individual fighting for justice. The dialogue, *'Bihad mein baaghi hote hain, dacoit milte hain parliament mein'* Rebels are found in the ravines, dacoits are found in parliament, (Tigmanshu Dhulia 2012, 26) underscores the power of sports in society. *Bhaag Milkha Bhaag* (2013) imparts profound lessons to society through the inspiring journey of Milkha Singh, the 'Flying Sikh'. The film highlights the transformative power of sports to overcome personal and societal challenges. Milkha's story, from a traumatized refugee to an Olympic athlete, teaches resilience, determination, and the importance of hard work. The dialogue, *Mujhsenahi hoga*, (Rakesh Omprakesh Mehra, 2013)which Milkha overcomes to say, 'Mujhse hi hoga,' symbolizes the shift from self-doubt to self-belief.

Despite numerous hardships, his relentless pursuit of excellence demonstrates that sports can be a powerful vehicle for personal growth and societal change, inspiring individuals to strive for greatness against all odds. *MS Dhoni: The Untold Story* (2016) portrays sports as a powerful symbol of change that transcends lines of identity, background, and societal expectations. The film portrays the journey of Mahendra Singh Dhoni from a small-town boy to the captain of the Indian cricket team, emphasizing that talent and determination can break barriers. Dhoni's story illustrates how sports can unify people across diverse backgrounds, inspiring millions.

The dialogue, '*Mujhe wicketkeeper nahi, batsman banana hai*', I do not want to be a wicketkeeper; I want to be a batsman, (Neeraj Pandey, 2016). This narrative encourages viewers to pursue their dreams and challenge the status quo, showcasing sports as a societal-transforming force. *Lagaan* (2001) depicts sports as a potent symbol of freedom and resistance against oppression. Set in colonial India, the film revolves around villagers who challenge their British rulers to a cricket match to avoid oppressive taxes. This act of defiance through sports symbolizes the struggle for autonomy and justice. The villagers, who initially know nothing about cricket, unite and overcome their fears and differences to take on the British team. The game becomes a metaphor for the fight against colonial rule, showcasing that courage, unity, and determination can lead to liberation.

A culture is remembered for its heroes and heroines; sport constructs them and continuously influences our perceptions of them. As Connell argues, hegemonic masculinity is naturalized by the hero, who is conventionally robust, aggressive, and brave. However, heroines are usually defined differently. She must be heroic—superior or exemplary in some way—and female inferior by definition (Jennifer Hargreaves 2013, 7) According to these characteristics, there is inconsistency in becoming sporting heroines. However, women are often undeniably heroic, even according to male definitions of heroism. Mainly, throughout the history of modern sport, there have always been a small number of women who have transgressed gender roles, taken up primarily sports such as boxing, wrestling, wrestling, flying, and soccer, and shown consummate skill and broken records equal to those of male sporting heroes.

Now sports films present women, along with other characters, as individuals with a strong will and determination who stand for what is written without shying away from voicing their opinions in a patriarchal domain. Though our society remains patriarchal to some extent, these films bring a fresh perspective to the audience, entertaining and educating them simultaneously. In a world that uses the phrase 'weaker sex' or 'second sex' synonymously with women, these characters have dared to make their voices heard and led their lives according to their own rules. Thus, sports films often highlight the extraordinary achievements of individuals from marginalized backgrounds who face socio-economic challenges, resonating with audiences on multiple levels. Now Stories of sports are almost exclusively stories of those in power. Now, 'games like the national international and the Olympics unite people from different states. They are social, interactive events that unite communities and provide a sense of identity.

Historically, Indian women faced significant social barriers in sports, but their unwavering determination has challenged the status quo and demanded recognition for their abilities. The year 2016 marked a pivotal moment for Indian women in sports: Sakshi Malik won a bronze medal in wrestling at the Rio Olympics, Sania Mirza claimed the Australian Open doubles championship, and Saina Nehwal was awarded the Padma Bhushan. Indian women sportspersons have emerged as beacons of inspiration, defying stereotypes and proving that women can achieve extraordinary feats in sports.

From pioneers like P.T. Usha to trailblazers like Karnam Malleswari, whose bronze medal at the 2000 Sydney Olympics ignited a lasting fire of inspiration, these athletes have paved the way for future generations. From breaking barriers to shattering stereotypes, Indian women in sports have shown the world that courage knows no bounds, Their journey inspires us to dream bigger, reach higher, and never back down from a challenge So, the sports films on females were made to highlight the strength and prowess of Indian women. *Panga* (2020), tells the story of Jaya Nigum, played by Kangana Ranaut, a former national-level Kabaddi player who decides to make a comeback after embracing motherhood.

Panga occurs when Jaya's husband, Prashant, expresses concerns about her decision to return to Kabaddi, saying, '*Tum puri zindagi is taraf ho, toh us taraf kaise dekh paogi*' If you're fully focused on this side, how will you look at the other side (Tiwari, 2020). This dialogue reflects the societal expectations placed on women to prioritize their roles as wives and mothers above personal aspirations. So, the concept of the 'motherhood penalty,' a term used to emphasize the disadvantages and discriminatory treatment that mothers experience in the workforce due to societal expectations

The concept of the 'second shift,' as discussed by Arlie Hochschild, becomes highly relevant when examining Jaya's character in the context of her household and caregiving responsibilities alongside her pursuit of Kabaddi. Hochschild's research, presented in her seminal work 'The Second Shift: Working Parents and the Revolution at Home' (Carol 1989, 34), underscores the disproportionate burden of unpaid domestic work and caregiving placed on women, which often continues even as they manage their careers or personal aspirations The dialogue, '*Kabhi Kabhi humein apni maa ke sapne poore karne ka mauka dena chahiye*', sometimes we should give our mothers the chance to fulfil their dreams (Tiwari 2020). This dialogue challenges conventional societal norms that often place mothers in caregiving roles, underscoring the significance of sons and society at large supporting women in the pursuit of their passions and dreams. This idea aligns with the concept that mothers may seek support from their children, particularly sons, to excel in their careers and personal aspirations, thus breaking away from traditional gendered roles. *Saand Ki Aankh* (2019), tells the inspiring true story of Chandro and Prakashi Tomar, two elderly women from rural Uttar Pradesh who break societal barriers and become accomplished sharpshooters. Through their journey, the film provides a nuanced exploration of the obstacles they face, such as the male-dominated sports culture, '*Humare khilaf sirf umar bolti hai, lekin jab hamare paas gun hota hai, toh hum kisi se bhi darr kar nahi rehte*', People only talk about our age, but when we have a skill in our hands, we fear no one (Hiranandani 2019).

This dialogue not only challenges ageism but also asserts their skill and confidence. It shows the characters' refusal to be defined by their age and their unwavering belief in their abilities. As De Beauvoir also noted, 'Representation of the world, like the world itself, is the work of men; they describe it from their point of view, which they confuse with absolute truth' (Beauvoir 2010, 116). Further, Prakashi's dialogue and actions resonate with the concept of feminist consciousness, as proposed by Patricia Hill Collins (Collins 1990, 214). It delves into how women's experiences and identities are shaped by intersecting systems of power, such as gender, race, and class.

Prakashi's character reflects a feminist consciousness as she confronts and challenges the stifling constraints of traditional gender norms that restrict women's autonomy and self-expression. Furthermore, Prakashi's dialogue also aligns with the iconic feminist phrase 'the personal is political', (Hanisch 1989, 89) emphasizing that personal experience and choices can have broader political implications. When Prakashi asserts her passion for shooting, stating, *'Humare liye toh yeh shooting, ek azaadi ki talwar hai'* for us, shooting is a sword of freedom), where she not only makes a personal choice but also sends a powerful message (Chadha, 2019). By pursuing her passion for shooting, Prakashi challenges not only the gendered division of labor that confines women to domestic roles but also confronts and defies the patriarchal norms that limit women's aspirations.

In addition to the dialogues, the theme of sisterhood and collective empowerment is beautifully portrayed through the characters of Chandro and Prakashi. These two remarkable women exemplify unwavering support and encouragement for each other throughout their transformative journey. One poignant instance that underscores this theme is when Chandro uplifts Prakashi after a disappointing performance, stating, *'Zyada jaldi haar maan li hai, abhi jitni baar uthegi, utni hi baar aur gir sakti hai'* you gave up too soon; as many times as you fall, you can rise the same number of times (Chadha, 2019). This dialogue encapsulates the essence of sisterhood, resilience, and collective empowerment among women, reflecting the core principles of feminist theories.

Within this context, we can draw upon the theory of "Relational Cultural Theory," (Jordan 2008,15) It emphasizes the significance of relationships and connections among women and posits that these connections are essential for personal growth and empowerment. Chandro and Prakashi's unwavering support for each other exemplifies the transformative power of their deep, nurturing relationship. Furthermore, the concept of collective empowerment aligns with Bell Hook's theory of sisterhood. In her work "Sisterhood: Political Solidarity Between Women," discusses how sisterhood can catalyze social change (Hooks 1984, 77). *Dil Bole Haddipa* (2009) is based on VeerKaur a cricket player who dressed as boy Veer Pratap Singh, and played to save India'spride in the Annual Aman Cup Match against Pakistan held every August 15, the date of India's independence. She performed at the Cricket World Cup in 1983 and added herself to the list of those who will do her region proud. As a Punjabi identity in the World Cup, she becomes a sign of authentic Indianess and a symbol of the Indian state's ostensible inclusiveness thus inscribes the local over the global, positing Veera as the appropriate bride for Rohan; in the end, rather than return to England, he decides to stay in India with his father which is the sign of true nationhood.

The film *Mary Kom* (2014) delivers a powerful message across the lines of identity by portraying the journey of a woman from a small village in Manipur who overcomes societal and personal challenges to become a world champion boxer. Through impactful dialogues like, '*haarna nahi hai, mujhe bas ladna hai*', I don't want to lose, I just want to fight, (Omung Kumar, 2014) emphasizes resilience and determination. It highlights the intersection of gender, regional, and socio-economic identities, showing how Mary Kom's success transcends these barriers. Her story inspires audiences to defy stereotypes, pursue their dreams, and assert their identity against all odds. In*Irudhi Suttru* (2016), Madhi beats an international player who is a three-time world champion. She is the inspiration and motivation for many women in the country who have and passion for sports.

Despite their occasional reliance on stereotypes, Indian sports films have played a crucial role in portraying individuals with disabilities as central protagonists and projecting their embodied nuances. The film *Iqbal* (2005) directed by Nagesh Kukunoor, has been one of the finest representations of disability in sports. It exemplifies that cinema can provide visibility and a platform for disabled individuals, showcasing their potential and resilience. The film tells the story of Iqbal, a deaf and mute boy who dreams of becoming a cricketer. Despite his disabilities, Iqbal's passion and determination drive him to overcome numerous challenges. Such as Mohit says, '*Jab log tumhare khilaaf bolnelage, samajh lo tarakki kar rahe ho*', When people start speaking against you, understand that you are progressing (Nagesh Kukunoor 2005), underscore the film's message of resilience and persistence.

By featuring a disabled protagonist excelling in a mainstream sport, the film breaks stereotypes and fosters empathy. Iqbal's relationship with his mentor, Mohit, highlights the importance of support and belief in one's abilities. Mohit's guidance and belief in Iqbal's talent demonstrate how mentorship and encouragement can play crucial roles in helping disabled individuals achieve their dreams. R. Balki's *Ghoomer* (2023) stands as an example of cinematic expression, questioning the notions of ability and normalcy through the manifestation of disability and resilience in cricket. Through an intersectional stance that takes representation and representativeness into account, the film examines how a physically impaired sportswoman debunks the trope of 'otherness' through her perseverance and indomitable spirit. 'sports invite transformations of the body as well as providing a site where the boundaries of the human body can be interrogated and challenged as well as possibly reinstated. In *Ghoomer* Anina's narrative of overcoming her impairment, the audience is prompted to contemplate the diverse encounters of non-abled athletes in sports and understand how their lived experience challenges prevailing norms. Furthermore, her resistance can be viewed as embodied (Powis 2020, 55).

Similarly, *Shabaash Mithu* (2021) through the story of Mithali Raj, a female cricketer who overcomes significant obstacles to achieve greatness, the film sends powerful messages that talent and passion can defy all odds, including physical limitations. Mithali's journey, marked by resilience and the support of her mentors and community, illustrates that anyone can excel anywhere with dedication and the right opportunities. The sporting body represents a pivotal form of 'physical capital', for disabled individuals, more so for disabled men than women. Pierre Bourdieu's concept of 'physical capital', suggests that the body possesses power, exhibiting value in different social fields. So, it invokes hope in disabled athletes, encouraging them to pursue their dreams and demonstrating that sports can be an inclusive and empowering field for all individuals, regardless of their physical challenges.

Furthermore, Haryana is a small state that has established itself as a significant contributor to India's success in the Olympics, with approximately 30-40% of the country's medals coming from the side of Haryana. Sports in Haryana have not only provided thousands of youngsters with opportunities to achieve glory but have also become a source of employment. Wrestling, in particular, runs in the blood of the people. The daughters of Chandgi Ram, the renowned wrestler who won gold in the 1970 Asian Games, were the first women from Haryana to take up wrestling. It was from the same akhara where Mahavir Singh Phogat, whose story was immortalized by Aamir Khan in the film *Dangal* (2016) trained his daughters. State initiatives like *Padhak Lao, and Pad Pao* (Bring Medals, Get Jobs), rewarded successful wrestlers with Class 1 and 2 jobs, Sakshi

Malik, who became the brand ambassador for the *Beti Bachao, Beti Pad-hao* (Save the Girl Child, Educate the Girl Child) campaign. Despite persistent challenges, including, it is remarkable that parents in rural Haryana support their daughters.

Most recently, 2016 wrestling gold medalist Vinesh Phogat was among a group of acclaimed wrestlers who gathered at Jantar Mantar in Delhi to accuse the head of the Wrestling Federation of India who harassed female sportspersons. It shows that sports have given them a platform to speak out at a global level. As activist Dipika Switch from Rohtak, a major wrestling belt in Haryana, notes, this shift is significant. Although the state was once dominated by male sports, every district in Haryana now supports women's participation in athletics.

As Rudraneil Sengupta says that in 'Haryana, *kushti* (wrestling) was a common sport among *sepoys* (soldiers) of the British Raj during temporary halts, giving rise to *akharas* (wrestling schools) where the art of *pahalwani* (wrestling) cantered on the importance of the body as a psychosomatic whole' (Sengupta, 2016). Thus sports have given girls freedom and recognition, allowing them to become heroines of their own stories. As one girl proudly says, *Hum apni film ke hero hai* (We are the heroines of our film). Their visibility makes them symbolic of success and inspiration and became models and heroes for the nation like, Neeraj Chopra, the champion of the javelin throw, Bajrang Poonia, the wrestling champion, Sakshi Malik and Antim Panghal are the nation's pillars. Their stories of success are the outcome of the determination and energy of individuals.

Dangal (2016)set in Haryana has inspired a generation in Haryana and across the world by showcasing the true story of Mahavir Singh Phogat, who defied societal norms to train his daughters, Geeta and Babita Phogat, in wrestling. The film delivers messages of perseverance, breaking stereotypes, and achieving greatness against all odds. Mahavir, portrayed by Aamir Khan, challenges traditional gender roles in a male-dominated society with impactful messages like '*Mhari chhoriya chhoron se kam hain ke?*' (Are my daughters any less than boys (Amir Khan, 2016) emphasized gender equality and the potential of women? The dialogue, '*Gold to gold hota hai, chhora lave ya chhori' Gold is gold*', whether a boy wins it or a girl (Amir Khan, 2016). The success of Geeta and Babita Phogat, who achieved international wrestling medals, serves as a powerful example for young athletes, inspiring them to pursue their dreams despite obstacles. *Dangal*, also brought global attention to the struggles and triumphs of female athletes in India, particularly in Haryana, showcasing how local stories of courage and determination can inspire audiences worldwide.

The film has sparked discussions on the importance of sports and education for girls, making the Phogat sisters' journey from a small village to the international stage a beacon of hope and empowerment. The film *Sultan* (2019) set in Haryana vividly portrays sports as a powerful catalyst for personal and social transformation. Through the journey of Sultan Ali Khan, played by Salman Khan, the film highlights how wrestling becomes a means of redemption and self-discovery. Sultan, once a humble villager, faces numerous personal setbacks and loses his sense of purpose. Wrestling offers him a path to regain his self-respect and rebuild his life.

Dialogues such as, '*Wrestling se mujhe duniya mein wapas laaya hai' and'* Wrestling has brought me back to life '(Khan, 2019) emphasize the profound impact sports can have on an individual's life. Wrestling is depicted not just as a physical activity but as a medium that installs discipline, resilience, and a fighting spirit. It transforms Sultan from a broken man into a symbol of perseverance and strength. *Soorma* (2018) set in Haryana is based on the life of Sandeep Singh, an Indian hockey player who makes a remarkable comeback after a life-threatening injury. While the film primarily focuses on Sandeep Singh's journey, it also touches on the broader theme of identity through sports. In the context of female identity, the film subtly addresses the role of women in supporting and nurturing the dreams of athletes.

Then there are also internationally acclaimed sports films like *Rocky* (1976), *Escape to Victory* (1981), *The Jesse Owens Story* (1984), *A League of Their Own* (1992), *She is the Man* (2006), *Bend It Like Beckham* (2002), *Pele: Birth of a Legend* (2016), and *King Richard* (2021) that have notably positioned sports as a pivotal force for addressing societal issues and historically served as a platform for social change and activism. Figures like Muhammad Ali, Jesse Owens, and Pele have used their sporting achievements to advocate for civil rights, racial equality, and other social causes, inspiring millions and catalyzing progress toward greater inclusivity and equality. Pele's *Pelé: Birth of a Legend* (2013) vividly illustrates how sports turned him from an ordinary man to a global icon. The film records his journey from the poor streets of Brazil to the grand stages of international soccer and explores how his dedication to the sport, hard work, and perseverance, awarded him greatness on the world stage. This narrative imparts crucial lessons to the youth of America as well as to the youth across the boundaries of the nation, that with passion and effort, one can overcome any obstacle and achieve their dreams. It facilitates the idea that one's background does not determine one's future. Pele's story is also a celebration of Brazilian culture and identity. The Jesse Owens film *Race* (2016) sets itself up as a standard Hollywood biopic: a straightforward telling of the life story of Jesse Owens, the African American sprinter who made history when he won four gold medals at the 1936 Olympics. Owens (Stephan James) overcomes an impoverished upbringing and racism to become the world's leading athlete, with the help of a bullish coach (Jason Sudeikis) and a burning desire to win.

The visibility of Sports icons on screen gave opportunities to Nigeria, Syriya Qatar, Turkey, and Ukraine's women to seek empowerment through national, regional, and international organizations. Muslim women create for themselves more opportunities within the confines of Islam through sports. Once, Quatri women in the stadium were spectators wearing full-length, traditional black dresses. There were very few of them; most women were prevented from attending by their husbands or fathers. However, because of cinema, media, and films, women from Islamic countries like Iran and Iraq Seria are participating more than ever before; they can now take part and compete in the same spots as Iranian men., and they can wear shorts and T-shirts. Before that, they are prohibited.

In Aboriginal communities, sports films give them new visions, enrich their lives, and help them transcend discrimination. Those who have acquired the status of sporting heroines have significantly contributed to the shaping and reshaping of aboriginal and national identities. Their motto is 'If you can achieve if you believe.' Sports superstars like Cathy Freeman and Michael Jordan can use their status to highlight issues of difference and discrimination. For the Aboriginal people, sports activity is an attempt to grasp the power to reverse the privileging of European culture over traditional culture, to revalue local culture, and to recreate and redefine communities and identities.

India in 1969–1970 made possible the rapid development of gay culture activities, and over the past two decades, there has been an explosion of lesbian and gay sports. Over the years, lesbians have suffered systematically from oppression and exclusion in sports, and to avoid discrimination, they have mostly kept their sexuality hidden. 'Coming out' in sport is, for them, a heroic quest. The lesbian struggle for identity in sport has been inextricably linked to 'gay liberation 'and 'women liberation.' The gay games are an open celebration of homosexual sporting identity and community that lesbians and gay men have created and claimed as their own The visibility of lesbian women in sports has significantly increased, leading to a more inclusive environment.

Lesbian athletes consciously promote inclusiveness rather than exclusiveness. Despite this, many lesbians, whether they are athletes, coaches, administrators, or faculty, often remain invisible for survival reasons. Icons like Martina Navratilova and Amélie Mauresmo have become inspirational figures embodying lesbian sporting womanhood. Munt (1998) argues that "lesbian" remains a powerful and strategic identity. These elite athletes have fostered the construction of a lesbian identity, creating a sense of community and belonging. They have helped transform negative perceptions of lesbianism into positive ones. This has sparked the growth of lesbian sports clubs, organizations, and competitions globally. Thus, sports elevate the profile of lesbians, create positive images, and offer a safe space for comfort and belonging.

After 2000, in India sports became a significant leisure interest for the working class and an essential expression of community and identity. Sociologically, sport and fitness loom large in the media. Sports programs, dedicated sports channels, sports pages, sports supplements in newspapers, and specialist sports magazines have become increasingly prominent. In both representational forms and lived practices, sport is one of the cultural spheres that most distinctively mark gender identities and differences (Whannel 2000, 12). Media coverage of sports arguably plays a significant part in constructing national identities. Further, innovations such as advanced wheelchairs, prosthetics, and exoskeletons have significantly improved the performance of these athletes, allowing them to compete at the highest levels with enhanced speed, agility, and precision. Virtual reality (VR) and augmented reality (AR) create immersive training environments, and biometric sensors provide real-time performance data, optimizing training and enhancing overall capabilities.

Liberalization was also accompanied by yet another phenomenon of Indian Hindi sports films becoming popular abroad. With an increase in the number of Indians moving overseas for study and employment, Hindi films transformed into a source of cultural sustenance for overseas Indians, preparing them perhaps for the 'return visit', which is an essential part of the migration experience (Baldassar 1997, 45). Bollywood films not only enable them to maintain ties with their geographically distant country of origin, but these 'ties to the old homeland' often even define 'the development of ethnic identity in the new homeland (Baldassar 1997, 50).

Thus, Indian sports films have been colored by questions of Indianness and identity, providing thus a redefinition of Indianness. These films worldwide spread the message of *Parampara* (translated into English as 'tradition'), which is the need to save one culture and tradition. In India, gendered heroism is being constantly challenged by sportspersons female who are appropriating the narratives of maleness and transforming themselves from victims into superstars.

However, as time has progressed, these barriers have been dismantled, ushering in an era where women are not just watchers but also players on the field of sports. They are breaking the glass ceiling in the male-dominated arena of sports like wrestling and have internationally unfurled the flag of India. In a state like Haryana, where, people practiced wrestling used to run *Akharas* and to prepare themselves to fight against the British as well as to project aggressive native masculinity considered to be 'an essential step for the success of the national struggle' Thus, sports films in India capture myriad issues that resonate with audiences on personal and societal levels. Through compelling narratives and powerful performances, these films confront identity, belonging, and aspiration issues, inspiring the masses to reflect on the broader implications of sports beyond mere competition. Ultimately, films mirror society, sparking conversations and driving awareness about the need for systemic change and equitable opportunities in sports.

Conclusion

Indian sports films transcend traditional lines of identity, offering profound commentary on the nation's evolving social fabric. They are cultural artefacts that entertain, inspire, and provoke thought, highlighting issues like gender discrimination, representation, and the transformative power of sports. These films have initiated crucial dialogues, advocating for gender equality and inclusivity. Globalization and advancements in technology have broadened their reach, enabling them to resonate with diverse audiences worldwide. By featuring athletes from various backgrounds, these films challenge stereotypes and promote social change, serving as metaphors for nation-building and the ongoing struggle for equality.

References

Aggarwal, V. B., and V. S. Gupta. 2001. *Handbook of Journalism and Mass Communication,* 28–29.

Ali, Shaad, dir. 2018. *Soorma.* India: Sony Pictures Networks Productions. Netflix.

Amin, Shimit, dir. 2007. *Chak De! India.* India: Yash Raj Films. Netflix.

Baldassar, Loretta. 1997. *Home and Away: Migration, the Return Visit, and Translation Identity: Home Displacement Belonging.* University of Western Sydney Press.

Balki, R., dir. 2023. *Ghoomer.* India: Hope Productions. YouTube.

Basrur, Rajesh M. 2008. *South Asia's Cold War: Nuclear Weapons and Conflict in Comparative Perspective.* Routledge.

Bhaag Milkha Bhaag. Directed by Omprakash Rakesh Mehra. 2013. India: ROMP Pictures. Netflix.

Brah, Avtar. 2005. *Cartographies of Diaspora: Contesting Identities.* Routledge.

Bora, Abhijit, and Perosh Jimmy Daimari. 2012. "Sports Films for Social Messages Communication."

Buck, William. 2019. *Mahabharata.* University of California Press.

Chak De! India. Directed by Shimit Amin. 2007. India: Yash Raj Films. Netflix.Chakravorty, M. N. 2012. "Nationalistic Transactions: Chak De! India and the Down-and-Out Sports Coach." *Continuum: Journal of Media & Cultural Studies* 26, no. 6 (2012): 845–58.

Collins, Julie. 1990. *Othermothering by African American Women in Higher Education at Predominantly White Institutions: How the Practice Affects Their Professional and Personal Lives.* DePaul University.

Connell, R. W. 1987. *Gender and Power.* Polity.

Dangal. Directed by Nitesh Tiwari. 2016. India: Walt Disney Pictures. Netflix.

De Beauvoir, Simone. 2010. *The Second Sex.*Vintage.

Dey, Debashrita, and Priyanka Tripathi. 2024. "Media Representations of Dis/ability in Sports." *Media Asia.* https://doi.org/10.1080/0129661 2.2024.2304972.

Dibyakusum Roy, and Pooja Radhakrishan. 2023. "Playing It the Nation's Way: Tradition, Cosmopolitanism, and the Native Masculine of Hindi Sports Films." *Contemporary South Asia* 31, no. 4: 533–46.

Dhulia, Tigmanshu, dir. 2012. *Paan Singh Tomar.* India: UTV Spotboy. Netflix.

Dubey, Madhu. *Signs and Cities: Black literary postmodernism.* University of Chicago Press, 2007.

Ghoomer. Directed by R. Balki. 2023. India: Hope Productions. You-Tube.

Goldman, Sally J. Sutherland, and Sheldon I. Pollock. *The Ramayana of Valmiki: An Epic of Ancient India-Kiskindhakanda.* Vol. 4. Princeton University Press, 1984.

Gowariker, Ashutosh, dir. 2001. *Lagaan.* India: Sony Pictures Classics. YouTube.

Hanisch, Carol. 1989. "The Personal Is Political." *Notes from the Second Year: Women's Liberation.* http://www.carolhanisch.org/CHwritings/pip.html.

Hooks, bell. 1984. *Feminist Theory: From Margin to Center.* South End Press.

Jennifer. *Heroines of sport: The politics of difference and identity.* Routledge,

2013.

Jha, Sonal. 2023. "Counter-Hegemonic Sport: Constructing Alternative Sports Narratives in Indian Cinema." *The Journal of Popular Culture* 56, no. 3: 719–30.

Jordan, Judith V., Linda M. Hartling, and J. Baker. 2008. "The Development of Relational-Cultural Theory." Jean Baker Miller Training Institute, Wellesley Centers for Women, Wellesley, MA. Accessed April 20, 2008. http://www.example-url.com

Lagaan. Directed by Ashutosh Gowariker. 2001. India: Sony Pictures Classics. YouTube.

Mandela, Nelson. 2000. "Speech at the Inaugural Laureus Lifetime Achievement Award." Speech, delivered May 25, 2000, in Monaco. Nelson Mandela Centre of Memory. https://archive.nelsonmandela.org/index.php/za-com-mr-s-1148.

Mehra, Omprakash Rakesh, dir. 2013. *Bhaag Milkha Bhaag*. India: ROMP Pictures. Netflix.

Negi, Mir Rajan. 2012. "From Gloom to Glory." *Bhartiya-Hockey*, August 18, 2012. https://www.bhartiyahockey.org.

Oza, Rupal. 2019. "Wrestling Women: Caste and Neoliberalism in Rural Haryana." *Gender, Place & Culture* 26, no. 4 (2019): 468–88.

Paan Singh Tomar. Directed by Tigmanshu Dhulia. 2012. India: UTV Spotboy. Netflix.

Powis, Benjamin. 2020. *Embodiment, Identity, and Disability Sport: An Ethnography of Elite Visually Impaired Athletes*. Routledge.

Radhakrishnan, Pooja, and Dibyakusum Ray. 2023. "Playing it the Nation's Way: Tradition, Cosmopolitanism, and the Native-Masculine of Hindi Sports Films." *Contemporary South Asia* 31, no. 4 (2023): 533–546.

Soorma. Directed by Shaad Ali. 2018. India: Sony Pictures Networks Productions. Netflix.

Tarlo, Emma. 2003. *Unsettling Memories: Narratives of the Emergency in Delhi*. Hurst & Co.

Tiwari, Nitesh, dir. 2016. *Dangal*. India: Walt Disney Pictures. Netflix.

Whannel, Garry. *Media Sports Stars: Masculinities and Moralities*. Routledge, 2005.

Shaping Her: Words, Affects and Identity Formation in H.D.'s *Hermione*

Anna Cadoni, PhD

Abstract

Susan Stanford Friedman defined HERmione, H.D.'s long-forgotten Bildungsroman—written in 1927 and published more than fifty years later, a "literally suppressed, figuratively repressed story of origins." Hermione Gart, H.D.'s fictional character whose experience strikingly resembles that of the image throughout the years of youth and her troubled relationships with Ezra Pound and Frances Gregg continuously shapes the world around her through the repetition of certain words that become, indeed, the psychological structure of her persona: "Her," "Tree," "Aum" permeates the whole narration and define the foundation of Hermione's understanding of life, so that "the mind of Hermione Gart was a patchwork of indefinable association." The initial inability to spell the name of certain things and events that surround HERmione's reality resolves eventually in the personal education that the woman goes through, adjusting herself around the words that she applies to the world and the people in her life. Drawing upon the critical frame of Affect Theory—and specifically around the political outcome of affective practice as Sara Ahmed intends it - this article contends that, shaping her own identity, Hermione Gart negotiates her position in relation to the outside. The affective limits of Hermione's identity identify at times with the institutions of school or marriage, social expectations or familial bonds. Focusing primarily on Hermione's presence in the novel as both a bodily and affective figure, as well as a socially constructed entity, this work will therefore explore the practices through which the

woman shapes her own identity and how that process
affects the reality around her, placing her character in a
liminal position, and therefore in a precarious and subversive stand.

Keywords: Affect Theory, Modernism, Coming-of-Age,
Women's Studies

Identity formation plays a central role throughout H.D.'s works, particularly when autobiographical elements interest the lyrical and fictional
production. The latter, almost entirely devoted to her existence, has only
recently found recognition, particularly through critical studies by Feminist scholars, such as Susan Stanford Friedman and Rachel Blau DuPlessis. When approaching the artistic figure of H.D. it is essential to recognize how the writer's life experiences profoundly influenced her work and
became, as in the *romàn a clef HERmione* (1981), the work itself.

Completed in 1927 but only published in 1981 - following a resurgence
of critical interest in H.D.—*HERmione*, or *HER*, is a "scandalous story
of forbidden desire" (Friedman 1990, 102) that follows the fictional reconstruction of Doolittle's sentimental journey, from her failure at Bryn
Mawr College to her engagement and breakup with Ezra Pound, and
romantic relationship with Frances Gregg. Throughout the novel, their
names are encoded in the characters of George Lowndes and Fayne Rabb,
who embody the intimate companions of H.D.'s in a turbulent portrayal
of relationships and breakups. Given the evident autobiographical information, *HERmione* has been rightly analyzed in regard to its vicinity to
Doolittle's life. Friedman defines the structure of *HERmione* as divided
into two substantial parts that can be summarized in the "making and
unmaking of H.D." (103) This process refers precisely to the artist's im-
pulsion to shape her own identity as a young woman in a specific cultural context, social environment, and historical background. The pursuit
of identity permeates the whole narration to the extent that the cyclical
structure of the novel—with Hermione Gart in a continuous spiral of ever-changing perspectives—resolves in fundamental failure in detecting
her own definition of self.

Focusing primarily on Hermione's presence in the novel as an affective character in search of an identity category to fit into, this work explores the practices through which the woman conceives and embodies her found identities and how that process influences the reality around her. The scope of this study is to identify how H.D.'s literary *persona* Hermione Gart defines herself through her continuous interaction with the other, to which she attaches an affective meaning. The process through which Hermione connects to the external reality, apart from her unstable consciousness, is substantiated in the affective movements that she directs to the significant figures in her life.

To consider the limits of Hermione's identity formation, this work delves into the potential qualities of infinite possibilities on which affects are based. Drawing upon the critical frame of Affect Theory, I argue that Hermione Gart negotiates her position in relation to society, her family and her community by shaping her own identity. The affective limits of Hermione's identity often overlap with the institutions of school or marriage, social expectations or familial bonds. Therefore, my analysis addresses determined categories of identity formation through which Hermione Gart builds her limits and possibilities.

Although the protagonist's corporeal presence is somehow deceiving and dwells on a basic ambiguity between "being there" and hiding behind a veil of mental instability, the role of the body will be central in this study. Hermione's body, in constant movement between being subject and object of the narrative, stands in continuous relationship with speech, capable of defining its own identity and subjectivity, but also in relation to other bodies. The numerous figures that populate *HERmione*, real and imagined, change and arise throughout the *Bildungsroman*, going on to form Hermione Gart's identity on the path toward self-awareness precisely through the way she interacts with the outside world. Her's affective body, profoundly touched and limited by the others and capable of modifying its condition, is thus observed through the relationship established with its ability to interact in infinite and "possible endpoints."

HERmione offers examples of the protagonist's identity formation process from the beginning of the novel: "Her Gart stood. Her mind still trod its round. I am Her Gart, my name is Her Gart, I am Hermione Gart, [...] I am Her Gart. Nothing held her, she was nothing holding to this thing: I am Hermione Gart, a failure." (H.D. 1981, 4) Here, Hermione's consciousness rises as she is continually oscillating between the condition of failure and vision. As a counterpart, she immediately latches onto the possibility that failure in the broadest sense offers: "Hermione Gart could not then know that her precise reflection, her entire failure to conform to expectations was perhaps some subtle form of courage." (H.D. 1981, 4) If the inability to conform to expectations is a fundamental feature on which the entire *Künstlerroman* is based, the possible semantic intersections of the concept of failure assume a relevant role in understanding the infinite endpoints to which Hermione is directed while asserting that her impossibility to define herself affect her standing in the society.

Hermione's initial inability to name and channel a reaction or feeling within a definition leads her precisely to name only what she knows: first and foremost, herself. Indeed, the novel opens with the figure of the protagonist who "went round in circles" (3) uttering the phrase "I am Her" which appears as performative. This first expression of self-representation accompanies the work and punctuates its timing in a syncopated manner, whereby the protagonist must always uphold, before herself, her own identity. On the other hand, the repetition of the utterance "I am Her" takes on an alternative value to that repetition of herself, approaching more to the function of the mantra, that is, the invocation in the Sanskrit language of the expression "AUM." Leaving aside for the moment psychoanalytic influences and links to Vedic literature, it is evident that the use of Her's name has, in addition to a possible performative and evocative function, a representative role of the self that, through negation, opens up the possibility of a new subjectivity formation. The first introductory paragraph closes with "She was not Gart, she was not Hermione, she was not anymore Her Gart, what was she?" (4) This "undoing," as well as the definition by negation, can be seen as an opening to the possible, ranging from "I am Hermione Gart, a failure" to "I'm too pretty. I'm not pretty enough." (5) This means that Her Gart's understanding of herself seems unable to reverberate beyond the name itself, which is repeated incessantly.

Seeing failure as an opportunity for action, Jack Halberstam has argued that "failure allows us to escape the punishing norms that discipline behavior and manage human development to deliver us from unruly childhoods to orderly and predictable adulthoods." (Halberstam 2011, 3) Here, failure is conceived as a unique opportunity and the only possible rupture that grants an alternative to a prescribed path. As a woman involved in a homoerotic relationship, Hermione fails with her family, society, and the other. Nonetheless, this performance unexpectedly opens up a break from an oppressive system to which she is inevitably attracted and to which she tries to belong.

In reference to the status of women within a given system of oppression, Halberstam has argued that "where feminine success is always measured by male standards, and gender failure often means being relieved of the pressure to measure up to patriarchal ideals, not succeeding at womanhood can offer unexpected pleasures." (4) The opportunities are, according to Halberstam, a direct consequence of the expectations with which women are burdened in a system of patriarchal values that require a rather rigid construction of society and leave little room for error and change, let alone female agency. For this reason, by offering a vision on failure through continuous negations, *HERmione*'s opening lines express the beginning of the rupture and, consequently, new possibilities in failure: "She wasn't now any good for anything" is a negation that, theoretically, should preclude from any opportunity for action.

Being "any good for anything" is not only to be declined in the academic context, in which Her Gart failed; it is also to be read in reference to her gender identity. The unexpected pleasure suggested by Halberstam is shaped throughout the entire novel as Her's gender is problematized (specifically through her engagement and erotic relation to her lovers) on several occasions. As a woman, Hermione offers a subversive perspective that collides with a normative gender narrative, revealing socially constructed roles as inherently fallacious. The path through which Hermione manages to overturn the delusory nature of gender structures is an arduous one and requires several phases in Hermione's bildungsroman to be endured.

Hermione's agency, which will eventually emerge as being deeply affective, is encoded in the continuous repetition of words that acquire different meanings throughout the novel. People's names, for instance, intensify Hermione's attachment to her reality and act as affects, thus bearing in themselves (semantically and phonetically) the power to affect and be affected.

The act of obsessively repeating one's name appears initially as the refuge of human essence, in which Hermione can hide as the bearer of a name. "Names are in people, people are in names" (H.D. 1981, 5) is the revelation that Hermione shares with herself, in what might be an attempt to seek stability through a closed structure (i.e., a person's name). However, associating people and names also means being able to modify a given environment, a condition, and a person. The active power of naming and ascribing a symbol to an entity, sustains Hermione in her discourse and allows her to view the outside through her perspective.

The attempt to establish an identity through which to define herself is expressed precisely in the attribution of new words, often at a high symbolic level, to which the protagonist traces her own individuality and that of the people around her. Consider the meanings attached to Pennsyslavia: "Sylvania. I was born here. People ought to think before they call a place Sylvania. Pennsylvania. I am a part of Sylvania. Trees. Trees. Trees." (5) Pennsylvania bears several meanings to the development of Her's consciousness, as it represents not only a geographical but also an affective connotation to her personal "history of origins." The region means the paralysis from which it is impossible to escape. Pennsylvania is the origin of Hermione's life and despair; the opposite of growth, of evolution. In an impossible vision of the expression of her individuality, Her is measured against a physically suffocating, claustrophobic land, populated with plants that deprive her of oxygen and undermine Hermione's attempts to free herself from the soil trampled by her parents.

Thus, Pennsylvania is not only the object of the mind but also the land, leaves, trees and smells of her family genealogy. The metaphor of Pennsylvania as an oppressive parent from which it is impossible to distance oneself is strongly supported by Her's mental connections. Unable to attribute the right name to her experiences and feelings, Hermione recognizes a maternal and paternal root (8) in her inability to belong to the place of birth.

Her's inadequacy and the constant reminder that she does not fit into a clear category shed light on her dual identification with parental figures who have engendered an underlying incompatibility with her land. If her mother Eugenia "had grown into the subsoil" (8) and her father Carl is "at peace in the green shadows after the inland prairies," no other possibility presents itself for Her than the physical severance of the roots that sink into the numbing security created by her parents, upon which she cannot lean—except from the perspective of remaining in perpetual captivity. Precisely because in Pennsylvania, "Carl Gart had found a sort of peace and a submergence" and "in Eugenia Gart, the fibers were rooted and mossed over and not to be disrupted," (9) every action and thought of Her directed outward from this rootedness with millennia-old features is a subversive act toward her parents, her status and herself. Indeed, the narrative is at a point where Hermione Gart has not yet achieved a true awareness of herself and she drags herself into a pessimistic consideration of her person, in describing all that she is not and cannot achieve.

Operating an analysis on affect as a force prior to intention, automatic, visceral, pre-subjective, and pre-political, the element underlying this observation is precisely non-intentionality. By linking the affect produced by and on Hermione in relation to Eugenia, Carl, and the Pennsylvanian to this factor, the presence of components affecting the status and exchanges between relationships can be traced to an affective nature of the event. What Hermione does not realize, indeed, is the inherent connection between the earthly spaces to which she and her parents belong; it is both a metaphysical and an earthly connection that links each "fiber" of her identity to any geographic origin.

The passage explores Hermione's "possible" origins, hers as much as anyone else's: "She could not realize that there was an affinity with Siberia when long nights beat them indoors and lamps shining upon tables were the same lamps that made Lithuanians look tenderly across dark tablecloths and that made sailors in Cornwall start, listening to sea-shouts. She could not know that no race is in itself integral but that each has its fibers elsewhere." (10) However, this background, of which Hermione is not aware, has an influence, albeit on an unconscious level, on the protagonist's inability to feel that she belongs to one family, community or nation. Although this awareness is still invisible to Hermione, the effect is already tangible through her restlessness and discomfort. If the sense of belonging is stripped of its geographical limits and contours, Her is left with the only security that sustains her: that of being a failure: "She only felt that she was a disappointment to her father, an odd duckling to her mother, an importunate overgrown, unincarnated entity that had no place here." (10)

From the sense of failure, a feeling that has a form and a concreteness and thus belongs to a conscious plane of self, Hermione can then build that base from which to emerge as a potentially subversive subjectivity, not framed in a norm. *HERmione* is, after all, a coming-of-age novel, and although declined innovatively, some narrative traits remain quite recognizable. If Hermione initially floats in such unconsciousness, she later manages to delineate her subversive action precisely through an incompatibility of understanding. The way in which Pennsylvania and the parental figures exclude her acts automatically on Her and is in turn modified, thus affectively attached toward change. Change that, in Massumi's understanding, is considered as the primary feature of affect. Massumi finds in the principle of affect a "qualitative difference," the contours of which he determines in *Parables for the Virtual* (Massumi 2002, 1).

Attributing physical, earthly, corporeal, and tangible meanings and valences to figures, human and non-human, thus allows us to consider the importance of these subjects as affective entities, capable therefore of affecting and being affected as they are open to the world and capable of provoking change; in the case of the relationship between Her and the land of her her parents, change originates precisely from the affect of exclusion, failure, and not belonging to one place or another. Inanimate, non-human, human, living material entities act, in the course of the work, in an active manner among them, allowing them not only to affect each other but to convey a real change definable as "political."

The encounters described in *HERmione* are multiple: we witness the affective exchange between Her and the "other" (i.e., the family, Pennsylvania, George, Fayne). These figures cannot always be considered as separate, in their representation, from Her. This is the case of the sentence uttered by Hermione during a conversation with George: "I love Her" (H.D. 1981, 170) pronounced by the protagonist leaving little room for ambiguity. Here the word *Her*, which includes the personification of Hermione, certainly refers to Fayne. Based on the figure of Frances Gregg, Fayne is identified, through the object pronoun "her," as part of Hermione herself. The affective encounters mostly take place on a level of self-representation toward Hermione, to the extent that what the protagonist establishes with *HER* (word and *personae*) is indeed a relationship with herself in the shape of external subjects. For this purpose, the episode that narrates the "literary" origins of Hermione is significant to understand the uninterrupted bond between Hermione and what enters her perspective.

Hermione Gart "learns" her own story from *The Winter's Tale* by telling herself how "I am out of this book" (32) The Shakespearean play, in which the name "Hermione" is linked to the Queen of Sicily, Leontes' wife, assumes a central role not only as content but also—and more importantly, as physical matter belonging to Hermione's household. Looking at two volumes that are sitting next to her mother's picture, Hermione studies both and from them, she undergoes an affective moment: the episode, which opens with "there was a small red Temple Shakespeare one side of Eugenia's picture, the other side was a blue book matching it. The *Mahabharata*," (31) represents a strongly symbolic moment to Hermione, who finds herself constantly searching for the source of her existence, real or imagined.

The discovery of the two volumes—the Shakespearean play and the Indian epic poem—, causes Her to open up to her history and herself, as if the two works generate her once more and give her a new origin to her identity as a daughter. After all, as Friedman has pointed out, "H.D. was fascinated with the question of origins." (Friedman 1990, 100) Here, as in most of her works, H.D. re-proposes a "narrative of beginnings." *HERmione* is defined by Friedman as a gestational narrative, where birth is twofold in that it implies a "birth and a rebirth" (101) as well as the continuous and infinite possibility of creation, artistic and vital. The *Temple* is a shabby volume as it has been worn out by time. Its leather, softened over the years, recalls olfactory memories in Her's mind: "Leather, smelling like that, wafted through and through innumerable compartments bringing dispersed elements and jaded edges together." (H.D. 1981, 32) It is thus the book, a tangible object with certain characteristics that Her connects back to the atoms that make up Hermione's own body, thus producing innumerable mental connections. Having made the first acquaintance with the shaping of her original identity, Hermione "picked up the other book. It had a like effect upon her but more potently." (33)

The *Mahabharata* too conveys a specific feeling of belonging to Hermione, who appears eager to absorb any possible information on her origins. By finding the books, Hermione gains affective power that collides with the limits of the representation of subjectivity, which evolves and assumes many different shapes and identities. The "carnality" of the Shakespearean volume becomes impalpable matter and metaphysical substance in the *Mahabharata*, thus in Hermione two different effects converge that describe the evolution of one to the other: "Water lying filled with weeds and lily-pads... lilies of all kinds... became even more fluid, was being taken up and up, element (out of chemistry) became vapour. The water lying so pure became vapour, she would be lifted, drunk up, vanished." (32) The change from liquid to gaseous state causes a reaction in Hermione, who suddenly "dropped the volume. This frightened her." The Red Book and the Blue Book provide Her with two opposing views of her nature, as well as alternatives to those handed down to her by her family. The vision of the two volumes causes a sudden reconsideration of who Hermione really is, "God is in a word. God is in a word. God is in Her. She said 'HER, HER, HER. I am Her, I am Hermione... I am the word AUM.'" (32) giving rise to an inner clash between the newly discovered identities.

An essential change takes place in the figure of Hermione in response to the finding of the two volumes about her bodily presence and, in particular, to the dual nature of this subjectivity (i.e., individual and relational, observed here in the exchange between Hermione and the two works, but also between the different *HER, GOD, AUM*). It is therefore appropriate to define the "bodies" that come into contact with Her's as agents of affect; when these act on themselves and the outside, modifying and being profoundly changed by physical or verbal contact, they produce an effect that, as Massumi argues, provides the necessary basis to understand affect. In this case, the change is that of the perception of bodies in a space, as well as the resulting dynamics between them. If Hermione's reaction, disturbed by the blue book (the *Mahabharata*), consists of turning around and turning her back to her parental figure (we read "Her back was to the desk, to Eugenia, to the *Winter's Tale*, to the other little volume,"(33) she will come out of this stance with a new name. It is no longer the word AUM, the one chosen by Hermione, that defines her identity; by abandoning it Hermione begins a new story of her name and a new version of herself. Influenced by her father and mother figures, as well as by the Shakespearean comedy and the Indian poem, the *Her* who finds a new definition in conjuring her name can begin a new form of herself.

Hermione relationship with George Lowndes mirrors the long-lasting companionship that united H.D. and Pound throughout the first decades of the twentieth century. George plays a central role in engaging with Hermione's understanding of her persona, simultaneously acting as an agent of control and a means to Hermione's emancipation. Similarly to the encounter with the volumes, George's entrance into Hermione's life brings up a sort of revelation about her meaning as an existing being. About to marry George, Hermione remarks "I am Hermione Gart and will be Hermione Lowndes." (112) In such a redefinition of one's name, it is possible to foresee a potential transfer from one name to the other, thus from body to body, in an affective continuum that overwhelms Hermione in her understanding of mobility and potentiality in the transfer of meaning between words and bodies is evident, especially when Her claims that "people are in things, things are in people." (112) In this statement it is possible to see that there is a real intention to act on the *affective entities* that are, in this case, the expressions attributed to herself and George, and to be influenced by them in turn. The power that Hermione wields over the bodies of others through the definition of their names thus works in a double direction, as in the case of the encounter between HER and her books.

The influence exerted by George Lowndes on Hermione is undoubted; the sudden appearance through a letter ("George is coming back" (28) is the only information given, although the tension caused by George's return is obvious) and the promise of a return to what is called "Gawd's own god-damn country" by the author of the missive himself, cause a major rupture, exacerbated later by the two-book episode; this effect is described by Her's stream as a division of her mind: "my mind is breaking up like molecules in test tubes. Molecules all held together, breaking down in this furnace heat." (31) On the other hand, the effect caused in the news finds a counterpart in Her's repetition of the man's name, declined in the possible existences conceived by the 'compartments' of the girl's mind: "George is George. George or Georgio. George is not Georg. [...] Georg is too hard, he is not Georg. Georges better suits him" (33)

In ascribing one name rather than another to Lowndes, the "infinite possibilities" of George's representation present themselves in Her's mind; from the way this passage shows, each utterance corresponds to a different conception of the man on the other end of the telephone when, shortly after the letter, the man contacts Hermione for a conversation without intermediaries. The affective factor of this action emerges precisely as a result of the formulation of the name; in rethinking the figure of George, Hermione considers the word by which the man is identified and what is involved in pronouncing it, thinking about it, and consequently enacting a change about it. In reporting to her mother, Eugenia, the news of George's return to Pennsylvania, Her realizes what is the extent of the thinking connected with the figure who, up to that point, appears only through the name, before the body: Hermione knew she must formulate George Lowndes.

It was going to be very difficult to formulate George Lowndes, to concentrate enough to get an image of George, to say, "I hate George" or to say, "I love George." She perceived het lightning wavering above the Ferrand oak trees and realized that now was the moment for some definition." (44) In this case, "formulating" George allows Her to attribute reactions and relationships to the given name. Naming the word, declined in its various pronunciations, leads Hermione to focus on the image of George and the emotions that arise from it, whether precisely of attraction or repulsion, as the protagonist herself observes. "The moment for some definition" is thus a point of no return, from which Her can begin a journey of understanding and influence to and from herself. The exchange between Her and George, based on each other's formulation, is indeed continuous and changing. One can see how the dynamics between the two figures change over time and precisely through first bodily absence and then presence, which decisively determine the relationship between the two.

If floral images such as the hibiscus[1] or belonging to the plant world are associated with George's name, such as the continuous presence of trees in Her's mental connections, on the other hand, the presence of the man is also profoundly real in his corporeality, the mere idea of which is capable of triggering in the protagonist disturbance and, at the same time, desire. If, from the moment of George's entry into the narrative, Hermione's mind is continuously pervaded by the presence of the man, it is again, a desire dictated by the reflection of herself in the other. Indeed, it is through continuous affective impulses (of movement, tension, change) toward bodies outside her own that Her produces a certain view of herself. As a result of observing Hermione's behaviors toward people close to her, such as her parents, George, or Fayne, it is possible to observe how Her's self-determination comes through her gaze on the other.

The desire to possess a body that is able to define and thus has the power

---

1   H.D., 118.

to alter one's own or external condition is an essential element of Hermione's relationship with George. The bond between Hermione and George describes not so much a submissive relationship toward the latter, but an individual growth through the intervention of a mentor. If Hermione's position is initially one of subservience and dependence (on George's definitions but also on his actions, as in the case of the forced kiss on her), the woman manages to reach a condition of awareness and self-determination. An exemplary episode of Hermione's independence occurs in the aftermath of George's marriage proposal; this is greeted by Eugenia with the predictable mockery encapsulated in the phrase "you can't *marry* George Lowndes," (74) which is repeated numerous times, and wreaks havoc on the already rather unstable family dynamics. In feeling accused by her mother, who, bewildered at the possibility of Hermione marrying a man of ill repute, inveighs by claiming "George Lowndes is *teaching* you, actually *teaching you* words, telling you what to say" (95) the protagonist takes an attitude in defence not only of the man but of herself.

Hermione's validity and credibility depend on her ability to utter the exact words that not only define, but act as the people and external events that surround and affect her. The affective power of words for Hermione is demonstrated in its intensity when she realizes that she cannot marry George. The breaking of the engagement in the novel is presented through the impossibility of "calling" herself by a name other than her own, which would cause Hermione to make an effectively unbearable change: "I can't be called Lowndes" (112) In rejecting the name Lowndes, Hermione once again reconstructs her person, which is neither the word spoken by George nor her mother's definition.

Hermione "recreates" herself by feeling a moment of unity between her head, her body, and her self-consciousness: "The back of her head was at one with the front of her head, a head fitted to a body that belonged to a head." (118) Through the sensation of her own body closely connected (and reunified) to another anatomical part (the head), Hermione leads back, or is led back, to an awareness of her own identity; the impossibility of a union with George Lowndes, metaphorized through the acquisition of a new surname, gives rise to a microscopic presence. Here "the back of her head prompted the front of her head, slid a fraction of a fraction [...] away from the front of her head, actually almost with a little click, separated from the front of her head like amoeba giving birth by separation to amoeba." (118)

By a process of splitting, similar to that of unicellular organisms that, being asexual, reproduce through their separation, Hermione reproduces herself "by breaking apart." If, then, "separating themselves from themselves" is how Her Gart recreates herself, the breaking apart of herself ends in rebirth; at the end of this process, she will be able to remember, or see for the first time, the new self. Hermione reconciles (after "breaking" herself) with her name "and she remembered *I am the word Aum* and I am Tree and I shall have a new name and I am the word tree." (119)

The continuity that can be observed in the ways in which the characters in Hermione shift and change their routes, deviating from a predetermined path can be observed on two levels: on the one hand, when Hermione abruptly changes her condition. While at the beginning of the novel, Hermione struggles to define herself outside of what she is not and beyond her failure, the epilogue leaves the possibility open to a linear, rather than cyclical, direction. On the other hand, reversals and dynamism within the narrative are also observed on a semantic level: the most obvious example of this is the use of the word "Her," which in the course of the work changes from the protagonist's proper name to possessive adjective to pronoun, until it refers, with all new implications, to Fayne Rabb, with whom Hermione enters into a relationship following her breakup with George. In this case, "Her" object/subject of the narrative never finds itself cornered into a single category that determines its use and meaning, but it incessantly alters and reforms, to the extent that it transfers its meaning from one person to another.

Fayne's reappearance, following a brief introduction early in the novel, is similarly situated to George's entry. Through the medium of epistolary communication, Hermione anticipates meeting the woman in the same way in which, previously, George had announced his return to "Gawd's own god-damn country": "Looking closer at the name written in the unfamiliar writing Her read 'Compliments of Fayne Rabb' and wondering at the oddness? of the name Fayne with Rabb so hard and casual, rather nice." (127) Again, the name takes on a meaning-laden value in Hermione's mind; it is from the sound of the two compound names that Hermione suggests her predisposition to meet Fayne. Following a brief reading of the letter, in which reference is made to the protagonist's name, Hermione is suddenly struck by a feeling of order and rule in her thoughts: "Things making parallelograms came straight suddenly." (H.D. 1981, 128) The sudden sensation that pervades Her's mind as she suddenly "sees straight" is that of a return to a calmness unknown to her until then.

The lining up of parallelograms is a strong sign of resolution for Hermione, who is used to juggling concentric circles, clusters of molecules and perturbing mental compartments. In this way, Fayne enters Her's field of vision through her name and makes space for herself among the protagonist's consciousness: "Fayne with a click for the first time in consciousness became part of these things," (130) where things tell of Hermione's usual and known elements, considered everyday certainties of existence.

Fayne's entry into the story introduces the second part of the novel; if the first was dominated by George's figure, the rupture that brings the relationship between the two women causes irreversible consequences. According to Diana Collecott, "lesbian desire is presented as the only basis of an alternative to patriarchy, since, like male homosociality, it displaces the sexual Other." (Collecott 1999, 63) Not only does the lesbian relationship shatter the heteronormative framework of relationships, but it also gives a voice to a passion for the other, which constitutes the drastic change between the first and the second section of the novel. The process of identifying the word *HER* with another person other than the protagonist begins with the attribution of the object pronoun to the figure of Fayne, whose entry into the conversation between Hermione and Nellie, her old college friend, brings at the same time a sense of rupture but also tranquillity. The relevance of the name, not only the one attributed to the specific person but also in the words and discourse between the two women, remains central to Hermione's understanding of the different realities that lie before her.

About the polysemic "her," especially ascribed to the relationship with George and Fayne, Friedman and DuPlessis stated that "the name Her has different valences in the two relationships. With George, Hermione's nickname 'Her'—always grammatically awkward as a subject—signifies her object status within conventional heterosexuality. With Fayne, however, the nickname signals a fusion, one that gives birth to two selves, subject and object indistinct." (Friedman and DuPlessiss 1990, 212) If the name at the center of the entire play not only changes its meaning, but is also able to direct the characters in different ways, it is precisely with the arrival of Fayne that Hermione can openly show herself with the intended meaning: no longer an object, but the subject of desire. Fayne routs Hermione's mental structure by making her realize, once again, that "names are in people, people are in names."

The affective significance of names for Hermione overlaps with the individual's value and becomes a force capable of influencing the other's reasoning and reactions: "'Do tell me all about it' meant to tell me all about *her*. How to get it across to Nellie for she is HER and I am HER. People are in names, names are in people. "Oh her name—the name of the girl who sent them." (H.D. 1981, 131) Fayne's name undergoes, in the process of rapprochement between the two women, numerous changes: while initially unknown and thus carrying interest and curiosity, it then raises reasoning in Hermione. Fayne becomes "Pauline" in her college friend's stories: "Oh Fayne. I call it so affected. Her name is Pauline really. Pauline Fayne Rabb. She has dropped the Pauline, calls herself Fayne now. I call her Paul despite everything." (132)

Nellie, who decides precisely to give Fayne the name with the masculine meaning *Paul*, recognizes in her companion an exceptionally indefinable figure, starting with the word through which she identifies her. Precisely because of this indefiniteness, Nellie claims "No Pauline is absolutely any cloud I know of. [...] She's like a sort of reflection of a stormcloud seen in water," (133) where "cloud" could be replaced with "person," or *woman*. Finally, the last image that Her associates with Fayne before their verbal encounter is that of Pygmalion. (138) Once again, Fayne's entrance into the scene abruptly shakes Hermione's sensibilities, whereby "she had realized her head [...] was two convex mirrors placed back to back.

The two convex mirrors placed back to back became one mirror...as Fayne Rabb entered;" (138) the act of recognition, repeated from the first meeting between college classmates, verbatim, to the "unmasking" of Fayne/Pygmalion plays a central role in the relationship between the two women. In this case, the "two mirrors" that form Hermione's mind become one reflection, pointed at Fayne, who becomes the sole object of Hermione's gaze. For this reason, the first conversation between the two -charged with the affectivity of the first meeting- is delineated on the theme of recognition: "'I'm glad I waited in this corridor.' 'Oh—then you recognize me?' '*Recognize* you? But I always knew you.'" (139)

The gaze, which goes through this process, is a pivotal element in the relationship between Hermione and Fayne. Friedman has argued that "*sight and seeing* are central to their love." (Friedman 1990, 115) However, it is necessary to recognize the subversive force of the female gaze in the novel. In the relationship with George, a hierarchy is established from the outset that unequivocally distinguishes the artist from the muse to the extent that in Hermione's shaping as a writer, the origin is to be found in the power that the man wields over her. Conversely, between Hermione and Fayne "the gaze is mutual, not hierarchical." (115) If the relationship between the two women is thus equal, and mutual in the exchange of each other's gazes, then Hermione's phases of lesbian desire presents itself as the artist's "mature period." Friedman argues that the shift in narrative—from heterosexual erotica to lesbian-rooted desire—allows the artist to emerge as such, in that she is no longer locked into a mentor/pupil relationship that imposes constraints but is free to express herself in a bond that fosters her flourishing.

By knowing Fayne, Hermione once more knows herself. She repeats, in an anguished and feverish rhythm, "I know her. Her. I am Her. She is Her. Knowing her, I know Her." (H.D. 1981, 158) By the affective use of the word *Her,* she conveys not only the possibility of knowing the object of one's discovery and love but also her ability to relate to that object. The effect of such a discovery of the other and its process is ephemeral, consuming themselves in the instant or even before the two realize it ("you are here and you aren't here;" (159)) if, as Friedman has argued, the act of seeing is central to the love between Hermione and Fayne, this is continually tested—perhaps by the fact that Her's mind seems elusive and therefore uncontrollable—and it is found in Fayne's words, which carry with them a rather disillusioned tone: "You *seem* to see. And then you quite escape me," (161) Fayne declares, knowing that defining Hermione's identity, surrounded by continuous and often impenetrable thoughts, represents a perhaps impossible task. For that reason, the moment that encapsulates the first erotic encounter between the two is similarly beset by a palpable sense of incompatibility that Fayne feels while approaching Hermione.

By defining her view of the other, Hermione imagines another possible subjectivity of Fayne's and describes it by imagining its contours: "You might have been a huntress. [...] I mean a boy standing on bare rocks and stooping to take a stone from his strapped sandal." (163) Fayne's *persona* is further affect through Hermione's gaze as it becomes a masculine figure, a boy ready to hunt; the first kiss between the two occurs just as Fayne is given her new name. No longer Paul, Pauline, or Fayne, Hermione is ready to create her new definition, that of the young hunter. Recognizing her lover as a huntress and creative artist ("You were so exactly right as that Pygmalion,"(163)) Hermione subverts while kissing Fayne, the roles she herself assigned, making herself the Pygmalion in love with the motionless statue before her: Her bent forward, face bent toward Her. A face bends toward me and a curtain opens. There is a swish and swirl of heavy parting curtains. Almost along the floor with its strip of carpet, almost across me, I feel the fringe of some fantastic wine-colored parting curtains. Curtains part as I look into the eyes of Fayne Rabb. "And I- I'll make you breathe, my breathless statue." (163)

To this purpose, it is relevant to observe how the shift from third-person narration to the "I" by Hermione produces a sense of continuity in the description of the event as sought by the protagonist. Suddenly, Hermione finds herself in a context close to her knowledge, where she knows that she can make her movements and feels in control. The vital breath, transferred through the kiss, is a part of the rather familiar dynamic for Hermione, that of a creator and his muse, established with George Lowndes. Referring to these passages on the first romantic union between the two women, Cassandra Laity focused on the influence of Romantic poetry, particularly that of A.C. Swinburne, arguing how "in narratives such as HER [...] the adolescent Romantic 'self,' under the influence of Swinburne in particular, discovers poetic and prophetic power through a homoerotic bond with a 'twin-self sister' who is boyishly androgynous." (Laity 1989, 473)

Laity refers in particular to the last stanza of the composition *Faustine*, which reads, "Curled lips, long since half kissed away,/ Still sweet and keen;/ You'd give him - poison shall we say?/ Or what, Faustine?" (473) The first verse is repeated on several occasions and punctuates the moments of tension and attraction between the two. In Laity's opinion, Hermione and Fayne rediscover the "Romantic self" subjected to the use of the polysemous power of words: "Hermione's articulation of her own and Fayne's 'double' sexual identities in the 'naming' of Fayne as the boy Ity-

lus releases her from the object position in the discourse of male desire."
(474) Therefore, the first kiss between Hermione and *Fayne/Faustine/
huntress* turns out to be a moment of profound liberation as well as deconstruction of the "patriarchal/textual politics represented by George
Lowndes." (476) Through the act of kissing, and through the "new identity" attributed to Fayne, Hermione determines her individuality no longer
as a muse, a pupil or a wife. In this regard, Friedman suggested that the
sharp division between the Her/George and Her/Fayne relationship is
fundamentally expressed through the liberation of the word *HER* from
George's "text:" "in the novel, Hermione is literally "HER" of Pound's
text. [...] Hermione is the "HER" of Pound's poem, an object in his text
and of his gaze." (Friedman 1990, 119)

The relationship of possession between George and his "artistic creation"
permeates the entire work and seems to find a resolution and consequent
emancipation of the woman from her name through the erotic and sentimental encounters between Hermione and Fayne. It is precisely through
the deconstruction of Pound's Hermione that "H.D. reconstructed
Hermione's identity through a forbidden love of doubled "Hers" which
changes the scene of desire from heterosexual to lesbian." (119) When
Hermione and Fayne kiss, the power dynamics are not reversed but ultimately broken down and "both women are subjects in the story of desire."
(123) Nonetheless, the meeting between the two women also stands as a
breaking point that foreshadows a dramatic development for Hermione:
betrayal by the two people with whom she is in love.

Fayne rightly embodies the figure of Faustine, the *femme fatale* of Swinburne's play when, once given "the name", takes her role by becoming the
woman impossible to reach and inevitably leaves Hermione behind, while
she struggles in despair and madness. Laity considers this "foreboding"
in Faustine's name as a "reentrance into the heterosexist discourse of the
novel," (Laity 1989, 476) where the kiss is not the climax of romantic passion but the beginning of the protagonist's downfall. From the moment
of the discovery of the betrayal of the two, Hermione succumbs to a long
psychotic episode ("She was delirious at my house" (H.D. 1981, 191))
during which it will be precisely the loneliness of her body confined to
bed for long months that will show her a path to rebirth and independence. On the process of rebirth from collapse, Friedman and DuPlessis
contend that "her illness is the creative madness through which she must

pass to discover an autonomous identity." (213) In other words, "madness" is the process through which Hermione Gart, failure, becomes Her, artist.

The constant change of meaning and position of the words circulating in Hermione's mind and in the imagery that she constructs for herself is a highly affective element. The ability of some of the most frequent names ("HER," "trees," "AUM") to make an effective change in the dynamics in which they are used - as they are shifted from one role to another -opens up to observations of affect as agent a bearer of a given meaning. The ever-changing affective force is never crystallizing, but rather moves and enters the words uttered, profoundly affecting Hermione's subjectivity. Just like the continuous oscillation of Hermione's voice, the novel offers an interesting example of the potential of the word as a messenger of infinite meanings. The word itself, used by Hermione as an obsessive chant, is devalued of its semantic quality and becomes a necessary repository for further meanings and thoughts. Through repetition, the word acquires a physical valence that once emptied of meaning, acts unconsciously—and effectively—on the other.

In a discourse that focuses on the affective capacity of the word, the body seems to occupy a subordinate, if not almost insubstantial, space in the novel. Episodes are numerous in which Hermione reflects on her own symbolic, metaphysical presence in an attitude that seems to "outgrow" her corporeality beyond a material connection to Pennsylvania, her parents, George and Fayne. How, then, is the body to be reinserted into an affective discourse on identity, as an integral and necessary aspect of the effects of words and symbols? It becomes necessary to consider the terms in which a consideration of corporeality must be understood, to analyze its consequences on affective encounters and exchanges.

If the concepts of body and mind in Hermione are not only inextricable but fundamentally interchangeable in their ability to produce affects, corporeality within the novel acquires a new, pivotal role. It must be treated as not complementary to the subjectivity of the protagonist and the figures who act on her with visceral forces, but rather as conjoined to the more abstract aspect of the work. By considering the word's affective force in these terms, not only the semantic factor is contained and problematized, but also the unthoughtful element, as well as the pre-conscious, unintentional gap that constitutes the expression of the word itself.

Massumi seems to find the centrality of the visceral affective force in the movement of a body, in its consequent change in space, and on this moment of motion he synthesizes the qualities of affect: "when a body is in motion, it does not coincide with itself. It coincides with its transition: its variation. The range of variations it can be implicated in is not present in any given movement." (Massumi 2002, 4) It is in the act of movement, then, that a factor of "openness to an elsewhere" (5) develops from which one can begin to consider the implications of change, of the evolving process. Since "in motion, a body is an immediate, unfolding relation to its nonpresent potential to vary," (4) it is a moving body - even when that body is incapable of maintaining a position located in a precise place - that holds the potential for transformation.

Reading Hermione's affective potentiality in terms of "recovery" of bodily motion opens possibilities of action, thus recognizing in the non-materiality of the protagonist's physical presence an equally effective agency in terms of intensity and force. If the gap between ideology and affect is bridged—or at least narrowed—through the inclusion of the body in the semantic discourse (specifically Hermione's, thus not complementary to thought but an integral part of it and equally capable of producing and receiving affects), then the "non-signifying, non-conscious intensity" defined by Massumi allows new representational modes through which a subversive conception of corporeal identity can finally be conceived as a powerful tool to understand a marginal subjectivity.

References

Ahmed, Sara. 2004. *The Cultural Politics of Emotions*. Routledge.

———. 2006. *Queer Phenomenology: Orientations, Objects, Others*. Duke University Press.

Burkitt, Ian. 1999. *Bodies of Thought: Embodiment, Identity and Modernity*. Sage Publications.

Collecott, Diana. 1999. *H.D. and Sapphic Modernism*. Cambridge University Press.

Friedman, Susan Stanford, and Rachel Blau DuPlessis. 1990. *Signets: Reading H.D.* University of Wisconsin Press.

Friedman, Susan Stanford. 1975. "Who Buried H.D.? A Poet, Her Critics, and Her Place in 'The Literary Tradition.'" *College English* 36 (7): 801–14.

———. 1990. *Penelope's Web: Gender, Modernity, H.D.'s Fiction.* Cambridge University Press.

H.D. 1981. *HERmione.* New Directions.

Halberstam, Jack. 2011. *The Queer Art of Failure.* Duke University Press.

Laity, Cassandra. 1989. "H.D. and A.C. Swinburne: Decadence and Modernist Women's Writing." *Feminist Studies* 15 (3): 461–84.

Leys, Ruth. 2011. "The Turn to Affect: A Critique." *Critical Inquiry* 37 (3): 434–72.

Massumi, Brian. 2002. *Parables for the Virtual: Movement, Affect, Sensation.* Duke University Press.

———. 2015. *Politics of Affect.* Polity Press.

The "Other Selves": A Journey of Growth and Self-Discovery in Young American Literature

Hannah Grace Wilson, MA.

Abstract

This literary analysis explores the concept of "other selves" as depicted in young adult literature and their impact on the process of growing up. By drawing upon a diverse range of literary works, including the three novels *The Last of the Menu Girls*, *The Liars' Club*, and *Sunny and the Mysteries of Osisi*, this paper identifies four distinct types of self: the inner self, the outer self, the ghost self, and the other self, along with their individual roles within a character. By taking a closer look at the novels, results show that the four different "selves" interact with each other and significantly influence the development and maturation of individuals as they navigate the complexities of growing up. Furthermore, these interactions between "other selves" provide insights into the psychological, social, and emotional effects on characters, thus shaping their identity, self-esteem, and view of the world around them.

Keywords: Other Selves, Growing Up, Self-Identity, Self-Esteem, Psychological Effects, Social Effects, Emotional Effects

Introduction

Growing up is difficult for adolescents, as it marks a time that is filled with questions, doubts, and uncertainties as maturing individuals struggle to find purpose and meaning in an ever-changing and terrifying world. Arguably one of the most difficult aspects of growing up occurs when adolescents must attempt to figure out who they are and provide themselves with their own sense of self. The concept of the self is a fundamental aspect of human psychology that has drawn interest from researchers for generations, and in recent years, young adult literature has emerged as a powerful tool for exploring and understanding the difficulties adolescents face when trying to discover their sense of self.

Analyzing several examples of young adult novels such as *The Last of the Menu Girls*, *The Liars' Club*, and *Sunny and the Mysteries of Osisi*, four distinct types of self—the inner self, the outer self, the ghost self, and the other self—become apparent, and the interactions between these different selves provide insight into the psychological, social, and emotional effects pressed upon adolescents, thereby shaping their identity, self-esteem, and trauma response. The examination of these different types of self provides us with a deeper understanding of the complexities of growing up and the important role that young adult literature plays in helping adolescents navigate this challenging process.

The first type of self that is most apparent in young adult literature is the inner self. The inner self is in charge of one's self-esteem, true emotions, moral agency, and connection to home and family. When talking to others, people share personal topics by deliberately choosing to engage in conversations based on their preferences. People can lie or pretend in conversation, but the inner self is like an honest internal diary that keeps all of a person's thoughts, experiences, and feelings in a safe and private place. By storing all of this information, the inner self helps a person to create an idea of what is right and wrong and what is true and false. According to Lumen Child Psychology, "moral development involves children's increasing compliance with and internalization of adult rules, requests, and standards of behavior." ("Moral Development" n.d.) When these rules and standards become internalized, they become a part of the inner self. Positive moral beliefs such as "murder is wrong" and "stealing is a bad thing to do" are all upheld by the inner self. Sometimes, however, a person might internalize standards that are unhealthy for normal living.

When aspects of a person's inner self cause beliefs that are not based on reality, irrational thoughts can be created. For example, in the book *The Last of the Menu Girls*, the main character, Rocio, has thoughts about sexual purity making someone more or less of a good person. This thought is irrational and causes Rocio to have a negative reaction toward her distant relative Eloisa, after she realizes the nature of her relationships with several different boys. Because of the irrational thoughts caused by a part of her inner self, Rocio, who struggles with her loneliness, pushes Eloisa away. At a young age, Rocio internalized the idea that only bad people have sex when not in a committed relationship. Thus, now as a teenager, her inner self abides by this irrational idea and decides that it is wrong to be around "impure" people. The inner self is what allows one to determine what is right and wrong, and Rocio determined her irrational belief about sexual purity to be correct, though this is not the inner self's only duty.

Alongside being a moral compass, the inner self can also act as a place of comfort. In Mary Karr's memoir, *The Liar's Club*, where Karr narrates her heavily abusive childhood, she describes how she "bore down on myself inside" when her mother, Charlie, drove over a bridge to escape a hurricane (Karr 1995, 91). This moment, like many others in her story, causes Karr to feel a traumatizing amount of fear, thereby forcing her into her inner self for comfort. In doing so, Karr elaborates that she does not have a clear memory of the situation, as it took her years for her to remember this much of her childhood. In intense situations, the inner self can serve as a place of safety and peace. Meditation, clearing one's mind, or retreating into happy thoughts are all ways that a person can enter into their inner self.

This process can be done both intentionally, as in the case of guided meditations, or unintentionally, as in the case of Karr going through a traumatizing situation. When done intentionally, a person can grow to understand more about themselves or a particular event. However, on the other hand, when a person is forced into their safe space because of a traumatic experience, oftentimes "the victim is rendered helpless by overwhelming force." (Herman 1997, 32) Going into one's inner self is a psychological safety measure to protect someone from whatever is happening around them. 'Many survivors report feeling completely overwhelmed or unable to cope with the feelings, sensations, emotions, and thoughts that they experience during traumatic events," and going into the inner self to disassociate can be effective at distancing oneself from a situation (Welkin 2013, 158). In doing so, memory loss can be extremely common but does serve as a shield from further trauma.

Overall, the inner self is exactly what its name suggests. It is a culmination of everything a person is on the inside. Moral code, self-esteem, connection to others, beliefs, and safety are all dealt with by a person's inner self. The inner self is what makes a person who they are. However, one of the most interesting aspects of the inner self is how it interacts with another type of self: the outer self.

Unlike the inner self, the outer self is more involved with external aspects of the self, such as socialization, existing relationships, physical health, the environment, and perception. If the inner self is a diary, then the outer self is the shiny, personalized cover. In total, the outer self represents how a person is portrayed to others. Appearance, speech patterns, energy levels, and outward demeanor are all very large parts of a person's outer self because they give others an idea of what one's inner self is like. Much like with birthday presents, a person might be more tempted to find out what is inside a gift if the wrapping is more intricate. The outer self is responsible for overcoming the snap judgments that people make upon first seeing a person.

According to the American Psychological Association, "children by the age of 5 make rapid and consistent character judgments of others based on facial features, such as the tilt of the mouth or the distance between the eyes." (American Psychological Association 2019) If one seems to frown a lot, people will most likely assume that that person is consistently upset. These rapid judgments are based entirely on a person's outer self. Of course, this process can create a lot of pressure for a person.

The outer self is consistently under pressure to succeed. Not only does the inner self rely on the outer self to provide ample social interaction, but self-esteem is built off of the inner and outer self-interacting. Because the inner self relies heavily on the outer self, the outer self is constantly changing parts of itself every day. The process begins with the inner self decorating the outer self, which may come across as "What should I wear today?" Appearance and style are all results of the inner self deciding on how to present itself. According to a study done by Niel Hester and Eric Hehman, this daily process of constructing a daily appearance, or outer self, is influenced by four factors: "social categories, cognitive states, status, and aesthetics." (Hester and Hehman 2023) These factors describe how an outer self is formed on a daily basis.

The first factor, social categories, deals with how certain dress items connect to groups. For example, black lipstick and clothes are associated with gothic groups. A person with a strong sense of inner self will unconsciously try to create an outer self that connects them with many groups of interest to maximize their chances at social interaction with similarly minded people. Funny shirts, merch from a concert, and even looks from a magazine are all examples of outer self decisions based on social categories.

The second factor, cognitive states, relates to how a person feels day-by-day. Is the person in question going out on a date, attending a funeral, or simply going to work? What the person wants, is doing, and is going to do will all contribute to their cognitive state. Cognitive state determines the outer self frequently, as different situations and locations change how a person wants to be perceived. The cognitive state allows people to fit in.

The next factor, status, comes from the idea that "one's social class could be easily and accurately inferred from one's dress" (Hester and Hehman 2023). The more access a person has to money, the more likely they are to attract others. According to Saint Mary's University, "It has been cross-culturally documented that women exhibit a preference for mates who possess resources or traits that signal potential wealth." (Hunter et al. 2020, 88) Wearing suits, elaborate outfits, and name-brand objects are all ways of signaling status.

The last factor discussed by Hester and Hehman is aesthetics, which is determined by a person's inner self. Any objects without a social connection and assigned to an outer self fit into this category.

Together, these four factors come together to design the outer self. Afterwards, like-minded people will either be enticed to come closer or stay far away. If the outer self is unsuccessful in bringing about social interaction, then the inner self will find the outer self inadequate, and changes will be made to the outer self and self-esteem levels. "Self-esteem comes from learning to accept who we are by seeing the insufficiencies and still choosing to like ourselves;" however, sometimes this discovery can be difficult to face (Newman 2020). If a person's self-esteem becomes alarmingly low, the outer self might not even resemble the inner self. This dysfunction creates a change in a person's cognitive state and thereby changes their style. The more a person's outer self fails to achieve its purpose of attracting social interaction, the more likely the outer self and style are to change in significant ways. Many young adult novels highlight the tension between the inner and outer selves as a common theme. Adolescents struggling to reconcile their true selves with the expectations and pressures of the world around them is an extremely popular plot point not only in the Young American genre but also in the lives of kids and teens all across the globe.

One example from *Sunny and the Mysteries of Osisi* occurs when Sunny becomes upset upon meeting her boyfriend Orlu's auntie, who berates her for being an albino and looking different. Sunny asks herself, "Why is it always about my being albino?" (Okorafor 2018, 37) Her conflict stems from an imbalance between her inner self-esteem and her outer self-image. Her outer self is pushing away someone whose approval she wants, thus making her inner self feel as if she is less than other people who are not albinos.

However, this negative reaction from Orlu's aunt was built off of Sunny's skin color, a part of her that she can not change. When the inner and outer self are targeted by something that they either feel is an impossible or extremely difficult change, then occasionally the inner and outer self can hinder each other's development. In the case of Sunny, she begins to disregard her input when creating her outer self, instead focusing more on her spirit face, Anyanwu. This shift occurs because of Sunny's weak inner self, which consists of low self-esteem. Throughout her story, Sunny's self-esteem continues to weaken to the point that she only recognizes herself through her spirit face. She becomes convinced that she herself is not behind any of her abilities and abandons her outer self in favor of Anyanwu. Sunny's outer self is misaligned because of turmoil caused within her inner self.

An example of this hindrance can be found when Rocio begins to rely on her home's bedroom closet for a place of comfort due to her underdeveloped inner self. Rocio has never had a biological father in her life, and her mother's first husband drank acid three days after the birth of her older half-sister and died. Because of Rocio's lack of a father and her missing connection to such an important part of her life, she begins to feel as if she is missing a part of who she is: a part that can only be found within her mother. So, rather than being able to find comfort within her own body, Rocío locks herself in the closet, which is filled with old pictures and memories that she refers to as "my mother's other life." (Chávez

2004) This physical room becomes her safe space and a supplement for her lacking inner self. Inside the closet, Rocio enjoys playing with her mother's shoes that she wears to school; however, every time she tries to wear the shoes, she finds that they are much too big for her. Rocio desperately wants to understand herself and attempts to wear her mom's shoes as a way to make her outer self feel complete. Only after Rocio begins to feel she has control over her narrative does she feel comfortable relaxing in her inner self again, rather than going into the closet.

In *The Liars' Club*, Karr's abusive mother does something especially hazardous to her inner and outer selves: she chooses to subvert both with her alcoholism. Ignoring the inner and outer selves is extremely unhealthy, and when characters neglect one or both, it negatively impacts their mental and physical health, eventually leading to the creation of the ghost self.

The "ghost" self in young adult literature is a concept that explores the deep connection between the inner and outer selves and how their constant shifting can result in a breakdown and a state of identity crisis where a person temporarily abandons their inner self for a more emotional counterpart. The ghost self is first mentioned in Mary Karr's memoir *The Liars' Club* when Mary says that "Mother had shifted into her ghost self," and though it is not directly mentioned in other works of young adult literature, its effects can still be detected and analyzed (Karr 1995, 253). The ghost self acts similarly to a mental health crisis, where periods of turmoil last for short amounts of time and the subject in question has brief moments of fogginess after the ordeal is over. However, unlike mental health crises, the ghost self in literature always ends in more problems to drive the plot forward. In the real world, the ghost self does not always result in conflict. Young adult literature often expresses that life is messy and frequently uses the ghost self as a way to provide a comforting explanation for some of life's less satisfactory moments, unlike most stories with their happily ever afters. The ghost self is often portrayed as a manifestation of the internal conflict and turmoil that characters undergo when their inner and outer selves are seriously out of balance, and when characters enter their ghost selves, something drastic always happens.

For example, in *The Liars' Club*, Mary's mother experiences a breaking point when she becomes dissatisfied as a housewife and reminisces about her wealthy past life in New York. Karr's mother came from a very wealthy background, and she continuously reminisces about what her life could have been like if she had made different choices. Because her unhappiness continues to build throughout the first half of the memoir with her husband leaving, the well-being of her inner self falters. Charlie becomes unable to continue creating an outer self for her family that hides her past, which continues to cause her inner self to spiral further into catastrophe. This imbalance eventually leads her to a breaking point, where she enters into her ghost self, burning her family's belongings and making false claims to the police about harming her daughters. Unlike with a regular mental health crisis, when characters enter into their ghost self, something bad always happens.

Another example of the ghost self can be found in *Sunny and the Mysteries of Osisi*. While seeking revenge on the strongest confraternity in Nigeria, the Red Sharks, for attempting to murder her older brother, Sunny loses her self-control due to an imbalance between her moral agency, or inner self, and her existing relationships, her outer self. Sunny has an extremely strong bond with her older brother, and such a vicious attack on his life causes her to abandon her usual inner self in favor of a more emotional and drastic counterpart. Sunny becomes significantly more violent and cold than usual, thus entering into her version of the ghost self. Sunny only returns to normal once her inner self's drive for justice and her outer self's need to reinforce her bond with her brother have been settled. Thankfully, unlike with Sunny and Charlie, the ghost self does not always cause characters to become violent.

The ghost self has different effects depending on a person's reason for abandoning their usual inner selves. Rather than becoming violent because of her ghost self, Rocio from *The Last of the Menu Girls* loses her ability to narrate her own story. This reaction occurs due to her inability to socialize about her true emotions. Her outer self is not succeeding in permitting her to find like-minded people to whom she can express her inner self, so after being stuck without genuine socialization for so long, Rocio enters into her ghost self. The ghost self's presence is always different depending on a character's situation and how their inner and outer selves are imbalanced.

It is also important to note that the ghost self is not a true representation of the afflicted person. Mary herself emphasizes that the voice of her mother in her ghost self is "a hoarse voice I don't think of as hers," (Karr 1995, 149) and Rocio describes her ghost self as a manifestation of a "personality trait" when "you just disappear." (Chavez 2004, 146) These quotations highlight the distorted nature of the ghost self and suggest that the ghost self is a manifestation of the character's internal conflicts and turmoil, which take on separate identities in narratives. This idea once again shares similarities with mental health crises, where people have been known to abandon their usual inner selves and say or do things that they usually would not. People going through mental health crises "may behave in confusing and unpredictable ways and may harm themselves or become threatening or violent toward others." (National Institute of Mental Health 2023) Some people might experience moments of rage where they might punch holes in the walls. Others might have slight differences, like not being able to engage in everyday chores. Thankfully, the ghost self is not a permanent state of being.

The ghost self can also be subverted or escaped through storytelling. Talking about mental health is extremely important, especially when emotional trauma is on the line, and Emily Swaim writes that "telling the story of your trauma can help you shift not only what those memories mean to you but also how they affect you in the present." (Swaim 2022) Through storytelling, individuals can confront and process their innermost thoughts and emotions, allowing them to connect with their inner selves and overcome the pain and trauma they may be suppressing. Young adult literature exemplifies this idea when Rocio becomes a writer and Sunny is continuously asked to share her stories as a form of respect and mythical payment. However, most interestingly, Mary Karr's mother, whose past "was as blank as the West Texas desert she came from," never tells any stories and thus reaps the consequences (Karr 1995, 23). Instead of opening up to her family about any of her traumas or insecurities, she remains silent and turns to alcohol to numb her pain, ultimately leading to her inevitable encounter with her ghost self. Though the ghost self is not a permanent state of being, there is no limit to how long a person might remain in their state of crisis. However, it is important to note that the ghost self is not entirely bad.

The ghost self serves as a catalyst for the creation of the final and most influential form of self, the other self. Other selves come about when characters learn something from their struggles and make a change as they "experience a new kind of self-realization." (Grant 2017) Other selves are also the self that humans use "to define our me-ness" because it takes into account all of the things a character has learned and dealt with in a conflict, and as people grow up, they can create multiple different other selves as they go through different phases and learn more important life lessons (Edwardes 2019, 173). This process can be seen when Rocio describes a scene where she is looking back on her memory "down the aisles of Woolworth's with my other self, Christmastime 1960." (Chaves 2004, 37) Rocio has successfully created another self since her time as a young girl in the 1960s, which is the reason why she refers to her past self as her other self. Mistakes inspire change, and as Cytowic notes, "[T] he human brain learns best by monitoring its mistakes and trying not to repeat them." (Cytowic 2014) Young adult literature is particularly effective in illustrating the creation of other selves, as the genre often focuses on characters who are still in the process of figuring out who they are and what they stand for. Furthermore, the protagonists in these stories often experience significant personal growth as they face challenges and confront their own flaws, thereby creating other selves.

For instance, Sunny begins her story as a troubled girl struggling to understand who she is meant to be. She lacks a true self-image due to the presence of her spirit face and struggles with her destiny after leaving her hometown and traveling to Lagos and eventually Osisi. However, by the end of her story, Sunny has successfully created an other self, becoming a more self-assured and confident person who no longer feels defined by her spirit face. This shift happens because she learned from her conflicts and has made positive changes to her life.

The theme of "other selves" in young adult literature plays a crucial role in the maturation of characters because it not only allows characters to navigate the complexities of identity formation and personal growth but also serves as insight for any readers who can relate to the ontological struggles presented by young adult literature. The other selves represent significant moments of growth and development for characters and often lead to new relationships, new goals, and new outlooks on life. The four distinct types of self—the inner self, the outer self, the ghost self, and the other self—provide readers with valuable insights into the psychological, social, and emotional effects of the different kinds of self on young adult characters as they navigate the challenges of growing up.

References

American Psychological Association. 2019. "Young Children Judge Others Based on Facial Features as Much as Adults." Accessed May 20, 2025. https://www.apa.org/news/press/releases/2019/04/judge-facial-features.

Chávez, Denise. 2004. *The Last of the Menu Girls: A Novel in Stories*. New York: Vintage.

Cytowic, Richard. 2014. "10 Lessons Learned the Hard Way." *Psychology Today*, June. https://www.psychologytoday.com/us/blog/the-fallible-mind/201406/10-lessons-learned-the-hard-way.

Edwardes, Martin P. J. 2019. "What Is a Self? There and Back Again." In *The Origins of Self: An Anthropological Perspective*, 163–89. London: UCL Press. https://doi.org/10.14324/111.9781787356306.

Grant, Megan. 2017. "The Complicated Psychology of 'Hitting Rock Bottom.'" *Bustle*. Accessed May 20, 2025. https://www.bustle.com/p/the-complicated-psychology-of-hitting-rock-bottom-67906.

Herman, Judith L. 1997. *Trauma and Recovery*. New York: Basic Books.

Hester, N., and E. Hehman. 2023. "Dress Is a Fundamental Component of Person Perception." *Personality and Social Psychology Review* 27 (4): 414–33. https://doi.org/10.1177/10888683231157961.

Hunter, H., T. Hill, G. Reid, C. Bourgeois, A. Tiller, and M. L. Fisher. 2020. "Hi, My Name Is Wealthy: Women's Dating Behaviors in Relation to the Perceived Wealth of Prospective Mates." *EvoS Journal: The Journal of the Evolutionary Studies Consortium* 10 (Special Issue 1): 88–105. https://evostudies.org/wp-content/uploads/2020/07/Hunter_et-al_Vol10SpIss1_Revised.pdf.

Karr, Mary. 1995. *The Liars' Club*. New York: Penguin.

Welkin, Leyla. 2013. "Who Holds the Key to Your Box? Trust, Safe Space, and Culture." *Group* 37 (2): 155–66. https://doi.org/10.13186/group.37.2.0155..

Lumen Learning. n.d. "Moral Development." Accessed May 20, 2025.

https://courses.lumenlearning.com/child/chapter/moral-develop ment-2/.

National Institute of Mental Health. 2023. *Understanding Psychosis.* NIH Publication No. 23-MH-8110. Revised February 2023. https://www. nimh.nih.gov/health/publications/understanding-psychosis.

Newman, Sherie. 2020. "The Importance of Self-Esteem." *Child Develop- ment and Family Center, Northern Illinois University.* https://www.chhs. niu.edu/child-center/resources/articles/self-esteem.shtml.

Okorafor, Nnedi. 2018. *Sunny and the Mysteries of Osisi.* Lagos: Cassava Republic.

Swaim, Emily. 2022. "How Narrative Therapy Could Help Heal Com- plex Trauma." *Healthline Media.* https://www.healthline.com/health/ mental-health/narrative-therapy-for-trauma.

Identity Articulations in Mohja Kahf's
The Girl in the Tangerine Scarf

Hamida Riahi, PhD.

Abstract

This paper analyzes identity representations in Anglophone Arab literature, particularly in Mohja Kahf's *The Girl in the Tangerine Scarf*, through the lens of postmodernism and Herman's Dialogical Self Theory. It examines how the protagonist articulates various identity categories and positions shaped by her intersectional identity, creating contesting identities to challenge Eurocentric narratives. The novel portrays Muslim identity diversely, influenced by religion, nationality, and ethnicity, including examples like Syrian, Egyptian, and Iranian Muslims. It underscores the complexity of Muslim identity, characterized by intra-differences. It further elucidates that identity is a *continual process* and does not have a static origin. Additionally, it investigates how identity is *hybrid* and encompasses different *I-positions*, including meta-positions and third positions, enabling the female Muslim protagonist to navigate diverse perspectives within her surroundings.

Keywords: Contesting Identity, Intersectionality, I-Positions, Hybridity

Introduction

The term "Contesting Identities" in Anglophone Arab literature pertains to the process of opposing and subverting the prevalent and oversimplified perceptions and misconceptions surrounding Arab Muslim identity as imposed by the dominant Western cultures. It represents a revisionary endeavor that disputes the conventional understanding of "Muslim" identity by critically examining and re-evaluating established beliefs and assumptions. Therefore, the examination of identity representation in Mohja Kahf's *The Girl in the Tangerine Scarf* as a case study concentrates on the representation of diverse identity formations which embody "revisionary spaces" challenging the essentialist Eurocentric gaze about Muslims and Arabs.

According to Susan Muaadi Darraj (2002), the writing produced by Anglophone Arab authors after the 9/11 events centers on matters of identity politics and global political developments. This is because Arab immigrants are often viewed as adversaries in their new homeland, which they must contend with while also striving to survive. As a result, they are frequently exposed to hostile imagery and experiences that are explored in their written works (124). Otherwise stated, these writers are engaged in the critical projects of writing back to the center, addressing the subject of identity to reflect on matters of belonging, and violence, without discarding their efforts towards gender justice. To put it another way, representations of identity in this chapter delineate the way in which these topics are responded to and addressed.

The examination of identity therefore fits under the "revisionary spaces" created in response to an urgent question in the aftermath of the 9/11 events: "Who those 'Arabs' really were." (Al Maleh 2009, 1) Self-definition has not always been a straightforward process for Arab Muslim women writers. They have had to confront a range of challenges in their creative writing about identity, which requires an understanding of the various factors that shape it. When writing back to the center, they have to contend with a variety of situations and contexts. As Amel Amireh and Suhair Majaj brilliantly posit in the introduction to *Going Global: The Transnational Reception of Third World Women Writers* (2012), the "contexts of reception" represent important determining variables that have an impact on their writing. The major problem is "how they are read, understood, and located institutionally which is of paramount importance." (2) How their works are perceived and read has been impacted by how they are mediated via translation, editing, publication, and marketing (2). All of these processes were impacted by a manufactured pre-given identity of the "third world woman," an identity formed by Orientalism and under which Arab Muslim diasporic women were positioned.

The events of 9/11 have forced Anglophone Arab writers to confront the "'write or be written about' imperative: Define yourself or others will define you." (Majaj 1999, 125) In a time when the west wanted to understand "who those Arabs were," and with the appearance of a Neo-Orientalist group of Arab writers producing "a victimization story," (112) they have found themselves in front of an ethical role of writing to fill that space and oppose all these powers and situations. Arabs in the diaspora are forced to write against the grain of Orientalist narratives and bigotry leveled at them, particularly in terms of deportation and monitoring.

The structure of the paper includes an introduction that provides a literature review on the subject, followed by analytical sections that delve into the various categories and I-positions of identity depicted in Kahf's novel. The analysis draws on postmodern theories, particularly the ideas of Avtar Brah and Stuart Hall, as well as Herman's Dialogical Self theory. The novel illustrates four primary articulations of identity: the multiplicity of Muslim identity, Muslim is multiple, Muslim is complex, identity as a process, and identity as hybridity and I-positions.

1. Muslim is Multiple: Rhizomic / Intersectional Identity

Rhizomic is a term used by Deleuze and Guattari in *A Thousand Plateaus* (1987) to describe a non-hierarchical, interconnected system. Unlike traditional roots, a rhizome is a "subterranean stem" that represents multiplicity and diverse forms (6-7). This concept, often interchangeable with "multiplicity," helps to understand how identity is represented as multiple and intersectional. Deleuze and Guattari also explore intersectionality, asking if the rhizome intersects with roots, a concept further developed by Kimberlé Crenshaw in the 1990s (13). Rhizomic identity thus reflects how Anglophone Arab women writers depict their identities as multifaceted and shaped by various categories.

Basic to the rhizometic dimension is the *principle of multiplicity* which states that when multiple elements are treated as a substantive entity, they no longer have any relationship to a single, unified entity. Multiplicities are interconnected and dynamic, rather than being organized in a hierarchical structure. There is no central point or unity within a multiplicity, only various determinations, magnitudes, and dimensions that change as the multiplicity grows. According to Deleuze, multiplicities have no subject or object, only different elements that interact with each other (8). Following this line of thought, identity categories such as gender, race, religion, ethnicity, and nationality, etc., are all significant components that come together to form a person's unique "rhizomic identity." A rhizomic identity is, therefore, an intersectional identity because it recognizes that an individual's identity is made up of many different and interconnected layers, each of which is considered of equal importance and cannot be separated from one another.

Vivian May (2015) suggests that intersectionality goes against mainstream thinking, challenging established political frameworks and contesting conventional understanding of subjectivity and agency. According to this approach, individuals possess "multiple and enmeshed forms of [...] identity," (X) which aligns with the concept of a rhizomic identity. Like a rhizome, one's identity is "interlaced with multiple forms and multiplicities." (3) Intersectionality's approach to identity is important because "one aspect of identity [...] is not treated as separable or as superordinate." (3) In other words, no single aspect of a person's identity is considered more important or superior to others. The idea of intersectionality brings to light all the aspects of a person's identity that are neglected or concealed when they are only defined by a single identifier, like "Muslim" in the case of the Muslim woman. This single-dimension approach ignores the complex, interconnected elements that form a person's identity, including their nationality, ethnicity, and others.

In *Muslim Diaspora: Gender, Culture and Identity* (2006), Haideh Moghissi argues that the Muslim diaspora is "heterogeneous," inter alia, "because of national-cultural idiosyncrasies." (xiv) Consequently, nationality constitutes another aspect that characterizes "Muslims," in addition to religion. Similarly, Saeed Rahnema (2006) posits that "Muslims are distinct in terms of ethnic and national groupings, such as Arabs, Pakistanis, Indians, Turks, Kurds, Algerians, Nigerians, Iranians, Somalis, Indonesians, Chinese and many others." (29) Despite belonging to a common ethnic group, there is substantial diversity even within it. For example, despite a shared Arab ethnicity, Arab American and Arab British individuals display marked differences due to their varying national origins. Hence, to identify them solely as "Muslim" without due consideration for the other elements of their intersectional identity is inadequately reductionist.

As Avtar Brah (1996) asserts, labeling someone's identity, such as "Ugandan" in her example, can be problematic because "this naming rendered invisible all the other identities—of gender, caste, religion, linguistic group, generation." (3) Speaking about all the other "multiplicities" is to challenge that identity that is "reduced to 'looks,'" as Brah explains about her own experience in the diaspora. In the context of Arab Muslim women in the diaspora, they challenge the notion of identity that is shaped by external factors such as appearance, language, and skin color, among others.

Mohja Kahf's *The Girl in the Tangerine Scarf* underscores the diverse identity within the Muslim community of Indianapolis. The Dawah center, a focal point of the community, reflects this diversity with families like the Al-Deens, Abdul-Khadirs, and a Cambodian family. Additionally, the Haqiqat family from Iran, Kuldip Khan from Pakistan, and the Nabolsy family, including a white American convert, contribute to the center's richness. The Shamy family, prominent members from Syria, and Uncle Abdullah, an Egyptian with two wives, are also notable members.

In this context, intersectionality is used to understand the multi-faceted identities of Muslims living in the diaspora. This approach explains that their identity is not solely defined by religion, but encompasses a variety of other factors and experiences that are integral to who they are. It highlights that these various elements of identity are interconnected and cannot be ignored or erased.

Kahf blends various ethnic, national, and religious identities. Indeed, Khadra Shamy, during a period of re-evaluation and self-discovery, chooses to embrace and celebrate the intersection of her Syrian heritage through honoring the embodiment of her grandmother Teta. Khadra remembers Syria only "in flashes of words and tastes." (15) However, it is represented by her grandmother Teta, who periodically visits them, as the Shamys, being political opponents of the Assad regime, are unable to return to their homeland and must live in self-imposed exile. For Khadra, "Syria was Teta, sitting on a wet wooden crate in the bath with a modesty cloth on her lap." (270) While soaping Teta's back and pouring warm water over it, Khadra embraces her Syrian self as she listens to the stories Teta shares.

Through Teta's stories and character, Khadra realizes she cannot discard other facets of her identity. The narrator reveals this through Teta's wisdom:

I'm telling you the truth. You are allowed to know the truth about yourself. Besides, you have to have an ego, te'ebrini-of course! You have to have one to live! Who can live without a self? Ego is not the same as an ego monster. You must nurture and guide your ego with care. You must never neglect it. To be unaware of it, how it is working underneath everything you do, to think of yourself as floating high above the normal level of humanity, selfless and pure-why, that is what gets you in the greatest danger. (270)

Teta plays a significant role in helping Khadra understand the significance of embracing her true identity, which is unique and separate from the various versions of herself imposed by the Muslim community, her parents, or society at large. Drawing on Stuart Hall's ideas on identity, Kahf highlights the concept of the "true self" and emphasizes the importance of staying true to one's authentic self. It is as he says, "some real self inside there, hiding inside the husks of all the false selves that we present to the rest of the world. It is a kind of guarantee of authenticity. Not until we get inside and hear what the true self has to say do we know what we are 'saying.'" (64)

Teta embodies the essence of life through her love for music and beauty, contrasting sharply with the joyless, rigid Islamic lifestyle of the Shamy family, who see music as frivolous and forgetful of God (77). Teta encourages Khadra to embrace her authentic self, including her Syrian heritage. Teta's marriage for love, despite traditional expectations, contrasts with the structured marriages endorsed by Khadra's parents. She questions Khadra's lack of romantic connection with her husband, longing for the passion she had with her Circassian husband, whom her parents had rejected. Teta's belief that "God is beautiful, loves beauty" underscores her vibrant personality and the harmonious coexistence of her national and religious identities. Her example as a practicing Muslim highlights the Dawah community's failure to recognize the importance of love, melody, affection, and physical allure in one's identity.

The emphasis on ethnicity as "substantive multiplicity" that adds to being Muslim is also clearly explained by Kahf when depicting Muslims of African descent. She explores the idea that ethnic heritage like religion is in addition a key component of identity in the lives of Muslim African Americans. In the novel, Hakim, a childhood friend of Khadra, reveals that he has been hiding a secret from his wife because of her strict Islamic Wahabi beliefs. He tells Khadra that he enjoys playing the trombone at a club downtown, but has had to give it up for a while due to his wife's objections. Kahf asks through Khadra's words, "why couldn't [he]... do both?" suggesting that one's religious and ethnic identity should not conflict and one should be able to express both aspects of his identity.

Combining different parts of one's identity can be a difficult task for those in the traditional Muslim community, mainly because of the rigid rules and views they hold based on their traditional understanding of Islam. As insinuated by the narrator, this discrepancy is revealed as such:

> She pictures him stepping up to the minbar and giving a moving khutba, then turning to a large black case on the floor and picking up a fat brass trombone. Putting it to his lips and sending shivers up and down the spines of a whole floor full of congregants. They start to smile and groove. Never happen. (394)

The perception of incompatibility between Islam and music stems from a traditional interpretation rather than a focal point emphasized by the religion itself. To counter this perspective, the author highlights the significance of the identity category of ethnicity.

Hakim's sister, Hanifa, shares a similar challenge in balancing multiple aspects of her identity. As a teenager, Khadra, who acts as a sort of watchdog for the behavior of her Muslim community, finds Hanifa guilty for "listening to music. UnIslamic music." Hanifa is also deemed guilty of taking the family car for "joyrides," and Khadra finds her engaging in "UnIslamic behavior" in the back seat of the wrecked car (129). Due to her violation of the boundaries set by the Muslim community, Hanifa is sent to live with "her non-Muslim grandmother in Alabama" and "leave Khadra in the lurch." (129)

Later on, as Khadra comes to accept her true self and realizes that her previous actions have not been genuine, she understands that Hanifa's actions are a part of her identity, and an aspect of her ethnic heritage as a Black girl from a cultural background of non-Muslims. Through the protagonist's voice, Kahf highlights the significance of ethnicity in the lives of Muslims:

> Well, she was related to non-Muslims, wasn't she? She was related to this music, to Lionel Ritchie, to some old non-Muslim grandmother in Alabama. She could just up and leave this life she had where Khadra was her friend, where you abided by the Total Islamic Lifestyle, and go somewhere else. Be some other person. (129)

In Kahf's perspective, the religious identity of Muslims from various ethnic backgrounds does not conflict with the cultural aspects that their ethnic identity contributes to their lives. According to her, there is no notion of incompatible identity categories.

In a similar vein, Kahf critiques the tendency of some traditional Muslims to try to force their beliefs onto others from different cultural and ethnic backgrounds. The Shamys serve as the embodiment of this judgmental attitude, as they act as radar, scrutinizing and criticizing other Muslims for retaining parts of their past. For example, when visiting Uncle Jamal and Aunt Khadija, Khadra's parents disregard the wall of music in the Al-Deen townhouse, which is a mirror image of the Shamys who fail to comprehend why this monument of their pre-Muslim years is still present (22).

Khadra envisions a mosque, known as the Teta's Mosque, where prayer can coexist with music and where members of the Muslim community from different ethnic and national backgrounds can freely practice their religion and embrace all parts of their identity. She shares this idea with her brother Jihad who has similar views on integration. In the Teta Mosque, the discriminatory attitudes will be changed and everyone will be treated as equals, regardless of religion, and they will connect as human beings under the sun, with a special lamplight that makes everyone beautiful:

> 'I'd like to build a TEta-mosque,' she said to Jihad on the phone. … 'You'd pray, then you'd listen to music and poetry and wisdom from all over the world. You'd go walking arm in arm with your counterpart in every other religion and just relate as humans under the sun. Everyone would be beautiful-there'd be a special sort of lamplight that made you beautiful. (328)

Kahf's perspective on the significance of embracing intersectional identity, encompassing nationality, ethnicity, and religion, is evident in the protagonist's dream of constructing a mosque that incorporates and acknowledges all these facets of individual identity.

Advocating for a rhizomatic approach to identity that incorporates national and ethnic categories aims to deconstruct the notion of a rigid and overly simplified "Muslim" identity. This is a form of resistance that critiques the Eurocentric perspective that generalizes and oversimplifies the Muslim experience by homogenizing it into a single, stereotypical category. It is a critique of the view that "Islam [is ...] an all-encompassing category." (Saliba 2000, 2) Muslim women authors are perceived as utilizing their literary works as a means of resisting reductionist categorization and demonstrating their multifaceted nature as individuals. They reject the notion of being confined to a narrow, limiting identity and instead seek to showcase the full range of their experiences, emotions, and humanity through their writing.

In the same vein, Kahf emphasizes the "multiple" nature of the "Muslim" identity as a means of pushing back against the cultural hegemony of certain ethnic groups, such as Arabs, over other Muslims from diverse nationalities. By emphasizing the intersectional pluralistic nature of identity, Kahf seeks to subvert attempts to impose a monolithic cultural identity on all Muslims and instead assert the diversity and complexity of their experiences and perspectives. Rahnema (2006) warns against the faith-based approach of multiculturalism, arguing that it neglects the internal diversity within the Muslim community by prioritizing conservative religious leaders. He cautions specifically about the dangers of having Islam represented predominantly by these conservative figures (29). Comparably, Kahf depicts the same issue through the opposition that Khadra faces with the customary beliefs of the Dawah Center and her family.

The identity "Muslim" becomes complicated with the addition of other intersecting factors such as nationality and ethnicity; a step that necessitates the further implementation of intersectionality as a strategy that has a fundamental impact in forming and shaping identity. In other words, "Muslim identity is no longer exclusively religious, but has ethnic [...] dimensions as well," (Shryock 2010, 6) which reflects the diversity and complexity of the Muslim community. Intersectionality serves as a resistance strategy, playing a crucial role in the formation of contesting identities aimed at challenging the Eurocentric Orientalist perspective on Muslims and Arabs. This role will be further examined in the subsequent sections.

2. Muslim is Complex: The Many Shades of Identity

The "Muslim-is-complex" identity suggests that there is no single, definitive representation of what it means to be *a Muslim*, and that the Muslim community is made up of a diverse range of groups and individuals with different beliefs and practices. That is because the concept of a universal and uniform understanding of *Muslims* is called into question. The representation of identity in Kahf's novel is a response to the reductionist, oversimplified, and stereotypical view of Islam that prevails in the West. This view is based on the assumption that the Muslim community constitutes a uniform and monolithic religious group, and is perpetuated by the notion that all members of this community are fundamentalists. *The Girl in the Tangerine Scarf* aims to challenge this essentialist perception and instead offers a complex and nuanced understanding of the Muslim identity, emphasizing that "being Muslim wasn't such a straitjacket." (344)

The protagonist's journey indicates a multifaceted identity. Khadra Shamy challenges the belief, held by three characters, that "Islam was rigid and homogenous." She contests her mother's beliefs and those of Cherif who "both wanted Islam to be this monolith, only for her mother it was good, for him bad." (344) Furthermore, she criticizes her friend Semi's ideas about Islam that it is similar to "Islamic fundamentalism." (332) The three characters depicted in the story each embody distinct perspectives: the mother embodies the views of conventional Muslims, Cherif represents the views of secular Muslims, and Semi, a Pakistani "agnostic," embodies the views of Neo-Orientalists.

The concept of complicating the category "Muslim" involves using the concept of "self-difference," as articulated by Jacques Derrida, to challenge the idea of a fixed or singular definition of what it means to be Muslim. Difference is axiomatic when grappling with identity. Each identity marker is full of differences. It is not augmenting an existing identity category, such as religion, with another disparate category, but rather complicating the existing category itself. It is an identity construction that aligns with Derrida's perspective, as articulated in the following statement:

'self-difference' structures every identity. 'There is no
culture or cultural identity [for example] without this
difference with itself '. Every invocation of identity (the
identity of democracy, of a nation-state, of a language,
etc.) has to occlude the fact that no identity is ever identical to 'itself'. (Lucy 2004, 52)

This approach recognizes the diversity and complexity within the Muslim community and acknowledges that the category of "Muslim" cannot
be easily reduced to a single, uniform understanding. In other words, the
idea that no identity can truly be identical to itself means that all identities are inherently dynamic and subject to change, and that there is always some degree of internal diversity and variation within an identity
group. This is because identities are not fixed, absolute categories, but are
instead constructed and maintained through social, cultural, and political
processes.

The diversity in religious identity within Islam is due to the various interpretations that have arisen from a complex interplay of historical, social, cultural, and political elements. Sectarian differences, ethnic-cultural
differences, political ideologies, and personal interpretations, inter alia,
intersect in the individuals' experiences to create a nuanced and multifaceted understanding of the faith. In other words, the identity of Muslims
can be complex due to the self-difference that exists within the concept *of
Muslim*. There are a variety of factors that contribute to this complexity,
including differences in cultural background, national origin, and personal beliefs and practices, among others.

This intersectionality that happens leads to the appearance of sects like
Sunni, Shia, Sufi and others, each with their own beliefs, practices and interpretations of Islamic teachings. Islam is a world religion and the way it
is practiced in many different countries and regions, each with their own
cultural traditions and practices, influences their interpretation of the religion. Moreover, it has often been intertwined with political movements
and ideologies, leading to differences in beliefs and practices. In addition,
it is open to personal interpretations, and individuals may have different
understandings of its teachings based on their own experiences and perspectives. These intersections can lead to diversity and complexity within
the Muslim community.

This intricate complexity of Islam is highlighted in Kahf's novel when the protagonist gradually comes to grips with the multifaceted nature of Islam over the course of various pivotal moments in her life. As a child, she engages in a conversation with her African American Muslim aunt who has changed her name from Kacey Tompson to Khadija. Khadra inquires if the transformation of her name from Kacey to various iterations, including Khadija X, Khadija Kareem, and finally Khadija Al-Deen upon her marriage to Uncle Jamal, signifies the moment in which she becomes a "real Muslim." The novel revolves around this central question as Khadra experiences different facets of Islam, divergent from the version practiced by her parents. Through these encounters, she realizes that there is no single, universal definition of what constitutes a "true Muslim," as Islam is a complex and dynamic faith that is shaped by individual interpretation and historical political factors.

Khadra answers Aunt Khadija that a real Muslim practices the five pillars, follows the teachings of the Qur'an and the Prophet, wears hijab, and lives according to Islamic principles, as taught by her parents and Uncle Tahar at the Dawah Center Sunday lessons when she asks her "[w]hat is a real Muslim Khadra?" (24-5) However, as she goes through different stages of life, interacts with diverse individuals, attends higher education classes, and reads various books, her understanding of what it means to be a true Muslim evolves and changes. She ultimately arrives at the realization that there is no singular, definitive definition of a "true" Muslim. The initial spark that prompts her to ponder the essence of Muslim identity occurs when Aunt Khadija informs her that declaring the "*Shahada*" is what makes one Muslim. This assertion leads Khadra to feel puzzled, as her parents have previously advised her that being a "real Muslim" requires actual practice of Islam (24).

Through the protagonist's journey, Kahf illustrates that Muslim identity is not static; it evolves, influenced by intellectual engagement and significant life events, leading to the formation of various sects and perspectives within Islam. In her teens, Khadra becomes with her friends "impatient with traditional Islamic scholarship, with its tedious, plodding chapters on categories of water purity and how to determine the exact end of menses." (149-50) She undergoes a "radicalization" process after immersing herself in the ideology espoused by Islamist revolutionary Said Qutb.

Similarly, following an encounter with the Shia Nabolsy family, she becomes sympathetic towards the Shia denomination. In an act of intellectual inquiry, she poses a query to her father regarding the historical event of Yezid's slaying of the Prophet's grandson, and expresses bewilderment as to why there is not widespread adherence to the Shia sect as a form of rebellion. Upon being apprised of the details of the massacre, Khadra's previously held convictions undergo a significant reevaluation. This historical event marks a turning point that has a big impact on her belief and religious identity later. The narrator implies that all subsequent Islamic scholarship, following the events of Karbala, is inherently influenced and shaped by the legacy of a violent dynasty:

> The whole rest of the early Islam after the life of the Prophet—including all the scholarship—had been formed under the government of a dynasty that had mercilessly slaughtered the Prophet's grandson and most of his remaining kin. (152)

Consequently, she aligns herself with the Haqiqat sisters, Nilofar and Insaf, to embark on a campaign of "radical activism" to rectify the historical injustices.

This newfound identity as a revolutionary is shaped by her reaction to the narrative surrounding the killing of the Prophet's grandson, much in the same manner as the formation of the Shia sect is rooted in political events, specifically the events of Karbala. The Shia, like the Sunnis, are a religious denomination with a long-standing historical rivalry. Their collective identity is forged in response to the massacre and manifests in distinct modes of worship and interpretation of Islam. During this period of transformation, Khadra, who has embraced Shiaism, collaborates with the Haqiqa sisters to produce "Islam Rules" buttons, which will be available for purchase at Islamic gatherings (155). During this phase, she "donned black headscarves with a surge of righteous austerity that startled her parents [...] Stern in dress and gaze." (149).

In addition, Kahf suggests that American Muslims differ from their predecessors due to assimilation and the first Muslim immigrants experience, resulting in a distinct type of Muslim identity. Khadra's self-perception undergoes a metamorphosis after her encounter with the Shelby family in Mishawaka, Northern Indiana, which comprises Muslims who have undergone the process of assimilation (184). Her shift into a neo-classical phase is evidenced by her changed attire, exemplified by the donning of a "white scarf with tiny flowers like a village meadow in spring, and a pale blue blouse and soft floral skirt," as opposed to her previous preference for a jilbab and plain black scarves, which have now been relegated to the back of her closet (193).

During this phase, she engages with various translated Hadith texts, including works by Ibn Kathir, and at university, she studies Muwatta Ibn Malik, Sahih Muslim, Ibn al-Qayyim al-Jawzia, and *usul al-fiqh* books. For Khadra, the fact that it has been translated by an American Muslim implies that she is reading a version of the text that is free from the patriarchal or misogynistic biases present in traditional tafsir books, as it is produced by an outsider's perspective.

This neo-classical stage is defined by Khadra's focus on studying traditional Islamic heritage, with a particular emphasis on gaining a deeper understanding of her faith. Her motivation arises from a conviction that truth exists somewhere there:

> It seemed to her that the answer lay in there somewhere
> —not in the newfangled Islamic revivalism of her par-
> ents and the Dawh, with its odd mixtures of the modern
> and the Prophetic, and its tendency to come off more
> like a brisk civic action committee than a spiritual faith.
> No, not there, but in the direction of the old Quranic and
> hadith sciences, the various branches of *fiqh* and shariah
> studies, and the spiritual wisdom that had been handed
> down with them for centuries—now *there* was some-
> thing! (194)

At this stage of her journey, Khadra's sense of self is influenced by her quest for a deeper understanding of spiritual faith, as expressed in ancient texts on *fiqh* and *tafsir* of hadith. She begins to challenge her parents' limited view of Islam, which is restricted to mere observances of rituals and practices like *wudu*, ablution, and *salat*.

Kahf emphasizes that Islam is not monolithic, highlighting the diversity within the faith, including various sects such as Sufis. The decisive moment in Khadra's shift in identity occurs when she enrolls in an elective course taught by a German Islamic studies professor. As the semester progresses, she begins to acknowledge that her prior education, which has consisted of lessons at the Dawah Center and Masjid Salam, has only scratched the surface of Islamic teachings. Previously, she had only approached Islam from an internal perspective. However, in Professor Eschenback's class, she begins to see her beliefs from an external viewpoint and gains a new perspective on her religion (231). Islam has been approached and understood in three different ways throughout history. Some have emphasized reason and developed Islamic theology, while others have emphasized revelation and hadith and produced jurisprudence. Some have sought a direct personal connection with God, known as Sufis. The Shariah is considered the divine order of the universe in Islam and *fiqh* is the body of Islamic legal scholarship. Sufis have a different view of the Shariah, but do not play a role in its formation (232).

At this juncture, Khadra comprehends that the interpretation of Islam imparted to her by her parents and their prevailing ideology represents but a single manifestation of the faith, and that Islam encompasses a multitude of diverse perspectives and expressions:

> So the belief system of her parents and their entire circle, including the Dawah Center, was just one point on a whole spectrum of Islamic faith. It wasn't identical to Islam, just one corner of it. What was difficult to accept was that these other paths had always existed beyond the confines of her world, and yet were still Muslim. (132-3)

According to this representation, the complexity of being Muslim is reflected in the diverse ways in which Islam is perceived and practiced, shaped by varying priorities and focal points among Muslims that result in various schools of Islamic thought. Khadra feels conflicted in Professor Eschenbach's class as she is being exposed to new perspectives on Islam which challenge her previous beliefs and understanding. This creates a feeling of instability and fear as her previously held views appear to be wrong and new ideas seem good, causing a rift in her understanding (234).

Kahf suggests in addition that the Islamic faith exhibits self-differentiation, particularly evident in the African-American understanding of Islam during periods like the era of Elijah Muhammad. Khadra consequently confronts her parents' narrow-minded perspective on various facets of Islam by emphasizing the multifaceted nature of faith. When her father disparages the doctrine of Elijah Mohammad as "nonsense," and that "it was good things Black Muslims like Aunt Khadija and Uncle Jammal converted to Islam or they would be wandering astray," Aunt Khadija offers a contrasting perspective by expressing her belief that everyone is born with an innate disposition towards Islam and that her return to the faith is simply a rediscovery of her inherent state of surrender to God. Thus, she prefers the terminology of "reversion" to that of "conversion." (24)

Similarly, Kahf uses intertextual allusion to contradict the idea that true Muslims are Arabs or that Islam is an ethnicity-specific faith. She refers to a saying by Malcom X where he defends the Elijah tradition:

> [T]he Honorable Elijah Muhammad's teaching ... is part of Islamic tradition, not an Isolated, unique invention of half-baked negro theology... Arabs have no monopoly on Islam. (23)

In essence, Kahf underscores the intricacies of the interplay between religion and ethnicity in the African American community, elucidating the multifaceted nature of the Muslim identity. She highlights the significance of the Elijah Muhammad's interpretation of the faith, which provides a nuanced understanding of Islam as perceived by a non-Arab ethnic group. Kahf endeavors to explain how sacred texts are perceived and interpreted differently by various cultural groups.

From the same perspective, the "Mishawaka Muslims" serve as a compelling illustration of the complex identity that arises from cultural differences. These Arab Muslims, who migrated as far back as the 1870s, gradually assimilated into the new way of life, and as Wajdy Shamy posits in "The Islamic Forerunner," over time, "they had mixed American things in with real Islam" (103). Kahf accentuates the impact of ethnicity on the understanding of Islam and the Mishawaka Muslims exemplify how Muslim Arabs transformed into American Muslims through the process of assimilation, imbuing elements of American culture into their faith.

Kahf critiques the assumption that birth Muslims have a monopoly on Islam, challenging the arrogance of those who feel entitled to dictate to African-American Muslims despite lacking an earlier "awakened Islamic consciousness." (31) Khadra's father exemplifies this prejudice, viewing Muslims who follow a distinct spiritual path, such as the Mishawaka community, as needing a "refresh course in real Islam" because they "didn't even look like Muslims." (103)

In this context, Khadra is depicted as opposing the belief held by her parents that they possess a dominant and exclusive control over the religion of Islam. She vehemently disagrees with her parents' perspective regarding Muslims who do not adhere to the same religious practices as they do, and this disagreement stems from their tendency to disapprove of these individuals, "[s]haking their heads and calling them 'lost Muslims, led astray by Satan, following their base ego desires instead of God's law'." (334)

As a result of her dissent, the protagonist embarks on a journey of personal growth and development, separating herself from her familial ties and the Dawah Center. This transformation is driven by a series of personal experiences, including a failed marriage, an abortion, and a divorce, all of which are caused by the misogyny prevalent in the culture of her Muslim community. The dissonance she experiences due to the contradictions between the principles of Islam and the actions of her community has a profound effect on her future beliefs, ultimately leading to her disillusionment. The writer uses the protagonist's encounters with sexism in the Muslim community to highlight the similarities between the behavior of "popular Muslims" and the "Modern Islamists such as the Dawah folk" who "revived many concepts from classical Islam," but perpetuate patriarchal values (251).

Kahf argues that identity is shaped by personal interpretations, including Islamic feminism. Her experiences and ideals are influenced by her education and friends like Semi and Blue. Before her disillusionment, Khadra lacks a distinct self, or Nafs. During this transformation, she learns to create space for her individuality, allowing her to make her own choices and understand Islam in a way that aligns with her beliefs. The narrator reports:

> *Hello, self? Can we meet at last?* It was not vainglorious to have a self. It was not the same as selfish individualism, no. You have to have a self to even start on a journey to God. To cultivate your *nafs* whom God invites to enter the Garden at the end of Surat *al-Fajr*. She had not taken

411

even a baby step in that direction. Her self was a meager
thing. (148)

During this newfound phase, Kahdra endeavors to free herself from constraints that have become oppressive to her. To embark on her spiritual
journey towards God, she must divest herself of prior learned beliefs and
practices.

Kahf explores moreover the spiritual dimension of Islam through Khadra's
changing perspective on rituals like *salat*, as she seeks a deeper understanding of her faith beyond her parents' superficial practices. Khadra's
American identity complicates her interpretation of Islam, creating tension with her mother's beliefs. She resents her mother's assumption that
she lacks true faith simply because she disagrees with her parents' version of Islam. She strives for a more spiritual comprehension of her faith,
finding fulfillment through introspection rather than traditional practices
(326-7). This inner nourishment allows her to sustain and grow her spiritual life independently of external influences. Kahf asserts moreover that
divine law can manifest in various forms and should not be confined to
a rigid "Islamic lifestyle." Through the protagonist, she emphasizes that a
personal connection to Islam arises from *love*, not *hate*, highlighting the
profound significance of the Qu'ran and ritualistic prayers (401-2).

The complexity of what Atar Brah (1996) refers to as "the intra-Muslim
differentiations" (47) highlights the multifaceted nature of the Muslim
identity. As demonstrated in Kahf's novel, the Muslim identity is not uniform and the interpretation and understanding of Islam is influenced by
a variety of historical, political, ethnic, and individual factors. "Muslim
is complex" therefore is a contesting identity that serves to counter the
reductionist and stereotypical Orientalist gaze, which oversimplifies the
Muslim community and fuels racist sentiments towards them.

3. Identity as Process: Between the Home(land) and Hostland

Kahf's perspective on identity formation involves transcending imposed
boundaries and questioning fixed origins. Khadra Shamy revisits Syria to
deepen her self-understanding and explore her identity's roots in both her
homeland and adopted country, creating a nuanced sense of self. During
her visit to Jobar Kanees, the oldest synagogue still in use, near Damascus, she meets a rabbi who speaks with a familiar Damascene accent. This

encounter profoundly impacts her, making her feel a familial connection and prompting her to rethink her previous notions of identity and origin:

> And then this whole other life opened up in her mind. It sent her whirling in mad agony. This incidental skin, this name she wore like a badge—glance down, check it—what was it again? Had it changed? Was it always changing? Who was she? What was she, what cells of matter, sewn up into this Khadra shape, this instar? Imagine! (306).

Kahf undertakes a re-examination of the concept of identity by scrutinizing its fundamental constituents, including the body, skin, name, and cellular composition, only to discover that they remain immutable, regardless of the protagonist's possible lineage as the granddaughter of a rabbi.

The protagonist's encounter prompts her to rethink her understanding of her identity, realizing that it transcends simple categorization based on race, geography, culture, and religion, among other identity categories. Previously, she has thought about Jews for instance as the "others" who are different from the self. However, as she reflects on her experiences, she realizes that these individuals are connected to her past and origins, thus blurring the perceived boundaries between "us" and "them." (305-6) This epiphany highlights the fluidity and interconnectedness of identity, challenging the notion of fixed and distinct categories of self and other.

The distinction between "them" and "us" has dissolved for Khadra, as she now recognizes a shared commonality with all individuals, regardless of their cultural or social background. She experiences a profound realization:

> She slept and woke. Slept again. Dreamt, cried and blessed. They came to her, all the people she had once held at bay, as if behind a fiberglass wall. Now the barrier was removed, and they all rushed into her heart, and it hurt: Livvy. Hanifa. I'm Litfy. Joy's Assyrian boyfriend, whose holocaust she'd denied. Droves of people, strangers and neighbors. We are your kin, we are part of you. Where are those who love one another through my Glory?" (308)

Khadra has come to understand that her identity is not confined to a singular, essential category but is instead the product of historical displacements. As Brah argues, origin is not fixed but a "matter of historical displacements." (194)

In this context, Kahf highlights a *syncretic* identity that merges various cultural and social categories into a new hybrid form. As Ella Shohat notes in *Unthinking Eurocentrism* (2014), the term 'syncretism' in postcolonial literature draws attention to the diverse identities created by the geographical displacements of the post-independence era. This concept is rooted in anti-essentialist poststructuralist theory, which rejects the enforcement of pure, singular identities. Diasporic intellectuals, who are often hybrids themselves, have played a key role in developing this hybrid identity framework (41).

Brah's definition of diaspora identity as a "process" is relevant in comprehending the representation of diaspora identity in this novel:

> [d]iasporas ought not to be theorised as transhistorical codifications of eternal migrations, or conceptualised as the embodiment of some transcendental diasporic consciousness. Rather, the concept of diaspora should be seen to refer to historically contingent 'genealogies', in the Foucauldian sense of the word. That is to say that the term should be seen as conceptual mapping which defies the search for originary absolutes, or genuine and authentic manifestations of a stable, pre-given, unchanging identity; for pristine, pure customs and traditions or unsullied glorious pasts. (193)

Brah argues that the development and expression of diasporic identities are not fixed or pre-determined but rather are shaped by a variety of historical and cultural factors. This definition emphasizes the fluid and dynamic nature of diasporic identities and recognizes that they are constantly evolving and changing over time.

The "cultural mixing" at the level of religion (Shohat 2014, 42) shows that "hybridity has existed from time immemorial, as civilizations conflict, combine, and synthesize." (43) In other words, cultural mixing that Shohat explains involves connecting disparate histories and geographies in ways that allow for new and different understandings of identity, as Amireh (2012) posits "Shohat creates a kind of a dialogue between geographies and histories that are usually kept separate." (20)

The novel also exemplifies the syncretic and hybrid nature of identity through the architecture and Sufi "*dhikrs*" of the mosque of Muhyideen Ibn al-Arabi, to which Khadra is drawn. As Shohat contends, "syncretism has always pervaded history and the arts," (43) and this is evident in the mosque's design and rhythms of dhikr, which reflect a fusion of different styles that have influenced Syria over time, including Ottoman and Arab influences. The narrator's description of the mosque's architecture highlights the contrast of dark brick and white stone, and dark and light skin tones, typical of traditional Damascus architecture: "Dark brick, white stone, dark flesh and white side by side, striped the arch-work of the mosque, as it did everywhere in Damascus's traditional architecture." Khadra's stillness as she listens to the faint rhythms of the dhikrs conveys a sense of reverence and appreciation for this syncretic blend of cultural influences (292).

Arab Americans who migrated and settled in their new host countries possess identities that are marked by syncretism, according to Shohat's framework. This syncretism is a product of a dialogue between the histories and cultures of their countries of origin and their new homes, which shapes their sense of identity. Kahf's novel uses the history of Arab Muslim immigration to establish their identity, frequently denied to them. It is through Khadra's friend Joy who belongs to the Mishawaka, an older group of Muslims who migrated as far back as the 1870s that Kahf explains how these early immigrants contributed in the making of society. In the beginning, Khadra's father has taught her that the Mishawaka had mixed American culture with Islam and needed a refresher course in real Islam. However, her perspective changes after she visits Syria and realizes that the idea of ethnic purity is a lie, as there is no such thing as pure origin or ethnicity.

Khadra learns to accept the Mishawaka Muslims as part of her community, despite their different practices like not wearing hijabs or having beards, and engaging in activities like volleyball and dancing (103). Kahf explains the assimilation of early immigrants through Joy's recounting of her family's history: "[I]t was a different era when my grandfather came over [...]

He was just a farm boy. Immigrants were more afraid back then [...]. Less educated. They did whatever the Ellis Island officer said [...]. If he told you Anglicize your name, you did. Sorry, it doesn't meet your standards of ethnic purity." (184) The novel underscores in addition the vital contributions of early Arab American immigrants, exemplified through Joy's family history of working in a steel factory. Joy's family album symbolizes their integral role in shaping identity and highlights the significance of the Arab American community in the country's history.

The Girl in the Tangerine Scarf illustrates that the Arab Muslim diasporic self's identity is a multifaceted construct shaped by the intersectionality of various categories. This construct is in a perpetual state of flux, as the diasporic self navigates its way through different social and cultural environments. Therefore, the diasporic self's identity can be understood as a dynamic process that is constantly evolving, rather than a fixed and static entity. Intersectionality serves thus as a methodological approach to construct this *contesting identity as process*, aiming to confront narratives and discourses rooted in racism and white supremacy. These narratives often advocate for Arabs and Muslims to adhere to a fixed homeland, and intersectionality is employed as a means of resistance against such perspectives.

4. Identity as Hybridity and I-Positions

Identity is also hybridity. This means that immigrant identity is not solely determined by the culture and identity categories of their homeland or their new hostland, but rather by a fusion of both. Homi Bhabha introduced the term "hybridity" and defines it as a "third space" that allows for the emergence of new positions, rather than simply tracing two original moments from which a third emerges. This third space challenges the histories that define it and creates new structures of authority and political initiatives that cannot be adequately understood through conventional wisdom (211).

Kahf for instance emphasizes this type of identity after the return of the protagonist after she visits Syria. The protagonist has a deep connection with her homeland, Syria. She is drawn to the soil, air, and architectural beauty of Syria, which satisfies a fundamental need within her and corresponds to the essence of her identity. However, though she loves her country of origin, she acknowledges that Syria's political situation is restrictive, and her path to return is blocked. Nevertheless, "she knew at last that it was in the American crucible where her character had been forged, for good or ill." Despite being brought involuntarily, she accepts that she is now on a path that leads to a new identity and a different way of life. She cannot go back to her old life or phone home (313).

Indeed, the protagonist's identity is not defined solely by her Syrian heritage or her experiences in the host country, but rather by the intersectionality of both cultures, resulting in a hybrid and newfangled identity. As Deleuze and Guattari (1986) explain, upon their "flight" or immigration, diasporic identities undergo a process of "deterritorialization according to which they change in nature and connect with other multiplicities." (9) As Brah (1996) argues in this regard, "diasporic journeys are essentially about settling down, about putting roots 'elsewhere.'" (179) This hybrid identity reflects the complexities of her experiences as an immigrant and the various social, cultural, and political factors that have shaped her worldview. As such, her identity represents a unique synthesis of both her origins and new context influences, rather than a simple binary or singular identity.

Being an Arab Muslim American diasporic woman constructs this "third space" that allows for the emergence of new positions and structures of authority, as Bhabha (1990) suggests. This "third space" challenges the Eurocentric gaze that defines her Syrian, Arab, and Muslim identity and creates new possibilities for her. This space can be understood by drawing on Hubert Hermans' Dialogical Self Theory. The dialogical self refers to the idea that the self is not a fixed entity, but rather a dynamic multiplicity of "I-positions" that emerge from the individual's interaction with their social environment. These I-positions are shaped by specific contexts and are not independent of time and space. The self, as an embodied entity, can move from one position to another as situations and time change. This process of positioning, repositioning, and counter-positioning can cause the self to fluctuate among different and even opposing positions within the self and between the self and others.

In the *Handbook of Dialogical Self Theory* (2012), Hermans declares that these positions are also involved in relationships of relative dominance and social power (2). I-positions are defined as follows:

> I-positions are stabilized routines that find their origin in
> highly dynamic processes of positioning. Such positions
> become 'identities' when they are an answer to the ques-
> tion 'Who am I?' or 'Who are we?' as defined by oneself
> or one's social environment. DST assumes that there is
> not only a multiplicity of I-positions but also, by implica-
> tion, a multiplicity of identities (I-dentities). (17)

Khadra Shamy's I-positions are shaped by her intersectional identity as a
woman, Arab, Muslim, and American, and they undergo a continual process of positioning and repositioning. The protagonist faces oppression
from Muslim misogyny due to her upbringing in a community that follows a strict Islamic lifestyle. To reflect on her situation, she adopts what
Hermans (2022) calls a meta-position; that is to say, "the I can leave a specific position and even a variety of positions and observe them from the
outside, as an act of self-reflection." (9) Khadra's journey, including her
trip to Syria, her visit to the Shelbys, her Islamic studies with professor
Eschenbach, her conversations with feminist Semi and secularist Cherif, and her struggles with marriage, abortion, and divorce due to Muslim
misogyny, among other experiences, leads her to adopt a meta-position.
This I-position involves revising her understanding of what it means to
be Muslim, rejecting the misogyny that she sees as originating from her
Arab ethnicity.

Upon returning to Indianapolis after seven years, Khadra is shocked to
find that the Muslim community still practices Islam in the same traditional ways, with segregation between the sexes. This realization underscores the ongoing struggle Khadra faces in reconciling her different
I-positions, as she seeks to navigate the tensions between her intersecting
identities and the various positions that she holds:

> So here they are. God, she thinks, surveying the rows
> in salah. My God, they're still pottering along the same
> way, the same old tired language, the same old restrictive
> ideas and crabbed beliefs. Oh sure, some people thought
> about changing the old mentality [...]. And, of course,
> the people of Dawah weren't all the same. Some were
> quite freethinking, on their own, when it came down
> to it. But the Dawah as an *institution* still is what it is.

> Institutions tend to be like that, holding on to systems
> and perpetuating them. And it's so-limited and cramped
> and-she sighs-just out and-out wrong. Always stressing
> the *wrong* side of religion, the fear-God side instead of
> love-God. Always stressing the outer forms over the in-
> ner light. (422)

The protagonist's perspective can be characterized as that of a liberal and progressive I-position, as she is critical of the Dawah institution and its teachings. She critiques the emphasis on the *fear* of God, as opposed to the *love* of God, which she feels is limiting and narrow-minded. She fur-ther suggests that the institution's emphasis on outward displays of religi-osity, such as strict adherence to rituals and rules, ignores the significance of one's inner spiritual life and personal connection with God. In essence, the protagonist advocates for a more all-encompassing and open-minded approach to Islam that places greater value on individual spiritual explo-ration and personal growth.

The novel portrays a "third position" in the protagonist's veiling and un-veiling positioning. As described by Hermans (2022), this position is:

> [w]hen there is a conflict between two positions in the
> self, this can be reconciled by the creation of a third po-
> sition that has the potential of unifying the two origi-
> nal ones without denying or removing their differences
> (unity-in-multiplicity). (10)

The protagonist experiences conflicting emotions regarding her veiling and unveiling. She is conflicted between her desire to remove her veil based on personal preference and her fear of losing her cultural identity as a Muslim woman.

During her trip to Syria, Khadra experiences a moment of enlightenment when her headscarf unintentionally falls off, symbolizing a "kashf" or un-veiling of light, as she realizes that veiling and unveiling are integral to her soul's development (309). On the plane, she drapes her "depatta" over her head to assert her cultural heritage at customs, countering the Orientalist view of Muslim women as oppressed (313). This act reflects her reconcil-iation of veiling and unveiling, integrating both into her identity.

Conclusion

Identity articulations are a response to the need for alternative spaces that offer nuanced and complex depictions of Arabs and Muslims in the US, from "an anti-homogenous lens," to use Conrey's (2014) words (534). The 9/11 attacks triggered an increase in racial profiling and discriminatory labeling of Arabs and Muslims leading to a homogenization of the group and the formation of negative stereotypes. In response to this, these literary works as this paper demonstrates aim to challenge these stereotypes and provide a more diverse and multifaceted representation that reject exclusionary Eurocentric Orientalist views about Arabs and Muslims. Kahf's novel is a fresh and alternative perspective on Muslims/Arabs, which frequently revolves around the concept of multiple, complex, dynamic, syncretic, and hybrid identities. Intersectionality therefore as practiced in Kahf's novel illustrates how identity can function as a form of resistance strategy. It proves how this methodology is a successful tool that creates different contesting identities that aim to achieve this resistance.

References

Al Malah, Layla, ed. 2009. *Arab Voices in Diaspora: Critical Perspectives on Anglophone Arab Literature*. Rodopi B.V.

Bhabha, Homi K., ed. 1990. *Nation and Narration*. Routledge.

Brah, Avtar. 1996. *Cartographies of Diaspora: Contesting Identities*. Routledge.

Conrey, Carol Fadda. 2014. *Contemporary Arab American Literature: Transnational Reconfigurations of Citizenship and Belonging*. New York University Press.

Crenshaw, Kimberlé W. 2011. "Demarginalising the Intersection of Race and Sex: A Black Feminist Critique of Anti-Discrimination Doctrine, Feminist Theory, and Anti-Racist Politics." In *Framing Intersectionality: Debates on a Multi-Faceted Concept in Gender Studies*, 23–51. Ashgate Publishing Limited.

Darraj, Susan Muaddi. 2002. "Writing Relocation: Arab Anglophone Literature of the Last Decade." *Iowa Journal of Cultural Studies*. University of Iowa.

Guattari, Felix, and Gilles Deleuze. 1986. *Kafka: Toward a Minor Literature.* Translated by Dana Poland. University of Minnesota Press.

———. 1987. *A Thousand Plateaus: Capitalism and Schizophrenia.* Translated by Brian Massumi. University of Minnesota Press.

Hermans, Hubert J. M. 2022. *Liberation in the Face of Uncertainty: A New Development in Dialogical Self Theory.* Cambridge University Press.

Hermans, Hubert J. M., and Thorsten Gieser. 2012. *Handbook of Dialogical Self Theory.* Cambridge University Press.

Kahf, Mohja. 2006. *The Girl in the Tangerine Scarf.* Carol and Craft Publishers.

———. 2011. "The Pity Committee and the Careful Reader: How Not to Buy Stereotypes about Muslim Women." In *Arab and Arab-American Feminisms: Gender, Violence, and Belonging,* edited by Rabab Abdulhadi, Evelyn Alsultany, and Nadine Naber, 111–126. Syracuse University Press.

Lucy, Niall. 2004. *A Derrida Dictionary.* Blackwell Publishing.

Majaj, Lisa Suhair. 1999. "New Directions: Arab-American Writing at Century's End." In *Post Gibran: Anthology of New Arab American Writing,* 45–58. Syracuse University Press.

May, Vivian M. 2015. *Pursuing Intersectionality: Unsettling Dominant Imaginaries.* Routledge.

Moghissi, Haideh. 2006. *Muslim Diaspora: Gender, Culture, and Identity.* Routledge.

Rahnema, Saeed. 2006. "Islam in Diaspora and Challenges to Multiculturalism." In *Muslim Diaspora: Gender, Culture, and Identity,* edited by Haideh Moghissi, 98–112. Routledge.

Saliba, Theresa. 2000. "Arab Feminism at the Millennium." *Signs* 24 (4): 1087–1092.

Shohat, Ella, and Robert Stam. 2014. *Unthinking Eurocentrism: Multicul-*

turalism and the Media. Routledge.

Shryock, Andrew, ed. 2010. *Islamophobia/Islamophilia: Beyond the Politics of Enemy and Friend*. Indiana University Press.

Transnational Consciousness as a Counter-Narrative to Essentialist Nationalism

Reliance Chekwubechukwu Enwerem, MA.

ABSTRACT

This paper explores identity by examining the intricate relationship between nationalism, essentialism, and the pervasive phenomenon of 'othering'. Through my analysis, I argue that transnational consciousness disrupts the essential in-group/out-group margin binaries for Asian (becoming) Americans. Drawing on scholarship in rhetoric/composition, communication and cultural/critical studies, I explore historical contexts, and contemporary manifestations of othering rooted in nationalist and essentialist discourses. Nationalism and essentialism have culminated in the construction of the "other" and emerge as ambivalent, demanding the fulfillment of certain criteria for belonging, inevitably leading to affirmations and marginalizations. This paper explores the discourse of Asian American identity with a focus on nationalism and essentialism as the grounds for othering and argues that a transnational consciousness, achieved through de-centering, translingualism, and embodiment, is key to disrupting the binary in-group/out-group margins for immigrants becoming Americans and particularly, Asian Americans.

Keywords: Transnationalism, Nationalism, Essentialism, Ambivalence

Introduction

Examining Western discourse, the term 'American' is frequently entwined with 'whiteness,' power, and supremacy. Meanwhile, the construct of 'Asian American' is entrenched in orientalism. While factors like nationality, ethnicity, language, gender, and religion contribute to shaping identity, it is also communicated through mechanisms of exclusion, inclusion, nationalism, and essentialism.

Marginalization, otherness, orientalism, affirmative action, the model minority, raciolinguistics, becoming, and exclusion amongst others are descriptive of the discourse of Asian American rhetoric. According to Jane Rinehart (1994), "the terms 'center' and 'margins' are defined in relation to each other and are most often used to refer to opposite locations about power and prestige; that is, what is centralized has importance and what is marginalized is discredited." (19) Over time, the rhetoric of Asian American identity has been relegated to the margins; and in many ways, Asian Americans have been dehumanized, strung through regulations and stereotypes meant to communicate their identity.

Nationalism and essentialism are relevant concepts used in the conversations around identity and marginalization across nations of the world. Over time, nationalism has been used to express love for one's country, culture, and a deep desire to uphold cultural values. "It has also been the banner, at which, all colors of skin have gathered before they picked up arms and went to war." This brings us to the notion of otherness described as "the dichotomist formation of an us-group and a them-group, or in some places an in-group and out-group... usually based on some external identifier; such as ethnicity, nationality, gender, accent, etc." (John Evans n.d, 2) However, these concepts have culminated in the construction of the "other." In identifying the "other", these groups (considered as other) are excluded and marked out as inferior.

Therefore, this paper aims to explore the discourse of Asian American identity with a focus on nationalism and essentialism as the grounds for othering. I deploy the concept of "becoming" to conceptualize identity as unfinished and contested, where certain people are consistently seen as "becoming" American but never fully "being" American. Through my analysis, I argue that transnational consciousness disrupts the essential in-group/out-group margin binaries for Asian (becoming) Americans.

Positionality Statement

This paper is inspired by a seminar class I attended at the University of Alabama focused on US rhetoric at the margins. Although the paper draws insights from Asian Americans' experiences, and I am an African, I understand that nationalism, essentialism and transnationalism are not limited to a specific geographical or cultural identity, but impact individuals globally. So, this is important to me because as a member of a minority group- *an Other,* I relate to similar experiences and aspire to contribute to a world where borders are permeable and "becoming" equals representation and equality.

Nationalism and Essentialism in Identity Formation

Nationalism, with its etymology in the old French word, *nation* and Latin *natio* means *to be born.* Nationalism is potent in binding groups of people together. According to Eugene O'Brien (1996), "the roots of nationalism lie in racial homogeneity, a homogeneity expressed and solidified by linguistic, cultural and religious practices, and by the exclusion of any other racial input." (4) This brings forward the desire for unity, belonging, socio-cultural, and self-identification. Hence, he questions: "Is nationalism an ideology, a philosophy, an epistemology or a faith?" (1)

Additionally, Plato's essentialism holds that people and things possess certain inherent and innate natural, important, and essential characteristics which are usually unchanging. (Şahin & Şahin 2018, 193) For Plato, "essence is the what of a thing, the substance and essence have been among the most fundamental concepts of metaphysics focusing on faith and reason as they are permanent, unchangeable and imperishable." (194). Essentialism in academia posits that essential knowledge such as cultural heritage and history must constitute the basis of a common core curriculum taught to students. This is aimed at preserving intellectual and socio-cultural norms, values, and standards.

O'Brien (1996) suggests that socio-cultural, religious, and linguistic factors serve as unique passwords exclusive to those sharing similar identities, leading to the birth of exclusion and otherness (4). These essential factors define and validate group identity. For instance, in my examination of the global spread of English, as globalization unfolded, certain countries like Japan resisted the English language due to its intricate connection with culture as the language of a people and their culture are interwoven. Hence, English was perceived as synonymous with Westernization.

The Japanese commitment to preserving their unique cultural essence gave rise to nationalism, resulting in the perception of westernization as an *otherness*. Consequently, English is considered a foreign language in Japan today. This case illustrates how cultural essentialism and the desire for cultural preservation and safeguarding cultural identity contribute to the formation of nationalistic sentiments and the rejection of external linguistic influences.

Ambivalence in Nationalism and Essentialism

The need to check certain boxes to belong results in affirmation and marginalization. According to Joshua Jones (2022), ambivalence is defined as the coexistence of contradictory feelings, emotions, or attitudes toward an object (1). In defining identity, nationalism becomes exclusive and the ambivalence of nationalism is reflected in otherness, "the ambivalent others," which revolves around national inclusion and exclusion, and thus "confronts the question of who is included in our national body and who is excluded as the other body?" (Roginsky 2006, 239) In discussing Asian (becoming) American experiences, Asian American rhetors explore the ambivalence of nationalism and essentialism. These conversations are usually rooted in essential concepts such as linguistic identity, citizenship, stereotypes, race, and racialization amongst others. Nationalism and essentialism as affirming foster a unique sense of pride in collective identity, fostering unity. Whereas as marginalizing, these ideologies take on an exclusionary role. In other words, the ambivalence of nationalism and essentialism is seen in its dual nature: affirming vs marginalizing.

The Ambivalent Nature of Otherness in Citizenship

The United States of America declares *e pluribus unum*. Whereas proposed to be a conglomerate of diverse states, tribes, religions, and cultures, nationalism and essentialism thrive based on race. Nationalism and essentialism are deeply rooted on the grounds of white supremacy and instead of a transnational consciousness, we are faced with national consciousness. Hence, we see terms like "Asian/American" (cf. Monberg and Young 2018), inclusion vs exclusion, alienation, forever foreigner, etc. This slash/ solidus acts as a border and a bridge.

The first significant law restricting Chinese immigration into the US was the Chinese Exclusion Act of 1882 signed by President Chester A. Arthur. The Chinese were expected to provide certifications upon entry and re-entry into the US, and Chinese resident aliens were denied citizenship (National Archives 1882). Over time, many acts such as the Geary Act made permanent in 1902, the Immigration Act of 1924 and the Immigration Act of 1965 among others were modified forms of otherness as they still bore the resemblance of desire for exclusion.

What then is the authentic identity of the Asian/Americans? Considered "yellow" as opposed to white, they are denied citizenship In the case of *Ozawa vs US*, Ozawa meets the criteria descriptive of a model US citizen. However, regardless of his demonstrated acculturation and integration, he is denied naturalization because he is considered racially "not white" ("Ozawa v. United States, 260 U.S. 178" [1922] 2019). On the other hand, Thind, an Indian American (of Caucasian descent and) racially white is deemed ineligible for citizenship because he would not be considered "white in the eyes of the common man" ("United States v. Bhagat Singh Thind, 261 U.S 204" [1923] 2019)

Historically, Asian (such as Chinese, Japanese, Korean, and Filipino) immigrants among others have played crucial roles in building and sustaining America. On the one hand, the American laws view Asians as persons to be integrated for economic purposes. On the other hand, these immigrants are also treated as unintelligible elements, deserving of marginalization, alienation, and even deportation. In becoming American, the Asian American rhetoric is dominated by the theme of being a "forever foreigner," consistently torn between identifying as an insider or outsider (Lowe 1996).

Linguistic Otherness as Ambivalent

Cathy Park Hong's (2020) *Minor Feelings* explores ambivalence as being embedded in the intersection of nationalism and essentialism within the context of Asian American identity, challenging simplistic narratives of belonging and unveiling the complexities that define the experiences of Asian Americans. In *Minor Feelings*, Hong (2020) describes how language symbolizes resistance and collective identity. In "Bad English," she explores how Asian Americans' difficulty in expressing themselves linguistically on the one hand contributes to otherness in the form of marginalization. On the other hand, it also creates a notion of national identity and resistance through Asian Americans' decision to essentialize their indigenous linguistic traits. Hence, she writes: "It was once a source of shame, but now I say it proudly; bad English is my heritage. I share a literary lineage with writers who make the unmastering of English their rallying cry- who[...] *other* it by hijacking English and warping it into a fugitive tongue. To *other* English is to[...] slit English open so its dark histories slide out." (95)

Furthermore, whilst the demand for linguistic justice by marginalized groups is resistance towards linguistic racism, it also affirms individuals' rights to their own (patterns and varieties of) language. Also, in most contexts, while code-mixing, code-meshing and code-switching might signify otherness, these terms also mark collective identity and enable these groups of individuals to reinforce embodiment, embodying their experiences in navigating and negotiating their linguistic and racial identities across multiple contexts. Hence, Jennifer Cho (2020) uses the term "mel-han-colia" in analyzing Theresa Hak Kyung Cha's *Dictée* to depict how Cha's description of her historical memory defies the expectations that minority populations somehow transcend their grievous pasts in becoming model American citizens.

Literacy as Ambivalent

The ambivalence of literacy is rooted in the interplay of the empowering and marginalizing dimensions of (written) language and narratives. When viewed affirmatively, literacy is a powerful tool for empowerment, providing access to opportunities, information, and integration. It mirrors nationalism by encouraging cultural and historical preservation and transmission. Literacy enables immigrants to assert and define themselves about their host cultures. This affirmative aspect creates a sense of identity and continuity. Thus, Iswari Pandey (2015) depicts language as rhetorical, deployed for unity and illustrates that "maintaining their cultural identity while 'fitting in' in their new home is a common challenge that immigrants face." (75) Sanskrit is identified as "preceding present-day differences and so is used as a heritage marker; a unifier of all who identified with the dominant South Asian faith and cultural traditions." (92)

As marginalizing, literacy when essentialized results in stereotyping and could also pose language barriers for minorities. When limited in the knowledge of the dominant language, the ideology of exclusion and otherness prevails. For Asian Americans, literacy is also associated with the model minority myth which is associated and a stereotype of minorities-in this case Asian Americans- who are high achievers, educated, and successful by (White) American standards. In "Bad English," Hong (2020) explores literacy through the lens of language and identity as relating to the challenges faced by Asian Americans. She interrogates how literacy, English proficiency in particular, is crucial to the minority myth, suggesting that Asian Americans' success is linked to their linguistic and academic performance. The term "bad English" is itself a form of linguistic/ literacy otherness.

Furthermore, literacy is used to reinforce the "forever foreigner" stereotype. Despite linguistic proficiency or the duration of stay in the United States, otherness enforces the idea that literacy alone is not a criterion for integration into the national narrative. Hence, in "Bad English," Hong (2020) writes: "Pity the Asian accent. It is such a degraded accent, one of the last accents acceptable to mock. How hard it is to speak through it to make yourself heard. I am embarrassed to say that I sometimes act like that white woman [...]." (99)

Deconstructing Otherness via Transnationalism

The transnational allows immigrants to move across, be present, and be a part of distinct worlds. Transnationalism is a term often used to refer to migrants' durable ties across countries. Although *diaspora* is often used interchangeably with *transnationalism, diaspora* is used to "denote religious or national groups living outside an (imagined) homeland" (Rainer Bauböck and Thomas Faist 2010, 9). Delphine Nakache (2008) posits that "Transnationalism leads to forms of "multiple belonging" [...] contributing to the formation and maintenance of relations which transcend national boundaries and create a transnational space of cultural, economic and political participation." (91) The argument is that transnationalism as a rhetorical concept has the potential to disrupt, contest, and complicate stereotypes, as well as challenge marginalization and exclusion in several ways.

Transnational consciousness has indeed provided a rich framework for rhetors to reshape narratives and challenge structures that perpetuate stereotypes. According to Huang (2021), "transnationalism highlights the complex spatiality within and across local, national, and global communication." (207) Pandey's (2015) *South Asian in the Mid-South* vividly illustrates the operationalism and dynamics of transnational consciousness.

429

He examines issues and experiences of immigrants concerning citizenship, migration, literacy, and language across borders. This exploration reveals how South Asian immigrants have at various times created agency for themselves to promote cross-cultural practices amidst globalization. Through his work, we see how transnational literacy practices reproduce a united community and representation by dismantling monolithic representations, decentering linguistic supremacy, and presenting immigrants' narratives as individual, unique experiences that contribute to the development of collective agency.

Firstly, to move past essentialist in-group/out-group binaries, we must dismantle monolithic representations. Hence, Huang (2021) posits that "a transnational perspective is an analytic that focuses on relationships rather than places." (208) Based on the consensus that transnationalism involves belonging across worlds, by acknowledging the diversity of experiences, languages, and cultures that span national borders, transnationalism challenges the tendency to view Asian Americans as a monolithic group. This disrupts the simplistic and essentialist stereotypes often used to characterize Asian Americans.

For instance, In "Genes and Jeans", Pandey (2015) describes how Sanskrit and Hinduism were utilized transnationally so that "people from different locations (including different native nation-states) would easily identify with a space and community thus imagined and its heritage" (97). Thus, "Hindu school literacies went beyond reflecting a people's native language or literacy[...] to indicate a new form of sociality and social formation that members could relate to in multiple ways. In this sense, cultural formations that have been traditionally restricted to... political and geographical boundaries have transgressed national borders." (Anderson, quoted in Pandey 2015, 97-98)

Additionally, transnationalism disrupts linguistic stereotypes by portraying language as a bridge rather than a barrier. Through translingualism, we can decenter the primacy of English as the lingua franca. As opposed to multilingualism which refers to the ability to use multiple languages, translingualism focuses on the communicative practices of people interacting across different linguistic and communicative codes such as borrowing, bending, and blending languages into new modes of expression. According to Ellen Cushman (2016), "translingualism can be defined as those meaning-making processes that involve students and scholars in translanguaging, translating, and dwelling in borders." (235) The "immigrant participants" translingual practices here push us to consider literacies on the move as the object of inquiry" (Pandey 2015, 22) Consequently, scholars in the field of rhetoric and composition encourage the need to emphasize translingualism in writing and composition studies (cf. Canagarajah, quoted in Pandey 2015; Cushman 2016; Gilyard 2016).

Furthermore, transnationalism presents migration narratives as dynamic, individual stories rather than a singular, homogeneous experience (Cha 2009; Hong 2020; Monberg & Young 2018). Humanizing the journeys of Asian Americans influences and requires that we rethink our histories, methods and essentialist stereotypes. Through this, we can see beyond nationalism to other groups on the margins. Consequently, we can then address feminism, sexuality, and disabilities (cf. Cha 2009; Wu 2018; Cedillo 2018). Transnationalism is intertwined with embodiment to project a nuanced understanding of identities not confined by geographical borders. The physical body becomes a vessel for the intersectionality of identities, disrupting simplistic categorizations and challenging the otherness imposed by essentialist perspectives. They saw themselves constantly at war with us.

Conclusion and Recommendations

Transnationalism is a rich and multifaceted framework rhetors can utilize in reshaping narratives and challenging structures that perpetuate stereotypes. Asian American rhetoric scholars continue to challenge and critique their positionality within the U.S. Aside from exploring nationalism and essentialism as the basis of otherness through citizenship, language, and literacy, this paper argues that a transnational consciousness disrupts the in-group/out-group margin binaries through decentering, translingualism, and embodiment.

With current trends in technological advancements and the emergence of Artificial Intelligence, human and media biases and stereotypes are being reinforced more than ever before (Arola and Wysocki 2012; Byrd 2023). Certain scholars such as Huang (2021) and Eguchi (2021) advocate for transnationalism as a theoretical and methodological intervention in communication and critical/cultural studies. However, in discussing transnationalism today, it is pertinent that we recognize the need for transnational consciousness in the digital landscape. Therefore, because technological advancement has permeated diverse communication and educational spaces, it is necessary to consider the contributions of digital spaces to nationalism and essentialism, and how virtual transnational spaces can impact the deconstruction of otherness. Consequently, future research could explore how artificial intelligence and technologies have influenced immigration policies and the representation of marginalized perspectives within the framework of transnational discourse.

References

Arola, Kristin L., and Anne Frances Wysocki. 2012. *Composing(Media) = Composing(Embodiment): Bodies, Technologies, Writing, the Teaching of Writing*. Logan: Utah State University Press.

Bauböck, Rainer, and Thomas Faist, eds. 2010. *Diaspora and Transnationalism: Concepts, Theories and Methods*. Amsterdam: Amsterdam University Press.

Byrd, Antonio. 2023. "Where We Are: AI and Writing Truth-Telling: Critical Inquiries on LLMs and the Corpus Texts That Train Them." *Composition Studies Journal*. https://compositionstudiesjournal.files.word press.com/2023/06/byrd.pdf.

Cedillo, Christina V. 2018. "Race, Disability, and Critical Embodiment Pedagogy." *Composition Forum* 39. https://compositionforum.com/ issue/39/to-move.php.

Cho, Jennifer. 2020. "Mel-Han-Cholia as Political Practice in Theresa Hak Kyung Cha's *Dictée*." *Meridians* 19 (S1): 410–34. https://doi.org/ 10.1215/15366936-8566067.

Cushman, Ellen. 2016. "Translingual and Decolonial Approaches to Meaning Making." *College English* 78 (3): 234–42. https://www.jstor. org/stable/pdf/44075113.pdf.

Eguchi, Shinsuke. 2021. "On the Horizon: Desiring Global Queer and Trans* Studies in International and Intercultural Communication." *Journal of International and Intercultural Communication* 14 (4): 275–

83. https://doi.org/10.1080/17513057.2021.1967684.

Evans, John. n.d. "Othering in Nationalism: The Use of Othering in the Formation of a Nationalist Society." Accessed October 24, 2023.

Gilyard, Keith. 2016. "The Rhetoric of Translingualism." *College English* 78 (3): 284–89. https://www.jstor.org/stable/44075119.

Hak Kyung Cha, Theresa. 2009. *Dictée*. Berkeley: University of California Press.

Hong, Cathy Park. 2020. *Minor Feelings: An Asian American Reckoning.* New York: One World.

Huang, Shuzhen. 2021. "Why Does Communication Need Transnational Queer Studies?" *Communication and Critical/Cultural Studies* 18 (2): 204–11. https://doi.org/10.1080/14791420.2021.1907850.

Jones, Joshua. 2022. "Ambivalence in Twentieth and Twenty-First Century U.S. Literature and Culture." *Current Biology.* University of California, Santa Cruz. https://doi.org/10.1016/j.cub.2022.10.035.

Lowe, Lisa. 1996. "Immigration, Citizenship, Racialization: Asian American Critique." In *Immigrant Acts: On Asian American Cultural Politics,* 1–35. Durham: Duke University Press.

Monberg, Terese Guinsatao, and Morris Young. 2018. "Beyond Representation: Spatial, Temporal and Embodied Trans/Formations of Asian/ Asian American Rhetoric." *Enculturation.* https://enculturation.net/ beyond_representation.

Nakache, Delphine. 2008. "The 'Othering' Process: Exploring the Instrumentalization of Law in Migration Policy." PhD diss., McGill University.

National Archives. 2021. "Chinese Exclusion Act (1882)." National Archives. September 8, 2021. https://www.archives.gov/milestone-documents/chinese-exclusion-act.

O'Brien, Eugene. 1996. "The Epistemology of Nationalism." *Irish Studies Review* 5 (17): 15–20. https://doi.org/10.1080/09670889608455554.

Ozawa v. United States, 260 U.S. 178 (1922). 2019. *Justia Law*. https://supreme.justia.com/cases/federal/us/260/178/.

Pandey, Iswari P. 2015. *South Asian in the Mid-South: Migrations of Literacies*. Pittsburgh: University of Pittsburgh Press.

Rinehart, Jane A. 1994. "Roaming in the Margins, Speaking with Broken Tongues." *Frontiers: A Journal of Women Studies* 14 (3): 19. https://doi.org/10.2307/3346679.

Roginsky, Dina. 2006. "Nationalism and Ambivalence: Ethnicity, Gender and Folklore as Categories of Otherness." *Patterns of Prejudice* 40 (3): 237–58. https://doi.org/10.1080/00313220600769505.

Şahin, Mehmet, and M. Şahin. 2018. "Essentialism in Philosophy, Psychology, Education, Social and Scientific Scopes." *Journal of Innovation in Psychology, Education and Didactics* 22 (2): 193–204.

United States v. Bhagat Singh Thind, 261 U.S. 204 (1923). 2019. *Justia Law*. https://supreme.justia.com/cases/federal/us/261/204/.

Wu, Judy Tzu-Chun. 2018. "Hypervisibility and Invisibility: Asian/American Women, Radical Orientalism, and the Revisioning of Global Feminism." In *The Routledge Handbook of the Global Sixties: Between Protest and Nation-Building*, 212–29. Abingdon: Routledge.

Revolutionary Potential in the Hybrid Self

Jamie Bollweg, MA.

ABSTRACT

With many existential threats haunting our daily lives, the individual feels hopeless in enacting societal change. Our imagination towards a better future has become near impossible under capitalist realism. Most theories plot a way for humanity to go back to stateless or hunter-gatherer societies when we were "more human." But humanity is forever severed from that possibility. Technology and modernity have worked us over completely. In our globally connected and technologically dependent world, "knowing thyself" necessarily involves an acceptance of our interconnectedness to technology, society, and Others, and perhaps even an Other as far-reaching as non-animate, material things. Such new conceptions of self are better understood and viewed through a posthuman lens. The posthuman breaks down the boundaries between ethnicity, gender, and binaries in general. Virginia Woolf breaks down conceptions of self in her novel *The Waves* which shows the trajectory of identity formation through the hybridity of six individuals. Donna Haraway's identification as a cyborg conflates the binary between human/machine. Gloria Anzaldúa deconstructs and reconstructs identity in the borderlands between societal distinctions. If we are to imagine a new future collectively, we must first imagine new versions of the self: a hybrid self in an interconnected world.

Keywords: Self, Other, Hybrid, Posthuman, Cyborg

> The ultimate, hidden truth of the world is that it is some-
> thing that we make, and could just as easily make differ-
> ently ... the ultimate revolutionary question: what are the
> conditions that would have to exist to enable us to do
> this—to just wake up and imagine and produce some-
> thing else? (Graeber 2024, 15)

With several existential threats haunting our lives—global pandemic,
AI, World War 3, climate change, economic collapse—much discussion
revolves around societal change. We are understandably compelled to
carry an opinion about what should be done at a societal level to avoid
such catastrophes. Implicit in these discussions is an assumption that if
enough voting people shared a similar corrective vision of the future, a
democratic society would make it happen. It's just a matter of convincing
enough people of socialism, libertarianism, technocracy, or whatever social ideology that seems reasonable enough to a person. To avoid despair,
we're compelled to hope for and imagine a better future. But it seems that
composing a coherent vision of a future outside of our technological capitalist society is practically impossible. Mark Fisher's *Capitalist Realism*
expounds upon the phrase, "it is easier to imagine the end of the world
than it is to imagine the end of capitalism." (Fisher 2009, 12)

Fisher argues we are stuck inside a dominant capitalistic ideology where
imagining utopia and criticizing capitalism is nothing more than coping,
or worse, counter-productive. Slavoj Zizek said he would "sell his mother
into slavery" (2023, 0:55) to watch a film named "V for Vendetta Part 2."
A joke to emphasize our inability to imagine what comes after revolution.
Popular media reflects this, as most post-apocalyptic depictions cannot
present a coherent vision without resolving to zombie apocalypse or rus-
tic hunter-gatherer worlds like in the popular video game and TV show
The Last of Us. It seems we cannot think of a future outside of whatever
stage of capitalism we are in without either depicting global catastrophe
or a return to a perfectly foreign version of humanity.

Visions of a simpler-technology future seem possible because at one
point humans did live this way. We can believe that societies unaffected by
capitalism and technology have existed, but we are more or less unable to
imagine enacting such systems today in our technological, interconnected world. We are our habits and our habits are dependent on technology.

Try persuading a person to give up running water, heating, cooling, washer, dryer, and medication—not to mention GPS, video games, Diet Coke and Van Gogh Exhibition: The Immersive Experience. The gap between the world of homosapians and our current condition is wide. Technology and media have "worked us over completely." (McLuhan and Fiore 1967, 26) The desire to return to a previous version of humanity must provide a conceptual bridge between the experience of our current bodies (and all of their organs of function) to the bodies of history, which is little more than a guess at what bodies were like according to anthropologists.

Idealizing hunter-gatherer societies for their "egalitarian" constructions feels like a common conservative notion that past structures were never fully realized. Or just sounds like Ted Kaczynski. Adaptable humans are completely severed from this past. If we hope to bring about the freedom or more-connected-to-nature that the stateless hunter-gatherers may have had, the route is not to go back, but to move forward with an understanding of what our bodies and minds are behaving like in the age of information. Social change requires a material understanding of our bodies which does not fetishize an idealistic past that is no longer attainable.

What is neglected from the discussion about potential societal fixes, is attention to the individuals that make up society. Before a new vision of a better future can be written we must first continue the discourse of how we understand our bodies as they are in 2025. Society as a whole is made up of individuals as parts. Society doesn't change unless the individuals that make up that society change. To be sure, society informs individuals as well, the process is indeed recursive. But discussion of societal change seems to rest on what needs to change in society, and neglects to address what needs to change in individuals. In the same way, discussions of changes in individuals, or self-improvement, don't frequently address how this change has any impact on society. When asked what his famous song "The Revolution Will Not Be Televised" means, Gil-Scott Heron said that "the catchphrase[...] that was about the fact that the first change that takes place is in your mind. You have to change your mind before you change the way you live and the way you move." (Scott-Heron 1971) The change required for revolution will not be something captured on film. The change revolution requires will happen first inside the individuals who have changed their minds about themselves.

From Graeber's simple yet provocative revolutionary question, it seems that for societal change to happen, one must first understand the self. The revolutionary task is not only coming up with better policies and social arrangements, but also honestly assessing who we are as the individuals that define society. Echoing Gil-Scott Heron's explanation of his song, Gloria Anzaldúa argues that "the struggle has always been inner and is played out in the outer terrains. Awareness of our situation must come before inner changes, which in turn come before changes in society. Nothing happens in the "real" world unless it first happens in the images in our head." (Anzaldúa 1987, 85) What has been played out in the outer terrains is the overwhelming crisis of climate change. It's the experience of a global pandemic. It's the potent collective experience of alienation, exploitation, and dehumanization of capitalism. It's the horrors of colonialism, whose effects still oppress millions around the world. We know the environment that our organs react to, but do we know our organs? Do we understand our new bodies post-industrialization? Have we understood the fragmentation of our identities, our tethering to technology, or how language is used to define our identities? We must recognize that,

> The "inner" and "outer" worlds of the subject is a border and boundary tenuously maintained for the purposes of social regulation and control...[they] constitute a binary distinction that stabilizes and consolidates the coherent subject. When that subject is challenged, the meaning and necessity of the terms are subject to displacement. If the "inner world" no longer designates a *topos* (place [Greek]), then the internal fixity of the self [...]become similarly suspect. (MediaBurnArchive 2025)

The idea here is not to place individual change in priority over societal change but to recognize that this binary is a simplification of the reality that makes up both the self and its relation to society. To challenge our systems, we must challenge the concept of identity we are prescribed. Let's divert the conversation from how the systems are not working to (with grace) how the systems have changed us individually. Having an "awareness of our situation" most acutely, is understanding the body first, then how that body interacts in the environment. If you understand your body, you will know how to adapt to (or create!) a new environment.

The task then is less so to convince individuals which political framework, or government system would work best, but to inspire individuals to know their power. We must ask ourselves, "Who am I?" with intense scrutiny. We won't have a viable vision for utopia if we rely on outdated conceptions of self and identity. This is why utopian arguments never quite pass the sniff test. They end up sounding like universal descriptions of human nature, treating humans like static, permanent inputs for a desired societal output. Instead of imagining utopias, let's imagine future versions of ourselves based on the technology, language, culture, and material reality that defines us as organisms in a changing environment. If we are to imagine a societal future, we must first imagine a future self.

It is then useful that we view human beings through a "posthuman" lens. The humanity that we understand now, is beyond the humanity of the past. We are cyborgs, hybrids, and a composite. The irony is that a posthuman self is not singular. Or at least, rejects individualism which promotes the individual as a self-centered, autonomous, isolated, rational, agent. Posthumanism breaks down the boundaries of gender, race, and all binaries. Donna Haraway's cyborg finds "pleasure in the confusion of boundaries and responsibility in their construction." (Haraway 1985, 151)

Rosi Braidotti says that the posthuman,

> rejects individualism, but also asserts an equally strong distance from relativism or nihilistic defeatism. It promotes an ethical bond of an altogether different sort from the self-interests of an individual subject, as defined along the canonical lines of classical Humanism. Posthuman ethics for a non-unitary subject proposes an enlarged sense of interconnection between self and others, including the non-human or 'earth' others, by removing the obstacle of self-centered individualism.   (Braidotti 2013, 2352)

Here we have a "self" that removes the weight of the world on our shoulders, but at the same time, is interconnected with the world. It's an acceptance of one's non-unitary subjectivity, while asserting that this is the case for me.

We must also reconceptualize what it means to have a body. In our online, technologically saturated environment, our bodies have extended beyond our own skin. Oppressors use conceptualizations of our bodies to keep them in places where they can be controlled. Judith Butler remarks, "Any discourse that establishes the boundaries of the body serves the purpose of instating and naturalizing certain taboos regarding the appropriate limits, postures, and modes of exchange that define what it is that constitutes bodies." (Butler 1990 2380) But by being comfortable in the traversing of the body's boundaries, we find that our so-called autonomous self is interconnected to our families, stories, tools, dialects, and all categorizations which make up our perspective. All of which point to a non-centralized self. The self is a collection of other selves and influences ever-changing through time. You are "you" at different spacetimes. Even candy bar advertisements know you are not "you" when you are hungry. Traversing the boundary of prescribed versions of bodies and self is revolutionary. Societal change begins with individuals who are deeply connected to their environment and positionality. Knowing thyself necessarily involves an acceptance of our inter-connectedness to technology, society, and Others, and perhaps even an Other as far-reaching as non-animate, material things.

The Hybrid Self

The fact that the self is non-singular, multiple and hybridical, is evident within the dynamics between our closest relationships. Modernist author Virginia Woolf illustrates how the self is a composite in her book *The Waves*, which reads less like a novel, but more like a Socratic method exploration wrestling with what it means to be a subjective self in a social world. Woolf provides a theory of self through six different voices that mirror her struggle to redeem internal consciousness with social existence.

The first thing to note about Woolf's conception of self is that it happens in stages. At first, when we are young, the self is assumed. We take in sensory experiences from our environments and construct ideas about our relation to them without thinking too much about them. The voices simply describe the world around them as they see it, "where the voices are children celebrating a sensorium and saying only the simplest things about their identities and fears." (Miko 1988, 69) Virginia Woolf's voices describe very basic sensory experiences, ""I see a ring," said Bernard. "I see a slab of pale yellow," said Susan. "I hear a sound," said Rhoda. "I see a globe," said Neville. "I see a crimson tassel," said Jinny. I hear something stamping," said Louis." (Woolf 1931, 1) It is possible to exist without asking the question, "Who am I?" But this is basic, and human consciousness inevitably becomes aware of itself and starts to interrogate what it means to be conscious.

It is not until section three of the novel when the question of self comes into the minds of our characters, at college (often a place of self-discovery): "The complexity of things becomes closer," said Bernard, "here at college, where the stir and pressure of life are so extreme, where the excitement of mere living becomes daily more urgent. Every hour something new is unburied in the great bran pie. What am I? I ask. This? No, I am that"(76) To answer the question "What am I?" we notice a unique distinction in ourselves in the differences in faces. I have this face. Other people have that face. When older, Bernard reflects on one of the first moments he noticed his distinct self:

> Faces loom. Dashing around the corner, 'Hullo,' one says, 'there's Jinny. That's Neville. That's Louis in grey flannel with a. snake belt. That's Rhoda.' She has a basin in which she sailed petals of white flowers. It was Susan who cried, that day when I was in the tool-house with Neville; and I felt my indifference melt. Neville did not melt. 'Therefore,' I said, 'I am myself, not Neville,' a wonderful discovery. (240)

But this "wonderful discovery" proves to be agonizing when explored further. It may seem simple at first. I am in this body. I have this face that is not like other faces. Yet, the voice of Rhoda says, "That is my face, in the looking-glass behind Susan's shoulder–that face is my face"(43) and from this, Rhoda can tell herself one thing or another about what this face is: "But I will duck behind her to hide it, for I am not here. I have no face."(43) This is Woolf's conundrum: is that stories, illusions, and delusions, are what define our concepts, and even our face is up for debate as to what makes us unique. Rhoda's lack of face is a story she tells herself. But we might ask, 'who is it that I am telling the story to?' What exchange between two objects is there a dialogue? I tell myself. I and myself. Two and one? Who is the subject? Who is the object? Who is doing the talking to whom? Where is this singular self? Attempting to talk to himself, Bernard says:

> But you understand, you, my self, who always comes at a
> call (that would be a harrowing experience to call and for
> no one to come; that would make the midnight hollow,
> and explains the expression of old men in clubs–they
> have given up calling for a self who does not come)…
> Underneath, and, at the moment when I am most dispa-
> rate, I am also integrated. (77)

The stories I hear from others are stories I can tell myself. The stories of my friends. The stories of my family. My history is the history of the stories I've heard. At this stage of searching, the self is something I can talk to. I can understand it by reading the stories that define me. But the mere fact that one can understand the self by acknowledging the stories that define the self, the singular nature of the self is exposed as a constructed illusion. The next stage that Woolf realizes about this exploration of trying to pin down the self, is that it is multiple. Paradoxically, the self is a hybrid of many selves. Reading *The Waves* metafictionally, we see that Woolf can hold six distinct voices in her head. She is composed of multiple stories, multiple metaphors, and multiple selves, all of which evolve and change over time. The self is not singular, isolated, or completely discrete. The voice of Neville expresses this idea early on when he notices:

> How curiously one is changed by the addition, even at a
> distance, of a friend. How useful an office one's friends
> perform when they recall us. Yet how painful to be re-
> called, to be mitigated, to have one's self adulterated,
> mixed up, become a part of another. As he approaches, I
> become not myself but Neville mixed with somebody—
> with whom?—with Bernard? Yes, it is Bernard, and it is
> to Bernard that I shall put the question, Who am I? (83)

This new self deletes the unitary, solitary self. To know ourselves, we of-ten look to others to define ourselves. Near the end of the novel, Bernard relates his multiplicity. I can't help but read it as metadrama, that is, Woolf speaking directly to the reader, because Bernard references himself in the third person:

> And now I ask, 'Who am I?' I have been talking of Ber-
> nard, Neville, Jinny, Susan, Rhoda and Louis. Am I all of
> them? Am I one and distinct? I do not know. We sat here

together. But now Percival is dead, and Rhoda is dead; we are divided; we are not here. Yet I cannot find any obstacle separating us. There is no division between me and them. As I talked I felt, 'I am you.' This difference we make so much of, this identity we so feverishly cherish, was overcome. (288-289)

If Woolf asks herself this question, "Who am I?", we can infer that her theory of self is not hyper-individualistic, isolated, and discrete. It is rather, multitudinous, hybrid, and connected. Yet, it is questions of multiplicity that lead one to not hear that voice inside our heads anymore. We cannot trust the stories, the faces, the names, because they are all made up. None of them are, objectively true. We notice them as constructions. Ones that we have made up, or ones that others have told us to believe.

The next stage that Woolf illustrates about consciousness, the self, and identity, is the deep dive into existential thought. After acknowledging the decentering of the self into a hybrid, Woolf realizes this is a harrowing experience. Through the voice of Bernard, she demonstrates how terrible it feels to talk to a self and no one responds. Accepting the hybrid self is something of an identity crisis. It involves decoupling assumed beliefs of what it means to be a subject in a chaotic world. It deconstructs the very paths of how we make meaning out of material reality. Identity crises come with depression, nihilism, and despair. As Bernard relates in this quote:

I spoke to that self who has been with me in many tremendous adventures; the faithful man who sits over the fire when everybody has gone to bed... This self now as I leant over the gate looking down over fields rolling in waves of colour beneath me made no answer. He threw up no opposition. He attempted no phrase. His fist did not form. I waited. I listened. Nothing came, nothing. I cried then with a sudden conviction of complete desertion. Now there is nothing. No fin breaks the waste of this immeasurable sea. Life has destroyed me. No echo comes when I speak, no varied words. This is more truly death than the death of friends, than the death of youth. (284)

Bernard becomes bored prescribing meaning to existence. A man defined by his love of stories, loses his trust in them:

> I must tell you a story—and there are so many, and so many—stories of childhood, stories of school, love marriage, death, and so on; and none of them are true. Yet like children we tell each other stories, and to decorate them we make up these ridiculous, flamboyant, beautiful phrases. How tired I am of stories, how tired I am of phrases that come down beautifully with all their feet on the ground! Also, how I distrust neat designs of life that are drawn upon half sheets of notepaper. I begin to long for some little language such as lovers use, broken words, inarticulate words, like the shuffling of feet on the pavement (238).

Bernard has come to the 'intolerable boredom'. The ability to see beauty is lost.

Nothing would happen to lift that weight of intolerable boredom. The terms went on. We grew; we changed; for, of course, we are animals. We are not always aware by any means; we breathe, eat, and sleep automatically. We exist not only separately but in undifferentiated blobs of matter. (246)

We are but bags of meat on a spinning rock floating in the indifferent universe. Taking the multiplicity of self to its end, in this moment, destroys the self. A true exploration of consciousness takes one down to the depths of thought. The darkest and most existential thoughts. Thinking, and questioning everything, takes one to the edge of reason. Analyzing this stage of consciousness in *The Waves*, Suzette Henke writes,

Exploration is no longer possible; accomplishment is defined and stratified; ultimate coherence has eluded the storyteller. Seeing his life as a drama that approaches culmination, Bernard surveys his past and sees nothing more than the "orts, scraps, and fragments" ... Bernard the storyteller is unable to finish the impassioned story of his own life. (Henke 1989, 465)

A true exploration of consciousness takes one down to the depths of thought where exploration seems futile and impossible. The darkest and most existential thoughts. The self and our conception of consciousness interact. We think, we learn, and we develop identities on these activities, but consciousness brings some to a useless skepticism. Albert Camus writes:

> Thinking is learning all over again how to see, directing one's consciousness, making every image a privileged place... From the evening breeze to this hand on my shoulder, everything has its truth. Consciousness illuminates it by paying attention to it. Consciousness does not form the object of understanding, it merely focuses, it resembles the projector that suddenly focuses on an image. The difference is that there is no scenario, but a successive and incoherent illustration. In that magic lantern, all the pictures are privileged. Consciousness suspends in experience the objects of its attention. Through its miracle it isolates them. Henceforth they are beyond all judgements. This is the "intention" that characterizes consciousness. But the word does not imply any idea of finality. (Camus 1942, 34)

What we desire is a permanent idea of self, but consciousness cannot grant us that privilege. Yet, as Camus says later with his analogy of imagining Sisyphus "happy" as he is condemned to push up the bolder up the mountain for eternity, the absurd hero stares directly into the face of death, the enemy, and rebels. Bernard finishes his summing up with resistance against death, the ultimate absurdity:

> What enemy do we now perceive advancing against us, you whom I ride now, as we stand pawing this stretch of pavement? It is death. Death is the enemy. It is death against whom I ride with my spear couched and my hair flying back like a young man's, like Percival's, when he galloped in India. I strike spurs into my horse. Against you, I will fling myself, unvanquished and unyielding, O Death! *The waves broke on the shore.* (Woolf 1931, 297)

This act of resistance is the only option besides suicide, if one, sadly, reaches this stage of consciousness. It then becomes an act of heroism to resist utter despair:

> Bernard's renewal is parallel to an impending dawn; what is positive in human life is parallel to something positive in the external world... he now transforms what is, after all, little more than an assertion that life goes on, into an act of heroism. (Miko 1988, 80)

Against the impending wash of the dark ocean of nothingness, the hero rebels. Henke continues, "Their [the voices] antagonist is oceanic–the threat that ushers in a revelation of nothingness. Guided by creative will, each of the six challenges ontological absurdity through a life-long project of heroic self-creation" (Henke 1989, 462) It is a heroic act to deconstruct and reconstruct the self.

What we've gained from Virginia Woolf, is that we are multiple selves socially, and embracing a self beyond the assumed individualistic version of the self is harrowing. But she emphasizes that going beyond individualism is a worthy adventure into a fight against the absurd, mutating the acceptance of the mundaneness of life into an act of heroism. It is a heroic act to rebel against the absurd and form new identities outside of the purity narratives we have inherited.

The Technological Self

With that happy(ish) ending, we must also acknowledge more ways that the self is composed. Deconstructing the self and developing a new conceptualization of the self even further also requires us to recognize how our identities are intrinsically tied to technology and modes of communication. To fully understand our situation and ourselves we must understand humanity's tethering to technology. Marshall McLuhan states that.

> All media work us over completely. They are so pervasive in their personal, political economic, aesthetic, psychological, moral, ethical, and social consequences that leave no part of us untouched, unaffected, or unaltered. The medium is the massage [message]. Any understanding of social and cultural change is impossible without a knowledge of the way media work as environments. (McLuhan 1967, 26)

Nothing will change in society if we don't understand our technology and its impact on our metaphysical/nominative frameworks. Human evolution is defined by our technology. There's a reason we call it "The Stone Age," "The Bronze Age," "The Industrial Age," "The Information Age," and most recently, Klaus Schwab's "Fourth Industrial Revolution," an "epi-digital" rather than "post-digital" age which "affirms that technological change is a driver of transformation relevant to all industries and parts of society" (Philbeck 2018, 17) If the Anthropocene defines our era as a planet, technology explains the species that make up the era. Technology defines our societies and the lives of the individuals within them.

Technology's grip on us can be evident in the way our human bodily faculties have been extended through technological mediums, often to fearful affect. Cars are extensions of our legs. Books are extensions of the stories that define us. Computers are extensions of our knowledge. Or the layering and combination of things like, "robotics, advanced materials, genetic modifications, the Internet of Things, drones, neurotechnologies, autonomous vehicles, artificial intelligence, and machine vision," expanding ideas of every sensory organ and intellectual faculty in our head. (18) In being extensions, they are a part of us. To function in 2024, we must embrace cars, smartphones, department stores, and algorithms. To live deep in the woods, severed from modern technology has become impossible for anybody born in our post-industrial world. We have changed. Characteristics of human nature isolated from technology have become increasingly obsolete. This may seem scary for some. Are we losing what it means to be human? Has technology changed us for the worse? Like the existential idea of a multiple self from Woolf, technology also fractures our bodies into an uncanny indiscernibility.

The fear of emerging technology is nothing new. Plato, in *Phaedrus*, tells the story of Thamus, who is skeptical of the advent of writing as an innovative technology. He worries that it will shorten our memory as we will rely on books to hold knowledge and then spread falsehoods. The thing is, Thamus was right. Writing took away our long-term memory and diffused knowledge. It changed our realities. Wouldn't it be splendid to recite the Iliad from memory? Or the Odyssey? Allegedly, Homer could do that. Humans were, at one point, capable of doing that. But if you want to do that again, you must give up reading and writing. Even if you could memorize ten epic poems, it might be the only stories outside of your personal experience that you have. Writing gave us more stories to read. More cultures and contexts to imagine and experience. This is why Neil

Postman clarifies that,

> The error [in Thamus' thinking] is not in his claim that
> writing will damage memory and create false wisdom. It
> is demonstrable that writing has had such an effect. Tha-
> mus' error is in his belief that writing will be a burden to
> society and nothing but a burden. For all his wisdom, he
> fails to imagine what writing's benefits might be, which,
> as we know, have been considerable. We may learn from
> this that it is a mistake to suppose that any technological
> innovation has a one-sided effect. Every technology is
> both a burden and a blessing; not either-or, but this-and-
> that. (Postman 1992, 9)

Therefore, it is imperative to understand our connection to the technologies that define us. With the onset of any new technology, it features a
grieving period of what is lost. But to move forward, we must embrace
what is gained. We cannot know how to navigate our new technological
realities unless we have a concept of ourselves that integrates our tools
without losing our love.

Walter Benjamin's essay "The Work of Art in the Age of Mechanical Reproduction" demonstrates how new technology, even if the language
about it is hijacked by fascism, can still find revolutionary potential in
understanding that technology. Technology's material effects give artists
new avenues of resistance.

Benjamin illustrates this by the example of photography. In photography's predominant characteristic of reproducibility, it contradicts the notion that art has, what Benjamin calls, an "aura." The aura is this idea that
the "original" work of art, i.e., the painting itself, not a print or replica, is
where the aesthetic value of the art resides in the original piece worked
on by the artist. Photography disrupts this as there is nothing authentic
or pure about a print from the film negative (and the film negative itself
is not what we, as art viewers, evaluate). It is in the photographic print,
infinitely reproducible, where our attention resides, severing the art from
the "aura" of origin. At first, this seems like photography is a lesser form of
art because of this loss of aura, because we feel the aura of standing in front
of DaVinci or Monet, or any amateur's painting. We want to feel a connection to the source. When we see replicas as our iPhone backgrounds, it's

not the same as standing in the room with the painting that was touched by the Genius. But because a photographic print has no original to bask in, we may want to assume that the "aura" feeling, that communicates to us the aesthetic value is reduced.

But what Benjamin argues is that the idea of the aura is somewhat arbitrary, along with the idea of making "art for art's sake." These ideas were emphasized as a "theology of art" in reaction, by fascist idealists, to the fact of the reproducibility of art. This theology of art rejects the social function of art and maintains it as non-political and "pure" (Benjamin 1936, 981) Capitalism neutralizes the concept of art. But art's aesthetic value is not only perceptible in the presence of its material essence, but in its basis in the ritual and context of the culture that values it. Therefore, "for the first time in history" Benjamin argues, "technological reproducibility emancipates the work of art from its parasitic subservience to ritual." (981)

With this, the debate centered around whether photography was art or not, can be expanded to "the more fundamental question of whether the invention of photography had not transformed the entire character of art." (984) The insight here is that through new technologies, conceptualizations of our realities are disrupted. Through this revolution, art, political identity, and literature are no longer solid concepts. From here we can move from one conceptualization of art that wants to keep art as apolitical and pure to maintain the fascist status quo, to a new conceptualization of art where it can be political.

The revolutionary potential of photography and film is also evident in that it is experienced collectively. Benjamin points out that "Painting, by its nature, cannot provide an object of simultaneous collective reception, as the epic poem could do at one time, and as a film is able to do today" (990) With this perspective now, we can see the revolutionary potential of reproducible art. This has become increasingly applicable with the advent of digital art. Even if there is a "master file" for a film completely filmed on hard drives, this is still not the "essence" of the art but diffused through every theater, laptop, and iPhone the film is enjoyed. The hope here is that in its reproducibility, it also opens up the door to a more democratic and collective interpretation of art and literature. Like film and photography's emancipation of rigid conceptions of art, we can witness this already happening with video games becoming less of a hobby (or a waste of time), but as art, literature, and sport, with the added powerful factor of interactivity and communication.

What is to glean from this for my argument is that Benjamin saw the revolutionary potential of a technological apparatus within a hegemonic capitalist machine. Benjamin exposes how the neutralization of concepts has had on our identities and societies, but then sees the chaos as an opportunity to deconstruct Western thought at its core, and rethink new ways of defining and enjoying art. To interpret the loss of "aura", or the untethering art from the purity of "art for art's sake," as harmful for the arts is to resolve to and be complicit with the typical conceptualizations of art. A more material perspective sees that when art loses its aura, is not necessarily a loss for art, but an opportunity for art to explore uncharted areas. Benjamin gathers the tools that our dominating structures have given us incidentally. It's seeing what is typically defined as ugly, as beautiful. Benjamin shows that the purity of concepts is often a fascist creation aiming to stifle creative, non-dualistic thinking. The blessing of new technology is discovering how it disrupts pure concepts of art and, more to my point, the self.

Like Benjamin's perspective on new technology as challenging totalizing notions of art, Donna Haraway does use totalizing ideas and strategies to interpret the way our technologies dominate us, but as an opportunity to reconstruct new ideas and strategies with a new image of ourselves. Benjamin shows how technology can change fundamental notions of art. Similarly, Donna Haraway shows how technology challenges identity. She writes this in her "blasphemous" and "ironic" "A Cyborg Manifesto". An essay on constructing new identities in a highly technological world. She says her essay is blasphemous because it takes "very seriously" what is happening, with apt knowledge of the doctrine, but proposes alternatives of knowing "while still insisting on the need for community." And ironic because two contradictory situations can both be "necessary and true" (Haraway 1985, 2043) A blasphemous and ironic cyborg as an escape from our totalizing, dualistic, rigid, binary thinking. She writes, "There is no drive in cyborgs to produce total theory, but there is an intimate experience of boundaries, their construction and deconstruction" (2064) Non-essentially, the cyborg finds "pleasure in the confusion of boundaries" because that is where they find political agency in this fragmented, technological world.

We've heard a common prescription to gain a healthy relationship with technology is to identify technology as a tool, asking ourselves something like, "do you control the technology? Or does the technology control you?" This idea wants to maintain a distinction between humans and machines. In order to maintain our essence as humans, we must be aware of how technology rules us. The typical image here is how much we are glued to our phones, television, and computer screens. Our screen-time report once a week reminds us of how much time we have "wasted." But this comes from a place where we want to maintain old ideas about what it means to be human. To remain pure, we must control our technology to keep it from corrupting us. This again falls to a binary, dualistic thinking of human/machine. Haraway problematizes this distinction by stating,

> From the seventeenth century till now, machines could be animated—given ghostly souls to make them speak or move or to account for their orderly development and mental capacities. Or organisms could be mechanized—reduced to the body and understood as a resource of the mind. These machine/organism relationships are obsolete, and unnecessary. For us, in imagination and other practice, machines can be prosthetic devices, intimate components, friendly selves. (2062)

Cyborgs confuse this distinction. To identify as a cyborg is to say, "We can be responsible for machines; they do not dominate or threaten us. We are responsible for boundaries; we are they" (2064). Seeing ourselves as cyborgs makes us consider ourselves as we really are in our technological world. Texting is an extension of my voice. Instagram is an extension of my social life. These are not simply tools, but prosthetics for our bodies. We are they. But it is not simply a positive attitude towards technology. Haraway points out that "it is not just that science and technology are possible means of great human satisfaction, as well as a matrix of complex dominations" (2064) We are enmeshed in webs of informatic domination, but we know we are. We are they.

Cyborgs are an amalgam of identifications, constructions or conceptualizations. Concepts like gender, a dominating force of identification, become obsolete. This identification releases us "to recognize the "historical contingency" of the social relations of gender, while allowing them to claim their own "truths," however partial or contingent." (Finke 1992, 4) Haraway proposes an "infidel heteroglossia" which highlights the complexity of being, but some level of ownership over language. Laurie Finke, writing on Haraway's work, adds that, "complexity describes a cultural poetics of indeterminacy, informed by contemporary theoretical debates in a variety of fields but without the political paralysis often attributed to poststructuralism" (4) By embracing complexity, we can exist in the in-between of the dualisms where fact is taken for granted. Embracing complexity denies "a demonology of technology, and so means embracing the skillful task of reconstructing the boundaries of daily life, in partial connection with others, in communication with all of our parts" (Haraway 1985, 2064) The infidel heteroglossia means "both building and destroying machines, identities, categories, relationships, spaces, stories." (2065) Identifying with anything creates the risk of adhering to some dogmatic, fascist, essentialist, objective, or pure vision of the self. But the cyborg's key identifying factor, is that it is not these things. It is rather agnostic, democratic, without origin, subjective, and unclean. And most importantly, grounded in a materialistic perspective. It provides individuals with a theory of self that empowers them to be organisms (or machines) in the reality that immediately interacts with them.

The Social and Material Self

The cyborg is ultimately challenging the restricting language that defines us. Similar to Woolf's vision of the self-being composed of multiple personalities, our interpretation of self is also a hybrid of the social constructions, and categorizations through language systems we find ourselves in. Our individuality exists at the intersections of race, class, gender, sexuality, and many others. We are given categorizations through our biology that society will attempt to keep us in. Society circulates molds about constructions that make up what we understand as our personality. We have a "clash of voices" telling us who we are, which "results in mental and emotional states of perplexity." (Anzaldúa 1987) Our dual or multiple personalities are plagued by psychic restlessness. But in the spirit of Haraway, Gloria Anzaldúa embraces a pleasure in the confusion of boundaries that has the potential to emancipate us from essentialist ideas given to us. What must be paramount in our construction of self is that we, as individuals, have the power to construct the image of our self for ourselves. If we are brave enough, we have the power to resist dominating structures that will do the work of identification for us. The activity we must take on is both deconstruction and construction in developing our power within these categorizations. Anzaldúa beautifully illustrates this point in this passage:

As a *mestiza* I have no country, my homeland cast me out; yet all my countries are mine because I am every woman's sister or potential lover. (As a lesbian I have no race, my people disclaim me; but I am all races because there is the queer of me in all races.) I am cultureless because, as a feminist, I challenge the collective cultural religious male-derived beliefs of Indo-Hispanics and Anglos; yet I am cultured because I am participating in the creation of yet another culture, a new story to explain the world and our participation in it, a new value system with images and symbols that connect us and to the planet. *Soy un amasameiento*, I am an act of kneading, on uniting and joining that not only has produced both a creature of darkness and a creature of light, but also a creature that questions the definitions of light and dark and gives them new meanings." (102-103)

In the in-between, there are new roads to identification. Let us be realistic about what makes up our personalities and behaviors. We cannot claim authority over these positions. We do not always choose them.

By acknowledging ourselves as hybrid, integrated creatures, we gain the authority to define ourselves. Homi Bhabha clarifies this by distinguishing a few things:

> The split space of enunciation may open the way to conceptualizing an international culture, based not on the exorcism of multiculturalism of the diversity of cultures, but on the inscription and articulation of culture's hybridity. To that end we should remember that it is the 'inter'– the cutting edge of translation and negotiation, the in-between space—that carries the burden of the meaning of culture. It makes it possible to begin envisaging national, anti-nationalist histories of the 'people'. And by exploring this Third Space, we may elude the politics of polarity and emerge as the others of our selves." (Bhabha 1994, 2171)

The 'inter', the space in our heads, the in-between, is what carries meaning. Finding a third space, a synthesis with our identifications, gives us political power. It gives us a political identity that is not reduced to the myopic identity politics of feminism, classism, or race. We subscribe to labels because unity is desired. Judith Butler, challenging the identity politics of feminism writes, "It is clear that coherence is desired, wished for, idealized, and that this idealization is an effect of a corporeal signification." Yet we think that "acts, gestures, and desire produce the effect of an internal core or substance" but they only "produce this on the surface of the body, through the play of signifying absences that suggest, but never reveal, the organizing principle of identity as a cause." (Butler 1990, 173) Identity is not a cause for our desires, but rather a label to define our desires through the repetition and performance of an identity.

This means that identity is non-essential, dynamic, and individualistically determinable. Our desire for a unified identity is just another desire that creates identity. But to think of our individual make-up as natural or essential, underdetermines our identity. It produces a "false stabilization" to regulate sex, gender, race and class into obligatory frames of being. In this framework, we do not have bodies that cause our political stance, but rather, strategic political forces define our bodies. Decoupling identity as the cause for our politics gives individuals the power to perform their strategies for resistance. In this way, an essentialist notion of gender is complicit with the system that maintains these boundaries of identification. To think of identity as performative, on the surface of our bodies, and an act of heroic self-creation, is to give power back to individuals to compose their political stance outside of fascist dualisms that regulate us.

At the core of this argument is an appeal to material reality. So much of our identities are shaped by restrictive, idealistic frameworks. To step outside the wire is to compose new idealisms based on our material existence, not the language systems that previously defined us. Thinking of our bodies materially helps us understand ourselves in the context of language and technology and create a new language that matches our experience.

Following a materialist tradition, Jane Bennett proposes that we "distribute value more generously" to all things, objects, and even debris, in hopes that in doing so, it would "raise the status of the materiality of which we are composed." Because if "each human is a heterogeneous compound of wonderfully vibrant, dangerously vibrant, matter." (Bennett 2009, 2444)

We obtain an ethics that distributes love not just to human personifications, but to the entire network of existence. In her manifesto, Haraway wants to blur the lines between human and machine by asking, "why should our bodies end at the skin, or include at best other beings encapsulated by skin?" (1985, 2063).

Similarly, Jane Bennett wants to expand our perceptions of self to more than just our organic bodies. It is not that we expand our consciousness to streams, rocks, and red solo cups to understand ourselves through metaphor, although that can be useful at times, but as an acknowledgement of the vitality of materials connects us to a wider framework of being. It is not, 'I am like a stream because I am fluid and dynamic.' It is, 'the stream is really there, being fluid and dynamic, and I can see it as an Other, with no condemnation, with an awareness of its mysterious consciousness and being.' This view entertains a realism that does not depend on subjective conceptualizations, but on a practice of being in the presence of the interconnectedness to all materiality. It does not dismiss a hierarchy of value of materiality that we place onto things subjectively but takes a leap of faith into a realist perspective about things (if we are brave enough to dethrone judgment as the monarch of understanding). Bennett admits that acknowledging the vibrant materiality of things "will not solve the problem of human exploitation of oppression, but it can inspire a greater sense of the extent to which all bodies are kin in the sense of inextricably enmeshed in a dense network of relations." (Bennett 2009, 2444) This is again thinking of ourselves as hybrid. It sees interconnection as a cornerstone of identification. A cornerstone, as vibrant as any material thing.

Conclusion

All these authors give us ways to identify ourselves in our interconnectedness to machines, material nature, and society. In this expansion of self, we obtain new ways of using our bodies. If our eyes have been extended by technology and hybrid identities, we may be able to see and imagine more for a world we would like to live in. Haraway gives us the cyborg imagery which "can suggest a way out of the maze of dualisms in which have explained our bodies and our tools to ourselves" (Haraway 1985, 2064) Bennett gives us a "world of vibrant matter," where "to harm one section of the web may very well be to harm oneself." (Bennett 2009, 2444)

Their theories maintain deconstruction as an ongoing process. Hybrid identities are messy, non-essential, and collective. What we have then, is a dynamic and flowing perception of self. Why does our foundation need to be solid? While the wise man did not build his house on the sand, even rocks erode over time. When we define our intersectionality ourselves and widen the boundaries of vitality and life, we see ourselves not as stagnant creatures, doomed to inevitability, but as materialistic, which is chaotic, yet authentic. Finke writes, "chaos is not disorder and meaninglessness but a form of complex information. The apparent randomness of that information results from the inadequacy of our linear representations of a historical narrative to comprehend, to represent, complexity."(Finke 1992, 24) Hybrid identity denies orderly narratives to define ourselves. In our integration with our closest friends, technology, language constructions, and vibrant materiality, we see ourselves as complex and not unchanging. Hybrids are "the people who leap in the dark [...] the people at the knees of the gods." (Anzaldúa 1987, 102-103) In our known chaos, we construct order for ourselves—providing new perspectives and realities that then, in turn, shape society.

References

Anzaldúa, Gloria. "From Borderlands/La Frontera: The New Mestiza." In *The Norton Anthology of Theory and Criticism*, edited by Vincent B. Leitch, 1987, 1987-1997. W. W. Norton & Company.

Bakhtin, Mikhail M. "Discourse in the Novel." Translated by Caryl Emerson and Michael Holquist. In *The Norton Anthology of Theory and Criticism*, edited by Vincent B. Leitch, 997-1030. 3rd ed. W. W. Norton & Company, 1934-35.

Benjamin, Walter. "The Work of Art in the Age of Its Technological Reproducibility." In *The Norton Anthology of Theory and Criticism*, edited by Vincent B. Leitch, 1936, 1955, 976-996. W. W. Norton & Company.

Bennett, Jane. "From Vibrant Matter: A Political Ecology of Things." In *The Norton Anthology of Theory and Criticism*, edited by Vincent B. Leitch, 2009, 2434-2450. W. W. Norton & Company.

Bhabha, Homi K. "The Commitment to Theory." In *The Norton Anthology of Theory and Criticism*, edited by Vincent B. Leitch, 1989, 2152-2171. W. W. Norton & Company.

Braidotti, Rosi. "From *The Posthuman.*" In *The Norton Anthology of Theory and Criticism*, edited by Vincent B. Leitch, 2013, 2329-2352. W. W. Norton & Company.

Butler, Judith. "From *Gender Trouble.*" In *The Norton Anthology of Theory and Criticism*, edited by Vincent B. Leitch, 1990, 2372-2388. W. W. Norton & Company.

Camus, Albert. 1942. *The Myth of Sisyphus*. Translated by Justin O'Brien, Penguin Classics.

Finke, Laurie A. 1992. "A Powerful Infidel Heteroglossia: Toward a Feminist Theory of Complexity." In *Feminist Theory, Women's Writing*, 1-28. Ithaca, NY: Cornell University Press.

Fisher, Mark. 2009. *Capitalist Realism: Is There No Alternative?* Zer0 Books.

Graeber, David. 2015. *The Utopia of Rules: On Technology, Stupidity, and the Secret Joys of Bureaucracy*. Melville House.

Haraway, Donna. "A Manifesto for Cyborgs: Science, Technology, and Socialist Feminism in the 1980s." In *The Norton Anthology of Theory and Criticism*, edited by Vincent B. Leitch, 1985, 2043-2065. W. W. Norton & Company.

Henke, Suzette A. 1989. "Virginia Woolf's 'The Waves': A Phenomenological Reading." *Periodicals Archive Online*, 73, no. 3: 461-472.

"Heteroglossia, n." *OED Online*, Oxford University Press, March 2023, www.oed.com/view/Entry/64762592.

McLuhan, Marshall, and Quentin Fiore. 1967. *The Medium Is the Massage*. Gingko Press.

MediaBurnArchive, "The Revolution Will Not Be Televised," Gil-Scott Heron" *YouTube*, https://www.youtube.com/watch?v=kZvWt29OG0s

Miko, Stephen J. 1988. "Reflections on The Waves: Virginia Woolf at the Limits of her Art." *Criticism* 30, no. 1: 63-90.

Philbeck, Thomas, and Nicholas Davis. 2018. "The Fourth Industrial Revolution: Shaping A New Era." *Journal of International Affairs* 72, no. 1: 17-22.

Postman, Neil. 1992. *Technopoly: The Surrender of Culture to Technology.* Vintage Books.

Woolf, Virginia. 1931. *The Waves.* Mariner Classics.

Žižek, Slavoj. 2023. "I'm ready to sell mother into slavery to watch the film 'V for Vendetta' 2.0." YouTube video, uploaded by The Zizek/ Chomsky Times, March 2023. Accessed June 29, 2024. https://www. youtube.com/watch?v=qOhTuaDTEsg

Authors' Short Biographies

Theodora Valkanou, PhD. is an adjunct lecturer and postdoctoral fellow in the School of English at Aristotle University of Thessaloniki, Greece. She holds an MA in Translation Studies from the University of Warwick, UK and a PhD in the same field from the School of English at Aristotle University. Her current research interests include the relationship between translation and identity, the translation of children's literature, translation and gender, postcolonial translation, and cultural studies.

Laxana Paskaran, MEd. is a PhD. student in the Gender, Feminist and Women's Studies program at York University, located in Toronto, Canada. Her research lies at the intersection of social reproduction and platform labour and contributes to current debates about how social reproduction, the social relations that reproduce labour power, is understood in diverse social contexts and how it can effectively advance analyses that integrate gender, race and class. She holds an MEd. and an HBSc. from the University of Toronto.

Guadalupe Ciocoletto, PhD. is an architect and urban researcher with a PhD. in Urban Studies from the Universidad de Buenos Aires and a Laurea Magistrale from Politecnico di Milano. Her work explores migration, diversity, city branding, and intercultural communication. She has published widely and collaborated with research teams in Buenos Aires and Milan. She is passionate about the academic field and held academic roles at the University of Buenos Aires, Universidad de la Matanza, and briefly at Politecnico di Milano.

Abdelhak Jebbar, PhD. is a full professor at the Faculty of Arts and Humanities at Sultan Moulay Slimane University in Beni Mellal. He earned his doctorate from Sidi Mohamed Ben Abdellah University in Fez, jointly with Nice Sophia Antipolis in France. He holds an MA. degree in Cross-Cultural and Literary Studies. He is an active member of the Doctoral Program on Interactions in Literature, Language, Culture, and Society (ILLCS), and a permanent member of the Research Laboratory in Literature, Language, Culture, and Communication (RLLLCC). He is a prolific speaker and author in both national and international academic circles. His research focuses on Cultural Studies, Literature, Translation Studies, and Academic Reading and Writing.

Najah Mahmi, PhD. is a full professor at Sultan Moulay Slimane University, Morocco. She holds a PhD. in English Studies from Sidi Mohammed Ben Abdellah University, a PhD. in Anthropology from Nice-Sophia Antipolis University, and an MA. in Cross-Cultural & Literary Studies. Her research interests cover issues related to cultural anthropology, translation studies, philosophy, literature and cultural studies. She has been a speaker at both national and international conferences and has published essays with esteemed publishers across these domains.

Sheila Collingwood-Whittick, PhD. is a former senior lecturer in the Department of Anglophone Studies, at the University of Grenoble III. She got her Ph.D. degree from London University. Her thesis was entitled: "The Colonial Situation in Algeria and its Literary Reflection". Since her retirement, she has become an independent researcher. Her main research interests and numerous publications are focused on (post)colonial fiction, and all aspects of Indigenous Australians' experience of settler colonialism.

Isabel Ekua-Thompson, MA. is a Lecturer in the European Studies BA Programme at the University of Amsterdam's Faculty of Humanities. She holds two MA degrees in Eastern European Studies and Comparative Cultural Analysis. Her work focuses on political identity construction and critiques of normative theory. Isabel applies philosophical concepts to empirical research, including a project on contemporary Estonia and a recent study on protest identity during the Black Lives Matter movement in the UK. Her interdisciplinary approach bridges theory and practice across diverse sociopolitical contexts.

Gary Forster, PhD., MA., BA. is an English academic who specialises in adaptations into and across various media, and whose most recent publication is a (post)feminist analysis of the hit TV show *Ugly Betty*. Forthcoming chapters include post-human subjectivities in the *Warhammer 40K* franchise; Freudian and Jungian ideas in the films of Roger Corman *and* in Vestron>s *Warlock* films; a postculturalist reappraisal of *The Color Purple*; and a psychoanalytic-feminist ideology critique of 20th- and 21st-century film adaptations of the Medusa myth.

Nishant Upadhyay, PhD. is an upcoming postdoctoral fellow at the Department of Political Science at Tsinghua University. He earned his PhD. from the University of Texas at Austin, where his doctoral dissertation focused on the responses of Shi'i Muslim individuals, religious leaders, and institutions to political events in India. Through this dissertation, Nishant's work contributes to the scholarship, dispelling the myth of the Hindu-Muslim binary. His research interests include nationalism and neo-nationalism in South Asia, critical theoretical thought, foreign and security policies of India, and relations with China, Africa, and the Middle East. His research articles have appeared in leading journals, such as *Sophia, Middle-East Critique, Journal of Political Power, International Critical Thought* and *Contemporary South Asia.* He published numerous co-authored books.

Maryam Farahani, PhD., MA., MAEd., MSc., BA. is a research associate at the University of Liverpool with 20 years of cross-disciplinary experience in humanities, education, and sciences. She has expertise in psychology of ancient civilizations, classical narratology,healthcare, contemporary leadership, aesthetic performance, nonlinear reflexivity, East-West philosophies, workplace psychology, and education leadership and management (inc. SEND methodologies). She has published on women's health narratives, sports, arts, literature, psychology of pain and medical histories. She has forthcoming publications on healthcare leadership, disability, the othering process, Oriental dance, and aesthetics.

Ian Schermbrucker, PhD., MSc. is a social psychologist and lecturer at the University of Liverpool. Over the past 20 years, he has contributed to the psychology of human behaviour, identity and social dynamics, group dynamics, conflict, and the influence of overlapping social identities on prejudice and out-group derogation. His expertise spans the psychology of leadership, multidisciplinary focus on conflict resolution, and the arts, sports, and identity. His research lies in the same area with focused past publications on conflict and forthcoming co-edited volumes on leadership, otherness, and primary care management.

Abdelali Jebbar, PhD. is a professor of English Studies at the Faculty of Arts and Humanities, Fez-Sais, Morocco. He earned his doctorate in Cultural Studies from the Dhar Mehraz Faculty of Arts and Humanities in Fes, 2016. He has participated in numerous national and international academic events and published articles and papers in various national and international contexts. He is also a permanent member of the Afro-Mediterranean Research Lab for Discourse, Communication and Cultural

Studies. His areas of research include Postcolonial Studies, Travel Narrative, Risk Society and Translation.

Abhisek Ghosal, PhD. currently works at the Department of Humanities and Social Sciences, Indian Institute of Technology (Indian School of Mines), Dhanbad, Jharkhand. He holds an M.A., an M.Phil and a PhD (IIT Kharagpur). His broad areas of research interest include Deleuze and Guattari Studies, Blue Humanities, South Asian Literature, and Indic Studies, among others. His latest book titled *Cartographies of Postcolonial Vegetal Politics* was published by Lexington Books (2024).

Jennifer Roth Miller, PhD. has served in administration, research, and faculty roles at the University of Central Florida since 2003. Jennifer's research has sought to better understand digital citizenship and social media engagement by exploring the convergence of communication, technology, philanthropy, and education in socially constructing collective views and actions for social justice. Jennifer's work has been published as articles in peer-reviewed communication-focused academic journals as well as book chapters in scholarly edited collections published by Brill, Routledge, University Press of Colorado, and Utah State University Press.

Rania Elshabassy, PhD. is an Assistant Professor of English at the Department of English, Faculty of Arts, Cairo University. Her research interests span ecocriticism, digital humanities, comparative literature, feminist, postcolonial and decolonial studies. Her recent publications include "Exploring Brain-Computer Interface Representations in Science Fiction.", "The Nation at a Wobbly Juncture.", and "An Interview with Dipesh Chakrabarty." She also co-edited a special issue of Cairo Studies in English titled "Conjuring up Decolonial Alternatives: Subversive Navigations of Transnational Colonialisms".

Prachi Priyanka, PhD. holds a doctorate in English literature. Her areas of interest include intertextuality and visual culture, Indian literature in translation and English, Partition narratives, eco-criticism and Victorian studies. Her research articles and chapters have appeared in prestigious edited volumes like Routledge, Lexington publications and reputed Scopus-indexed journals. She has five books to her credit. She is an Assistant Professor in the School of Humanities and Social Sciences, at Sharda University, India.

Manisha Poonia, PhD. is a Junior Research Fellow and PhD. scholar in the Department of English and Cultural Studies at Panjab University, Chandigarh, India. She holds an M.Phil. degree in Partition Literature from Kurukshetra University, Kurukshetra, Haryana, (India) and has also completed a one-year Postgraduate Diploma in Translation (PGDT) from the same university. Her academic contributions include research papers published in reputed journals and presentations at national and international conferences. Her research interests span gender studies, cultural studies, translation, and the representation of sports in Indian cinema.

Anna Cadoni, PhD. holds a PhD in American Literature from the University of Roma Tre. During her PhD program, she conducted research on Modernist writers through the theoretical frame of Affect Theory and Feminist Studies. She is currently teaching Anglo-American Linguistics and Literary Translation at the University of Messina and she holds a research fellowship at the University of Cagliari. She was a teaching fellow at Bowdoin College, Maine, for two semesters. During her PhD program, she was a visiting scholar at JFK Institut in Berlin and Stony Brook College while completing her dissertation. Her field of study includes Feminist literature and Gender Studies, Affect Theory, Black Studies, Modernist literature and Queer studies.

Hannah Grace Wilson, MA. holds a BA in English and is earning her master's degree in English at ACU. A passionate writer, she has recently published her novel *Wormwood* and six short stories. She is also working to improve West Texas schools through her article "Swipe, Tap, Distract: Depolarizing Phones in Education." Hannah strives to continue pursuing her studies in literature and aims to inspire her students to pursue their academic dreams.

Hamida Riahi, PhD. is a lecturer of English literature in the Department of Languages and Translation at Northern Border University, Saudi Arabia. She holds a PhD. in English literature, focusing on Anglophone Arab novels by Muslim women writers in the diaspora. Her research interests include Muslim feminism, intersectionality, and the strategies employed by Arab and Muslim women writers to counter anti-Muslim racism, Muslim misogyny, and Orientalism. Additionally, she has written unpublished short stories in English and is actively engaged in civil society initiatives in Tunisia, particularly advocating for the rights of rural Tunisian women.

Reliance Chekwubechukwu Enwerem, MA. has a master's degree in English from the University of Alabama, with a focus on Composition, Rhetoric, and English Studies. She is committed to exploring innovative approaches in digital literacy and access, and her research merges critical digital (AI) literacy, critical embodiment pedagogies, rhetoric at the margins, and digital humanities.

Jamie Bollweg, MA. holds an MA in English Literature and a BA in English Literature and Language from Western Michigan University. Their research focuses on identity studies and rhetoric. Bollweg's teaching approach stems from a passion for education and a commitment to fostering critical thinking in first-year writing students. Outside academia, Jamie is an avid gamer and enjoys creating ambient music and DJing.

Related Titles from Westphalia Press

The Limits of Moderation: Jimmy Carter and the Ironies of American Liberalism

The Limits of Moderation: Jimmy Carter and the Ironies of American Liberalism is not a finished product. And yet, even in this unfinished stage, this book is a close and careful history of a short yet transformative period in American political history, when big changes were afoot.

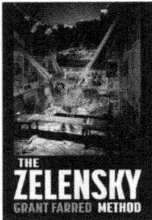

The Zelensky Method
by Grant Farred

Locating Russian's war within a global context, The Zelensky Method is unsparing in its critique of those nations, who have refused to condemn Russia's invasion and are doing everything they can to prevent economic sanctions from being imposed on the Kremlin.

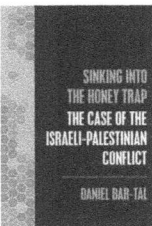

Sinking into the Honey Trap: The Case of the Israeli-Palestinian Conflict
by Daniel Bar-Tal, Barbara Doron, Translator

Sinking into the Honey Trap by Daniel Bar-Tal discusses how politics led Israel to advancing the occupation, and of the deterioration of democracy and morality that accelerates the growth of an authoritarian regime with nationalism and religiosity.

Essay on The Mysteries and the True Object of The Brotherhood of Freemasons
by Jason Williams

The third edition of Essai sur les mystères discusses Freemasonry's role as a society of symbolic philosophers who cultivate their minds, practice virtues, and engage in charity, and underscores the importance of brotherhood, morality, and goodwill.

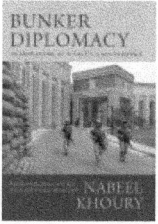

Bunker Diplomacy: An Arab-American in the U.S. Foreign Service
by Nabeel Khoury

After twenty-five years in the Foreign Service, Dr. Nabeel A. Khoury retired from the U.S. Department of State in 2013 with the rank of Minister Counselor. In his last overseas posting, Khoury served as deputy chief of mission at the U.S. embassy in Yemen (2004-2007).

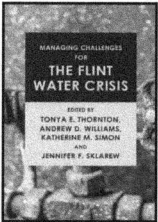

Managing Challenges for the Flint Water Crisis
Edited by Toyna E. Thornton, Andrew D. Williams, Katherine M. Simon, Jennifer F. Sklarew

This edited volume examines several public management and intergovernmental failures, with particular attention on social, political, and financial impacts. Understanding disaster meaning, even causality, is essential to the problem-solving process.

User-Centric Design
by Dr. Diane Stottlemyer

User-centric strategy can improve by using tools to manage performance using specific techniques. User-centric design is based on and centered around the users. They are an essential part of the design process and should have a say in what they want and need from the application based on behavior and performance.

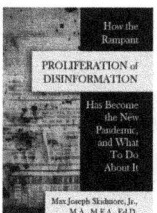

How the Rampant Proliferation of Disinformation Has Become the New Pandemic, and What To Do About It by Max Joseph Skidmore Jr.

This work examines the causes of the overwhelming tidal wave of fake news, misinformation, disinformation, and propaganda, and the increase in information illiteracy and mistrust in higher education and traditional, vetted news outlets that make fact-checking a priority.

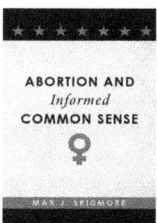

Abortion and Informed Common Sense
by Max J. Skidmore

The controversy over a woman's "right to choose," as opposed to the numerous "rights" that abortion opponents decide should be assumed to exist for "unborn children," has always struck me as incomplete. Two missing elements of the argument seems obvious, yet they remain almost completely overlooked.

The Athenian Year Primer: Attic Time-Reckoning and the Julian Calendar
by Christopher Planeaux

The ability to translate ancient Athenian calendar references into precise Julian-Gregorian dates will not only assist Ancient Historians and Classicists to date numerous historical events with much greater accuracy but also aid epigraphists in the restorations of numerous Attic inscriptions.

Siddhartha: Life of the Buddha
by David L. Phillips,
contributions by Venerable Sitagu Sayadaw

Siddhartha: Life of the Buddha is an illustrated story for adults and children about the Buddha's birth, enlightenment and work for social justice. It includes illustrations from Pagan, Burma which are provided by Rev. Sitagu Sayadaw.

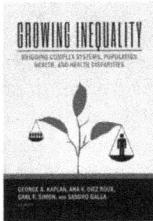

Growing Inequality: Bridging Complex Systems, Population Health, and Health Disparities
Editors: George A. Kaplan, Ana V. Diez Roux, Carl P. Simon, and Sandro Galea

Why is America's health is poorer than the health of other wealthy countries and why health inequities persist despite our efforts? In this book, researchers report on groundbreaking insights to simulate how these determinants come together to produce levels of population health and disparities and test new solutions.

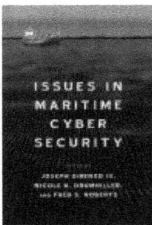

Issues in Maritime Cyber Security
Edited by Dr. Joe DiRenzo III, Dr. Nicole K. Drumhiller, and Dr. Fred S. Roberts

The complexity of making MTS safe from cyber attack is daunting and the need for all stakeholders in both government (at all levels) and private industry to be involved in cyber security is more significant than ever as the use of the MTS continues to grow.

Female Emancipation and Masonic Membership: An Essential Collection
By Guillermo De Los Reyes Heredia

Female Emancipation and Masonic Membership: An Essential Combination is a collection of essays on Freemasonry and gender that promotes a transatlantic discussion of the study of the history of women and Freemasonry and their contribution in different countries.

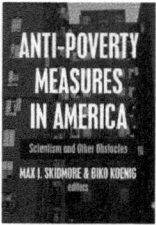

Anti-Poverty Measures in America: Scientism and Other Obstacles
Editors, Max J. Skidmore and Biko Koenig

Anti-Poverty Measures in America brings together a remarkable collection of essays dealing with the inhibiting effects of scientism, an over-dependence on scientific methodology that is prevalent in the social sciences, and other obstacles to anti-poverty legislation.

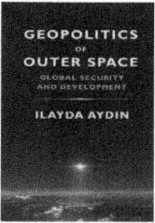

Geopolitics of Outer Space: Global Security and Development
by Ilayda Aydin

A desire for increased security and rapid development is driving nation-states to engage in an intensifying competition for the unique assets of space. This book analyses the Chinese-American space discourse from the lenses of international relations theory, history and political psychology to explore these questions.

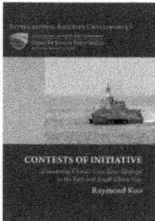

Contests of Initiative: Countering China's Gray Zone Strategy in the East and South China Seas
by Dr. Raymond Kuo

China is engaged in a widespread assertion of sovereignty in the South and East China Seas. It employs a "gray zone" strategy: using coercive but sub-conventional military power to drive off challengers and prevent escalation, while simultaneously seizing territory and asserting maritime control.

Discourse of the Inquisitive
Editors: Jaclyn Maria Fowler and Bjorn Mercer

Good communication skills are necessary for articulating learning, especially in online classrooms. It is often through writing that learners demonstrate their ability to analyze and synthesize the new concepts presented in the classroom.

westphaliapress.org

Policy Studies Organization

The Policy Studies Organization (PSO) is a publisher of academic journals and book series, sponsor of conferences, and producer of programs.

Policy Studies Organization publishes dozens of journals on a range of topics, such as European Policy Analysis, Journal of Elder Studies, Indian Politics & Polity, Journal of Critical Infrastructure Policy, and Popular Culture Review.

Additionally, Policy Studies Organization hosts numerous conferences. These conferences include the Middle East Dialogue, Space Education and Strategic Applications Conference, International Criminology Conference, Dupont Summit on Science, Technology and Environmental Policy, World Conference on Fraternalism, Freemasonry and History, and the Internet Policy & Politics Conference.

For more information on these projects, access videos of past events, and upcoming events, please visit us at:

www.ipsonet.org

www.ingramcontent.com/pod-product-compliance
Lightning Source LLC
Chambersburg PA
CBHW050642270326
41927CB00012B/2832